AF327110

Classes, Class Conflict, and the State

Empirical Studies in Class Analysis

Edited by

Maurice Zeitlin
University of California at Los Angeles

Winthrop Publishers, Inc.
Cambridge, Massachusetts

Library of Congress Cataloging in Publication Data

Main entry under title:

Classes, class conflict, and the State.

Includes bibliographies and index.
1. Social classes—United States—History—Addresses, essays, lectures. 2. United States—Economic conditions—Addresses, essays, lectures.
3. Capitalism—Addresses, essays, lectures. 4. Social conflict—Addresses, essays, lectures. I. Zeitlin, Maurice
HN90.S6C57   301.44′0973   79-23040
ISBN 0-87626-122-5

For the old mole

Cover design by Karyl Klopp

© *1980 by Winthrop Publishers, Inc.*
17 Dunster Street, Cambridge, Massachusetts 02138

10   9   8   7   6   5   4   3   2   1

Contents

Preface

The original studies in class analysis in this volume grew out of a common intellectual effort and represent, to a great extent, a collective intellectual product, unified by a common theoretical perspective. The contributors have been my often recalcitrant students, all but two in the Department of Sociology at the University of Wisconsin at Madison; most participated in the continuing Colloquium of the Center for Social Organization, which I directed, and from which I learned so much. (The Social Organization Training Program was funded by a grant to the University of Wisconsin by the National Institute of Mental Health. Many of my friends and colleagues in the Department of Sociology, but especially Robert Alford, who preceded me as Director of the Program, and Michael Aiken, were vital participants in this common effort.)

At the Center, the studies were conducted, from conception through execution, in a highly charged, exciting, demanding, but supportive intellectual atmosphere. Drafts of papers, from research proposals to finished studies alike, were critiqued by other participants in the Colloquium; each author's work was exposed to a formidable array of careful, exhaustive, and constructive written criticisms and intensive discussions. In a real sense, then, the ideas expressed, the methods used, and the substantive explanations proposed in any single study are the product of a genuine community of scholars.

At the same time, these studies, drawn from their original doctoral dissertation research, are—in the last instance—the works of individuals guided by their own instincts of intellectual craftmanship and standards of scholarly excellence. It is understandable that this sort of cooperative intellectual community was created at a university that was the focus of the new left struggles of the late 1960s. A continuing commitment to the radical, egalitarian, and democratic social objectives of these struggles infuses not only the theory and substantive content of the works presented here, but their very method of creation: each is the product of freely cooperating yet highly individual labor.

Ms. Marsha Thomas, then secretary in the Department of Sociology at UCLA, deserves special thanks for her assistance in assembling the manuscript for this volume.

MAURICE ZEITLIN

On Classes, Class Conflict, and the State: An Introductory Note

Maurice Zeitlin

*Class is defined by men as they live their own history,
and, in the end, this is its only definition*—Thompson
1963:11.

The general theory underlying the empirical studies in this volume is that classes and their contradictory interrelations are the constitutive units of the social whole and the decisive elements in historical development. It is a *social* theory, then, whose originating questions are essentially *historical* questions, and its core propositions and analytical categories are simultaneously sociological and historical.

The theory aims not only to explain the specific historical forms of social domination, but also to reveal the conditions for self-emancipation from them; for this reason, it aims also to penetrate and demystify the coercive illusions (including the dominant social theories) that sustain these historic forms. In short, the theory is simultaneously scientific and *critical*, and carries its own radical, democratic, and egalitarian implications.

The theory originated with Marx, but it now exists in many and quite distinct, if not hostile, variants, and has been both enriched and vulgarized by many hands since. Its essence, in my view, its unique core as a social theory, is its inherently dialectical conception of social reality: Human beings are both bound and free, historical development is both determined and contingent, and human capacities can be realized only through the struggle to realize them and to abolish the social relations and material conditions that stunt and deform humanity's reach.

In this essay, I outline my conception of the most important questions, propositions, and concepts of a historically specific, critical, and dialectical class theory of political relations and historical development. I do so in close reference to the empirical studies in class analysis presented in this volume.

The discussion is organized around six topics:

Classes
Exploitation: coercive and commodity forms
Contemporary capitalism

The consent of the exploited: class hegemony and the state
The capitalist democratic state
Class conflict and state policy in recent American capitalism

Classes

What, then, are classes? Classes are constituted by the objective location and practical activity of men and women in the entire productive process, and by their specific differential relations to the means of production—that is, to the land, materials, and equipment with which men and women produce. The productive process is understood as a social process, not merely a technical one, in which the transformation of the material conditions of existence is simultaneously the production, reproduction, and transformation of social relations between the direct producers (engaged in actual productive labor) and the appropriators of their "surplus product" (those who control the means of production). These social relations of production, in short, are intrinsically exploitative relations—the essence of social domination in every *class society.* "Exploitation," in this sense, and in the precise meaning Marx gave it, refers to the social process by which the surplus product of the direct producers (that is, the product over and above what they require, in specific historical circumstances, for their continued laboring existence) is appropriated by the dominant, owning class.

As Lewis Feuer has observed,

> "Exploitation" is as characteristic of class systems as "parasitism" is of the fungi in the plant kingdom. The two ideas are equally significant in scientific terms. Just as there are organisms which live off the bloodstream of others and contribute no labor of their own, there are likewise those who in the social world take something for nothing (1959:xv).

It is precisely the specific historic form of this exploitative social relationship, given the specific material basis of the productive process, that defines both the basic classes themselves, since *neither exists apart from this relationship between them,* and the entire social whole, or mode of production.

This inherently *contradictory set of social relations* and the men and women actually involved in them—that is, their *"incumbents"*—are *conceptually* distinct; but "class" refers not to the one or the other, but to both simultaneously, in their specific historical connection: *the exploitative and contradictory productive relations and practical activity in which men and women are involved historically.* No adequate social theory can be so restricted as to focus either on the so-called structures or their agents. Nor certainly are real men and women merely the supports or determinate effects of abstract structures bereft of subjects, as in so-called structuralist Marxism, much as they once appeared to be no more than the emanations of immanent and self-moving historical ideas (see Althusser and Balibar 1970; Poulantzas 1973a). On the contrary, real individuals actively create and recreate social structures within given material conditions and historical circumstances, which themselves have been produced historically by prior human activity. Men and women make the social relations and material conditions of life that make them.

Classes, therefore, are inherently distinguished by their latent historical content, or their history-making potential, which is centered in the struggle over exploitation and its reduction or intensification. This struggle, in turn, enters into and conditions these relations and the process of class formation itself. It simultaneously shapes and realigns the internal relations *within* classes and the relations *between* them. Therefore, and this may be considered the red thread running through these theoretical notes, classes and class "interests" are both "objectively given" and are themselves dialectical historic products. In this sense, and to this extent, classes possess an inherent *relatively contingent historicity.* They are determined both by their place in a historically specific ensemble of productive relations and by their self-activity, which constitutes and reconstitutes these relations and their place within them. They are shaped by and in specific struggles, and by the consequences of these struggles (intended and unwitting), as well as by unique circumstances and events (including decisive defeats) that "load the historic dice," as Max Weber once remarked.

For example, the class relations that were consolidated in the American South after the Civil War, as Wiener shows (chapter 1), resulted, in part, from the defeat of the political strategy of the Radical Republicans, who wanted to use the coercive power of the federal state to break "the old agricultural basis of aristocratic power." Had the Radicals' strategy for the confiscation of the plantations of Confederate officials and their distribution to the freedmen won, the new forms of exploitation (sharecropping and debt peonage) might never have been established in the New South, nor would the "interests" of the white yeomen and black sharecroppers have been splintered with all its fateful implications for the future.

Exploitation: Coercive and Commodity Forms

Exploitation in precapitalist societies has generally taken explicitly coercive historic forms, in which the process of appropriation is relatively transparent (such as in ancient mining and plantation slavery, or the peasant's labor dues on the medieval demesne). With the advent of capitalism, in contrast, this process is characteristically mediated and obscured by the commodity form. Consequently, the place of the state in the entire exploitative process is qualitatively different under capitalism and in precapitalist social formations (as we shall discuss again in a later context).

Under Western European feudalism, to take a clear historic instance, the political unit and the productive unit tended to coincide, and exploitation was an intrinsically political process. The division of labor on the lord's domain (the basic unit of production) was limited. The immediate productive units were small scale, relatively self-contained, and scattered. The tools and other implements of production, including draft animals, necessary to carry out agricultural and craft production were owned by or in the immediate possession of the peasantry; but it was characteristic that the land itself (whether the peasant was bound to it or not) was owned by the lords. Only because the aristocracy appropriated the means of violence, political power, and administration, could it also appropriate the surplus product of the direct producers, the peasantry. These means of domination were ordinarily direct attributes of property, both for the individual and the class as a whole. The aristocracy's political power was mediated through the possession of fiefs—the territories within which, as Weber emphasized, individual lords held political and juridical rights and controlled their own fiscal and military means of domination and rule (see Zeitlin 1960). In short, the state, in the specific sense of the monopoly of the means of legitimate violence within a territory (Weber 1946:78), and the lord's domain tended to coincide. In this form of "dismembered political sovereignty" (Vernadsky 1939), state and dominant class were not clearly separable: The monopoly of the means of legitimate violence was a class monopoly.

The right to rule was a class right, granted, as were other rights in the feudal order, by a contract of asymmetrical but mutual fealty between free (and armed) men with reciprocal obligations. Exploitation itself, therefore, was a political right, and political means, outside the immediate productive process, were required to complete the act of appropriation from the petty producer. It was, to subtly rewrite Marx, an "extraeconomic" form of exploitation. Even analytically, the line between the political and economic aspects of the exploitative process under feudalism tends to be imperceptible. The appropriation of the surplus labor of the peasantry and the appropriation of their political rights by the feudal lords were transparently coalesced features of class domination and class rule.

In contrast, under capitalism, a system of *generalized commodity production* and exchange with private ownership of the means of production, the exploitative process takes place not nakedly but hidden, not directly but indirectly through the mediation of the market. Not extraeconomic coercion but ostensibly free exchange relations characterize the exploitative process; as a result, the economy itself appears as a relatively separate sphere of existence.

Capitalism, both logically and historically, originates with the transformation of the productive capacity or potential labor of the direct producer into a commodity. Labor has become "free" in a double sense: the direct producers are now free of juridical and customary encumbrances on their labor; they are now also free of any possession of the means of production and realization of their labor, including the land. As a consequence, they *can* and *must* sell their *productive capacity*, or "labor power," to capital. They can produce only by selling their capacity to produce; they can, and therefore must, produce only with the means of production owned and controlled by capital. "It is in contradiction to the *essence* of capitalism, and the *development* of capitalism is impossible," in Weber's formulation, "if such a propertyless stratum is absent, a class compelled to sell its labor services to live" (1961:208, emphasis added).[1] The basic split in capitalist society is that between the owners of capital, who, as a class, monopolize the means of production, and the workers, who, as a class, are *compelled to produce for capital so they can produce for themselves*. This split in social life is the basic "sociological datum" of capitalism as a mode of production (Lange 1935:69, 78). It is only because the workers neither own nor control the means of production, that what they produce in excess of what it costs to produce their own capacity to produce goes to capital, that this surplus product (now in the hidden form of "surplus value") is appropriated by capital.

Surplus value is equivalent to the workers' unpaid labor time: It is the difference between the amount of socially necessary labor time (that is, labor in accord with the prevailing standard of efficiency in production) embodied in the totality of commodities produced by the working class and in the sum they can buy with their wages (or paid labor time). In Marx's famous metaphor, the worker is paid for "a day's work"; that is, a day of the worker's productive capacity, during part of which he works for himself, producing his and his family's means of existence, and the rest of which he spends working for the capitalist, producing surplus value. The first is therefore the worker's necessary labor; the second, surplus labor or surplus value.

Of course, this *is* merely a metaphor; for in contrast to the identifiable and tangible necessary and surplus product of the individual peasant producer under feudalism, individual workers not only do not and cannot characteristically produce their own means of subsistence under capitalism,

---

[1] "[T]he physical whip assures the exertion of the slaves lodged in barracks," as Weber put it (1968:1010), "and the wage whip and threat of joblessness guarantees the effort of the 'free' worker. . . ."

but no product is truly their own. The workers as a whole, only as a class, in a complex and increasingly socialized division of labor, with the "factory" as its characteristic immediate productive unit, produce the social product in common, only part of which they receive back in the form of wages. The overall social ratio of unpaid labor time (surplus value) to paid labor time in production, or of surplus to necessary labor, is the *rate of exploitation.*

Surplus value can be realized by the capitalist only through the sale of the commodities produced by labor. That is, appropriation by the class takes place only through the market. The entire pool of surplus value appears in the single homogeneous form of money; it is through the relative prices of commodities, and in the payment of profits, interest, and rent (as well as taxes and the uses to which they are put by the state) that the surplus product is divided among various claimants in the capitalist class.

Structurally, that is, based on their location in the primary phases of the reproductive process of capital, the main claimants to a share of the profits of productive (or industrial) capital have been commercial and loan (or banking) capital. *Historically,* depending on the specific precapitalist forms in which it developed, productive capital has also been subject to the claims of large landed property, in the form of ground rent (whether or not land and capital have actually coalesced). These contending claimants to the surplus product may appear, depending on the phase of capitalist development, as distinctive "class segments" (Zeitlin and others 1976). These segments of the class are differentiated by their relatively distinct locations in the process of production and appropriation of surplus value. As a consequence, they may have specific political economic requirements and concrete interests in contradiction to those of other segments of the class, although they share a common relationship to the means of production.

Class segments, therefore, have the inherent potential for developing a specific variant of intraclass consciousness and common action in relation to other segments of the class. Whether or not their relatively distinct and contradictory "intraclass situations," as Weber (1946:181–186, 301) might have said, become manifest in actual struggles or in explicit political relations, depends on specific historical circumstances and on the nature of the other social relationships that differentiate or integrate the class segments. In a phrase, it depends on the extent to which *contradictory interests* and *social cleavages* tend to coincide.[2] These intraclass divisions within the dominant

---

[2] The working class and other subordinate classes, such as the peasantry, are also internally differentiated into segments having contradictory "immediate" interests, that is, as elements of an exploited class *within* the prevailing class relations, although they share a common "historic" interest in their emancipation from capital. These intraclass contradictory interests originate in (a) the historically specific development of the various capitalist social formations (for example, black versus white workers in the United

class, and subsidiary ones based on various forms of combination and coalition in the competitive struggle, bear a special structural relationship to the political process under capitalism, as will be discussed below. How the various segments of the capitalist class are recombined or transformed with the ascendance of the large corporation is another critical question addressed below.

Contemporary Capitalism

The exploitative relationship between labor and capital is the *differentia specifica* of capitalism and at the center of its internal movement, but its actual historic form varies markedly from one capitalist country to another. Every real capitalist society has its own unique constellation of classes, or distinctive "social formation." This is the result, on the one hand, of the *uneven,* and, on the other, of the *combined* nature of the real historic development of capitalism (Trotsky 1932). Emerging at different historic moments in different states, when their own development is already conditioned by the relative development of capitalism elsewhere, the various capitalisms develop at different rates and spread unevenly and unequally within their state borders. Different industries lead and successively displace others in the competitive struggle as various capitalisms develop; their specific development, in turn, shapes and is shaped by the distinctive class and intraclass relations of these countries. Capitalism is also profoundly conditioned by the historic forms of precapitalist production and agrarian relations it confronts in its development—and this, too, distinctively shapes every specific capitalist social formation. Such a social formation is split not only into the constituent classes unique to the capitalist mode of production (that is, labor and capital), but also incorporates, as Marx remarked of western European capitalism, "strata of society which, though belonging to the antiquated mode of production, continue to exist side by side with it" (1967, 1:765).

States or white labor in the Transvaal versus the Cape of South Africa); or derive from (b) labor's location in the process of the expanded reproduction of capital (i.e., "productive" vs. "realization," or sales, labor; agrarian versus industrial labor; or labor in competitive, small-scale, and labor-intensive versus "monopoly," large-scale, and capital-intensive production), and (c) the extent of labor's subordination to capital in the immediate labor process (craftsmen versus operatives and laborers). The extent to which such contradictory interests and social cleavages coincide within the working class is a historic and essentially political question, depending on how the class organizes itself: it may accentuate these contradictory interests and transform them into the basis for durable internal divisions, or it may find an organizational means for enhancing its internal cohesion and common, unified action as a class.

For instance, if the enclosures and rapid destruction of the peasantry typified England, as the original home of capitalism, this pattern was not characteristic either in France, where the bourgeois revolution preserved and consolidated peasant production, or, in varying ways, in central and southern Europe, or, especially, Japan. In every capitalist country, then, whatever the general tendency toward the concentration and centralization of capital, there will be an historically specific articulation of productive forms; the relative balance of large-scale capital and small, industry and agriculture, craft and mass production, and of landed estates, agribusiness and independent farming will vary. Therefore, the constellation of class and intraclass relations will be distinctive.

Such differences, in turn, may have far reaching historic implications. Esping-Andersen shows, for example (chapter 11), how the contrasting paths of social democracy in Denmark and Sweden have been shaped by the different patterns of capitalist development in these countries. The relative centrality of independent farming and small manufacturing in Denmark contrasts with Sweden's high level of capital centralization, large scale of industry, and the preponderant size and internal cohesion of the Swedish working class. This has meant that the types of political class alliances *necessary* and the relative independence *possible* for the Social Democrats in these countries has also varied markedly. In turn, this has provided the Swedish Social Democrats with an historical option: by basing themselves squarely on the organized labor movement, they have been able to pursue a form of radical "production politics," including the public steering of capital flows, rather than confining themselves to the merely ameliorative redistribution politics of their counterparts in Denmark—and elsewhere in the capitalist world.

Corporate Capital

Whatever the differences between specific capitalist countries, the major economies, especially the United States and England, are now characterized by the decisive ascendance of the large corporation. Production is carried out on an immense scale and is mediated by complex bureaucratic forms of organization. In turn, these bureaucratic forms themselves obscure the exploitative relations on which they rest. Consequently, it is in these countries that a certain plausibility attaches to the notions of the "postcapitalist society" or "new industrial state" (Dahrendorf 1959; Galbraith 1971), and in which a functionalist theory of social stratification has been the prevailing conception of classes. That capital retains its exploitative nature and that its accumulation remains the mainspring of the entire society is now veiled not merely by the commodity form, or market, but also by the corporate form itself.

The illusion now appears that not capital but bureaucracy, not capitalists but managers control the large corporations. With this usurpation of their capitalist predecessors by the managers, class domination is replaced by a differentiated occupational order, which is intrinsically based on merit: "Rewards" are distributed by "society" according to ability, or the scarcity of the skill involved and the occupation's "functional importance."

Clearly, in functionalist theory (Parsons 1956; Davis and Moore 1945; cf. Tumin 1953; Blau and Duncan 1967), classes lose their previous historical meaning; they become merely quantitatively ranked *strata* that are both *essential* in any complex society and *just,* because their differential rewards accord, except for occasional "dysfunctional" variations, with their social "contribution to the maintenance of the system." With capital dissolved and a rational occupational order now headed by professional managers, the contradiction between labor and capital also disappears, as does, in managerialist doctrine, even the drive for profit in the large corporation: growth replaces profit as the corporation's *primum mobile.* Labor and management are, then, just members of the same team, playing different positions. Of all the pseudofacts behind the notion that classes have withered away in America and other so-called postcapitalist societies, none is as persistent or as fundamental as this illusion of the managerial revolution.

To dispel it, several closely related ways that capital really controls the corporations and dictates production must be grasped (see Zeitlin 1974; 1976). First, the real owners do not actually have to *manage* the corporation, or even be formally represented on the board, to have their objectives realized—that is, to exert control. How much stock it takes to control a corporation is not fixed. It depends on the size of the holdings of other stockholders—and who they are and how they are connected—and how dispersed the rest of the stock is; it also depends on how much the firm is indebted to the same few large banks or other creditors. What sorts of ties the corporation has to others, and especially to big banks and other financial institutions allied with it, is also crucial. A large corporation is just one node in a network of relations tying it together with others and the proprietary interests rooted in them (see chapters 2–4). The critical holdings and real connections that make control possible are simply invisible to the uninformed eye and often even to the seasoned investigator. The holdings of even the leading families (such as the Mellons or the Rockefellers) in corporations they have been known to control are hidden in a welter of accounts held by brokers, foundations, other companies, associates, intermediaries, or nominees. The extent of a principal capitalist family's holdings is also concealed by a finely woven though tangled web of kinship relations. Apparently unrelated persons can be part of a single cohesive set of kindred united to control a corporation, as considerable recent evidence indicates. My own learned guess is that in most corporations that appear to be under management control, there are real controlling owners.

However, even if large corporations were not controlled by *particular* owning interests, the higher executives would still have only relative autonomy in their activities and would be bound by the *general* interests of capital. The heads of the large corporations are the main formal agents and functionaries of capital. Their personal careers, interests, and commitments are closely tied to the expansion of capital. High managerial income and status depend, directly and indirectly, on high corporate profits. Some executives are among the principal shareholders of the companies they run, and most own stock that not only provides much of their income but ranks them among the population's largest stockowners—and puts them in the propertied few. Typically, the managers also move in the same closed circles as the very rich. Intimate social ties and entangling kinship relations, common interests and overriding commitments, unify the families of the heads of the largest corporations and their principal owners into the same relatively cohesive dominant class.

Finally, even if management alone had full control of the corporations, it would still have to try to extract the highest possible profits out of their workers and make the most of their investments. The conduct of management is shaped above all by the imperatives of capital accumulation— the competitive struggle among the giants (now global rather than national), the types of investments they make and the markets they penetrate, and the relations they have with their workers (organized and unorganized). Whatever their so-called professional motivations or power urges, their technocratic teamwork and bureaucratic mentality, managers' decisions on how to organize production and sales have to be measured against the bottom line. They dare not imperil corporate profitability. They must unflinchingly act as "trustees" only for the top investors and real owners who control the large corporations.

In sum, the corporations are units in a class-controlled apparatus of private appropriation; the whole gamut of principal owners and functionaries of capital participate in varying degrees, and as members of the same social class, in its direction. The corporations both administer production and command labor to enforce the extraction of surplus value, which in turn is appropriated by private capital (see Zeitlin and Norich 1979).

If managerialism has posed a false problem and a false solution, the ascendance of the large corporation does, unquestionably, have a critical impact on the structure of the capitalist class. The large corporation is a new form of class-property: a form of social rather than private capital. In it, the ownership of capital has been partially dissociated from the actual direction of production. A critical question then, is how the dissociation of these functions of capital affects internal relations within the capitalist class. The so-called managers themselves are socially differentiated; they are not identically situated in the class and in the expanded reproduction of capital as a whole. Empirically, to answer this question requires analyzing how the principal owners and functionaries of capital are related within the concrete ensemble of social relations that emerge in the class. What are the real internal relations in the dominant classes of specific capitalist countries? Theoretically, such research has to proceed from the recognition and specification of the objectively distinct locations in the productive process occupied by different types of owners and functionaries of capital and the *consequences* that flow from these distinctive locations.

Alongside the dissociation of the functions of capital, the large corporation has also unified, although in contradictory forms, the essential phases of the reproduction of capital: the production, appropriation, and realization of the surplus product of labor. Industrial, banking, and commercial capital have coalesced and combined in a host of ways; in fact, conceptualizing the largest banks, insurance companies, merchandising firms, and industrials as independent organizations may hide the actual coalescence of these differing forms of capital. These corporations and banks are frequently themselves principal shareholders in each other; and they may also have as their principal shareowners the very same individuals, associates, and families. These corporations may also be linked by an apparatus of interlocking directorates that both bind them together organizationally and provide mechanisms for the coordination and reconciliation of their contending interests.

The implications of these relations for the process of capital accumulation, for the internal structure of the capitalist class itself, and for its relations with other classes have, however, yet to be systematically specified theoretically.

Several questions are critical. First, what elements of the capitalist class have effective control of the large corporations and how does this control affect the disposition of the surplus product and the process of capital accumulation? Is, as even certain Marxists argue, "real power" in the corporation held by a "self-perpetuating" management—and is it, therefore, valid to "abstract from whatever elements of outside control may still exist in the world of giant corporations because they are *in no sense essential* to the way [capitalism] works"? (Baran and Sweezy 1968:16, 20; emphasis added.) Does, for example, the rate of internal accumulation (that is, the retention of earnings versus the payout of dividends) in the large corporation differ depending on the types of proprietary interests involved in it? What role do so-called "outside control centers" (proprietary interests) versus "inside managements" (in Baran and Sweezy's words) have in determining this? Assuming that both principal owners and managers strive to maximize the supply of capital under their immediate control to minimize their dependence on external financing and the consequent intervention of the large banks in their corporate affairs, the question becomes: Do putatively management-controlled firms succeed to the extent that owner-controlled firms do in retaining their earnings, given the same pressures for higher dividend rates exerted by financial institutions on behalf of their trust holdings (much of which are in tax exempt pension funds)? The answer, according to Norich's analysis (chapter 3), is that when a single dominant owner (or owning family) controls the corporation, a larger proportion of its profits are retained than in the putatively management-controlled corporation. The nature of the "elements of outside control" in the large corporation is, therefore, quite essential (contrary to Baran and Sweezy) in determining the rate of internal accumulation (though how this affects the overall rate of accumulation remains to be examined).

A second critical question is what implications does the concrescence of the various moments or forms of capital and the emergence, in particular, of finance capital have for the internal organization of the capitalist class? Neither financiers extracting interest at the expense of industrial profits nor bankers controlling corporations, but *finance capitalists* on the boards of the largest banks *and* corporations preside over the banks' investments as creditors *and* shareholders, organizing production, sales and financing, and appropriating the profits of their integrated activities. To the extent that the largest banks and corporations constitute a new form of class property—of social ownership of the means of production by a single dominant class—the finance capitalists interlocking them become the leading organizers of this system of class-wide property. This would be reason enough to predict, as I have (1974; 1976), that they "represent a special social type in contrast to other officers and directors of the largest corporations and banks."

Moreover, the coalescence of financial and industrial capital does not eliminate the contradictions between them, nor the claims of the former to a share of the profits of the latter; rather it produces a *self-contradictory class situation,* in which the individuals who personify this coalescence are constantly confronted with the inherent problem of reconciling these contradictory interests. No structural mechanism ensures their reconciliation, although interlocks between the banks and corporations facilitate it. Thus, there is reason to believe that precisely those individuals whose interests personally span finance and industry, as principal owners of capital in both, would especially strive to occupy the directorships that interlock the large banks and corporations, so that they could actively shape corporate strategy to accommodate their specific self-contradictory interests. In short, those who are finance capitalists, in the limited sense that they are directors of both large banks and large corporations, should also be far more likely than ordinary corporate executives to be drawn from the core of interrelated principal owners of capital. Obtaining the relevant data is a research task yet to be systematically undertaken in the United States or any advanced capitalist country. However, by using several interrelated indicators, it is possible to estimate whether or not the various directors are drawn, as Soref puts it (chapter 2), from "the older, more established, families of the capitalist class" whose interests most probably span both finance and industry.

In a sample of directorships from a prior sample of 40 of the 200 largest industrials, Soref found that those who are also directors of any financial company are about twice as likely to be from the established capitalist families as ordinary executives; and those who are directors of either one of the 50 largest banks or 50 largest insurance companies or a partner of an investment bank (a highly restricted group of finance capitalists) are only slightly less likely than the broader category to be disproportionately drawn from the leading families of the class. In fact, the finance capitalists are also more likely to sit on the boards of a sample of the largest *Fortune* 500 corporations, to have more directorships in firms in the "key industries . . . at the heart of manufacturing," and in the firms most centrally located in the interlocking corporate network. The evidence is thus quite consistent with the hypothesis that finance capitalists constitute a distinctive segment of the class.

A third critical question examined here on the political economy of internal relations in the capitalist class is: What consequences result, directly or indirectly, from differential control over capital flows within that class? More precisely, how are the spatial location, social composition, and internal differentiation of the working class and other subordinate classes affected by the ascendance of specific elements in the capitalist class? For instance, the reciprocal processes of suburban expansion and inner-city decay have characterized the recent history of American cities. These are structural reflections of mutually reinforcing state policies and private investment decisions (see Castells 1977:380–401), specifically the high rate of investment in affluent areas and suburbs and the high rate of disinvestment in inner-city and other working-class neighborhoods.

In fact, as Ratcliff shows in his analysis of the processes in St. Louis (chapter 4), they are also the measurable consequence of the explicit investment policies of particular dominant capitalist elements. That is, the large banks leading the disinvestment process, through their home loan mortgage policies toward low- and moderate-income areas of the city, are not merely large banks: they most clearly embody the organizational form of *finance capital,* in that they are the banks which are most closely interlocked with the largest nonfinancial corporations. Through the mediation of these banks, even the savings of the workers are reappropriated from them and converted into capital at the disposal of the large corporations; in turn, this capital is diverted from the workers' neighborhoods into more profitable investments elsewhere, thereby accelerating the deterioration of their living conditions.[3]

Obviously, these results of the contradictory calculus of profitability in the competitive struggle should not be given a merely voluntaristic interpretation: investment decisions are determined both by the constraints and compulsions of the contradictory accumulation process and by the specific location in that process of decisive units of capital and dominant elements of the capitalist class. (See also the related study by Yago, chapter 13, of the decline of public transit in Germany and the United States.)

The Consent of the Exploited:
Class Hegemony and the State

A critical aim of class analysis is to reveal, as it has here, the otherwise hidden "connections between the causes and the consequences of the 'class situation' " of the exploited. Only by recognizing these real connections can they "react," in Weber's words, "against the class structure not only through intermittent and irrational protest, but in the form of rational association" (1946:184). Consequently, the common meanings that men and women impute to their social activities and relations, particularly their production relations, and how these meanings become the accepted and standard interpretations and definitions of social reality, are, in fact, an essential aspect of the relations between classes. These ideas, concepts, or forms of social consciousness enter into class relations as an *intrinsic* and even *constitutive* feature of these relations; they are not some "superstructure" resting on a "base," as Marx put it in a poorly chosen metaphor (1970:20–21); nor, certainly, are they a free-floating, self-moving, but functional value system. On the contrary, the various ideational forms—legal, philosophic, moral, religious, aesthetic, political, and so on—are merely different aspects (or "moments") of the actual practical activity of men and women. In producing their real existence, they also produce these ideational products of their own thinking—some of which, as mystified forms of consciousness, or ideology, actually disguise and obscure or even substitute an imaginary existence for their real existence.

To the extent that the forms of thought in any society provide false

---

[3] In the sense that even a portion of the workers' necessary product, in the form of savings, is reappropriated from them by capital, this constitutes a method of "secondary exploitation, which runs parallel to the primary exploitation taking place in the production process itself" (Marx 1967:3, 609).

explanations, distorted understandings, and inner justifications for the relations of domination that inhere in it—conceiving them as inevitable, natural, or rational—these relations become acceptable, or *legitimate.* Recognized social practice takes the form of an abstract or universally valid principle; the particular interests of the dominant class turn into the general social interest, and its own ideas of its dominance become the dominant ideas of society. In this ideological process, the dominant class achieves its hegemony by consent. It secures, in short, the basis for its own *legitimate class domination* (cf. Marx and Engels 1947:40–41; Weber 1968:946; Gramsci 1971). How "the consent of the exploited" is obtained and perpetuated, in what ideological form exploitation is legitimated, and how and under what conditions such *exploitative legitimacy* is eroded and subverted and inchoate revolt or self-conscious political action emerges among the exploited, is the primordial political question for every class society.

The making (and unmaking) of classes is, in this sense, simultaneously an ideological and political process. Every dominant class has to devise a repertoire of social arrangements to ensure the continued reproduction of the exploitative relations on which its dominion in society rests, including the essential legitimations of these relations. To "devise," however, does not necessarily mean (although it certainly does not exclude) explicit and self-conscious attempts to create these means of domination. On the contrary, to the extent that they are the products of an *ideological* process, the real origins of these means of domination remain hidden; and precisely because they encompass the full panoply of social relations, which is the real terrain of class conflict and political action, the means of domination are the unintended and refracted product of the contradictory class relations they tend to uphold. In the broadest sense, then, *the "state" is a concept for the concentrated and organized means of legitimate class domination,* whether or not these are explicitly *recognized* as political in any given historical society.

Of course, class hegemony never rests merely on the consent of the exploited—whatever the ideological forms consent may take and whatever its substantive legitimations. "Every state is founded on force," as Trotsky said at Brest-Litovsk; or, as Weber put it: "The state is a relation of men dominating men, a relation supported by means of legitimate (i.e., considered to be legitimate) violence" (1946:78). Ultimately, control of the means of violence, of the physical means of coercion, is the indispensable means of class domination; without it, consent can always be withdrawn; with it, consent can be enforced or imposed.[4] Of the concentrated and organized

---

[4] It is not only the "expropriation of the workers from the means of production" that assures their so-called consent to capitalist production relations, but also, as Weber put it succinctly, "that the appropriation of the means of production by the owners is to be protected by force" (quoted by Mommsen 1974:66).

means of legitimate class domination, one alone is specific to the "state" and is its defining feature: the monopoly of the major means of violence.

Every real state is a historical product: It is, in Marx's celebrated phrase, "the official *resumé* of the antagonism in civil society," but under historically determinate circumstances. As such, it is the product of the historically specific constellation of class relations and social conflicts in which it is implicated; it may, therefore, indeed it must, if it is not to rest on its monopoly of the means of coercion alone, incorporate within its own structure the interests not only of the dominant but of the subordinate classes. In this quite specific sense, then, every real state, as Engels long ago argued clearly, has an *"inherent relative independence."* The state is "endowed with a movement of its own," but within the varying constraints imposed by the contradictory productive relations and historical situation in which it is situated. Its relative independence (or "relative autonomy"), Engels argued, has two fundamental sources. First, the political authorities necessarily have "particular interests" that are "distinct . . . from the interests of those who empowered them"; the state therefore "strives for as much independence as possible." Second, and most important, its relative autonomy appears precisely because its own activities simultaneously create opposition to it by those who originally empowered it but over whom it also rules, and which it strives to deal with independently to ensure its own independence (Engels 1973:491). The proximate limits of any state's autonomy, then, are set both by its own particular structured interests and by its location in the existing political relations themselves, even as the ultimate limits are imposed by the contradictory class relations underlying them.

Nonetheless, our own conception of the state is itself mediated by our bourgeois historical epoch. Historically, it is only with the emergence of capitalism that the state appears as an "independent sphere" and "civil society" loses its directly political character. In contrast to the varying precapitalist forms of class domination and corporate appropriation of political rights, political power under capitalism is characteristically neither privately appropriated, a direct attribute of productive relations, nor a distinctive and inherent function of property ownership.

In precapitalist states, the control of the means of coercion and the means of administration, on the one hand, is inseparable from control of the means of production, on the other. And the so-called internal relations of authority and official activity of the state tend to coincide with corporate class relations outside it. This occurs even when the state (in contrast, for instance, to a long period in medieval political relations) does constitute an identifiable institution.

In the ancient state, for example, the Lex Judiciaria under the second of the Gracchi specifically incorporated within the structure of the republican state in Rome the changed class relations between the patricians and *equites,* the armed imperial financiers and traders of the late second century B.C.: these laws granted the class of equites control of judgeships that previously had been the exclusive prerogative of the preeminently patrician Senate. The transfer of judicial functions from the Senate to the corporate body of equites was a direct translation of changed class relations into changes in the internal relations of authority within the state itself (*pace* Weber 1968:1309). On the other hand, the Roman state also retained a relative autonomy within the relations of classes, as is evidenced, particularly, by the famous Gracchian agrarian codes, the Lex Sempronia Agraria and Lex Frumentaria, and their historic precursors, the Licinian Rogations: these laws responded, as did the specific institution of the Tribune, to centuries of active class struggles and violent eruptions by small holders, tenants, and the landless against the latifundia.

The separation of the economic and the political as relatively distinct spheres of social existence is the specific historical product of the development of capitalism, precisely because the act of appropriation itself is no longer inherently political but is mediated instead by economic relations. In this lies the historical specificity of the bourgeois state, a point to which we return below. "Capitalism," in Weber's sharp imagery, "subjects the worker" to a form of "masterless slavery." Because "the domination of capital appears in such an indirect form that one cannot identify any concrete master" (1968:1186), the real relations between capital and labor tend to be concealed ideologically. Although every dominant class strives for the ascendance of its own conceptions as the conceptions of the producers themselves, the connection between them is peculiarly opaque under capitalism. It is for this reason that the imaginative activity or *theoretical thinking* involved in identifying the "master" and the "slave" as capital and labor, as exploiter and exploited, is also an inherently *political* activity in which *classes become defined as social realities.*

Classes are constituted in contradictory productive relations, but these relations never exhaust the range of social experience in which the consciousness of class emerges and organized classes are formed. Rather, the productive relations set objective limits to potential historical development and, at the same time, as Przeworski observes, constitute "a structure of choices given at a particular moment of history. Social relations are given to a historical subject, individual or collective, as realms of possibilities . . . a set of conditions that determine what course of action have what consequences for social transformations" (1977:377). Theory, in other words, is always an integral element of the social transformation any radical movement aims to bring about; and only the transformation itself can validate the movement's theory. However inchoate or incoherent its expression in organized consciousness, every social movement has such a theory, and it heavily influences its practical political action. Marxian socialist parties, in particular, have always had such a self-conscious conception of the "unity of theory and practice." The consciousness that classes have of themselves is the consciousness expressed in their real political struggles; and these struggles, in turn, condition and transform their consciousness, and therefore the actuality of the class relations themselves.

Chile is only the most recent historical example of how a socialist movement's theory of the social formation it aimed to transform, itself hampered the struggle for its transformation. It "conditioned the policy of class alliances proposed by the various parties of the Left," as Roxborough observes (chapter 16), and "initiated and reinforced propensities to act in certain general directions," which imposed often unrecognized limits on the left's concrete political practice. Especially when the left won the presidency, its theory of classes and the state in the Chilean social formation was to have far-reaching historical consequences for the future shape of the social formation itself. Class conflict and class formation are, then, aspects or moments of the same social process; neither follows from the other as an effect or is necessarily prior (*pace* Przeworski 1977); rather, they interact and reciprocally interpenetrate in the real historic movement. "Classes," in Sartre's succinct formulation, "do not naturally exist, but they are made" (1968:96).

Although every dominant class strives to secure its rule as "permanently organized consent" (Gramsci 1971:80), none gains its ideological hegemony, or legitimates its domination, without reiterated struggle. Capitalism's ideal working class, an ideal constantly confronted by a recalcitrant reality, would be one "which by education, tradition, habit, looks upon the conditions of that mode of production as self-evident laws of Nature" (Marx 1967, 1:737). The identification of hard work with virtue, docility with civility, merit with "success," technical complexity with hierarchy, rationality with profitability, individuality with possessive individualism, and personal freedom with private property are all closely related components of the basic legitimations of capitalism; these ideological conceptions make capitalism itself appear to be self-evidently natural if not desirable, and organize the workers' consent to their own exploitation.

A critical political question for every working class, therefore, is whether or not it has the *capacity to organize its own consciousness*, rather than submit to the reproduction among its members of the ideological conceptions that conceal their own real existence—their common existence as a class—from themselves. Can the workers fashion, as their conscious creation, a distinctive political culture for their class, one which simultaneously provides them with a contrary *explanation* of their common situation and an alternative *vision* of their possible future? Historically, only socialist conceptions rooted in an organized labor movement and sustained by the workers' own political party have provided a durable basis for such an authentically self-conscious working-class political culture. Mass-based social-ist parties in the West have erected a relatively separate public sphere through which to instill socialist content in the everyday lives of the work-ers under capitalism—a public sphere "including," as Esping-Andersen writes (chapter 11) of the Swedish and Danish Social Democrats, for in-stance, "cooperatives, workers' centers, sports clubs, boy scout movements, schools, and newspapers designed to integrate the working class, educate it politically and insulate it from bourgeois society."

Once socialist conceptions have taken hold among the workers, the connection between the accumulation of capital and their own class situa-tion is rendered transparent. The source of capital's creation in their own productive activity is no longer a mystery, obscured by the appearances of the market, veiled by the corporate form, or mystified by the labor process itself. They recognize and reject both their exploitation and alienation in the productive process. Capitalist relations of production have a dual as-pect: Capital dictates both the social process of production as a whole, through its control of the means of production, and the "immediate labor process," through its control of the concrete organization of production within the plant itself. Capital appropriates not only the means of produc-tion but the very rationality of the direct producers. Not labor but capital plans, organizes, and controls the expenditure of labor; it appropriates the workers' common "knowledge, judgment and will" and lodges it in a man-agerial-technical apparatus that directs and enforces production (Marx 1967:1, 360–63). This alienated labor process distorts the workers' con-sciousness of the entire process and their place within it; but socialist con-ceptions demystify the process for the workers and make it transparent (see Zeitlin 1967, ch. 8). This can be seen, for example, in Haas's analysis (chap-ter 12) of workers' views of self-management (or "workers' control") in Sweden and the United States. The American workers interviewed typi-cally deny both their *right* and their *ability* to have a "bigger role in deci-sions" where they work, whereas Swedish workers affirm both, by a large majority. Americans accept the legitimacy of private property and the rationality of hierarchical authority; in marked contrast, Swedish workers (whose political culture, shaped by 50 years of struggle, is permeated by so-cialist conceptions) recognize both the creative power of their own labor and the emancipatory possibilities of their own control of the labor process.

These contemporary differences between the workers' explicit com-mitments and implicit understandings in these countries are certainly not historic constants; nor do they reflect some inherent American exceptional-ism. The labor movement in the United States has often fought self-con-sciously against the imposition of values and institutions it saw as hostile to its own democratic and egalitarian temper. Yet it is clear that, although so-cialists have played a crucial role in the organization and leadership of many major industrial unions in the United States, a radical or specifically socialist political culture has so far been a rare and ephemeral creation among American workers. Where it has been implanted, its roots usually have been in the distinctive ethnicity of working-class immigrants—the *landsmanschaften,* workmen's circles, and mutual aid (and burial) societies of the working class neighborhoods of the major industrial cities—though even the timberlands, mines, and tenant farms of the southwestern states formed a mass base for the "gospel of socialism" in the early decades of this century (Green 1978).

One of the most significant regional socialist political cultures in the American working class was created in the Midwest's Mesabi iron mining range by Finnish immigrants at the turn of the century—a political culture that they consciously sought to wield as "a weapon," as Blee and Gedicks put it (chapter 7), "in the struggle for hegemony in capitalist America." In their workers' halls, newspapers, clubs, barbershops, saloons—and even in their own socialist temperance leagues—they constituted an autonomous consciousness of themselves as a revolutionary class; indeed, they established socialist Sunday schools, where their children were taught not a catechism of possessive individualism and self-blame for "failure" (see Piven and Cloward 1980), but a "Socialist Child's Ten Commandments"—and from which emerged a generation of socialist worker-intellectuals. While the socialist miners of the Mesabi range ran their own Work-People's College and Sunday schools, workers elsewhere in the country fought actively against the imposition of a public school system often explicitly designed to reproduce class inequality.

From the 1890s through the 1920s, for example, Chicago was the scene, as Wrigley shows (chapter 6), of "extensive and bitter conflict over the control, funding, and curriculum of the public schools." The labor movement actively fought against organized capital's open attempt to impose vocational and moral (rather than academic) education on the workers' children, which aimed to turn them, as the Chicago Federation of Labor charged, into docile and "perfect parts of an industrial machine." Yet even such relatively self-conscious political struggles by the labor movement were entirely fought out *within* and limited by the prevailing ideology. In contrast to the socialist political culture that sustained and was sustained by the Mesabi iron miners' struggles against capitalism, an alternative social vision was not borne by labor.

But even where such a world view prevails in the working class, consent and class-consciousness can coexist uneasily within it; the real limits to consciousness are imposed as well as created by the material conditions it strives to transcend. Not only the realm of possibilities constituted for the workers by their objective class situation, but the quite concrete control of the means of violence by the state, assure their practical, if not theoretical, consent. Consent, in other words, has a double antinomy: Class consciousness is its negation, but coercion is its reaffirmation. Consent, to paraphrase Moore (1966:486), has to be created anew in each generation, often with great pain and suffering. To enforce it, human beings are punched, bullied, sent to jail, thrown into concentration camps, cajoled, bribed, tortured or shot. The course of post–World War Two Germany in the West, for example, and of working-class political action in particular, was decisively affected both by the Nazi regime's murder or incarceration of the workers' most class-conscious cadre and leaders and by the postwar occupation by the armed forces of the advanced capitalist countries. With the German capitalists politically paralyzed after the Nazi defeat, and with a renascent workers' political movement demanding major socialization measures, the intervention of the military authorities—the suspension of new state laws transferring certain industries to public ownership, the abrogation of the Workers Council acts, the harassment of the left and the hindrance of union organization, the forcible suppression of the major postwar strike wave, the careful selection and appointment of anticommunist politicians to administrative positions and support for their political organization— was the *sine qua non* for labor's consent to the restoration of capitalism and · bourgeois hegemony in West Germany, as Ahlemeyer and Schellhase show (chapter 14).

Here, once again, much as in the post–Civil War American South, for example (allowing for substantial historical differences), the hegemony of a prostrate dominant class was restored through the sustained deployment of state power. As Wiener shows (chapter 1), the planters, despite the abolition of slavery, were able to use state power (in this instance, their control of the legislature) to "reconstitute the region's economy on their own terms, in their own interests, against a new class [the merchants], which threatened their dominant position." The state, in short, was critical not merely in preserving or restoring, but actually creating new social relations of production—precisely because the old relations were in disarray and the nature of the new ones could only be determined politically.

This partially *originative role of the state* occurs especially, as the instance of the post–Civil War South suggests, when unwonted forms of social production and their concomitant class relationships are originally being forged, and which class, or class segment, gains command of state power and uses it effectively can be decisive in the consolidation of new social relations. In every historical transition between modes of production the effective deployment of state power is critical, but in none more than revolutionary transformations. Certainly, "the *overthrow* of the existing ruling power and the *dissolution* of existing social relationships . . . is a *political* act," in Marx's phrase (1956:238); but so, too, is the actual creation of the new relationships (within given material and historical limits, of course).

The *organizing activity* of the revolutionary state itself shapes the nature of the new social formation. In postrevolutionary Mexico, for example, the state not only established the "conditions for capital accumulation and the financial basis of the state itself, . . . but contributed directly and indirectly," Hamilton argues, "to the creation of the new capitalist class" (chapter 15). The new state, under such conditions (that is, with the old state apparatus smashed, the landed class politically paralyzed and economically wounded, and the peasantry unable to assert itself as a unified class), achieved an extraordinary level of autonomy.

The Capitalist Democratic State

Under capitalism, as I have already emphasized, class domination is characteristically mediated by a state in which the means of coercion and of administration have been formally separated from the officials, and official activity from private life. The independent individual appears in the state only as a citizen, and the relations between such independent individuals are regulated by law rather than by their corporate identity (Marx 1956:235). In fact, it is precisely by abstracting from the class divisions in social life that the bourgeois republic creates the fictive common identity and formal legal equality of its citizens. The legal system attains a relatively independent internal development of its own, for it has to be in harmony with the ideological *conceptions* of justice and *principles* of jurisprudence of bourgeois society; the law has to be not merely an "official expression" of existing social relations, but also, as Engels put it (1973, 3:491–92), an *"internally coherent* expression." Because the law now appears to be the codified embodiment of popular sovereignty, the state now appears to be no more than its veritable official form. In this way, the relative autonomy of the bourgeois state is internally buttressed by its own legitimate, and legitimating, legal order.

It bears emphasis that the attainment of formal juridical and political equality—of equal personal, civil, and political rights under the law (for men)—is the historic product of the specific relations between classes *within* bourgeois society; it was not "inscribed" in the capitalist mode of production as an inherent functional necessity. The abolition of class encumbrances or property qualifications (or their surrogates, such as literacy requirements) on the franchise and on legal entitlement to higher officer ranks in the military or to bureaucratic posts and political offices has been achieved only through popular struggle. In the process, the various historically durable forms of representative capitalist democracy have been constructed. As the immediate connection between dominant class and state became increasingly attenuated, the translation of its social hegemony into political power and state policy also became, in comparison to prior types of state, relatively problematic.

As citizens before the law, capitalists also must be "represented." The translation of the interests of capital into state policy, especially in contemporary capitalist democracies, involves specifically political means. Their representation is the mediated product of a complex, visibly pluralistic, political struggle that also partially structures and redefines what those interests are and often renders the political power of capital invisible, even to the capitalists themselves. Class interests are certainly objective, but they are never merely expressed; they are also *produced,* as I have emphasized throughout, during the political struggle for their political realization.

"Pluralism" is no mere "phenomenal form of political conflict in capitalist societies" (*pace* Esping-Andersen and others 1976:217). On the contrary, the extent to which the political struggle *appears* to be no more than a society-wide pluralist process is itself a practical political *reality.* The *political* reality is constructed so as to deny the *social* reality of classes, to the extent that organized classes *are* absent from it. How, and to what extent, the working class is able to organize politically under advanced capitalism to transform the otherwise opaque split in society between it and capital into a transparent conflict within the political arena, and thereby to make pluralist politics into class politics, is a primary political question for that class. Thus, it is always an empirical question as to how and within what limits the struggle for the representation of the interests of capital in state policy actually shapes, as well as is shaped by, the interests themselves. Nothing in the *structure* of the state itself ineluctably assures the realization of the interests of capital by the state.

However, the contradictory requirements of the accumulation process constrain and direct the state's response to the plurality of class and intraclass interests and cross pressures. The autonomy of the state is inherently relative to the extent that capitalist class relations and the accumulation process they set in motion are presupposed. They set intrinsic limits to political realism: The range of so-called rational alternatives for state policy is immanently bounded by what is rational, only given these relations. These structural limits are double-edged: On the one side, the concrete constellation of class interests on which state policy impinges constitutes an always present potential source of political opposition to any encroachment on private property. On the other, the accumulation process itself, and the multiplicity of private investment decisions based on a calculus of profitability through which it is manifested, requires the predictability and stability of state policies that sustain it.

If state policies were even sporadically, let alone systematically, to provide "disincentives" to private investment, whether through taxation, fiscal, or monetary policies, or through social policies that raised the reproduction costs of labor for capital (the "wage bill"), this would tend to rupture the cycle of production, realization, and reinvestment of profit; doubt among capitalists about the profitability of reinvestment tends to propel disinvestment throughout the interrelated but anarchic productive process. A lowered rate of accumulation, disemployment and underemployment, shortages and rising prices, and even popular disenchantment and hostility, and not merely the opposition of capital, would result from the activities of a democratic state that thwarted capital and its reproduction. The narrow limits on state policy imposed by the accumulation process are therefore transparent only when state officials attempt to exceed them; and such officials would likely find their tenure in office rather tumultuous and short, unless these policies were reversed.[5] For these reasons, not merely conservative and liberal, but labor and social democratic governments in democratic capitalist states ordinarily pursue their social objectives through state policies that are also designed to ensure a "healthy business climate." Any state policies intended, for example, to increase labor productivity, spur economic growth, clean up the environment, reduce poverty, renew the cities, or provide mass transit are rational under contemporary capitalism only if they also imply the profitable expansion of

---

[5] Were an elected left or labor government to put through reforms that impinged on capital and threatened its prerogatives, this especially would disrupt the economy, not only for the reasons noted, but also because of the specific implications for class relations of labor's newly won political power: the prospect of enhanced workers' control over the immediate production process and a declining rate of exploitation. The paradox is that such a government would then face the probability of economic stagnation, if not severe crisis—for which it, and not capital, might well be held responsible by the electorate. For to the extent that a left government must act within the confines of liberal democracy, even in the rare situation when it actually has a cohesive majority in parliament, it cannot act decisively to meet the crisis. It has neither the authority nor the power (assuming it has the will) to compel investment and control production, sales and pricing; and, to the extent that it strives for such power, this in itself would exacerbate the crisis. For capital, highly concentrated and centralized in the largest corporations whose activities reverberate immediately throughout the economy, has the capacity to act willfully (and not merely anarchically) to create economic chaos designed to wound the left government and bring it down.

The dilemma of a democratic left government is clear: Either it capitulates and seeks to manage the economy on behalf of capital rather than labor, or the travail of its efforts at reform may dissipate the very popular support that brought it to office in the first place. Its only alternative is to take measures which, at best, are extralegal, to gain control of the economy's commanding heights. This, in turn, means accelerated social polarization and economic disruption (and sabotage). Yet such a struggle can only be waged successfully, assuming the left's commitment to it, with the active support and initiative of a conscious, cohesive, and thoroughly alert working class. The source of the workers' travail and of the crisis must be clear to them, and their struggle against capital must be unwavering. This is a struggle, however, for which the left's previous participation in parliamentary politics and labor negotiations can only ill prepare it.

capital and the reproduction of its legitimate domination of labor; social needs can be served only by serving the needs of capital in the process. Rationality, therefore, can only mean *capitalist rationality.*

Whatever the class situation, social origins, or personal predilections and interests of political officials and bureaucratic functionaries in the democratic capitalist state, they must ordinarily act within narrow objective limits to confront the problems posed by the contradictory accumulation process governing the political economy. Certain policy options, as rational as they might be in the abstract, can scarcely be considered, because implementing them would, in Gramsci's apt phrase, "touch the essential" and endanger the prevailing relations of domination. Therefore, the personnel of the state do not have to be conscious of the class interests involved or have explicit social allegiances to act politically in a way that ensures the realization of the interests of capital. So long as the state is assumed to be the mere arbiter of the "public interest," a mere regulator of "social problems" and mediator of social conflicts *within* the existing order, the interests of capital must define the universal interest and be served objectively by the state. Under these conditions, in which the accumulation process itself closely constricts the range of variation in state policy, the capitalist class does not have to "govern" in order to "rule" (Kautsky 1903:13). The capitalist class that *can* govern least, governs best, for capital.

Of course, none of this is meant to hypostatize the so-called capitalist state, nor to treat it as a reified object whose functions inhere in and self-determine its structure, as is done in recent structuralist Marxist formulations. In these, the so-called relative autonomy of the state exists as if by definition, and is, therefore, untouched by the relative autonomy of real political practice itself. The claim is not only a sort of complicated structural reductionism (Hindness and Hirst 1975:38), but it is also wrong that, for the so-called capitalist state, "the participation, whether direct or indirect, of the dominant class in government *in no way changes things*" (Poulantzas 1973c:246; italics in original). On the contrary, the proximate—maybe even the ultimate—limits on the activities of the state are not static; they shift in response to changes in the balance of forces, within and between classes.

The context of public expectations in which state policy is made and in which concrete political decisions are seen as reasonable is not spontaneously generated. Rather, it emerges and is formed in the struggle for political power between contending interests, in the course of which the so-called public interest is defined and shifts in the standards of political realism and rationality are legitimated. Consequently, *intra*class political activity may be crucial in defining and actualizing a given set of interests within the capitalist class. Any adequate class analysis of political relations under contemporary capitalism should try to grasp the connections between (both short- and long-term) state policy and the political activities, in whatever form, of the internal segments of the capitalist class. Within the class, a specific segment may gain political ascendancy, thereby not only representing the class as a whole, but transforming *its* interests into *class* interests. In this sense, it becomes the dominant or "hegemonic" segment of the class (Zeitlin and others 1976:1009; cf. Poulantzas 1973b:44). The immediate and even long-run interests of contending elements of the dominant class, and their conceptions of these interests and of the state policies they consider appropriate to their realization, often differ sharply. The democratic state, therefore, is ordinarily an arena for struggle between special interests, spheres of influence, interest groups, and distinctive segments of the capitalist class itself, as well as between it and labor and other subordinate social elements. To this extent, the relative autonomy of the state derives from these plural intraclass conflicts, as well as from its place within class interrelations as a whole.

How clearly (and sharply) specific state policies, or the lack of relevant and proper policies, affect the interests of distinct elements of capital—which, obviously, is also conditioned by their relations with labor—will determine to what extent they find it essential, or desirable, to participate directly or indirectly in government. This question is primarily historical. Much of the actualization of dominant intraclass interests does not require the mediation of the state, but can be effected through the peak associations (such as the Business Council or National Association of Manufacturers) of the class, or through various forms of corporate combination (such as cartels, trusts, gentlemen's agreements) and concrete corporate coalitions that ensure the realization of their interests and the subordination of those of other contending elements in the class.

Whether or not such self-organization within the dominant class and the active effort to shape state policy go together—either indirectly through participation in the "voluntary associations" of the class (Domhoff 1979) that formulate, advocate and organize its political strategy on a closely linked set of issues (such as the Council on Foreign Relations, the Committee for Economic Development, and the Trilateral Commission); or directly through active intervention in the electoral arena, political party activity, and actual participation in government—also varies with the historical situation. It depends especially on the extent to which distinct intraclass interests transparently require state intervention for their realization—which, in turn, depends on the relative position of these elements in the competitive struggle, the specificity of their class situation, and the concrete political configuration. This is clear, for example, from Yago's analysis (chapter 13) of capital's intraclass political struggles around "motorization" and the displacement of the old modes of transit and the industrial interests deeply involved in them, both in Germany and the United States.

Such dominant intraclass struggles and their specific resolution can have far-reaching effects on social life and the very contours of the social formation itself. No adequate theory of the state under contemporary capitalism can dismiss such political activity by capitalists and their close associates as a mere effect or epiphenomenon of structures; nor is it sensible to claim that any class theory that seriously attempts to grasp the meaning of such activity thereby reduces "the role of the State to the conduct and 'behavior' of the members of the State apparatus" (Poulantzas 1973c:246). The question is rather what they are *doing* there, and what the real social *consequences* are of their participation, "whether direct or indirect, in government." The initiatives taken by the dominant class through its politically active representatives are always critical and may be decisive determinants of state policy.

Yago shows, for example, how critical the self-organization and political activity of the "corporate car complex" was in the defeat of rival industrial interests from the 1920s on in the United States. The resilience of public rail transit in the large cities and the saturation of the private automobile market in the 1920s led the auto, rubber, and oil industries' largest firms to ally in a long-term corporate strategy designed to create demand for their products, and, in fact, society's dependence on them. The corporate car complex secretly bought control of electric and rail systems of mass transit and then dismantled and replaced them with gasoline-run buses; which, successively, impelled the rapid growth of private automobile transportation. Coupled with these private investment decisions were public policies to offset the competitive advantages of electric lines and initiate federal highway construction to facilitate "automobilization." In short, here was an intraclass coalition of capital whose corporate strategy was threefold: It made concerted private investments that immediately served the coalition's interests; in turn, these investments created a social context that virtually required state policies favoring its interests; and, aside from *creating* these "structural determinants," the coalition assured its control over relevant state policies by active and systematic "instrumental" participation at the highest levels of government.

Perhaps the most effective way to translate specific dominant class interests into state policy, as this example also suggests, is to have agencies established within the state itself (such as the Bureau of Public Roads), which incorporate these interests into their organizational routine by regularly taking them into account in their normal activities. In this way, political questions become defined as "technical" or "administrative" problems, requiring "experts" rather than "politicians" for their solution—and, not incidentally, insulating the interests involved from popular pressures. This is especially important for those agencies of government whose activities regularly and obviously impinge not only on the competing interests of segments of capital, but on the contradictory and conflicting *class* interests of capital and labor. With *the routinization of capitalist class interest within the state itself,* only *opposition* to it appears to be political—an illegitimate intrusion of politics into supposedly socially neutral state agencies.

To effect this institutionalization of class domination within the official forms of public authority themselves, the active intervention of representatives of capital at critical phases in the organization of specific state agencies may be crucial. Defining an agency or department's objectives and the range of its legal authority, determining the size and content of its budgets, establishing its lines of authority and types of accountability, centralizing or decentralizing it, as DiTomaso argues (chapter 5), are each crucial phases of the formation of the apparently classless character of agencies of the state that routinely serve dominant-class interests. This has been particularly clear, as she shows, in the history of the Department of Labor. It originated out of the late nineteenth-century struggles of the incipient labor movement, which aimed to institutionalize *labor's* class interest within the state, by establishing an "executive department of government" which would, as the Knights of Labor demanded, scrutinize "the means by which employers or moneyed men acquire wealth" and put an end to "illegitimate profitmaking."

With the active intervention and political struggle of organized capital, however, it was to become instead, as its first and long-time head put it correctly, a means within the state to "harmonize . . . divergencies between capital and labor." It was also to remain, so as to prevent its being in any way an "enclave of labor" within the state, one of the smallest, most fragmented, and least effective cabinet-level departments of government. Only with the growing militance of labor in the 1960s, and especially with the eruption of the poor and black segment of the working class, did the Department of Labor's organization, authority, and programs—along with other agencies of the state—once again become immediate objects of political class conflict.

Class Conflict and State Policy in Recent American Capitalism

Everywhere, late capitalism is now characterized by the extensive intervention of the state. The relative independence of the state and economy and of civil society and the state, which once constituted the distinctive hallmark of capitalism in the West, has eroded historically at an accelerating pace. Such intervention is a response to popular struggles, on one hand, and the contradictory demands of capital, on the other. With the ascendance of a small number of units of capital that are now decisive in the entire productive process, the reverberations of their competitive struggle and the scope of the social consequences of their activities require active regulation by the state. It intervenes to regulate demand and create profitable outlets for private investment, stabilize wages and prices, and increasingly socialize the costs of private accumulation. Labor, too, as it becomes centralized in large unions and, as in Europe, organized into its own political parties, increasingly strives to realize its class interests through state policy, such as social welfare, full employment programs, public health and medical services, low-cost housing, and redistributive policy in general. Thus, the state's expanding activities have been impelled by and are the distorted reflection of the struggle between labor and capital for the realization of their contradictory interests through the state.

The "state" in the United States is a complex federal rather than unitary structure, whose separate state, county, and city levels also mediate and shape state policy as a whole. Their relatively independent roles vary, of course, with the substantive content of the specific policies involved. Each of these levels of the state is, therefore, also the terrain of class and intraclass political conflict. How the federal government responded, for example, to the insurgence and quickening political mobilization in the cities in the late 1960s was mediated by the city's own political and administrative structure; in turn, as Friedland shows (chapter 8), the city's "public policy" (in this case, the level of poverty program funding) was partially determined by the relative organized class power of labor and capital, gauged by the local organizational presence of major corporations and national unions.

State governments also play a crucial role in the activity of the state as a whole in the United States. They spend roughly a third of total expenditures and raise about a fourth of the total tax revenues of all levels of government. In particular, they have a central place in the national redistributive policy that emerged since the Great Depression as a critical means of stabilizing and legitimating American capitalism. Understandably, therefore, the relatively specific organized relations between classes, especially as Hicks shows (chapter 9), between their decisive internal segments, "monopoly capital" and organized labor, have been critical in determining the level of redistribution by state governments over the past few decades.

A multiple regression analysis of "fiscal direct" redistribution shows that the extent to which tax and spending policies have had the net effect of redistributing income to the poor has varied closely with these organized class relations in the 48 mainland states. In the 1930s, it was the unemployment rate, a proxy measure for the militantly organized unemployed of the time, that had a strong effect on redistribution, while monopoly capital (measured by private commercial bank assets in the state) had a moderate negative impact. In the 1940s, it was precisely the relative balance of forces (or ratio of organizational capacities) between monopoly capital and organized labor that had the only strong effect. In contrast, in the 1950s, the state structure itself, already fashioned by the class struggles of the previous years, played a relatively autonomous role in the redistributive process. Organized labor, which had sealed a postwar compact with corporate capital, binding itself to rising productivity as the basis for higher wages, had no independent measurable political effect. Thus, we see that even at the state and city levels of government, public policy is largely the refracted product of the contradictory interests and organized demands of labor and capital and of their internal segments; such policy not only mediates but also shapes and reshapes their relations.

The late 1960s witnessed unparalleled mass insurgency among poor and black workers in America's major cities, the campus-based mobilizations against the war in Vietnam and imperial foreign policy, and the efflorescence of an increasingly broad radical, egalitarian and democratic movement. It was also a time, though less remarked, of rising labor militancy at the point of production in plants across the country. During the sustained boom and tight job market of that decade, wages rose rapidly while productivity slowed, as workers were able more effectively to resist the intensification of their labor.

The typical postwar corporate response had been to raise prices so as to offset such increased labor costs, but rising international competition made this risky even for the largest corporations. As a result, between 1965 and 1969, both the ratio of profits to wages and the share of profits in national income apparently dropped.[6] With demand high but profits

---

[6] There is some question concerning the validity of the measures used to show a declining rate of profit for the largest corporations in the 1960s. Perlo (1976) argues that the standard calculations used to show such a decline are inaccurate because they usually exclude from the definition of profits such categories as inventory valuation adjustments, capital consumption (or depreciation) allowances, profits distributed as interest and rents, and foreign profits. By partially correcting for some of these inadequacies in the profits data reported, Perlo finds that "the share of profits has been stable throughout the period" since World War Two (1976:60).

Whether or not real "declining profits" impelled the intensification of the exploitation of labor, the *threat* of such a decline as the result of rising competition from foreign capital would have been sufficient to impel it. As soon as major international rivals appear on the scene, the large corporations have to strive to protect their competitive positions, and one of the most basic prerequisites for any long-term competitive strategy is to increase their discipline and control of labor and to raise labor productivity, either through speed-up or mechanization and automation. The late 1970s are not only a pe-

squeezed, the corporations found it hard to compensate for reduced profits by labor-saving investment, because existing plant and equipment had to be used to the optimum as retained earnings declined. This required increased corporate borrowing if the level of investment was to be maintained, which, in turn (as dependence on external financing rose quickly in the late 1960s), became another drain on industrial profits.

Given all this, the corporations tried to speed up production to extract more unpaid labor from each worker daily. This precipitated the first rise in the rate of industrial accidents in 50 years and a leap of 28 percent between 1963 and 1970 alone. In response, workers' strikes (whether authorized or wildcat) and other forms of resistance rose even more dramatically. The number of "man-days" lost to strikes in the same period more than tripled, and the number of workers involved in work stoppages to protest "speed-up" specifically also went up three and a half times. With the boom continuing but profits still eroding as the workers resisted speed-up, the role of state policy in the struggle became critical. The so-called wage-price freeze was imposed to discipline the workers so profits could recover. The purpose of the controls, as the government's administrator put it bluntly, was to "zap labor." Strike activity fell as wages fell, and by 1973, work stoppages were again at the level of the early 1960s (Boddy and Crotty 1974; Gordon 1977). Beneath its classless legitimation as a "fight against inflation," the state's economic policy was a transparent political form of labor repression.

Of the workers' wildcats during this period, the most numerous as well as the most explicitly political were the massive coal miners' strikes. The number of miners' walkouts went up ten times, from 111 to 1,039, between 1964 and 1973; and nearly all (94 percent) of the major work stoppages took place during the term of the contract—a figure over three times the average for other industrial workers (Marschall 1978:88). These strikes, which brought down the regime of Tony Boyle and led to some internal democratization of the United Mine Workers, won the miners the right to vote to ratify their contracts; but the right to call their own strikes at the local level continued to be denied them, and was again a major issue in the 1975 walkouts. Bound by contract not to strike while it is in force, the UMW itself had to try to discipline the miners, whose only means of combatting repeated company violations of their agreement is the wildcat strike.

But with the UMW no longer able to assure labor discipline, the

---

riod, as discussed below, of renewed antiunion attacks by the large corporations, but of increasing labor displacement through computerization, automation and "unimation" (replacement of human labor by robots). (See, for instance, "UAW fears automation again," *Business Week*, March 26, 1979:94–95.)

companies had to turn increasingly to the federal courts to mediate their labor relations for them, through injunctions ordering the miners back to work. This cycle was ruptured by "the great anti-injunction strike of 1976" (Worth, chapter 10), in which 120,000 miners in Appalachia and the West struck against repeated company violations of the 1974 contract with the Bituminous Coal Operators Association. The miners stayed out for several weeks despite the opposition of the UMW itself. (Endorsement of the strike would have opened the union to company lawsuits that could have bankrupted it.) Only by bypassing the UMW bureaucracy and taking the initiative themselves in an explicitly political strike were the miners able to stem the escalating use of state power against them, to make the federal injunction an ineffective company weapon, and even to have previous charges and fines levelled against militant miners dismissed. But without the effective deployment of the union's resources, the miners' working conditions continued to deteriorate.

This wildcat strike was followed by the official UMW contract strike—the 113-day-long "great coal strike of 1978"—barely two years later. Although they lost some hard-won rights, such as their industry-wide health program which was converted into a fragmented company-by-company plan, the miners held out against and defeated the coal companies' demand for a "labor stability" clause to prevent and punish wildcat strikes. The miners' strike also sparked the first nationwide acts of labor movement solidarity in decades, through widespread local and national financial contributions by other unions to the UMW strike fund, "food-for-miners" convoys, and strike support rallies. The strike set an example of fiery insurgence and militant solidarity before which even the federal government stood all but mute—representing a sharp break with the postwar period of organized class collaboration.

The strike came, in fact, at a moment of renewed antiunion attacks by organized capital—including a rising number of decertification elections, the National Association of Manufacturers' establishment of a Committee for a Union Free Environment, the "business community's" stiff opposition to even moderate labor-reform legislation, and the Chamber of Commerce's announced intention to try to roll back longstanding labor laws. With it, a language of class and "class warfare" not heard at such levels in four decades began to reappear among top labor officials. For example, in May 1978, AFL-CIO Secretary-Treasurer Lane Kirkland denounced the corporations' "civilized cooperative discourse with labor" as a mere "veneer of civility" to hide "the bed-rock primitive honing for the master-servant relationship." He accused American corporations of launching "a campaign to kill the hopes of the most oppressed and deserving workers in this country. It is class warfare ... launched by the most privileged and powerful in our society." Similarly, Douglas A. Fraser, president of the 1.5 million-member United Auto Workers union (UAW), the nation's largest industrial union, condemned the "business community" in unusual class terms. In July 1978, he resigned from the quasi-official Labor-Management Group with these words: "I believe leaders of the business community, with few exceptions, have chosen to wage a one-sided class war today in this country—a war against the unemployed, the poor, the minorities, the very young and the very old and even many of the middle class in our society."

With this sudden awareness of "class war" taking hold among labor's higher echelons, even talk of an independent labor party and concrete initiatives to form an independent political coalition of the left were begun. In October 1978, a coalition of 104 liberal, radical, "minority" (black and Chicano), and labor organizations began a hesitant but important counterattack against what its leaders called "the growing threat of right-wing corporate power in America." The coalition ranged from "hard-hat" construction unions to the left-wing National Lawyers Guild, brought together under the leadership of the UAW's Fraser, and included over 30 labor unions. It saw itself, as Fraser said, "on a collision course with the Democratic Party unless it makes changes" to support labor's demands; and, although muted, the possibility of forming a labor party was raised by many delegates at the coalition's founding convention in Detroit. "Down the road, perhaps, if nothing else works," Fraser said, "we might have to give consideration" to that possibility. Other labor leaders at the convention, like Sol Stetin, vice-president of the Amalgamated Clothing and Textile Workers Union, publicly proclaimed: "It is time for these organizations here today to give serious consideration to either getting full control of the Democratic Party or forming a party of our own." It was, in fact, already a significant change in American politics when one of its most prominent labor leaders could speak in blunt terms of the need to "transform the Democratic Party," in Fraser's words, "into a genuinely progressive people's party" (*Los Angeles Times:* July 20, 1978; October 18, 1978).

The workers' wildcat strikes and union militance in the late 1960s and early 1970s, and the miners' struggles and reawakened solidarity in the labor movement coupled with an incipient independent political organization as the decade drew to a close, indicate the contradictory relationship unions generally have to the working class: the unions both fragment and discipline the workers *for capital,* and integrate and unify them as a class, as *organized labor.* In the United States, the union is the workers' only *independent class organization;* without it, the workers would regularly confront capital only as isolated individuals. With it, they tend to act as a class.

On one hand, insofar as the union acts as a "trade" union and confines its conception of workers' interests and its action to promote them to their trade or industry, it both fragments the class and, in Gramsci's acute phrase, "concretely coordinates the interests" of labor and capital (1971:184); it identifies the interests of the industry (or even of the firm) and the interests of the union as one. This is enhanced by the union's ensnarement in a complex legal framework, reinforced by the coercive power of the state, which now interposes itself between labor and capital. As a consequence, labor and management take on the ideological appearance of merely free parties to a contract and fictive equals under the law. The result is class collaboration rather than class conflict; struggle is displaced from the point of production, where the workers' initiative is decisive, to the process of negotiation and compromise, where union officials, as labor statesmen rather than workers' leaders, become preeminent.

The contract itself becomes a set of binding contraints and regulations to which the union consents, and which it is legally compelled to enforce even against the workers themselves. The workers' common interests are redefined as individual grievances to be adjudicated rather than won through class struggle. The state reappears between labor and capital in the form of an "internal state" (Burawoy 1980), with its own fictive "industrial citizenship." It independently reinforces, by a veritable form of decentralized legal class domination—ostensibly resting on private contractual rights and obligations—capital's prerogative in production.

On the other hand, if the internal state ideologically converts workers into imaginary industrial citizens, the connection between the rights entailed in such citizenship and their source in class struggle has also become transparent. For even in this fictive form, such "citizenship" and the workers' common class situation are clearly the product of their own struggles, with the union the singular organizational weapon by which their rights are protected and advanced. The result is the real conversion of *individual* workers into *class* individuals.

In this sense, the union, and its place within the internal state, dialectically constitutes the workers into a *political class,* thereby reuniting their dual existence within capitalist democracy, as expropriated producer but bourgeois citizen, into one. Only as common members of organized labor do they appear in bourgeois legality itself not merely as citizens but as a class.

The expanded jurisdiction of the state over society under contemporary capitalism tends increasingly to convert class relations, once again, into explicitly political relations and to repoliticize civil society. Class and state are again transparently connected. Not an invisible hand but representative political authority is increasingly held responsible for "man's fate" under late capitalism. The question can now be put historically: Not whether the political economy shall be governed self-consciously, but how and by whom and for what social objectives.

References

ALTHUSSER, LOUIS, and R. ETIENNE BALIBAR
  1970   Reading Capital. London: New Left Books.
BARAN, PAUL A., and PAUL M. SWEEZY
  1968   Monopoly Capital: An Essay on the American Economic and Social Order. New York: Monthly Review Press.
BLAU, PETER, and OTIS DUDLEY DUNCAN
  1967   The American Occupational Structure. New York: Wiley.
BODDY, RAFORD, and JAMES CROTTY
  1974   "Class Conflict, Keynesian Policies, and the Business Cycle." Monthly Review 26 (5):1–17.
BURAWOY, MICHAEL
  1980   "The Politics of Production and the Production of Politics: A Comparative Analysis of Piecework Machine Shops in the United States and Hungary." Political Power and Social Theory 1.
CASTELLS, MANUEL
  1977   The Urban Question: A Marxist Approach. Cambridge, Mass.: MIT Press.
DAHRENDORF, RALF
  1959   Class and Class Conflict in Industrial Society. Stanford: Stanford University Press.
DAVIS, KINGSLEY, and WILBERT MOORE
  1945   "Some Principles of Stratification." American Sociological Review 10 (2):242–49.
DOMHOFF, G. WILLIAM
  1979   The Powers That Be: Processes of Ruling Class Domination in America. New York: Vintage.
ENGELS, FRIEDRICH
  1973   Karl Marx and Friedrich Engels: Selected Works, volume 3. Moscow: Progress.
ESPING-ANDERSEN, GÖSTA, ROGER FRIEDLAND, and ERIK O. WRIGHT
  1976   "Modes of Class Struggle and the Capitalist State." Kapitalistate 4/5:186–220.
FEUER, LEWIS S.
  1959   "Introduction." Marx and Engels: Basic Writings. Garden City, N.Y.: Anchor.
GALBRAITH, JOHN KENNETH
  1971   The New Industrial State, 2d ed. Boston: Houghton Mifflin.
GORDON, DAVID
  1977   "Capital Vs. Labor." Pp. 525–38, in M. Zeitlin (ed.), American So-

ciety, Inc. Studies of the Social Structure and Political Economy of the United States, 2d ed. Chicago: Rand McNally.

GRAMSCI, ANTONIO
1971   Selections from the Prison Notebooks. New York: International.

GREEN, JAMES R.
1978   Grass-Roots Socialism: Radical Movements in the Southwest, 1895–1943. Baton Rouge and London: Louisiana State University Press.

HINDESS, BARRY, and PAUL Q. HIRST
1975   Pre-Capitalist Modes of Production. London and Boston: Routledge & Kegan Paul.

KAUTSKY, KARL
1903   The Social Revolution. Chicago: Charles H. Kerr.

LANGE, OSCAR
1935   "Marxian Economics and Modern Economic Theory." Review of Economic Studies (June). Pp. 68–87, in D. Horowitz (ed.), Marx and Modern Economics. New York and London: Monthly Review Press, 1968.

MARSCHALL, DAN
1978   "The Miners and the UMW: Crisis in the Reform Process." Socialist Review 8 (4–5):65–115.

MARX, KARL
1956   Karl Marx: Selected Writings in Sociology and Social Philosophy, ed. T. B. Bottomore and Maximilien Rubel. London: Watts.
1967   Capital, volume 1. New York: International.
1970   A Contribution to the Critique of Political Economy, ed. Maurice Dobb. New York: International.

MARX, KARL, and FRIEDRICH ENGELS
1956   The German Ideology, parts I and III. Ed. R. Pascal. New York: International.

MOMMSEN, WOLFGANG J.
1974   The Age of Bureaucracy: Perspectives on the Political Sociology of Max Weber. Oxford: Oxford University Press.

MOORE, BARRINGTON, JR.
1966   Social Origins of Dictatorship and Democracy. Boston: Beacon.

PARSONS, TALCOTT
1953   "A Revised Analytical Approach to the Theory of Social Stratification." Pp. 92–128, in R. Bendix and S. M. Lipset (eds.), Class, Status, and Power. Glencoe, Ill.: The Free Press.

PERLO, VICTOR
1976   "The New Propaganda of Declining Profit Shares and Inadequate Investment." Review of Radical Political Economics 8:53–64.

PIVEN, FRANCES FOX, and RICHARD A. CLOWARD
1980   "Social Policy and the Formation of Political Consciousness." Political Power and Social Theory 1: 117–52.

POULANTZAS, NICOS
1973a   Political Power and Social Classes. London: NLB and Sheed and Ward.

1973b   "On Social Classes." New Left Review 78:27–54.

1973c   "The Problem of the Capitalist State." Pp. 238–53, in R. Blackburn (ed.), Ideology in Social Science: Readings in Critical Social Theory. New York: Vintage.

PRZEWORSKI, ADAM

1977   "Proletariat into a Class: The Process of Class Formation from Karl Kautsky's The Class Struggle to Recent Controversies." Politics & Society 7(4):343–401.

SARTRE, JEAN PAUL

1968   The Communists and Peace. New York: Braziller.

THOMPSON, E. P.

1963   The Making of the English Working Class. New York: Pantheon.

TROTSKY, LEON

1932   The History of the Russian Revolution. New York: Simon and Schuster.

TUMIN, MELVIN M.

1953   "Some Principles of Stratification: A Critical Analysis." American Sociological Review 18:387–93.

VERNADSKY, GEORGE

1939   "Feudalism in Russia." Speculum 14:303–323.

WEBER, MAX

1946   From Max Weber: Essays in Sociology, ed. Hans Gerth and C. Wright Mills. New York: Oxford.

1961   General Economic History. New York: Collier.

1968   Economy and Society (3 volumes) ed. Guenther Roth and Claus Wittich. New York: Bedminister.

ZEITLIN, MAURICE

1960   "Max Weber on the Sociology of the Feudal Order." Sociological Review 8:202–207.

1967   Revolutionary Politics and the Cuban Working Class. Princeton: Princeton University Press.

1974   "Corporate Ownership and Control: The Large Corporation and the Capitalist Class." American Journal of Sociology 79 (5):1073–1119.

1976   "On Class Theory of the Large Corporation." American Journal of Sociology 81(4):894–903.

ZEITLIN, MAURICE, W. LAWRENCE NEUMAN, and RICHARD E. RATCLIFF

1976   "Class Segments: Agrarian Property and Political Leadership in the Capitalist Class of Chile." American Sociological Review 41: 1006–29.

ZEITLIN, MAURICE, and SAMUEL NORICH

1979   "Management Control, Exploitation, and Profit Maximization in the Large Corporation: An Empirical Confrontation of Managerialism and Class Theory." Research in Political Economy 2:33–62.

I Class, Politics, and Historical Development in the United States

Political Economy and Internal Relations in the Dominant Class

1 Planters, Merchants, and Political Power in Reconstruction Alabama

Jonathan M. Wiener
University of California–Irvine

In the prevailing view, the Civil War brought about the transformation of the South's class structure, the abolition of the dominant landed class, and its replacement by a new class of merchants. The "downfall" and "destruction" of the antebellum planters brought the region's class structure into line with that of the rest of the nation (Woodward 1951a:179; 1951b:52). Because the bourgeois North seemed to have destroyed the American version of a prebourgeois landed aristocracy, the Civil War has been interpreted as "the last capitalist revolution" (Moore 1966:111–55; cf. Wiener 1976b:166–67).

The war did indeed represent a bourgeois victory in national politics, as industrialists won active state support for rapid capitalist development that had previously been blocked by southern planter representatives (federal aid to railroads, tariffs to encourage manufacturing, homesteads to spur the expansion of a domestic market). But the consequences of the war within the South were different.

The destruction of slavery and the defeat of the planter regime in war did not bring the abolition of the planters as a class and a genuine bourgeois revolution within the South. All the planters lost their slaves, and some lost their land; what occurred, however, was not the "downfall" or "destruction" of the old planter class, but rather its persistence and metamorphosis. The postwar planters were a new class because they were in new social relations of production. But they were a new class made up of families which to a significant extent had been part of the antebellum elite. The old families persisted in a quantitative sense; in a qualitative sense, their relation to production had been transformed. Yet they were not a northern-styled bourgeoisie.

The persistence of the planters as the South's dominant class was the key obstacle to the establishment of liberal democracy in the region during the century which followed the Civil War. The northern working class found its political freedoms radically incomplete, but it did not experience the kind of oppression practiced by the South's dominant class. Northerners had their votes manipulated by political machines, but they were not disfranchised by literacy tests; almost a million voted socialist at the turn of the century. Northern blacks were discriminated against, but they did not live with an ever-present fear of lynching. Northern workers fought bloody battles to organize unions, which they often won; southern workers lost their bloody battles. This greater oppression practiced by the South's dominant class, this relatively greater freedom in the North, was recognized by southerners, millions of whom migrated North when the opportunity arose. To study planter persistence is to study the root of this situation.

The manuscript schedules of the U.S. census of population are the kind of source Marc Bloch (1953:61) called "witnesses in spite of themselves." They provide a basis for identifying the South's largest planters, and for studying their transformation through the Civil War decade. In 1850, 1860, and 1870, the census asked each individual for the "value of real estate" he or she owned (Wright and Hunt 1900:152). The responses can be used to identify the wealthiest landholders in each census year, to study persistence and change in the composition of this group, and to compare antebellum patterns with the developments that accompanied war and Reconstruction.

The black belt of Alabama, along with Mississippi and Georgia, was the economic bastion of the planter class of the deep South; its planters took the lead in the secession movement, and it provided the first capital for the Confederacy (Barney 1974; cf. Johnson 1977). It was a region where landholding was extremely unequal: in 1860, the top 5 percent of landowners held 24 percent of the improved acreage, 26 percent of the slaves, and 30 percent of the farm value (G. Wright 1970). Five adjacent counties in the western half of the Alabama black belt were selected (Greene, Hale, Marengo, Perry, Sumter); in 1860, they had a population of 114,000, of which 74 percent were slaves.

I focus here on the group of 236 planters with the greatest wealth in real estate in each of the three censuses. It included all planters with at least $10,000 in real estate in 1850, $32,000 in 1860, and $10,000 in 1870. This group constituted approximately the top 8 percent of the landholders in the western Alabama black belt and 3 percent of white adult males. Their mean real estate holding in 1860 was roughly 1,600 acres; the smallest holding was around 800 acres, and the largest, close to 9,000 acres. (The top 10 percent of real estate holders in the five counties are called "big planters" in this chapter, but this statistically defined group by itself did not necessarily form a self-conscious social class, nor was membership in the actual planter class solely a matter of the value of individuals' real estate holding.)

Table 1-1. Black belt population and planter persistence

	1850	1860	1870
Total population	103,807	113,765	115,426
White population	32,007	29,467	27,122
Top planters	236	236	236
Top planters remaining in area at end of decade	110	101	NA
Percentage remaining (planter resistance rate)	47%	43%	NA

Note: Figures from five Alabama counties: Greene, Marengo, Sumter, Perry, Hale.

Since Roger Shugg's pathbreaking work (1937), historians have accepted the view that the plantation survived the Civil War and Reconstruction, but they have argued that the antebellum planter class was destroyed. C. Vann Woodward (1951a:179; 1951b:52) writes that after the war a "revolution in land titles" signaled the "downfall of the old planter class"; most subsequent studies have accepted this view (cf. Woodman 1967:313; Maddex 1970:xii; Hackney 1972:213; Eaton 1968:139; Harris 1967:32).

The census manuscripts show that, of the 236 top plantation owners in western Alabama in 1860, 101 remained in the group in 1870; their persistence rate through the decade of war and Reconstruction was 43 percent (table 1-1). The war thus appears to have destroyed more than half the big planters of 1860, but the situation was more complex. The planters' persistence rate for the war decade was in fact similar to their antebellum persistence rate. Of the 236 wealthiest planter families of 1850, only 110 remained at the top a decade later; the antebellum planter persistence rate was thus 47 percent. Fewer than half of the prewar big planters maintained their status in the region for more than a decade.

These figures lead to two noteworthy conclusions: first, the similarity of the antebellum and wartime persistence rates, which suggests that war and Reconstruction did not significantly alter the antebellum pattern of planter persistence and social mobility; second, the relatively low persistence rate of the antebellum big planters, which is usually thought to have been as stable a social group as could be found in nineteenth century America.

The internal units of a social class, particularly a dominant one such as the planters, are not individuals but families, as Maurice Zeitlin has recently argued (1975:21–28). Individual planters die, but as long as their property remains in their families, the social composition of the planter class is not transformed. Thus "persistence" has been defined here as family rather than individual persistence; if a planter did not appear in a subsequent list of the top planters, but his wife or son did, it was counted as a case of planter persistence. Still, because not all elderly planters had heirs, and not all heirs kept the old plantation intact, dying was one source of nonpersistence. And death may have made a significantly greater contribution to planter turnover between 1860 and 1870, when a quarter of a million southerners died in war.

Almost all of the wealthiest planters of 1870 had been among the antebellum big planters. Of the 25 planters with the largest holdings in 1870, 18 (or 72 percent) were in top planter families in 1860, and 16 had been in top planter families in 1850 (table 1-2). Only seven of the top 25 planters in 1870 were not among the top planter families in 1860 in the black belt of western Alabama, and they may well have come from such families in other areas.

This phenomenon of planter persistence did not escape the notice of contemporaries. The *Montgomery Alabama State Journal* (April 4, 1871) noted that "the old oligarchies have come to the surface again." The *Montgomery Advertiser* (June 20, 1866) reported on "the disinclination of planters . . . to sell any portion of their lands." It added that a majority of planters were responding to the economic collapse by "curtailing their outlay of expenses, and contenting themselves with a smaller but surer income." Robert Somers' firsthand descriptions (1871:114–15, 127) of widespread devastation of the plantations in 1870 should not overshadow his more telling observation that "generally the old homesteads and the old families continue to be the centres of reviving industry and cultivation."

The planter families that did not persist were not necessarily destroyed, nor were they necessarily "skidders" down the social scale. Few of those who remained in their county lost enough real estate (relatively) to move them below the top 236; the great majority simply moved out of the western Alabama black belt. Of the 1860 planter families that did not persist to 1870, only 9 percent could be identified as skidders, cases of downward social mobility within one county. The other 91 percent had left their county altogether; whether they maintained their high status is unknown. This suggests that, even during the war decade, geographic mobility was much more frequent among the largest planters than downward social mobility in the locality. Skidding may have been a relatively infrequent phenomenon among top planters, even between 1860 and 1870. The small number of planters who dropped from the top between 1860 and 1870 did not fall very far. Almost all of them ended up in 1870 in the top 25 percent of county landholders, and all were in the top half. To the extent that they could be identified, even those who were "downwardly mobile" during the sixties were not "destroyed"; they remained among the wealthier landholders of their counties.

Although the big planters persisted at approximately the same rate in

Table 1-2. The 25 wealthiest planters in 1870

Name	County	Real Estate Holdings 1870	1860	1850
Minge, G.	Marengo	$85,000	—	30,000
Lyon, F.	Marengo	75,000	115,000	35,000
Paulling, William	Marengo	72,000	150,000	29,000
Hatch, Alfred	Hale	70,000	120,000	40,000
Alexander, J.	Marengo	69,000	38,000	10,000[a]
Whitfield, B.	Marengo	65,000	200,000[a]	100,000
Terrill, J.	Marengo	62,000	93,000	—
Taylor, E.	Marengo	61,000	—	—
Robertson, R.	Marengo	60,000	—	—
Dew, Duncan	Greene	52,000	200,000[a]	41,000
Walton, John	Marengo	50,000	250,000	25,000
Collins, Charles	Hale	50,000	201,000[a]	30,000
Hays, Charles	Greene	50,000	113,000	—
Brown, John	Sumter	50,000	69,000	13,000
Pickering, Richard	Marengo	50,000	42,000	15,000
Withers, Mary	Hale	50,000	40,000	75,000[a]
Jones, Madison	Hale	50,000	36,000[a]	27,000
Nelson, A.	Hale	48,000	—	10,000[a]
Taylor, J.	Hale	48,000	—	—
Pickens, Wm.	Hale	45,000	210,000[a]	51,000
Reese, Henry	Marengo	45,000	52,000	24,000
Walker, R.	Hale	42,000	55,000	—
Smaw, W.	Greene	42,000	32,000	—
Blanks, E.	Marengo	41,000	—	—
Walker, Morns	Marengo	41,000	—	—
Number		25	18	16
Percentage present among top planter families			72%	64%

Note: Rounded off to nearest thousand; as reported in U.S. Census of Population, manuscript schedules.

[a] Wealth of father or husband

the 1850s and 60s, many have argued that the biggest landholdings were considerably smaller in 1870 than they had been in 1860—that the big planters, who had the most to lose in war and Reconstruction, lost the most, and emerged from their ordeal relatively poorer in comparison to other groups in southern society. Between 1860 and 1870, the loss in land value in the western Alabama black belt was staggering. The aggregate value of real estate owned by the 236 top planters declined from over $15 million in 1860 to not quite $5 million in 1870. The value of the median holding fell from $48,700 to $15,300. The reports of both contemporaries and modern historians correspond to these figures (Gates 1965:373; Lerner 1955).

Earlier historians argued that this decline was the consequence of wartime destruction of plantation property. Ransom and Sutch (1975), however, have recently shown that the destructive impact of the war on plantation agriculture has been greatly exaggerated. Emancipation was a fundamental cause of declining land values; the free black chose to work less than the slave had been forced to, and the resulting fall in tilled acreage "created a supply of 'redundant' land which acted to depress land prices." Land prices fell also because of the high taxes imposed by Radical legislatures (Williamson 1965:155).

Although losses in land value were devastating to all southern landowners, the top planters in 1870 were, in fact, relatively wealthier than they had been in 1860. As a group, they held a greater share of the real estate value five years after the war than when it began. The big planters' share of the land value held by county residents increased about one-seventh between 1860 and 1870, from 55 to 63 percent (table 1-3).

This relative expansion of the land value held by the big planters came at the expense of the upper-middle group of county landholders, the small planters and big farmers. Although the top planters of 1870 had increased their share of the real estate value by eight percentage points, the upper-middle group—those landowners below the top 10 percent but within the top 40 percent—lost a total of six percentage points. The top 10

Table 1-3. Shares of wealth

	Share in Year[a]			Change in Share	
Decile	1850	1860	1870	1850–1860	1860–1870
1 (top 10%)	57%	55%	63%	−2	+8
2	18	19	17	+1	−2
3	10	10	8	0	−2
4	4	6	4	+2	−2
5	4	4	3	0	−1
6	3	2	2	−1	0
7	2	2	1	0	−1
8	1	1	1	0	0
9	1	1	1	0	0
10 (bottom 10%)	0	0	0	0	0
Number	811	989	828		

[a] Marengo County only. Share is share of value of real estate holdings.

percent was the only decile to improve its position as a result of the war; the nine lower deciles either lost part of their share, or did not change.

The improvement in the relative position of the top planters becomes even more striking when it is compared to the trend for the antebellum decade 1850–1860. In that period, the top 10 percent were actually falling behind somewhat, their share dropping from 57 to 55 percent of the real estate value held by county residents, while the three upper-middle deciles were on the rise, increasing their share from 32 to 35 percent (cf. G. Wright 1970; Ransom and Sutch 1977:78–79).

During war and Reconstruction, then, the big planters reversed the antebellum trend toward a relative increase in landholding by the upper-middle group. They not only regained ground that had been lost between 1850 and 1860, but increased their share considerably, all at the expense of the upper-middle group. Between 1860 and 1870, they gained four times the share they had lost in the preceding decade. Though their losses were staggering, the big planter families of 1870 were not only relatively persistent, but also relatively wealthier than those in 1860, in their share of real estate holdings.

Although the pattern of landholding reveals the persistence of the old families in the postwar planter class, the structural basis of their wealth and power had been altered. This metamorphosis was a consequence of the creation of new economic levers for plantation agriculture: above all, the establishment of the crop lien for supplies as the basis for financing postwar cotton production on the tenant plantation. And, because the liens were held by merchants, the crop lien system gave the merchants an opportunity to challenge planter profits, planter control of the black labor force, and, eventually, planter land ownership itself—the structural basis of the planters' existence as a class.

With the collapse of southern banks and the decline of the cotton factors who had marketed the prewar cotton crop, postwar planters had difficulty obtaining the credit necessary for financing the crop to buy the seed, implements, and provisions necessary for their tenant farmers. The rural merchant, linked to northern wholesalers and cotton manufacturers, was the one most able to extend the necessary credit to the tenant. The legal provisions for financing the postwar cotton crop were established in crop lien laws, legislated in all southern states at the war's end. Alabama's law, passed early in 1866, did not distinguish between planters who advanced supplies to tenants, and merchants; the law gave a lien on the crop to "any person" who advanced provisions, tools, or draft animals to a farmer or tenant. A subsequent amendment gave merchants the same "rights and remedies" landlords had to collect from tenants (Acts of Alabama 1865–66:44; 1866–67:211).

Thus the crop lien appeared as the universal basis of credit in the rural South: a tenant pledged his crop as security against supplies advanced during the year. The tenant signed a crop lien contract with a supply merchant at the beginning of the season and did business only with that merchant; the merchant kept an account of the tenant's purchases, and, when the crop was harvested, the merchant took the portion he determined was due him. The tenant also owed rent to his landlord, for which cash tenants paid cash, and sharecroppers paid a share of the crop. Two-thirds of the crop went to the cropper if he could furnish his own tools, stock, seed, fertilizers, and other necessities; less if the landlord furnished some or all of these supplies.

The alternative to merchants supplying the black tenantry was for each planter to supply his own tenants, at a plantation store. The planter could obtain store stock directly from wholesalers, and thus avoid dealing with local supply merchants. Planters with such stores usually required that their tenants use it for all their purchases; some planters paid their laborers in scrip good only at the plantation store. Other planters loaned cash to their tenants for them to spend on supplies bought from the local merchant; such loans were secured by crop liens.

If it was not clear from the beginning, it rapidly became clear to both merchants and planters that the crop lien for supplies was a major new lever for the extraction of the surplus produced by the black tenantry, and that it was superior in many ways to the landlords' traditional lever, rent. The crop lien for supplies gave whomever held it much more flexibility in squeezing the tenantry. The amount the tenant owed for rent was fixed at the beginning of the season, but the amount he owed for supplies was never clear—to him, at least—until the crop had been harvested and the accounts figured. The unscrupulous merchant could adjust the amount of the debt to match the value of the tenant's crop. And the accounts of travelers and contemporaries abound with descriptions of unscrupulous merchants. C. Vann Woodward (1951a:180) has described the unusual flexibility of the crop lien for supplies: "the seeker of credit . . . [obtained] a loan of unstipulated amount, at a rate of interest to be determined by the creditor."

The newly freed slaves' inexperience with the workings of the system, and, more important, their powerlessness to challenge it, were a second major reason for the superiority of the lien for supplies over rent as a method of squeezing the tenantry. These new consumers lacked the skills necessary to check over the year's account books, and thus often were denied the opportunity to do so. The lien contract often provided that the merchant's accounts were incontestable, and more than one contemporary reported that a tenant who challenged his account was murdered (Rosengarten 1974:29; Gutman 1976:438).

The lack of distinction in the Alabama law between planters who advanced supplies and merchants meant that merchants were competing with planters as legal equals. The merchants' greater ability to extend credit gave them the opportunity to make substantial inroads on the planters' position. Thus, although the 1866 crop lien law ostensibly favored neither merchants nor planters, the merchants had a decisive advantage at the beginning of the ensuing six years of conflict, as the two groups competed for the profits from supplying black tenants.

The crop lien allowed the postwar merchants a source of additional profit that had previously been reserved for the planters. Under the antebellum system, the planter had been able to hold back his cotton, speculate on market fluctuations, and pay merchant suppliers in cash. Under the postwar system, the merchant lienholder got his share of the cotton as soon as it was baled; this allowed him to acquire any profit that could come from market speculation.

Of course the merchants themselves were not completely independent; they too needed credit. Before the war, the rural merchants' credit had come mainly from cotton factors in the port cities of the South who were social and political allies of the planter class. The postwar crop lien system gave the merchants considerable independence from these local powers, for which they traded greater dependence on northern manufacturers and wholesalers.

Although the crop lien gave merchants the opportunity for great profits, not all merchants prospered. The key to success for crop lien merchants was constant surveillance of each tenant-customer's activity, personal knowledge and detailed information about each. Merchant enterprises as a result were small and localized, but gave established merchants local monopoly power (Ransom and Sutch 1972:652–53).

The merchant who held the tenants' liens for supplies not only obtained a large share of the profit from black tenants' labor; he also had the power to determine which tenants stayed on the plantation and which were forced off. If a merchant wanted a hardworking or compliant tenant to remain, the account books could show a debt to the store at the close of each year. And the books could be made to balance exactly for those who were to be asked to move on (Woodward 1951a:184; Shannon 1945:92).

As a result, although the planter made a profit from the labor of black tenants either in cash rent or a share of the crop, both of these amounts were fixed beforehand, while the merchant, the holder of the lien for supplies, was able to squeeze the tenants with a wide variety of techniques: indeterminate but high interest rates, double pricing, and dishonest weighing and bookkeeping. The postwar merchant had gained considerable economic independence from the planter class and its local allies, had an opportunity for the first time to increase his profit by speculating in the cotton market, and even had the power to decide which tenants remained on the plantation. Merchants in such a position "divorced landownership from its age-old prerogatives" (Woodward 1951a:184). The crop lien for supplies thus became a crucial means of acquiring the surplus produced by the freedmen, and, in years of low cotton prices or a poor crop, merchants often had a greater opportunity for making a profit from plantation agriculture than planters.

The crop lien law that offered Alabama merchants such opportunities was not passed during Radical Reconstruction, under the influence of northern capitalists. It was passed in February 1866, before Radical Reconstruction began, by the same Alabama legislature that defied the Radical Congress by refusing to ratify the Fourteenth Amendment. The original crop lien law was thus not a Radical antiplanter program for merchant power, but rather seems to have been accepted by the planters as a necessary concession to finance the cotton crop after the antebellum system had been destroyed. In the words of a black belt newspaper, it was "an act of wise, practical statesmanship" (*Montgomery Daily Advertiser,* March 8, 1866).

Historians have argued that the crop lien law brought about the "merger" of landlord and merchant classes, that a new landholding group, which combined the economic roles of planter and merchant, arose from the crop lien system (Woodward 1951a:21, 184; Woodman 1967:332; Rogers 1970:17; Hicks 1931:42; Bond 1939:121; Shannon 1945:89). But it makes a great deal of difference whether merchants became landlords, or planters became merchants. If merchants became landlords, they tied their clients to them more securely by taking over ownership of the land, driving out the traditional landowners who had been competing for control of the surplus created by the tenants. Landownership for these "merchant-landlords" became a way of tying their crop lien customers into the credit system more securely; it also allowed the merchants to extract rent in addition to interest and profit from their store customers. This "merger" meant, in fact, the triumph of merchants over planters, the destruction of the old planter class, and its replacement in the agrarian economy by the new merchant class. When merchants became merchant-landlords, the crop lien law appears to have been the means by which this transformation took place.

But this is not what happened in postwar Alabama. There was no basic transformation of the dominant class. Rather, the planters defeated a merchant thrust for power, and, in the process, took over the right to grant credit to tenants.

However, because the planters had a qualitatively new lever for extracting the surplus, their class relation to their tenants was transformed; they became by definition a "new class" with new means of surplus extraction. Thus it would be erroneous to conclude that nothing had changed in the planters' defeat of the merchant challenge. On the one hand, the planters' relation to their tenants underwent a metamorphosis. On the other, the planter class retained much the same social composition, the same history and traditions, and the same patterns of social intercourse. The most significant feature of postwar social developments was thus the persistence of many of the antebellum planter families in the new dominant class, while they had gained an additional lever for extracting an economic surplus from the underlying population.

For six years after the conclusion of the war, Alabama's merchants and planters competed as legal equals in the contest over control of the black tenants. During this period, both groups organized to protect their interests. An 1871 newspaper article headlined "Crisis in the Credit System" asked, "how shall merchants protect themselves? . . . A policy of self-preservation impels them to the adoption of some measure" (*Montgomery Daily Advertiser*, January 22, 1871). A subsequent letter titled "Important to Merchants" proposed that they "adopt measures similar to those other cities have adopted, for protecting themselves." It was signed "merchant" (*Montgomery Daily Advertiser*, February 13, 1871). The *Union Springs Herald and Times* (May 29, 1872) announced that country merchants "have organized a Protective Society," and that "the commercial interests of Union Springs" formed a "Board of Trade."

Although such organizations ostensibly had as their first task sharing information about credit risks, the planter press saw the potential for class-conscious political action in the merchant organizations. The *Montgomery Advertiser*, a consistent defender of planter interests, argued (July 11, 1868) that

> the merchants of the country have their "chambers of commerce" and "boards of trade," for the purpose of fixing the value of their wares . . ., whilst the poor cotton growers plod along, every one on his own course . . ., sell for what they can get, and pay out of the proceeds for supplies at whatever price may be demanded of them. . . . Concert of action must be attained to protect the interest of the cotton grower.

The newspaper called for the organization of "farmers' clubs," writing that the planters "must now band together, or be immolated by the cormorants, loan sharks, and skinflints, infesting every village, town and city, throughout our land" (July 26, 1868). The paper printed the resolutions of planter organizations; a typical one declared that "we, a portion of the planters of Bullock county . . . [seek] concert of action" against "middle men . . . our enemies . . . and their schemes" (September 23, 1868).

Throughout Reconstruction, the planter press argued that all whites were united against the Radicals—planter and merchant alike. And, given the overwhelming developments in national politics in 1867, 1868, and 1869, with the advent of Radical Reconstruction and the impeachment of

President Johnson, it is surprising that merchant-planter conflict would receive any attention at all in the southern press. Thus the relatively few articles dealing with planter-merchant conflict that appeared in the southern press in the late 1860s and early 1870s are particularly significant; they made explicit what planter spokesmen had good reasons to conceal.

The planters' antimerchant argument was summarized early in 1871 by the class-conscious *Mobile Register,* the most authoritative voice of planter interests in the state. The paper reported (February 26, 1871), predictably, that the freedman was rapidly "degenerating." The newspaper's analysis of the cause was less predictable: the carpetbaggers were not responsible for the black's immorality, lack of thrift, and poor health, but rather "a low, unprincipled class of traders, keepers of small shops." These "cunning" merchants, "by a little flattery and poisonous whiskey, easily cheat him out of the little his bad management and indolence permit him to make." The paper complained of the blacks that "their share of the cotton crop they sell without prudence or proper calculation of the supplies they may want at the little stores that have arisen everywhere, and they buy trash of all kinds at extravagant prices. . . . Whether this evil can be reached by law or not remains to be seen." The lesson was clear: the freedmen were being cheated by merchants; they were unable to act in their own best interest; control by the paternalistic planter class was necessary. Legislation, however, was required.

The argument that merchants' crop liens were responsible for the region's labor problems was also put forward by the *Montgomery Advertiser.* As early as 1866, the *Advertiser* wrote, under the headline "Cheating the Freedmen," that "traders are taking advantage of the ignorance of pecuniary matters existing among the freedmen" (March 9, 1866). At the end of 1867, the *Advertiser*'s antimerchant tone became stronger: " 'The freedman' comes to town, purchases a gallon of whiskey, a flask of powder, a shot gun, and a piece of cheese, and a few crackers. In this way, his money is soon gone, and he apparently forgets that his wife and children have no 'massa' to look to, as in the good old days gone by" (Dec. 22, 1867).

The merchants were accused even more strongly in another article in the *Mobile Register* (Jan. 10, 1871) under the title "Now What?"

The negroes were encouraged and invited by our local merchants to lease land and make crops on their own account. They readily advanced to the freedmen . . ., taking liens on the negroes' crop and stock. The negroes, true to nature, being clothed and fed without work, would not work to pay for it. . . . The merchants are seizing corn, cotton, and stock, and the negroes are stealing cotton and stock of every description. . . . And with all this, they now swear they will neither hire nor crop on shares with a white man. . . . Now what?

The planters' objection to merchant competition was summed up concisely by a Mobile planter testifying before a congressional committee: "these shark storekeepers . . . swallow up the whole thing" (U.S. Senate 1885:IV, 74).

The planters' conception of the proper relationship between themselves, their tenants, and the local supply merchants was expressed on at least one occasion by the *Montgomery Advertiser.* "The planter, as the representative class of the South . . . performs the office [for the black] of being his intermediary with the capitalist" (December 20, 1867). A whole theory of class relations is expressed in this sentence: the planters do not view themselves as capitalists; capitalists are part of the economic structure of the South, but they should not have direct economic relations with the black tenants; instead, the capitalists should do business with the planters, who act as the representatives of their tenants. Statements like this indicate that the slaveowners' paternalistic, antibourgeois ideology survived the destruction of slavery.

Another antimerchant theme in the planter press was opposition to young men's interest in joining the merchant class:

> A large number of young men, instead of cultivating their land with their own hands, always an honorable calling . . . have taken to little country stores, where the temptation to cheat the ignorant negro is too strong for the virtue of many, and they become degraded by consciousness of making money in unjust and low ways, lose their self-respect and sense of honor, form a low standard of virtue and honesty, and will soon become an inferior class of citizens (*Mobile Daily Register,* February 26, 1871).

The *Selma Southern Argus,* another leading voice of planter interests, joined the chorus in its article, "Young Men Choosing a Profession." "Scores and hundreds of strong and hardy young men are dragging out the best and most important years of their lives . . . in our towns and cities, making barely enough to live upon, groping along as slavish subordinates, and wearing out their energies of body and mind in unmanly . . . employments" (May 19, 1870).

What is noteworthy in these profoundly antibourgeois statements is the concern with "honor," "virtue," and "manliness," with the danger of being "degraded," not by wealth itself, but by "consciousness of making money," and, finally, the explicitly class-conscious statement that merchants form an "inferior class" to planters. The planter press did not mince words when dealing with an antagonistic class.

The merchants did not suffer the planters' attacks in silence. Although they lacked the well-organized and skilled ideological organs the planters found in the Mobile and Montgomery press, merchant spokesmen did defend the interests of their class. The *Mobile Register* occasionally printed letters to the editor from such merchant spokesmen. One, written in 1871, dealt with the planters' argument that merchants were responsible for the blacks' degeneracy:

> Some writers attribute the lethargy among them to . . . these cross-roads merchants, to be found everywhere. . . . This is not the cause. . . . The negro is fooled, the cross-roads merchant is fooled, in fact everyone is fooled except the planter, who turns out to be the fooler, the sharpest of the lot. . . . The great and vital cause for dissatisfaction among the negroes lies in the planter . . ., who promises one thing and fails to comply with it.

The letter was signed "Cross-Roads Merchant" (Oct. 7, 1871).

With the crippling of Reconstruction in Alabama by 1871, the planter class apparently had regained enough economic and political power to mount a political campaign to weaken the legal position of merchants holding crop liens. A new antimerchant law was proposed in Alabama in 1871 by an obviously class-conscious "planter convention." The convention met in the state House of Representatives; the *Montgomery Advertiser* reported (February 10, 1871), "the attendance of this important meeting was large and extremely gratifying." One speaker complained that

> the agricultural fraternity . . . must continue to grovel subserviently to a class who derive their support and business from products of their soil and their labor. . . . The commercial world is growing into affluence to the impoverishment of our agriculturalists. This would seem to be the reverse of legitimacy and an exaltation of the creature into superiority to the creator.

Whereas the 1867 statute had given the landlord a lien for the year's rent, the new law gave the landlord a lien "superior to all other liens, for rent and advances" made to tenants. When a debtor was insolvent, and after his rent had been paid, this law required that his crops go first to pay for the supplies his landlord had advanced, and only after that to pay for supplies advanced by the local merchant. A letter to the editor of the *Advertiser* (February 14, 1871) argued that the planters convention bill "was demanded by the present condition of the planting interest. . . . An Act, giving to the planter who undertakes in good faith to supply his hands, a lien superior to that of an interloping 'advancer.'" The bill was voted into law by a sizeable majority in the legislature (Act of Alabama 1870–71:19; Rogers 1970:15–20; Going 1951:94–102).

For the merchant, this legislation created two types of credit customers: tenants who had landlords, the great majority of whom were black in 1871; and yeomen who owned their own land, who didn't have landlords, virtually all of whom were white. If both a planter and a merchant advanced supplies to a tenant, the planter had the right to be repaid first. In an economy where the profits of small producers were usually marginal, this legislation was a serious blow to all merchants competing with planters to supply black tenants. Its effect was to weaken the black belt merchants, and to pressure the merchant class to shift toward the white yeoman areas outside the black belt where they could continue to take crop liens without fear that the debtors' crops would go to planters instead of themselves.

Thus the Alabama planters' success at making their lien for supplies legally superior to that of the merchants restricted future merchant gains primarily to the white yeoman areas. It divided those working the land by race, and reserved the profit from the blacks' labor on the great cotton plantations for the planters, giving the merchant class, as a sort of consolation prize, the right to appropriate by means of the crop lien the surplus created by the white yeomen. The subsequent transformation of independent yeomen in the hills into tenants was accompanied by the transformation of hill merchants into merchant-landlords.

This was indeed a merger of landlord and merchant methods of appropriating the surplus, but there were two distinct versions of the merger in two different areas, with opposite social consequences for the merchant class. In the black belt, the planter appears to have obtained for himself the merchants' method of appropriating the surplus produced by the black tenantry; the planter became a planter-merchant by pushing the merchant class out of any position of substantial landed power in the black belt. This was a combination of economic levers for extracting the surplus, but the levers remained in the hands of a single class; it was not the merger of social classes. It marked not a transformation of the structure of power, but rather the return to the planters of their traditional position of domination over the black plantation labor force—one which entailed a metamorphosis of the planters.

It was in the hills that a major transformation of the social structure took place. There, merchants became merchant-landlords, but again there was no merger of social classes, because there had been no planter class in the hills, a region of small farmers. The rise of a new class of merchant-landlords entailed the fall of the white yeoman farmers to tenant status.

The manuscript schedules of the U.S. Census list individuals' occupations, making it possible to identify merchants, and to follow their rising or declining fortunes from one census to the next between 1860 and 1880. The merchants studied included those of the five contiguous black belt counties and six contiguous hill counties in northwestern Alabama (Colbert, Fayette, Franklin, Lamar, Lawrence, and Marion). The changing place of merchants in the postwar agrarian economy was measured in three ways. The number of merchants increased 70 percent in the black belt in the 1860s, and decreased 80 percent in the 1870s, while in the hills the

Table 1-4. Merchants in black belt and hill regions

	1860		1870		1880	
	Black Belt	Hills	Black Belt	Hills	Black Belt	Hills
Total population	113,765	56,579	115,476	59,289	138,841	78,386
Black	74%	32%	76%	26%	79%	26%
Merchants	146	97	247	92	148	108
Merchants per 10,000 population	13	17	21	16	11	14

number of merchants increased between 1870 and 1880 by 17 percent (table 1-4). The share of land owned by merchants in the black belt almost tripled in the 1860s, rising from 0.9 percent of all land owned by county residents in 1860 to 2.6 percent in 1870. And the number of landless merchants who stayed merchants in the area (an indication of the general prosperity of merchants) decreased during the 1870s in the black belt, from 33 to 23 percent, while rising in the hills, from 19 to 24 percent (cf. Wiener 1976a; 1978:109–135).

This evidence supports the argument that, as a result of the crop lien law, merchants were making considerable gains in the immediate postwar years, especially in the black belt; and that the planter-sponsored legislation was effective in restricting the number and prosperity of black belt merchants, limiting merchant gains to the hills during the 1870s. The crop lien was developed in the immediate postwar years as a new lever for extracting the surplus from the agricultural labor force. The surplus, the labor beyond that which is necessary for the subsistence of the actual producer, is the "life-blood" of every dominant class, Maurice Dobb writes (1963:15), and, as a consequence, "its particular relationship to the labor process [is] crucial to its own survival." The merchants' challenge to the planters over control of this new lever for extracting the surplus was a life-and-death matter for the planter class.

Yet it would be a mistake to see the defeat of the merchants by itself as the key to the weakness of liberal democracy in the South. Bourgeois revolutions have succeeded in establishing bourgeois freedoms when workers and peasants fought for them alongside (and often in front of) segments of the bourgeoisie itself. The planter regime could have been destroyed and replaced by a more democratic one only by an alliance of the South's relatively weak bourgeois forces with its potentially more powerful classes of farm laborers and yeoman farmers. Blacks would have been critical in such an alliance.

Radical Reconstruction had precisely such a strategy. The economic basis of planter political power had to be attacked, and a coalition forged between the newly freed blacks and the white Republicans, who often included merchants among their ranks (Williamson 1965:174). Thaddeus Stevens had the clearest understanding. He favored the confiscation of the plantations of Confederate officers and officials, and their distribution to freedmen, arguing that the freedmen's political power would be insecure as long as they did not have a solid economic foundation in the ownership of small farms (U.S. Congress 1866:2460, 2544; Foner 1974). Charles Sumner agreed that "the great plantations . . . must be broken up, and the freedmen must have the pieces" (Pierce 1893:198), and Congressman George Washington Julian argued, "of what avail would be an act of Congress totally abolishing slavery, or an amendment of the Constitution forever prohibiting it, if the old agricultural basis of aristocratic power shall remain?" (U.S. Congress 1864:2251; Cox 1958; Riddleberger 1955) Freedmen and poorer southern whites understood the significance of the proposal; the *Philadelphia Press* reported that, in Alabama, if confiscation of the plantations were submitted to a vote, "a majority of both blacks and whites would vote for it" (McPherson 1964:249–65, 410–12). The failure of this strategy was largely the consequence of the defeat of the Radicals in Congress by conservatives; they feared that northern workers might draw some lessons from the Radical attack on the South's dominant class (Montgomery 1967).

But the political battle over the fate of the planters was fought most intensely in the South. Its outcome has significant implications for Marxist theory: a dominant class suffered a decisive, near-fatal blow to its economic base—the slave plantation. But despite its economic prostration in the immediate postwar period, this planter class held tenaciously to political power in the state legislatures and governorships. And they were able to enlist the state in reconstituting the region's economy on their own terms, in their own interests, against a new class that threatened their dominant position.

Politics at this critical juncture was not simply a mirror of production; political power was not a passive reflection of economic power. The state played a critical role in creating new social relations of production; control of the state apparatus by an economically weak planter class permitted it to reestablish its domination, albeit on an altered basis. In this way the planter regime held on for a century after the Civil War, until the second Reconstruction, the civil rights movement, finally brought a measure of democracy to the South.

References

BARNEY, WILLIAM L.
   1974   The Secessionist Impulse: Alabama and Mississippi in 1860. Princeton: Princeton University Press.

BLOCH, MARC
    1953   The Historian's Craft. New York: Knopf.
BOND, HORACE MANN
    1939   Negro Education in Alabama: A Study in Cotton and Steel. Washington: Associated Publishers.
COX, LAWANDA
    1958   "The Promise of Land for the Freedmen." Mississippi Valley Historical Review 45:413–30.
DOBB, MAURICE
    1947,   Studies in the Development of Capitalism. New York: International
    1963   Publishers.
EATON, CLEMENT
    1968   The Waning of the Old South Civilization. Athens: University of Georgia Press.
FONER, ERIC
    1974   "Thaddeus Stevens, Confiscation, and Reconstruction." Pp. 154–83, in Stanley Elkins and Erik McKitrick (eds.), The Hofstadter Aegis: A Memorial. New York: Knopf.
GATES, PAUL W.
    1965   Agriculture and the Civil War. New York: Knopf.
GOING, ALLEN
    1951   Bourbon Democracy in Alabama, 1874–1890. University, Ala.: University of Alabama Press.
GUTMAN, HERBERT G.
    1976   The Black Family in Slavery and Freedom, 1750–1925. New York: Random House.
HACKNEY, SHELDON
    1972   "Origins of the New South in Retrospect." Journal of Southern History 38:191–216.
HARRIS, WILLIAM C.
    1967   Presidential Reconstruction in Mississippi. Baton Rouge: Louisiana State University Press.
HICKS, JOHN D.
    1931   The Populist Revolt. Minneapolis: University of Minnesota Press.
JOHNSON, MICHAEL P.
    1977   Toward a Patriarchal Republic: The Secession of Georgia. Baton Rouge: Louisiana State University Press.
LERNER, EUGENE M.
    1955   "Southern Agriculture and Agricultural Income, 1860–1880." Journal of Political Economy 62:20–40.
McPHERSON, JAMES M.
    1964   The Struggle for Equality: Abolitionists and the Negro in Civil War and Reconstruction. Princeton: Princeton University Press.
MADDEX, MACK P., JR.
    1970   The Virginia Conservatives 1867–1879: A Study in Reconstruction Politics. Chapel Hill: University of North Carolina Press.
MONTGOMERY, DAVID
    1967   Beyond Equality: Labor and the Radical Republicans, 1862–1872. New York: Knopf.

MOORE, BARRINGTON, JR.
  1966   Social Origins of Dictatorship and Democracy: Lord and Peasant in
           the Making of the Modern World. Boston: Beacon.
PIERCE, E. L.
  1893   Memoirs and Letters of Charles Sumner. Boston: Roberts Brothers.
RANSOM, ROGER, and RICHARD SUTCH
  1972   "Debt Peonage in the Cotton South after the Civil War." Journal of
           Economic History 32:641–69.
  1975   "The Impact of the Civil War and of Emancipation on Southern
           Agriculture." Explorations in Economic History 12:1–28.
  1977   One Kind of Freedom: The Economic Consequences of Reconstruc-
           tion. New York: Cambridge University Press.
RIDDLEBERGER, PATRICK W.
  1955   "George W. Julian: Abolitionist Land Reformer." Agricultural His-
           tory 5:108–15.
ROGERS, WILLIAM WARREN
  1970   The One-Gallused Rebellion: Agrarianism in Alabama, 1865–1896.
           Baton Rouge: Louisiana State University Press.
ROSENGARTEN, THEODORE
  1974   All God's Dangers: The Life of Nate Shaw. New York: Knopf.
SHANNON, FRED A.
  1945   Farmers' Last Frontier: Agriculture, 1860–1897. New York: Farrar.
SHUGG, ROGER W.
  1937   Origins of Class Struggle in Louisiana. Baton Rouge: Louisiana
           State University Press (reprinted 1969).
SOMERS, ROBERT
  1871   The Southern States Since the War, 1870–1. New York: Macmillan.
U. S. CONGRESS
  1864   Congressional Globe. 38th Congress, 1st Session. Washington, D.C.:
           Government Printing Office.
  1866   Congressional Globe. 39th Congress, 1st Session. Washington, D.C.:
           Government Printing Office.
  1867   Congressional Globe. 40th Congress, 1st Session. Washington, D.C.:
           Government Printing Office.
U. S. SENATE
  1885   Documents. 48th Congress, 1st Session, No. 1262.
WIENER, JONATHAN M.
  1976a   "Planter Persistence and Social Change: Alabama, 1850–1870."
           Journal of Interdisciplinary History 6:236–60.
  1976b   "Review of Reviews: Social Origins of Dictatorship and Democ-
           racy." History and Theory 15:146–75.
  1978   Social Origins of the New South: Alabama, 1860–1885. Baton
           Rouge: Louisiana State University Press.
WILLIAMSON, JOEL
  1965   After Slavery: The Negro in South Carolina during Reconstruction,
           1861–1877. Chapel Hill: University of North Carolina Press.

WOODMAN, HAROLD D.
1967   King Cotton and His Retainers. Lexington: University of Kentucky
         Press.
WOODWARD, C. VANN
1951a   Origins of the New South, 1877–1913. Baton Rouge: Louisiana State
         University Press.
1951b   Reunion and Reaction. Boston: Little, Brown.
WRIGHT, CARROLL D., and WILLIAM C. HUNT
1900   The History and Growth of the U.S. Census. Washington, D.C.:
         Government Printing Office.
WRIGHT, GAVIN
1970   "'Economic Democracy' and the Concentration of Wealth in the
         Cotton South, 1850–1860." Agricultural History 44:63–93.
ZEITLIN, MAURICE, and RICHARD EARL RATCLIFF
1975   "Research Methods for the Analysis of the Internal Structure of
         Dominant Classes: The Case of Landlords and Capitalists in Chile."
         Latin American Research Review 10:5–61.

2   The Finance Capitalists

Michael Soref
University of Wisconsin–Madison

Most social scientists seem to think that "finance capitalists" have gone the way of the nickel cigar and the trolley car. Certain Marxists, including such eminent theorists as Paul Sweezy (1942; 1972) share this view. Others (e.g., Fitch and Oppenheimer 1972) claim that finance capital is central within the political economy, and that finance capitalists constitute a powerful group within the American capitalist class. Data from a sample of corporate directors, however, show that finance capitalists occupy a central position within the class. These data raise two important questions: First, do the finance capitalists form a "core group" of the monopoly segment of the capitalist class? Second, do their positions enable them to coordinate intercorporate activity?

Two Problematic Views

There are two problematic views of the relationship between banks and the industrial sector—the first view is that industrial and other nonfinancial corporations have gained independence from banks; the second view is that they are controlled by banks. The few managerialists who address this

I wish to thank Monika Hey, Alex Hicks, David James, Charles Palit, Jane Niece, Erik O. Wright, and the members of the Social Organization Training Program colloquium for helpful comments. The research was partially supported by grants from the E. A. Ross small grant fund and the Social Organization Training Program of the Department of Sociology at the University of Wisconsin-Madison. Linda Davis, Bonnie Schuman, and especially Mary Vandenbrook deserve thanks for diligent research assistance.

question argue that the increase in the internal generation of funds and the declining power of investment bankers during the Depression freed industrials from financial control (Gordon 1946:214–221).

The relationship between the major banks and industrials has changed in the last half century, the forms and bases of financial control have changed, and the composition of financially influenced community of interest groups has changed, but financial control has not withered away. Critics of this part of the managerialist argument have cited three kinds of counterevidence. First, as Lintner (1959) points out, major corporations today do not rely more on internally generated funds. The proportion of funds internally generated now is about the same as at the turn of the century (Kotz 1975:69).

Corporate stock controlled by bank trust departments is a second base of control over nonfinancial firms. Bank trust departments control large amounts of stock in personal trusts and in pension fund stockholdings. For example, the Patman Committee "found that the largest banks surveyed in ten major cities . . . held five percent or more of the common stock in 147 (29 percent) of the 500 largest industrial corporations" (Zeitlin 1974:1101). Supplementing stockvoting information with data on interlocking and reliance on external debt, David Kotz (1975) studied control in the top 200 nonfinancial corporations in 1969. He classified 69 as under some sort of financial control. The Metcalf Committee (U.S. Senate 1978:1–3) examined stockvoting rights of institutional holders in 122 of the nation's largest companies, finding that institutional holders (most of the largest were bank trust departments) held 5 percent or more of the stockvoting rights in 19 of them. Five or fewer institutions can vote 10 percent or more of the stock in 24 other companies. Morgan Guaranty Trust had more than 5 percent of the stockvoting rights in 27 of these companies.

A third type of evidence is based on evidence on interlocking directorates between financial and nonfinancial companies. For example, Allen (1974:403) found that the top 200 nonfinancials (in 1970) average 3.4 interlocks with financial companies; large industrials average 4.1 interlocks.

Non-Marxists are not the only ones who espouse this portion of the managerial thesis (that is, independence from bank control in large corporations). One of Baran and Sweezy's premises (1966) is that monopoly corporations operate more or less autonomously; corporate decisions are made from inside the corporation, without banker interference. Although Baran and Sweezy did not agree with the entire managerial thesis, they did agree that the internal generation of funds led to the eclipse of the finance capitalists.

The managerial thesis was posed during a period when the relative power of finance was declining, but the managerialists exaggerated the decline, and did not notice the resurgence of financial control during the 1950s and 60s. The organizational form of the major financial centers and their bases of influence over large corporations underwent change, but, as Kotz's sketch of the history of financial control (1975:27–80) indicates, these changes did not bring about the eclipse of the finance capitalists.

According to Kotz, the development of financial control occurred roughly during the 1865–1914 period. Banks served as intermediaries for the infusion of European capital, and at first they dealt primarily with railroads. These New York banks, led by the house of Morgan, later branched out into industrials and utilities. Their basis of influence was their ability to loan money and to place securities offerings. Some of the major interest groups of today (Rockefeller, Morgan, and Mellon) developed during that period. With the decline in debt formation resulting from the 1930s Depression (and from the state sponsorship of debt formation during World War Two), the power of the major financial groups suffered a decline.

Some New Deal financial reforms also affected the bargaining position of some major investment houses. Since then, however, the rate of external indebtedness increased, and the major banks recovered their power. However, the major interest groups are not quite so concentrated in the Northeast, as they were before World War One. The organizational form of the dominant financial interest has changed from investment to commercial banks. The basis of influence has changed, to stockvoting in addition to the other types of debt. Bank trust departments control large amounts of stock in personal trusts, and in recent years their stockvoting rights in pension funds have increased rapidly.

The second problematic position is the "bank control" formulation. Robert Fitch and Mary Oppenheimer's article "Who Rules the Corporations?" in *Socialist Revolution* (1970) is a recent example of this theory. Fitch and Oppenheimer argue that bankers and industrialists not only constitute contradictory strata but that debt and stockvoting enable banks to control industrial and other nonfinancial firms. They contend that banks do not allow firms to maximize profits and that banks direct the flow of investment funds into unproductive sectors, thus decreasing the rate of accumulation. Aside from shortcomings of inference and evidence (Sweezy 1972), Fitch and Oppenheimer's formulation is susceptible to a basic conceptual shortcoming of bank control formulations—bank control and finance capital are not synonymous. Finance capital is better conceptualized as the form that the coalescence of bank and industrial capital takes in the monopoly stage of capitalism (Zeitlin 1974: 1102–3; DeVroey 1975; Poulantzas 1975). DeVroey (who applies this criticism to Fitch and Oppenheimer) and Poulantzas (who does not mention them) argue that there is a kind of merger of bank and industrial capital in monopoly capitalism, but that neither will necessarily dominate; the form of the coalescence between them varies according to historical circumstances.

Hilferding's Theory

Hilferding's *Das Finanzkapital* ([1910] 1970) is probably the principal Marxist theoretical contribution on the "joint stock company" or corporation and the role of banks. Hilferding understood the joint stock company much better than did later writers. The joint stock corporation is the pooling of many capitals, but is dominated by a few large capitalists; "capitalists form a society in the direction of which most of them have nothing to say" (Hilferding in Sweezy 1942:262). The development of the joint stock company facilitates the process of centralization (the standard economic term is "concentration").

When firms can fix prices and rationalize output, their profits are greater and more reliable. Here is where the banks come in. Because industrial profits become more profitable, banks see that industrials are worthwhile investments (Hilferding 1970:316–17). Industrial companies come to depend on banks for additional funds. Because of their control of indispensable capital, banks gain influence over the behavior of industrial corporations. "In what direction will this influence be exercised? Always towards the abolition of competition" (Sweezy 1942:265). Capital in this form is neither bank nor industrial capital: it is finance capital. Finance capital for Hilferding is "capital controlled by the banks and utilized by the industrialists" (tr. by Sweezy 1942:266). Finance capital remains under the control of bankers, but it is productive.

Three of the main elements of Hilferding's theory are that "finance capital" is a new stage in capitalist development, that finance capitalists are bankers involved in both banking and production, and that finance capital is a synthesis of both bank and industrial capital.

First, Hilferding argues that finance capital is a new stage in the development of capitalism—that is, previous stages of capitalist development were dominated by commercial capital and later industrial capital. Money capital loaned by usurers is instrumental in bringing about the transition from commercial to industrial capital. The bank replaces the usurer during the industrial capital stage and comes to dominate the industrial capitalist enterprise (1970:318–19).

Second, finance capitalists are bankers who are involved in both banking and the organization and direction of production. In Zeitlin's words:

With this coalescence of financial and industrial capital . . . there also tends to emerge a new social type, the "finance capitalist." Neither financiers ex-

tracting interest at the expense of industrial profits nor "bankers" controlling corporations, but finance capitalists on the boards of the largest banks
and corporations preside over the banks' investments as creditors *and* shareholders, organizing production, sales and financing, and appropriating the
profits of their integrated activities (1976:900).

Thus the original conception of the finance capitalist can be characterized
as "positional." Zeitlin follows Hilferding in provisionally defining finance
capitalists as "representatives of banks who sit on boards of the large
American corporations" (1974:1103). This definition might have applied to
the time and the place which Hilferding had in mind for his model.[1] For
example, in 1910, the six largest German banks had 751 interlocks to industrial corporations (Hilferding 1970:181). At about the same time, "the interlocked Morgan-Stillman-Baker combination held a total of 341
directorships in 112 major U.S. corporations" (Corey 1930:355–56).

Third, although the banker is the senior partner in the synthesis of
banks and industrials, finance capital is also a synthesis; it is neither strictly
bank capital nor industrial capital. The interests of finance capital rise
above those of bank and industrial capital. Marxists who work on the
problem of finance capital disagree about other elements of the thesis, but
most commentators on the thesis consider finance capital a synthesis of
bank and industrial capital (DeVroey 1975; Zeitlin 1974).

Community of Interest Groups

What does the theory of finance capital have to do with interest groups?
Hilferding may have been the first theorist to explain the development of
interest groups (or, more faithful to his wording, "community of interest
groups"), although I think that it would be an overstatement to say that
they are central to the theory. In any case, Hilferding does not describe
them in great detail.

The development of communities of interest is bound up with the
joint stock company and the domination of industrials by banks. A wealthy
investor can control one corporation with an investment which is small in

---

[1] However, the definition might be less applicable today. Many bankers now sitting on boards of nonfinancials may be merely representatives of their banks, not the
embodiments of the coalescence of bank and industrial capital into finance capital. Accordingly, this research will use two operationalizations of the finance capitalist, one
strictly positional, the other attempting to capture the notion of the "heavy of the heav-
ies"; in the second measure only financiers from the largest intermediaries, and nonfinancial executives who hold seats on the largest financial institutions, are counted as finance capitalists.

comparison with the assets of the firm; it would be in his interest to control the first corporation with a relatively small investment and spread his risk by investing in other corporations. Stockownership enables such a person to get a seat on the board of directors. One would expect that he would attempt to coordinate the actions of the interlocked firms.

Banks often receive a seat on the board of directors as a result of their influence on industrial firms. Whenever possible, the bank exerts its influence via interlocking directorates to coordinate the policies of the companies that it influences:

> There is formed a circle of persons, who, thanks to their own possession of capital or as representatives of concentrated power over other people's capital (bank directors), sit upon the governing boards of a large number of corporations. There thus arises a kind of personal union (*Personalunion*), on the one hand between the different corporations themselves, on the other between the latter and the banks, a circumstance which must be of the greatest importance for the policy of these institutions since among them there has arisen a community of interests (translated by Sweezy 1942:261).

A community of interests may include more than one bank. The creation of a community of interests among industrial corporations can have the consequence of also creating mutual interests among hitherto competitive banks (Hilferding 1970:315–16). The community of interest group is one of the organizational forms of finance capital (that Sweezy and later writers have renamed monopoly capital), which act to reduce competition. The community of interest group is sometimes the forerunner (or substitute) for more routinized organizational forms of coalescence (Sweezy 1942:261).

Hilferding suggested that some groups, including financial and non-financial corporations, develop common policies, have elements of control in common, and are connected by interlocking directorates. Recent writers on community of interest groups in the U.S. economy (e.g., Allen 1978; Sonquist and Koenig 1975) introduce their research reports by setting up contrasting models of the economy. One of their models is labeled the "finance capital" model; they do not realize that their own assumptions in seeking interest groups come from the theory of finance capital.

There has been almost no systematic empirical study of finance capitalists, except for Maurice Zeitlin's work-in-progress on finance capitalists in Chile. Work on finance capitalists has been incidental to investigating the interest group structure of the economy. Studies of interest groups have identified and described finance capitalists in the process of delineating interest groups. These studies show that interest groups are still important economic groupings and that the economy's interest group structure has not been static; some of the old names, based in investment banking, such as the Kuhn-Loeb interest group, have declined, and some regional interest groups relatively independent of New York–based finance have developed.

The interest group studies (both quantitative and qualitative) find similar results. The studies of Perlo (1957), Menshikov (1969), Sonquist and Koenig (1975), and Allen (1978) cover the entire economy. They all find a group centered around a set of Chicago-based corporations, and most find a Mellon interest group, a Morgan group, one or more Rockefeller groups, and several regional groups centered around such "regional metropolises" as St. Louis and Cleveland.

Students of interest groups argue that the members of community of interest groups divide up territory and fix prices. Knowles compared the products of a set of petrochemical companies in the Rockefeller group with those of a set of companies outside the group. He found that the companies in the Rockefeller group had significantly more product duplication, which indicates that there might have been some conscious coordination among the companies in the group; petrochemical product duplication serves the functions of pooling research and development, preempting antitrust by understating market concentration, and spreading the risk among the firms in the interest group (Knowles 1973:36–40).

Although research on interest groups yields roughly the same picture of interest group structure, no consensus has been reached on the conceptualization of the interest group. The conceptualization of Knowles and of Zeitlin (1974) seems to me to be consistent with Hilferding's theory and with much of the evidence on interest groups. This research assumes that interest groups can be conceptualized as more or less loose alliances of major family-controlled holdings.

Knowles describes the process by which a family sphere of influence becomes affiliated with other family spheres out of the requirements of doing business:

> the descendants of the original "robber barons" . . . have established huge financial centers of power by making alliances with other wealthy inheritors and by forming closely integrated "interest groups."
>
> The organization of an interest group begins with the members and representatives of wealthy families who sit on the board of directors, usually as major stockholders, of a large urban bank. . . . Although some of these families have made their original fortunes in banking, most constitute the dominant stockholder in one or more large nonbanking corporations. By sitting on the board's bank of directors, these families are in a position to serve the bank by giving to it the business of the family corporation and are served in turn by the banks in three ways; they are assured of a supply of credit for their family corporations, they are in a better position to maintain control over their family corporations because they can count on the support of the large stockholdings in the bank's trust de-

partment, and they may benefit from their corporation's participation in monopolistic trusts which are based in the bank.

The bank and its wealthy directors tend also to form alliances with other banks and wealthy families, and with one or more life insurance companies. This alliance of banks and insurance companies constitutes the core financial institutions of the interest group. There will usually be a set of law firms, investment banking firms, foundations, universities, and other institutions of power and influence associated with the group. All of these institutions together are able to control in turn a network of other financial and nonfinancial corporations (Knowles 1973:3).

Thus community of interest groups can be characterized as alliances of family spheres of influence. The question of bank control versus family control (see Allen forthcoming), then, is a false issue. Some families might be based on banking, and others might be primarily industrial. If community of interest groups are conceptualized as alliances of family spheres of influence, the banking family spheres might or might not dominate the community of interest group; the industrial families might be the equal of the banking families depending on historical circumstances.

Questions and Hypotheses

Finance capitalists bring together formally independent corporations, and participate in the direction of concentrations of capital. Judging from their structural position within the capitalist class, one would expect them to be especially wealthy, powerful, and socially established capitalists. Thus, the first research question is, Are finance capitalists a "special social type" (Zeitlin 1976)? Zeitlin has suggested studying the shareownership, wealth, social status, and kinship relations to principal owners of capital, compared to that of other capitalists. Although data on wealth and kinship are not available, membership in the upper class and some dimensions of directors' propertied interests insofar as the latter is reflected in board memberships can be used to categorize social types. I hypothesize that finance capitalists will be more likely to belong to the "upper class," and that they will hold more of each type of directorship.

The second research question concerns the role of finance capitalists in coordinating the common affairs of groups of corporations. Hilferding and Zeitlin suggest that finance capitalists influence pricing and the allocation of markets and factor inputs. I hypothesize that finance capitalists are more likely than other capitalists to hold positions that link interdependent companies. To my knowledge, this study is the first systematic attempt to investigate potentially anticompetitive interlocking, to compare the interlocking of the finance capitalists with that of the nonfinance capitalists, and to compare the coordinative interlocking done by finance capitalists with that done by nonfinance capitalists.

Dependent Variables

Simple lists of positions on directorships are inadequate for answering these questions. It is difficult to interpret the number of directorships held by an individual or group because some directorships are important and others trivial. Some directors considerably influence the operations of a company, while other directors are powerless compared to other insiders connected with the firm. Moreover, simple lists of positions do not tell the roles of directors in coordinating corporate business. Consequently, I have disaggregated measures of positionholding according to the following typology (see Soref 1979):

1. horizontal (interlocks between competitors)
2. vertical (interlocks between customers and suppliers)
3. local (interlocks between companies headquartered in the same city)
4. interest group (interlocks between corporations which belong to the same interest group)

The data come from a study based on a sample of directors of the top 200 industrials (sales rank for 1964, from the 1965 *Fortune* listing). Although not representative of all sectors of monopoly capital, the data can be considered a sample of corporate capitalists because it includes owners and top managers of the nation's largest corporations. Using publicly accessible sources, I gathered social background data, information on their home companies, and information on their positions in other companies. The observation units will be the directors of the top 200 industrials (including inside and outside directors). The independent measures are dichotomous measures of finance capital. The dependent variables will be a measure of social status, measures of the importance of the directors, and measures of positions that tap potential for coordinating corporate behavior. The finance capitalists will be compared to the other corporate directors in the analysis.

Data on horizontal, vertical, and interest group interlocks will be presented in the second hypothesis. The first hypothesis will be tested with data on the social status of directors, their local interlocks, and several measures of the importance of the directorships held. These latter measures will operationalize the size and centrality of the companies and their links to companies in basic industries.

Sample

Forty corporations were selected from the top 200 industrial firms in 1965. The 40 were treated as sampling units—300 directors were selected from the 40 sampling units. The 200 companies were divided into 20 strata according to the number of directors on the board. Two companies were selected from each stratum (without replacement). The two-stage sampling design introduced the possibility of a bias toward directors of large companies. But sampling procedures were devised, as described in detail elsewhere (Soref 1979), to ensure that the probability of such biases is small.

The unweighted sample was really a sample of directorships, not directors. A sample of directors would be a sample taken from a list of directors in which duplicated names were eliminated. In my sample, a director with, for example, three directorships on top 200 industrials had three times as great a probability of being selected as a director with only one directorship on a top 200 company. This problem was solved by weighting the sample, so that a director with one top 200 position was assigned a weight of unity, a director with two top 200 positions was assigned a weight of 0.5, and so on. (N for most tabulations is 196, while the sample size is 273, of 301 directors selected.)

Operationalization of finance capitalist

Two operationalizations of the "positional" aspect of finance capitalist will be used. In the first, a finance capitalist is any director with a directorship on both a financial and a nonfinancial company (62 of 196 were finance capitalists by this measure). The second operationalization is more selective; a director must sit on the boards of both a major nonfinancial firm and a major financial firm. Because the entire sample holds seats in top 200 industrial firms, the criteria for the second operationalization will refer only to their positions on financial firms; to be defined as a finance capitalist, the director had to be either a partner of an investment bank, a director of a top 50 commercial bank, or a director of a top 50 life insurance company. Eighteen directors fit these criteria.

Analysis

The results compare the positions of finance capitalists to the positions of nonfinance capitalists. The data are quite simple; they are merely comparisons of means between the two groups. At this point in the state of knowledge on finance capital, multivariate analysis seems unnecessary; because the literature does not suggest a model of positionholding, I see no reason to control for the possible effects of other variables.

The data will consist of three types of comparisons between the finance capitalists and the other directors (that is, the nonfinance capitalists) on measures of positionholding: (1) comparison of their mean positionholding; (2) comparison of the mean positionholding of finance capitalists with that of nonfinance capitalists with at least one board position outside their home companies (This comparison is an attempt to circumvent a technical problem; because finance capitalists are defined by their holding of an outside position—to be classified as finance capitalists bankers must sit on the board of a nonfinancial company, others must hold a seat on the board of a financial company—the independent variable is defined in terms of the dependent variable. Excluding directors with seats on only one board makes the nonfinance capitalists comparable to the finance capitalists, because in this comparison, all the nonfinance capitalists sit on at least one board in addition to their home company's board.); (3) comparison of number of positions (of a given type) as a *proportion* of the total number of outside positions held (for example, the number of positions on top 200 companies as a proportion of all outside positions held).

Defining the dependent variable as a proportion keeps the independent variable from being defined by the dependent variable. The difficulty with comparing means of finance capitalists and nonfinance capitalists is that the finance capitalists have at least one outside position by virtue of the definition of the category; if the dependent variable is a rate, the finance capitalists do not have that definitional advantage. These data are presented in table 2-1.

Are Finance Capitalists a Special Social Type?

If finance capital is a central segment of capital, finance capitalists should be more important than the other corporate capitalists; they should also be socially integrated into their class and have positions on more important companies.

Finance capital and the upper class

I used three of Domhoff's criteria (1970) for classifying membership in the upper class. These criteria refer to *Social Register* listings, attendance at one of a few very exclusive preparatory schools, or to membership in one of a few exclusive gentleman's clubs listed in *The Higher Circles* (1970:21–24). About two-fifths of the directors met one or more of these criteria. Using the broad measure of finance capitalist, finance capitalists were about twice as likely to be members of the upper class as nonfinance capitalists. Using the narrow measure, finance capitalists were 1.76 times as likely to be mem-

*Table 2-1. Positionholding of finance capitalists and
nonfinance capitalists (means)*

	Broad Definition[†]		Narrow Definition[†]		Total
	f.c.	n.f.c.	f.c.	n.f.c.	
1. Outside positions held					
Outside positions held	4.021*	2.089	4.123*	1.092	3.260
Verified outside positions held	3.412*	.445	4.909*	2.911	1.377
2. Size of interlocked companies					
1. Positions on top 200 companies					
(a)	.913*	.152	1.291*	.301	.394
(b)	.913*	.506	1.291*	.638	.756
(c)	.259*	.107	.367*	.133	.155
2. Positions on top 500 companies					
(a)	1.143*	.248	1.727*	.409	.532
(b)	1.143	.834	1.727*	.868	1.024
(c)	.303*	.162	.368*	.133	.207
3. Positions on large (assets $0.5 billion) industrials					
(a)	.491*	.071	.736*	.149	.204
(b)	.491*	.230	.736*	.313	.390
(c)	.123*	.049	.164*	.064	.073
3. Positionholding in key companies					
(a)	.903*	.271	1.355*	.380	.471
(b)	.903	.923	1.355*	.813	.911
(c)	.227	.162	.322*	.167	.182
4. Measures of centrality					
1. Home company in interest group	.449	.485	.553	.465	.471
2. Number of positions on companies in an interest group					
(a)	.992*	.112	1.368*	.291	.392
(b)	.992*	.357	1.368*	.609	.747
(c)	.281*	.058	.319*	.109	.129
3. Number of *Fortune* interlocks of home company					
(a)	18.034*	14.540	27.948*	14.646	15.446
(b)	18.034	16.366	27.948	15.668	17.355

Table 2-1—Continued

	Broad Definition[†]		Narrow Definition[†]		Total
	f.c.	n.f.c.	f.c.	n.f.c.	
4. Number of *Fortune* interlocks of outside position companies					
(a)	40.004*	4.102	61.309*	10.691	15.441
(b)	40.004*	13.655	61.309*	22.768	29.773
5. Interest group interlocks					
Membership in same interest group (composite measure)					
(a)	.359*	.019	.373*	.101	.127
(b)	.359*	.064	.373*	.217	.245
(c)	.191*	.017	.116*	.068	.072
Membership in same interest group (Perlo measure)					
(a)	.851*	.034	1.468*	.172	.293
(b)	.851*	.115	1.468*	.367	.566
(c)	.331*	.022	.330*	.098	.120

* Greater than nonfinance capitalists, $p < .05$, one-tailed test
   (a) entire sample
   (b) directors without outside positions excluded from tabulation
   (c) rate of positionholding (standardized by total verified outside positions)
† Broad definition of finance capitalists: Those holding a position on a financial company (or partnership in an investment bank). Narrow definition: those holding a partnership in an investment bank, directorship in a top 50 commercial bank, or a directorship in a top 50 life insurance company.

bers of the upper class (cross-tabulations not shown). In this context, Domhoff's upper class can be seen as a status group composed of the older, more established families of the capitalist class.

Number of directorships

Part 1 of table 2-1 presents the means for total number of positions held by finance capitalists versus nonfinance capitalists. Two measures of the total number of directorships (not counting the director's seat on the board of his home company) were used: first, the total number of positions on independent companies; none of the companies listed in the director's biographical entry (in *Who's Who*, or *Poor's Register of Corporations, Directors, and Executives*) could be a subsidiary of the director's home company, or of any other company listed in the entry. The second measure was based on the first measure, but included only companies listed in a publicly available corporate reference book. I consider the second measure somewhat more valid than the first (see Soref 1979 for more detailed description of the measures).

Finance capitalists have more directorships than nonfinance capitalists in every comparison in part 1, and the difference between means is significant in each case. So far, these results are little more than descriptive, however.

Size

Three measures of the size of companies were used. All three refer to *Fortune* 500 industrials. Two measures were based on size measured by sales, the third on size measured by assets. The means for these measures for finance capitalists and nonfinance capitalists are given in part 2 of table 2-1. In every comparison the means for finance capitalists were larger. The difference between means was significant in every comparison except the comparison between the mean number of top 500 positions held by finance capitalists (broad measure) versus top 500 positions held by other directors with at least one outside position. Finance capitalists hold positions on more big companies than other directors.

"Key" companies

Averitt (1968:2–3) argues that "American industries are divided into a hierarchy of economic importance. . . . Manufacturing forms the critical component of U.S. industry, and the key industries are at the heart of manufacturing." Key industries include, for example, primary metal processing industries, petroleum refining, the electronics industry, and industrial and agricultural chemicals. This variable measures the economic importance of director's positions and the results are presented in part 3 of table 2-1.

Although finance capitalists (broad measure) had more directorships in key companies than the other directors in two of three comparisons, the differences were not significant. Using the narrower measure of finance capitalist, the differences between the group means are significant. Thus finance capitalists who directed major financial intermediaries held more positions than other finance capitalists and nonfinance capitalists. These results do not clearly show that finance capitalists hold positions in more economically important corporations than the nonfinance capitalists.

Centrality

A third dimension of the importance of a director is centrality. Most recent interlocking studies have used some form of the concept of centrality (e.g., Allen 1978; Sonquist and Koenig 1975; Mariolis 1975). Using sociometric concepts and techniques, these studies search for an underlying clique structure, using interlocks as information on the strength of ties among companies. The centrality of a company depends on the centrality of its position within networks and the importance of its network(s) within the structure of intercorporate cliques. Measures of the centrality of a company tell how a given company fits into the clique structure.

Centrality itself can be separated into three dimensions, all of which are aggregated in the centrality measure—the number of firms with which a firm is interlocked, the intensity of the interlocks between the firms (that is two interlocks with a given firm signify a more intense relationship than one interlock), and the centrality of the firms with which a given firm interlocks (Bearden and others 1975:32). The measure also standardizes for the companies' board sizes. I will use a proxy for this measure. Using the universe of 797 *Fortune* companies for 1969, Mariolis (1975:430) found that the number of interlocks to *Fortune* companies had a correlation of .91 with the centrality measure. I used the number of *Fortune* interlocks of the home company and the total number of *Fortune* interlocks of the companies for which the director held positions as measures of centrality.

Two other measures of centrality were used—a dichotomous measure of the home company's membership in an interest group, and the number of positions in companies that belonged to an interest group (without respect for whether the position was in the *same* interest group as the home company or any other position). The first measure used several studies of interest groups, while the second used only an updated version of Perlo's study (1957).

The results for the measures of centrality are presented in part 4 of table 2-1. It was inappropriate to use rates for the proxy measures of centrality and summed centrality of interlocked companies because not all directors' outside positions were on *Fortune* corporations. It was obviously inappropriate to standardize the dichotomous variable of the home company's membership in an interest group.

Although the finance capitalists have greater centrality on all measures in part 4 of table 2-1, not all differences between means are significant. The results for the measures relating to outside positions, however, for the measures of summed centrality of outside positions, and for community of interest links measures seem clearer. The differences between means for those measures were significant. Overall, the results on centrality suggest that finance capitalists have more access to networks of coporations; although the data do not clearly show that finance capitalists' home companies are more central than those of others, they do show that the finance capitalists' positionholdings are more central.

Overall, finance capitalists hold more positions, and more important positions, than other corporate capitalists. Except for seats on key companies, their means were consistently greater on every measure of importance and social integration into the class. These data indicate that finance capitalists indeed constitute a "special social type" within the capitalist class.

Coordinative interlocks

Hilferding and those who followed him argue that finance capitalists play central roles in the creation of communities of interest among companies. Finance capitalists should be particularly likely to participate in decisions on pricing, product lines, and the allocation of markets and raw materials. If finance capital coordinates intercorporate behavior, it could be expected that finance capitalists occupy positions that enable them to participate in the coordination of the common affairs of several companies. I use three types of measures of such positions—horizontal interlocks, vertical interlocks, and interest group interlocks. The data cannot show that finance capitalists actually set prices and allocate territory, but rather that they hold positions which might enable them to do so.

The second research question on finance capitalists dealt with the coordination of the activities of formally independent corporations. The data presented here do not show that finance capitalists actually coordinate intercorporate relationships, but that they are more likely to hold positions which enable them to do so. I present data on two types of dependent variables: data on horizontal and vertical interlocks, and data on interest group interlocks. These dependent variables measure the extent that directors hold seats on companies with a vendor or customer relationship to each other, and the extent that they link corporations in their home companies' interest group with their home companies.

An *indirect interlock* between companies occurs when a director of two companies has a position on the board of a third company. I expect that finance capitalists will connect companies with a potential interest in such a linkage; I hypothesize that finance capitalists will get in a position to bring together competitors and to bring together vendors with customers. Accordingly, the appropriate data for this hypothesis are the relationships among a director's outside positions. For example, if a businessman sits on the boards of two steel companies, that is an *horizontal indirect interlock*. If he serves on the board of a steel company, and on the board of an iron ore mining company, that would be a *vertical indirect interlock*.

I judged a pair of firms as potential competitors if any of their four-digit Standard Industrial Classification (SIC) codes were identical. SIC codes for companies were taken from the 1965 *Standard and Poor's* reference volume.

Figures for 1967 input-output of the economy were used to operationalize potential vertical interlocks. The input-output table (U.S. Department of Commerce 1974) gives the proportions (inputs) of a given product coming from every other industry for 367 industries. The SIC codes were translated into the classifications used in the input-output table (details are given in Soref 1979).

I classified a pair of companies as vertically interlocked if any industry of one company supplied at least 1 percent of the output of any of the other company's industries. I also used a more stringent criterion, 2 percent. Both cutoff points might appear too small to the reader, but actually one or two percentage points is an unusually large contribution to the value of product. For example, in the auto industry, of a dollar's worth of autos (motor vehicles and parts), $0.032 came from the blast furnace and basic steel products industry, $0.025 came from the iron and steel foundries industry, and $0.012 came from the iron and steel forging industry. In turn, for example, $0.059 of the value of a dollar's product in the blast furnace and basic steel products industry came from the iron mining industry (iron and ferroalloy ores, mining), and $0.025 of a dollar's product of the blast furnace and basic steel industry from the coal mining industy (U.S. Department of Commerce, 1974:87, 143).

Previous studies (U.S. Senate Governmental Operations Committee 1978; U.S. Federal Trade Commission 1951) of interlocking directorates between vendors and customers have relied on educated guesswork to ascertain the companies likely to be customers and companies likely to be suppliers for a given company. Previous investigations identified direct and indirect interlocks among companies, and the researchers suggested that some appeared to connect potential suppliers with potential customers. These studies found many interlocks between customers and suppliers; the FTC study concluded that, of those interlocks detected which potentially suppressed competition, "The most common interlocks were those that linked a seller of goods or services with a buyer thereof" (1951:3). The last Metcalf report (U.S. Senate 1978) also noted many interlocking directorates between vendors and customers. The procedure for identifying vertical interlocks in the present research is not without deficiencies. For example, the categories used in the input-output table are slightly broader than four-digit SIC codes. The procedure cannot take into account the proportion of business a company does in any of its SICs.

I hypothesized that finance capitalists would be more likely than the others to interlock competitors and to connect customers with suppliers through interlocking directorates. The appropriate test would be to look at the interrelationships among the companies on which a given director holds positions. However, such a test would entail about 1,100 comparisons (using the distribution of known interlocks to calculate the combinations of companies taken two at a time), which are far too many to do without machine readable data on the SICs of each interlocked company, software for converting the SICs into the classifications used for the input-output table, and a program for using the input-output table. Accordingly, I took subsamples of finance capitalists and nonfinance capitalists.

I selected three subsamples from the sample of directors—10 nonfinance capitalists, 10 finance capitalists with financial home company, and 10 finance capitalists with nonfinancial home company (the broad definition of finance capitalist was used). I decided to divide the finance capitalists in that manner because I suspected that there might be a difference between the finance capitalists with nonfinancial home companies and the finance capitalists with financial home companies. Because of the complicated weighting that would have been required, tests of significance were not calculated. Seven of the 30 had any vertical or horizontal indirect interlocks—4 were financial finance capitalists, and 2 were nonfinancial finance capitalists.

Although only 1 nonfinance capitalist had any vertical or horizontal interlocks, there were no differences between the subsamples on indirect interlocking with competitors—each subsample had one indirect horizontal interlock. Therefore, the first part of the hypothesis was not supported by the data.

The nonfinance capitalist subsample had only one vertical interlock. With the 1 percent criterion, both finance capitalist subsamples clearly had more vertical interlocks than the nonfinance capitalists; the financiers had 15 interlocks, and the other finance capitalist subsample had a mean of 13. The more stringent criterion separated the two finance capitalist subsamples; the financiers still clearly had more vertical interlocks than the nonfinance capitalists with 12. However, the subsample of finance capitalists with nonfinancial home companies only had three vertical interlocks by the more stringent criterion. Overall, the financiers average more than one vertical interlock apiece, and the nonfinancial home company finance capitalists seem to have more vertical interlocks. Thus, the data support the second part of the hypothesis, although results on such small subsamples should be interpreted with caution.

Interest group interlocks

An interest group interlock occurs when a director holds a seat on the board of a company that belongs to the same interest group as the director's home company. Because finance capitalists are personifications of the fusion of bank and industrial capital into community of interest groups, finance capitalists could be expected to have more community of interest group interlocks.

I used results from the studies of Perlo (1957), Menshikov (1969),

Chevalier (1970), Knowles (1973), and Allen (1978) to assign companies to interest groups.[2] Although Perlo's findings are old, his study was the most useful; its coverage of companies and interest groups was the most detailed. I used two measures of interest group interlocks—the results using the Perlo data alone, and the results using all five of the studies.

The results for interest group interlocks are presented in part 5 of table 2-1. These results consistently support the hypothesis. Finance capitalists hold more interest group interlocks than nonfinance capitalists in all comparisons, and the difference between means is significant in every comparison. Not only do finance capitalists hold more positions, but their position holding follows a pattern; to a significantly greater extent than other directors, their positions result from alliances between the interlocked firms.

The data on horizontal, vertical, and interest group position holding support the view that finance capitalists hold positions that enable them to coordinate intercorporate activity. Neither finance capitalists nor nonfinance capitalists hold horizontal interlocks, so results for that measure did not support the hypothesis. Finance capitalists were more likely to link customers with suppliers than were nonfinance capitalists. Finance capitalists' interlocks were likely to link corporations that belonged to the same interest group.

Conclusion

A central segment of the American capitalist class located in the large corporations has been analyzed in this chapter. I have argued that there is a group of capitalists who combine financial and industrial holdings. Finance capital does not mean bank control, but rather the integration of financial and nonfinancial capital. The community of interest group, an alliance of the representatives of family holdings in corporations, is the unit for understanding finance capital. In this chapter, I have shown that the finance capitalists are a special social type, in that they are socially established and hold important positions. These positions allow them to coordinate the affairs of formally independent corporations.

Further empirical work on finance capital should include investiga-

---

[2] Except for the Allen study, these studies were primarily qualitative; their delineations of interest groups were based on concrete information about the relationships among companies rather than only on interlock data. I attempted to update the Perlo study; assuming that the makeup of interest groups remained unchanged from 1955 (the date for his study) to 1965, the year of our data on the corporations, I used information from the Moody's Manuals to account for name changes, mergers, and absorptions.

tions of the major interest groups, and their constituent family spheres. If the interest groups are indeed significant economic groupings, this means, among other things, that even aggregate concentration figures understate the concentration of economic power. Further theoretical as well as empirical work should explore the political and economic implications of such great concentration of economic power.

References

ALLEN, MICHAEL
1978   "Economic Interest Groups and the Corporate Elite Structure." Social Science Quarterly 58:597–615.
Forth-   "Continuity and Change within the Core Corporate Elite." Sociolog-
coming   ical Quarterly.

AVERITT, ROBERT T.
1968   The Dual Economy. New York: Norton.

BARAN, PAUL, and PAUL SWEEZY
1966   Monopoly Capital. New York: Monthly Review.

BEARDEN, JAMES, WILLIAM ATWOOD, PETER FREITAG, CAROL HENDRICKS, BETH MINTZ, and MICHAEL SCHWARTZ
1975   "The Nature and Extent of Bank Centrality in Corporate Networks." Paper delivered at the Annual Meeting of the American Sociological Association.

CHEVALIER, JEAN-MARIE
1970   La Structure Financiere de l'Industrie Americaine. Paris: Cujas.

COREY, LEWIS
1930   The House of Morgan: A Social Biography of the Masters of Money. New York: G. Howard Watt.

DeVROEY, MICHEL
1975   "The Separation of Ownership and Control in Large Corporations." Review of Radical Political Economics 7:1–10.

DOMHOFF, G. WILLIAM
1970   The Higher Circles. New York: Random House.

FITCH, THOMAS, and MARY OPPENHEIMER
1970   "Who Rules the Corporations?" Socialist Revolution (July-August): 73–107; (September-October):61–114; (November-December):33–94.

GORDON, ROBERT
1945   Business Leadership in the Large Corporation. Washington: Brookings.

HILFERDING, RUDOLF
[1910]   Le Capital Financier. Tr. Marcel Olliver. Paris: Les Editions des Minuit, 1970.

KNOWLES, JAMES
1973   "The Rockefeller Financial Group." Warner Modular Publications, No. 343.

KOTZ, DAVID
  1975   Bank Control of Large Corporations in the United States. Ann
           Arbor: Xerox University Microfilms.
LINTNER, JOHN
  1967   "The Financing of Corporations," Pp. 166–201, in Edward Mason
           (ed.), The Corporation in Modern Society. New York: Atheneum.
MARIOLIS, PETER
  1975   "Interlocking Directorates and Control of Corporations: The Theory
           of Bank Control." Social Science Quarterly 56:425–39.
MENSHIKOV, S.
  1969   Millionaires and Managers. Moscow: Progress Publishers.
PERLO, VICTOR
  1957   Empire of High Finance. New York: International Publishers.
POULANTZAS, NICOS
  1975   Classes in Contemporary Capitalism. London: New Left Books.
SONQUIST, JOHN, and THOMAS KOENIG
  1975   "Interlocking Directorates in the Top US Corporations: A Graph
           Theory Approach." Insurgent Sociologist 5:196–229.
SOREF, MICHAEL
  1979   "The Internal Differentiation of the American Capitalist Class."
           Ph.D. thesis, University of Wisconsin–Madison.
SWEEZY, PAUL
  1942   The Theory of Capitalist Development. New York: Monthly Review.
  1972   "The Resurgence of Financial Control: Fact or Fancy?" Socialist
           Revolution 8:157–191.
U.S. DEPARTMENT OF COMMERCE, BUREAU OF ECONOMIC ANALYSIS
  1974   Input-Output Structure of the U.S. Economy: 1967, volume 2; Di-
           rect Requirements for Detailed Industries. Washington: Government
           Printing Office.
U.S. FEDERAL TRADE COMMISSION
  1951   Report of the Federal Trade Commission on Interlocking Director-
           ates. Washington: Government Printing Office.
U.S. SENATE COMMITTEE ON GOVERNMENTAL AFFAIRS
  1978   Voting Rights in Major Corporations. Washington: Government
           Printing Office.
ZEITLIN, MAURICE
  1974   "Corporate Ownership and Control: The Large Corporation and the
           Capitalist Class." American Journal of Sociology 79(5):1073–1119.
  1976   "On Class Theory of the Large Corporation: Response to Allen."
           American Journal of Sociology 81(4):894–903.

3 Interlocking Directorates, the Control of Large Corporations, and Patterns of Accumulation in the Capitalist Class

Samuel Norich
University of Wisconsin–Madison

Who controls the large corporation? How is this control related to the internal structure of the capitalist class? What consequences does it have for differential patterns of capital accumulation? Two theories of control propose different sets of answers to these questions. According to one view, control of the large corporation is typically exercised by its "board of directors plus the chief executive officers"—that is, "the insiders, those who devote full time to the corporation and whose interests and careers are tied to its fortunes" (Baran and Sweezy 1966:15–16). Proponents of the second view locate the effective control not in a firm's management or insiders, but in a family that owns a large block of its stock, in a bank, or in an "interest group"—that is, a clique of financial and nonfinancial corporations, perhaps themselves dominated by one or a few families. Compared to the theory of insider control, theories of proprietary control imply a far greater degree of centralization of economic power and a more pronounced hierarchy within the very top ranks of the capitalist class.

To test the competing claims of these two perspectives, we conducted several empirical analyses of data on the leading 300 U.S. industrial corporations of 1964. These analyses suggest that a substantial proprietary interest affects not only the pattern of a corporation's director interlocks with other firms, but also its dividend payout ratio. These findings, we shall argue, cast doubt on the plausibility of the notion of insider control and reinforce the hypothesis that the large corporation is controlled by princi-

Michael Schwartz generously permitted the use of his data on interlocking directorates for this article. Samuel Bacharach provided not only an ideal place to work, but frequent and judicious advice as well. He, David James, and Steven Martin Cohen also made valuable comments on an earlier draft. Whatever merit may be found in the present one owes much to their critiques; its remaining deficiencies are the responsibility of the author alone.

pal capitalist families, or by interest groups, or by some amalgam of proprietary interests.

These is, of course, another perspective on corporate control, "managerialism," which stands opposed to the two theories discussed in this chapter. (See Zeitlin and Norich 1979 for an extensive discussion and analysis of this theory.)

Managerialism proceeds from the claim that control of the large corporation has passed from its owners to its professional managers, who may choose to ignore or even oppose the interests of the owners. Contrary to the theories of insider and proprietary control, both of which—in the versions considered here—are informed by a class theory of historical development, managerialists deny the applicability of class theory to any advanced industrial society. They contend, as Zeitlin has pointed out, that class theory "cannot explain, nor serve as a fruitful source of hypotheses concerning the division of the social product, class conflict, social domination, political processes, or historic change in these countries" (1974:1075).

Against this claim, we have shown, in an analysis of 300 corporations, that the rate of profit of industrial capital is primarily related to the "rate of exploitation" of their workers (Zeitlin and Norich, 1979). Industrial profit is a part of the surplus product of labor. Our focus here is on the disposition of this part of the surplus product, once it has already been extracted and realized, and the extent to which this is determined by the pattern of corporate control. Specifically, we examine the proportions in which industrial profit is divided between dividends, to be directly appropriated by members of the capitalist class, and retained earnings, to be ploughed back for internal accumulation within the given firm. The theoretical and empirical premise of this analysis, in other words, is that the surplus product of labor is extracted by capital in the production process. The question at issue, however, is how the surplus product is accumulated or appropriated by different elements of the capitalist class. This dispute rests, in turn, largely on opposing theories of corporate control: in particular, which elements of the capitalist class exercise effective control of the large corporation and are, thereby, able to *determine* the proportion of industrial profits that is directly appropriated by capitalists in the form of dividends, and what is retained for investment and accumulation within the firm? We begin, therefore, with the controversy over corporate control.

Insider versus Proprietary Control: The Work of Paul Sweezy

The most important empirical support for the interest-group model of control is still the 1937 study by Paul M. Sweezy for the National Resources

Committee (1939). The most important theoretical refutation of that model may also be found in Sweezy's work, though some years later. As Sweezy's changing perception of the locus of control marked the main lines of the debate over insider versus proprietary control, we shall focus our review of this controversy on Sweezy's relevant writings during the past 40 years.

The notion that financial institutions go beyond their intermediary, credit-providing functions, to exert influence and even control over industrial capital, originated in the work of Rudolf Hilferding, an Austrian Marxist theoretician, at the turn of the century. Hilferding noted the tendency of "finance capital" to centralize control over production in "the hands of an ever smaller number of the largest associations of capital" (1910:503). He attributed their predominance, particularly in Germany and the United States, to the fact that the process of capital accumulation began much later there than it did in England, the first industrial capitalist country. Despite—because—indeed of their "backwardness" [*Zuruckgeblie-benheit*], these economies could not compete with England by retracing the path that the "advanced country" had taken. "Rather," Hilferding wrote, Germany "had to take the level [of accumulation] already attained in the advanced country as a point of departure, and proceed from there" (1910:413). Accumulation on such a large scale, however, required

> the mediation of banks, which could concentrate not only the unused money of capitalists, but also that of other classes, and provide them to industry for its utilization.... This internal bond between industrial and bank capital became ... a significant element [*Moment*] in the development toward higher capitalist forms in Germany and America (1910:414–15).

This "internal bond between industrial and bank capital," forged by the requirements of accumulation on a large scale, manifests itself on the level of class structure as a group of principal owners and bankers that interlock the boards and coordinate the policies of many corporations. In Hilferding's words,

> A circle of persons is formed who, through the power of their own capital or as representatives of the concentrated power of others' capital (bank directors), sit on the supervisory boards of a large number of corporations. Consequently, a kind of personal union arises, among the various corporations themselves, on the one hand, and, on the other, between the latter and the banks. This circumstance must be of the greatest importance for the policies of these corporations since a common proprietary interest [*gemeinsames Besitzinteresse*] is formed among them (1910:157).

The first demonstration that these "higher capitalist forms," joining industrial and bank capital, actually existed in the United States, came in the report of the Pujo Committee of 1913 (U.S. Congress, House Banking and Currency Committee 1913). The Pujo Report documented the broad influence of the Morgan interests, acting through several financial institutions, over railroads, public utilities, and manufacturing corporations in several heavy industries.

Although quite influential (it led to the passage of the Clayton Antitrust Act in 1914), the Pujo Report was not as broad in its scope as the study of "Interest Groups in the American Economy" carried out by Paul Sweezy some 25 years later for the National Resources Committee (reprinted in Sweezy 1953). Sweezy found that fully 106 of the 200 largest nonfinancial corporations of 1935 were linked to one or another (and occasionally to two or more) of eight interest groups. At least three groups were controlled through ownership of the stock of their constituents by families whose name they carried (Rockefeller, Mellon, and DuPont). In most instances, firms belonging to a group were linked through interlocking directorates. Indeed, the Chicago group was defined by their interlocking directorates; the Kuhn, Loeb group, however, abstained almost completely from this means of assuring control and coordination. The members of the Morgan–First National group, preeminent among the eight for the broad range of its interests, were controlled by one or, more usually, both banking houses after which it was named—a control based "upon longstanding financial relations" and interlocks (usually multiple interlocks).

Sweezy's findings clearly indicated a far greater "degree of concentration of economic leadership" (1953:188) than one might judge from what economists call "overall concentration" or from the market shares of individual firms. As Sweezy put it, retrospectively, some 30 years later (Sweezy and Baran 1966:17):

> In traditional usage, an interest group is a number of corporations under common control, the locus of power being normally an investment or commercial bank or a great family fortune.... The members of an interest group would naturally coordinate their policies; and in the case of conflicts, the interests of the controlling power (or of the whole group as interpreted by the controlling power) would prevail.

But above and beyond the evidence of *economic* concentration, Sweezy's study also implied the existence of a very sharp stratification *within the capitalist class.* Of course, even by the strictest of definitions, this class consisted, even in those days, of many hundreds of thousands of families, and just those who exercised control over the largest 200 corporations must have numbered several thousand men, at least.

But even within this most select and dominant segment of the capitalist class, there were marked gradations of power and relations that subordinated some to (a few) others. That is, even those who appeared to (and in some respects surely did) manage the affairs of 106 of the largest 200 corporations were themselves allied with *and subject to* a handful of truly dominant families, or financial institutions, or amalgams of the two.

Moreover, to the extent that these eight interest groups could be regarded in some sense (be it economic, political, or geographic, or even social) as competitors—of which Sweezy gave no indication—this might constitute important lines of cleavage at the "commanding heights" of the capitalist class.

Withing a few years of the publication of the NRC study, Sweezy expressed doubt about the continued validity of its main findings. He proclaimed "the decline of the investment banker" during the "decade of depression and social reform" of the 1930s, and attributed this decline to four factors: (1) the recent economic contraction, which curtailed investment banking activity; (2) the avoidance of the capital markets by large corporations relying on "vast internal financial resources" as the source of new investment; (3) the increasing frequency of "private placement," i.e., the sale by large firms of their stocks and bonds directly to other large institutions, usually to insurance companies, without the mediation of investment banks; and (4) the expanding role of the federal government as a source of investment capital, displacing the banks (1953:192).

At the same time, however, that the power of investment bankers seemed to be declining, Sweezy noted the expanding "scope of industrial empires based on family ownership and control of key corporations and banks" (1953:194), on the one hand, and, on the other, the development of what he was later to call insider control:

> a more or less stabilized, and hence closed and self-perpetuating, group of corporate executives (including bank and insurance company executives) which is to an increasing degree engrossing the key positions in those corporations which are owned not by particular family groups, but rather by the capitalist class at large (1953:195).

In his latest formulation, the theory of insider control, Sweezy dismissed both investment bankers and principal owners as in control. Although these groups controlled the large corporation during the period of their formation in the last few decades of the nineteenth century and the first few of the twentieth, this phase had now passed. No longer were large corporations forced to rely on investment bankers for their funds. As Baran and Sweezy wrote: "the giants, reaping a rich harvest of monopoly profits, found themselves increasingly able to take care of their financial needs from internally generated funds."[1] Nor were these "giants" any longer subject to dominant owners:

> the domineering [*sic*] founders of family fortunes were dying off, leaving their stockholdings to numerous heirs, foundations, charities, trust funds and the like, so that the ownership unit which once exercised absolute control over many enterprises became increasingly amorphous and leaderless (1966:18).

The resulting "independence" allowed large corporations increasingly to shape their "policies . . . each to its own interests rather than being subordinated to the interests of a group" (1966:18). This, in turn, meant diminished centralization of economic power in the economy as a whole. Indeed, the notion of "interest groups," and the hierarchies and cleavages within the owning class it implied, are now "obsolete." If some interest groups still exist, "they are of rapidly diminishing importance and . . . an appropriate model of the economy no longer needs to take account of them" (1966:18). While acknowledging the continued representation of "outside interests" on boards of directors, Sweezy dismisses this as immaterial:

> Outside interests are often (but not always) represented on the board to facilitate the harmonization of interests and policies of the corporation with the customers, suppliers, bankers, etc.; but *real power* is held by the insiders, those who devote full time to the corporation and whose interests and careers are tied to its fortunes (Italics added; 1966:15–16).

Before we consider what "real power" might mean and how we may gauge it, several observations on the cogency of the notion of insider control are in order. When Sweezy originally put forward the theory of interest groups, it was in "tentative" terms, with no "claim to either completeness or finality" (1953:164). The conclusions were tentative, despite their obvious foundation on a large volume of evidence. Yet when Sweezy recently dismissed the theory of interest groups and replaced it with the notion of insider control, he asserted it with finality, despite the absence of any evidence to sustain it. The main reasons he offered were the alleged increasing reliance on internal financing and the progressive dissolution of dominant blocks of stock.

---

[1] By 1942, Sweezy had already dropped the term "finance capital" entirely for "monopoly capital." Unlike the former term, the latter did not suffer from what he considered the now misleading connotation of banker dominance over industrial capital. Monopoly capital does, however, retain the notion of a "coalescence" of bank and industrial capital (1942:269).

But on both of these issues, the evidence available before and since 1966 is either equivocal or flatly contradicts Sweezy's premises. Lintner (1959) showed that even large corporations had *not* decreased their reliance on external sources of capital over the first half of this century. Perlo (1957) documented the persistence of interest groups into the 1950s, based on modifications of data drawn from the Temporary National Economic Committee study of 1941, so these conclusions are also tentative.

Recent empirical studies (Menshikov 1969; Knowles 1973; Kotz 1978; U.S. Congress, House Banking and Currency Committee 1975; 1976; 1978) provide evidence of the increasing importance of financial institutions as voters of potentially dominant blocks of stock, as sources of expansion capital (particularly in the wave of conglomerate mergers) and as "hubs" around which groups of interlocking nonfinancial institutions "cluster" (Bearden and others 1975). Burch (1972) demonstrated the continuing prevalence, into the 1960s, of family ownership and control in the large corporation. Although these studies were not explicitly addressed to Sweezy's work, their bearing on it could not have escaped him, in view of the rigor and breadth his scholarship has consistently shown. Yet despite this array of evidence, all suggesting owner or financial control, marshalled in these studies (and in his own of 1937); despite criticism of his position (Fitch and Oppenheimer 1970) and a challenge to defend it (Zeitlin 1974:1079–80), Sweezy continues to stand by his later view (1972). It is now, moreover, a view that is not uncommon, even among Marxists.

The notion of insider control can be subjected to two novel empirical tests. We try to ascertain not whether insiders do, in fact, control the largest industrial corporations, but whether the corporations behave as if they are controlled by them. What Baran and Sweezy mean by "the real power" they attribute to insiders is never stated, but two inferences are reasonable. First, the pattern of a large firm's director interlocks, and especially of the outside interests represented on its board, should reflect its relationship with the "customers, suppliers, bankers, etc." whose "interests and policies" it must seek to "harmonize" with its own, but this pattern should not be affected by the distribution of the firm's stock.

Thus, if insiders do wield "real power," it should enable them to select the "outside interests" to be represented on their boards; such a selection should reflect their firm's resource dependence and market position, but it should not depend on the presence or absence of a dominant stockholder. Second, the real power, or control, held by insiders ought to enable them to dispose of the firm's profit in a manner calculated to serve their own interests. They should be able to minimize the dividend payout ratio, so as to augment the internal sources for new investment funds and thereby diminish their dependence on external funds and those who provide them.

The pattern of director interlocks and the dividend payout ratio are used as our dependent variables because they seem to be suitable and valid criteria of the relative power of insiders versus other capitalist interests, be they principal owning families, financial institutions, or the latter utilized as instruments of the former. We find that the pattern of interlocks and dividend payout ratios in the leading 300 industrial corporations of 1964 (ranked by sales) do not support the notion of insider control.

Interlocking Directorates: Economic and Class Factors

Previous studies of determinants of interlocking (Pfeffer 1972; Allen 1974) have generally proceeded from an interorganizational perspective. These studies have therefore focused exclusively on such intercorporate factors as firm size and measures of resource dependence (such as the debt-equity ratio), while ignoring such "extracorporate" relations as the distribution of stock ownership. However, the literature on this issue does provide us with another perspective. In a study of interlocks among the 37 largest nonfinancial corporations in Chile in 1966, Zeitlin and others (1976) consider the corporation not simply as a large-scale organization, but as "an administrative unit of production and command over labor and a decisive unit of ownership, control, and accumulation of capital, [so that] it is inherently located in both the 'economy' and 'class structure'" (1976:2). This leads the authors to consider interlocks not only as a means of "regulating competition among large corporations," but also as a way to facilitate the "reconciliation of interests among their principal owners." To assess the importance of the former, the authors examine such economic determinants of interlocking as a firm's size and market share; to assess the importance of the latter, they consider such class determinants as the firms' "interpenetrating and common ownership, including bank ownership." Although the data available for this analysis are somewhat different, we will follow the rationale of Zeitlin's study of interlocks among Chilean firms.

Aside from their theoretical limitations, previous studies of interlocking also suffer from empirical shortcomings, with obvious substantive ramifications. Without information about the historical, economic, ownership, or financial relationships upon which specific interlocks are based, these are difficult to interpret. Thus, Sweezy recently dismissed the claim that corporate interlocks with banks demonstrate bank control: "Taken by themselves it is certainly true that they [the interlocks] could just as easily prove the corporations' control of the banks as vice versa—or rather, taken by themselves, they don't prove anything" (1972:170).

We can, however, alleviate this difficulty by considering the *direction* of the interlocks. We ask, for instance, if an interlock is sent to a bank or received from a bank. We may plausibly assume that when Bank *A* "sends" one of its directors, whose principal business affiliation is with Bank *A,* to a seat on the board of Industrial Corporation *B,* the influence or element of control involved would be exerted by *A* over *B,* and not vice versa. Therefore, we analyze the pattern of interlocks, classified by direction (sent or received), and the kinds of firms interlocked. This will suggest (not prove) the relative dominance or subordination of firms in the intercorporate system, and the ways in which some of their economic and class characteristics account for their apparent position in the system.

What, then, are the specific hypotheses we must test concerning the relative validity of the theory of insider versus owner or financial control?

Sweezy, in his later work, does not deny the existence of linkages and alliances among firms, nor does he assert that interlocks are without pattern. He does, however, maintain that "the relevant line-ups are determined not by ties to outside control centers, but by the rational calculations of inside managements" (Baran and Sweezy 1966:20). Put as a hypothesis on interlocking, the inference is that a corporation's interlock pattern should reflect the degree of its interdependence with other firms, but not be affected by the presence or absence of a dominant proprietary (family) interest.

Following Zeitlin and others (1976), we may regard interlocks as serving two purposes. First, they are a means of regulating competition and facilitating coordination among large corporations. With the concentration of capital—that is, as productive units grow in size and acquire a degree of market power—"their interdependence increases markedly and their activities touch on each other in many ways, so that each firm can, and must, try to take into account the response of the others to its own policies" (1976:8). Firms must try to assure themselves a continuing supply of credit and of raw materials. They strive to calculate, if not to guarantee, the future demand for their products. Pricing and marketing decisions must be aggressive enough to maintain or even extend a firm's market share, but at the same time moderate enough to avoid provoking one's large competitors into a mutually ruinous struggle. Each of these tasks, imposed on corporate managements by the concentration of capital, require coordination among large firms. Such coordination may be accomplished by the exchange of directors between corporate boards, among other means.

The larger a corporation, the greater the number of other large firms affected by its decisions, on one hand, and the more other large firms that it must take into account when the focal corporation formulates its decisions, on the other. Hence, the first hypothesis is: The larger a corporation, the more corporations with which it will share one or more directors (with which it will have "ties," or one or more primary or secondary interlocks).[2] Size should be positively related both to the aggregate number of primary interlocks and of primary interlocks with financials and primary interlocks with other industrials. Increasing size, after all, entails increased interdependence (and the concomitant need for coordination and interlocks) not only among large industrial firms who may be each other's customers, suppliers or competitors, but also between them, on one hand, and financial firms that may provide their credit, on the other.

Market power, the other aspect of the concentration of capital, may be expected to have a positive effect on the number of primary interlocks for much the same reasons. Firms with a degree of market power with respect to certain goods thereby acquire a measure of potential influence over other firms, dependent on a secure supply of those goods. Such influence may be exercised by placing a member of one's board onto the board of the dependent firm. Our second hypothesis, then, is: Market power will be positively related to the number of primary interlocks, and particularly to the number of primary interlocks *with other industrials,* as well as to the number of interlocks *sent.* (There seems to be no reason to expect market power to be related to the number of primary interlocks with financial firms.)

These first two hypotheses, or sets of hypotheses, are completely congruent with both the proprietary control perspective and the theory of insider control. Both views acknowledge interlocks to be a means of regulating economic relationships among large firms. What distinguishes the two views is the claim of the proprietary control perspective that interlocks among firms also serve a second purpose: They are a way of coordinating and reconciling the interests of their principal owners. Sweezy, for one, explicitly rejects this claim, however.

The centralization of capital (distinct from, but simultaneous with concentration (Sweezy 1942:254–57) can take various forms. Independent enterprises may be merged into one large firm under a single management. Alternatively, two or more ostensibly independent corporations may in fact be owned by the same family or other controlling interest (even through a minority holding of their stock), thereby coming under central control despite their different managements. When the proportion of stock held in two or more firms by a single family, financial institution, or group is large but not sufficient to exert control, the influence of even the moderate own-

---

[2] Sweezy defined these terms as follows:

> A primary interlock exists between companies X and Y if a director of X, *whose main business interest is with X,* sits on the board of Y. If this same person also sits on the board of Z, then a primary interlock also exists between X and Z. These two relations, however, necessarily involve an interlock between Y and Z, and this we call a secondary interlock (1953:162).

ing interest may be reinforced through director interlocks with firms that are more securely controlled by the family or group in question. (This feature was, indeed, typical of the interest groups Sweezy described in 1937.) Moreover, where no single principal owning family or group holds enough stock to be dominant, a number of such large owners, in coalition, could direct the corporation's affairs. Where a firm is influenced by such a range of proprietary interests (financial institutions with sizable trust holdings, large but not dominant shareholders, and so on), each is likely to seek formal representation on its board to protect its individual stake. And when proprietary interests share influence over but do not singly control a number of large corporations, their representatives are likely to interlock the set of large firms to reconcile and coordinate their respective interests in the various firms.

Thus, the proprietary control perspective would lead us to expect more frequent interlocks among corporations that have no single dominant proprietary interest than among firms that (singly or jointly) do. Specifically, we are led to hypothesize that the absence of a discernible dominant proprietary interest among a firm's stockholders is positively related to the number of large corporations with which it has ties, and especially to the number of interlocks it *receives* from other large firms in general, and from financials in particular. This third and crucial hypothesis will help us to ascertain the relative plausibility of the insider, as opposed to the proprietary, control thesis. The insider thesis, of course, would lead us to expect no relationship between proprietary control and the pattern of interlocks.

To assess the impact of proprietary control on interlocking and measure the effects of size and market power, we performed a series of multiple regression analyses. In each, a different measure of interlocks was regressed on the same five independent variables. The independent measures are as follows:

Size

This was operationalized as the natural logarithm of assets (in millions of dollars) in 1964, reported in *Fortune* (July 1965). We used the logarithmic form of asset size for the argument that the number of interlocks would probably increase with size, but at a decreasing rate.

Number of directors

Clearly, the number of interlocks a firm maintains with others is to some extent affected by the size of its board of directors (although the need for interlocks may independently affect the number of its board members). This administrative characteristic of the firm is therefore included as a control variable in the regressions.

Market power

This measure was based on a weighted average of the barriers to entry in the industries in which the firm is principally active.[3] We reasoned that the need for coordination through interlocks would increase up to some moderately high level of the barrier-to-entry scores, and decrease thereafter, as the sheer dominance of the firms in their markets would make interlocks less useful as a means of assuring cooperation. A plot of the frequency of interlocks by increasing composite barrier-to-entry scores indicates this is true, with a peak at a score of 0.60. Our measure of market power, then, is the absolute value of the *difference* between the firm's actual barrier-to-entry score, and 0.60. The greater the deviation from a peak barrier-to-entry score of 0.60, the less numerous are the firm's interlocks expected to be. Thus, our second hypothesis above, concerning market power, predicts a negative coefficient for this measure.

Management and possible family control

We used Burch's classification (1972) of the 300 leading industrial corporations of 1964 by type of control: "probable family control" where (a) 4 or 5% of the voting stock was discernibly held by a single individual or family; and (b) there was evidence of representation by the family on the firm's board of directors over the early to mid-1960s; "possible family control" where one or the other of these criteria was met, but not both; and "probable management control" where neither of them was met. The three categories are represented by two dummy variables, one for "management control" and one for "possibly family control."

Our regression equations, which differ only in their dependent variable, may therefore be summarized by the following model:

$$INT = a + b_1 S + b_2 ND + b_3 MP + b_4 MGR + b_5 POSS + e$$

where INT = the number of one of various kinds of interlocks, to be specified; S = the natural logarithm of assets, in millions of dollars; ND = number of directors; MP = market power; MGR = management control dummy; and $POSS$ = possibly family control dummy. The predicted values of the regression coefficients, of course, depend on the dependent variable characterizing each equation.

Four regression equations in which this model is used to predict the number of interlocks with one of four kinds of firms are shown in table 3-1. In equation 1.1, the dependent variable is *number of ties*—that is, the num-

---

[3] John Palmer kindly provided his barrier-to-entry scores for the use of Maurice Zeitlin and his students.

Table 3-1. Relationship between the absence of owner control and the number of various types of interlocks

	Dependent Variables							
	Equation 1.1		Equation 1.2		Equation 1.3		Equation 1.4	
Independent Variables	Number of Ties		Primary Interlocks		Primary Interlocks with Financials		Primary Interlocks with Industrials	
Size (natural log of assets)	$.2991^a$	4.2650^b $(24.959)^c$	.2591	1.6499 (16.903)	.2368	.7846 (13.288)	.1879	.8653 (8.605)
Number of directors	.1809	.3035 (10.078)	.1125	.0843 (3.519)	.1215	.0473 (3.858)	.0682	.3696 (1.252)
Market power	−.0235	−.7069 (.184)	−.1255	−1.6867 (4.750)	−.0278	−.1944 (.219)	−.1536	−1.4923 (6.882)
Management control dummy	.2126	2.5370 (14.297)	.1002	.5337 (2.863)	−.0332	−.0922 (.297)	.1624	.6259 (7.287)
Possibly family control dummy	.1398	2.2265 (6.131)	.0028	.0201 (.002)	.0322 (.276)	.1192 (.276)	−.0193	−.0990 (.102)
Constant		−9.1806		−2.3730		−1.2516		−1.1214
R^2	.2373		.1547		.1020		.1269	
Corrected R^2	.2238		.1398		.0862		.1115	

Note: $N = 290$ cases (10 cases with incomplete data were excluded).
[a] Standardized regression coefficient
[b] Unstandardized regression coefficient
[c] *F*-ratio

ber of other firms (others among the 300 leading industrials, 50 largest banks, or 50 largest insurance companies) with which the focal corporation has one or more primary or secondary interlocks. Our model enables us to account for a fifth to a fourth of the variance in the *number of ties*. As predicted by our third hypothesis, the absence of a single dominant proprietary interest ("management control") is associated with a greater number of ties with other large firms. This result is, of course, in keeping with the proprietary control perspective, and not with the theory of insider control.

Equation 1.1 supports our hypothesis concerning the effects of size. The larger a firm, the more other firms with which it is tied—that is, the more other firms with which it has primary or secondary interlocks.

When we examine the relationship of *primary interlocks* as such to our economic and owner control variables (equation 1.2), we observe similar results. Again, as predicted, the size of a firm is positively related to the number of primary interlocks it has with other firms. Market power is also related to the number of primary interlocks, as predicted. Though it was not specifically hypothesized, firms under management control (those without any discernible dominant proprietary interests) maintain a larger number of primary interlocks, but the regression coefficient for this variable is not statistically different from zero at the 5 percent level. This occurs because primary interlocks are the sum of interlocks received and interlocks sent. Although management-controlled firms *recieve* more interlocks than family-controlled firms, they do not *send* more interlocks than the latter, as we shall show.

In equations 1.3 and 1.4, *primary interlocks with financials* and *primary interlocks with industrials*, respectively, are the dependent variables. Our hypothesis concerning size is supported by the results of both equations, and, as predicted, market power is strongly related to the number of primary interlocks with large industrials. Though we did not expressly hypothesize it, we find a strong positive relationship between management control and the number of *primary interlocks with industrials*, but none between the former and the number of *primary interlocks with financials*. But again, if we separate the latter dependent variable into interlocks sent to and received from financials, we see that management control is indeed related to the second, but not to the first.

The analysis of interlocks categorized by their direction (all of which, of course, are primary interlocks by definition), as reported in table 3-2, consistently supports our hypotheses, particularly on the effects of control. The absence of a discernible dominant proprietary interest (management control) is positively and strongly related to the total number of interlocks a corporation receives (equation 2.1), and to the number it receives just from large financial firms (equation 2.3). It is not related to the number a firm sends (equation 2.2).

Table 3-2. Relationship between the absence of owner control and the number of various types of directional interlocks

	Dependent Variables					
	Equation 2.1		Equation 2.2		Equation 2.3	
Independent Variables	Interlocks Received		Interlocks Sent		Interlocks Received from Financials	
Size (natural log of assets)	.2044	.7543 (10.245)	.2121	.8956 (10.611)	.1779[a]	.3329[b] (7.158)[c]
Number of directors	.1009	.0438 (2.754)	.0816	.0405 (1.731)	.0590	.0129 (.868)
Market power	−.0639	−.4972 (1.197)	−.1335	−1.1894 (5.033)	.0586	.2314 (.930)
Management control dummy	.2101	.6486 (12.262)	−.0325	−.1145 (.282)	.1250	.1958 (4.007)
Possibly family control dummy	.0439	.1810 (.532)	−.0341	−.1608 (.309)	.0527	.1101 (.706)
Constant		−1.4364		−.9366		−.6557
R^2	.1320		.0976		.0590	
Corrected R^2	.1167		.0817		.0424	

Note: $N = 290$ cases (10 cases with incomplete data were excluded).
[a] Standardized regression coefficient
[b] Unstandardized regression coefficient
[c] F-ratio

Assuming that the direction of interlocks indicates the direction of influence, then management-controlled firms (which have no single, discernible proprietary interest in control) are subject to the influence of far more large firms in general, and of large financials in particular, than firms in which an evident family owns interest. This conclusion contradicts the theory of insider control in a double sense: Not only is ownership related to the interlock pattern of large corporations, but the interlock pattern itself—in firms without a single dominant owner—suggests that control is held not by the inside management, but by a range of outside interests represented on its board. Admittedly, this conclusion is quite tentative, because it is based on a set of inferences from the pattern, especially of the direction, of interlocks. In the next section, this conclusion is solidly supported by an analysis of the effects of stock ownership and financial interlocks on the disposition of parts of the surplus product of the large corporation. We shall show that the notion of insider control is simply incompatible with the actual dividend payout practices of supposedly insider-controlled firms.

Dividends: The Appropriation of Surplus Product

The owners of the means of production have the right to appropriate and dispose of the surplus product created by their workers. Of course, there is a constant struggle between capital and labor to increase or decrease the portion of the total product that will become surplus; and even after the rate of exploitation has been fixed, there are still multiple claims on the surplus product. The owners must satisfy the claims of creditors, of those who possess the patents or the land they utilize in the productive process and of government, in the form of taxes. But once these juridically stipulated claims on the surplus product have been met, the owners have the exclusive right to appropriate and dispose of the remainder of the surplus product. They can determine how much of this remaining surplus product is to be reinvested in the enterprise and in what way, and how much is to be taken out of the enterprise for consumption or for investment elsewhere. This feature of capitalist property relations is so fundamental that we may regard it as an indicator of corporate control. That is, if control of a corporation is defined as the capacity of "an identifiable group . . . to realize their corporate objectives over time, despite resistance" (Zeitlin 1974:1091), we may postulate the ability to dispose of the firm's portion of the surplus product (after juridically stipulated claims upon it have been met) to be among the most basic of those objectives.

In managerial theory, control of the large industrial corporation has passed from its legal owners to its managers. Certainly this control and the power it confers are never absolute: like creditors, the owners of a corporation's stock do have a claim on its surplus product. But the power to determine precisely the proportion of the surplus product that stockowners receive, and the proportion the corporation retains, has now allegedly passed to management. That is, in the managerialist view, it is not capitalists that control and dispose of the surplus product created "in the heartland of the industrial economy," but managers.

In contrast, Sweezy regards the insiders who control the large corporation to be capitalists in their own right; indeed, he refers to them as the "leading echelon" of the capitalist class. But they base their control not on their ownership of capital. Owning the firm's stock may or may not have enabled them to acquire their position, but it is precisely their status as incumbents of the offices at the top of the corporation's formal hierarchy that confers on them the power to control and dispose of its surplus product. Their control rests on the authority pertaining to their organizational positions—the "institutionalization of the capitalist function." In this conception of capitalist control, the capitalist *class* has disappeared. In this limited sense, it is akin to the theory advanced by Dahrendorf (1959) and other managerialists.

Baran and Sweezy suggested an hypothesis concerning the dividend policies of the large corporation that, as it happens, can also be used to test their theory of insider control. Quite rightly (cf. Elton and Gruber 1970), they argue that large stockholders have an interest in a low dividend payout rate (1966:35). Effectively, the large stockholders have the corporation save for them; if they need cash, they can sell the appreciated stock and pay a capital gains tax that is lower than the tax on dividend income. Small stockholders, on the other hand, are more likely to want a higher dividend payout rate, for their consumption or other purposes. In this instance, management, according to Baran and Sweezy, is aligned with the large stockholders in preferrring a low dividend payout rate (1966:35). They not only want to avoid a high tax rate on their own dividend income, but even more to maximize control over their supply of capital and minimize the influence of such external suppliers of capital as financial institutions.

Baran and Sweezy therefore conclude that dividend policies are the result of a compromise between the opposing pressures of management and large stockholders, on the one side, and small stockholders, on the other, and that "managements as a rule hold the upper hand in determining the terms of the compromise, maintaining payout rates of 50 percent or less in most management controlled industrial corporations" (1966:35). Although Baran and Sweezy provided no evidence for this claim, it does have the clear implicit hypothesis that management-controlled corporations should have, on the average, the same dividend payout rate as corporations with a dominant stockowning interest.

If, as we argue, proprietary interests are in control, then there should be a higher dividend payout rate in so-called management-controlled firms than in firms with a dominant proprietary interest. Dominant stockholders, who can control the surplus product appropriated by their firms, tend to pay out less of it in dividends, not only to avoid taxes, but also to avoid diluting their control by recourse to outside sources of capital.

Management also certainly wants to minimize the dividend payout rate, but not really being in control, they would not be able to do so. Instead, in firms lacking a dominant proprietary interest, management would still be subject, in significant measure, to the influence of other extrafirm interests, particularly financial institutions represented on the board of directors.

Financial institutions, moreover, would probably exert their influence in the direction of a higher dividend rate. Between 1945 and 1974, financial institutions increased their trust stockholdings from about 16 percent to some 33 percent of total corporate stock outstanding. Most of this increase has been in the accounts of "private noninsured pension funds," usually managed and voted by large commercial bank trust departments (Kotz 1978:65, 66). Tax-exempt pension funds probably have at least as much interest in maximizing the flow of dividend income for their beneficiaries as they do in the steady appreciation of their holdings. Therefore, financial institutions may well have put their influence on the side of small stockholders—that is, on the side of higher dividend payout rates.

Consequently, the proprietary control perspective leads us to predict that (a) management control is associated with a higher dividend payout rate; and (b) in management-controlled firms, the number of interlocks received from financials would be associated with a higher dividend payout rate.

To assess the impact of proprietary control and interlocks received from financial institutions on the dividend policies of large industrial corporations, we performed the regression analysis reported in table 3-3. The above hypothesis clearly predicts an interaction effect between management control and the number of *financial interlocks received.* Testing for such an effect requires two separate equations, one of which does not include the interaction variable (3.1) and the other of which does (3.2). We must also consider several other possible influences on the dividend payout rate. We therefore included in the equations measures of firm's growth rate, debt ratio, size, and profit rate.[4]

---

[4] The reasons for the inclusion of these variables, and the specific measures used, are as follows:

Growth rate. In the classic study of the determinants of dividend payout behavior of large firms, Lintner (1956) specifies "the growth prospects of the industry, and more

Our regression model therefore has the following form:

$$DIV = a_1 + b_1G + b_2D + b_3S + b_4P + b_5FIR + b_6MGR + b_7POSS + b_8FIR \cdot MGR + b_9FIR \cdot POSS + e,$$

where DIV = amount of dividend paid out to stockholders, as a percentage of net income, 1964; G = the firm's growth rate of sales, 1955–1964; D = the ratio of debt to total assets; S = the natural log of assets, in millions of dollars; P = net income as a percentage of invested capital, 1964; FIR = the number of financial interlocks received; MGR = management control dummy variable; $POSS$ = possibly family control dummy variable; $FIR \cdot MGR$ = an interaction term between the number of financial interlocks received and the management control dummy; and $FIR \cdot POSS$ = the same interaction term, with the possibly family control dummy.

The overall results in table 3-3 once more give strong support to theories of proprietary control. In equation 3.1, without the interaction effects, the dummy variable for management control is seen to be positively related to the dividend rate, and the relationship is significant at the 5 percent level. That is, the *absence* of a single dominant family owning interest in the firm is associated with a *higher* dividend payout rate than the presence of such a proprietary interest. If both dominant owners and putatively controlling insiders have the same interest in higher rates, our findings seem consistent with the hypothesis that dominant stockowners are far

---

importantly, the growth and earnings prospects of the particular firm" as the first of a series of determinants of a firm's "target" payout ratio. Having no measure of our firm's growth *prospects*, we used what seemed the best approximation thereto, the firm's growth rate of sales over the preceeding 10 years (1955 to 1964). The greater a firm's growth rate, the more of its net income it is likely to retain for reinvestment, and hence the smaller its dividend ratio is expected to be. The regression coefficient for this measure should therefore be negative.

Debt-asset ratio. As Sweezy points out (1972:165), one of the most frequent stipulations of loan agreements between banks and corporate borrowers is a limitation on dividends, "to make sure that companies have enough money to service already existing loans." The more highly leveraged the firm (i.e., the greater the ratio of debt to total assets), the lower its expected dividend payout rate. Thus, the coefficient for this measure should also be negative.

Size. Fitch and Oppenheimer (1970, part 3:39) cite data that seem to indicate a positive correlation between the payout rates and the size of corporations. There is no clear indication as to why this should be so, but on the chance that the relationship is genuine, we decided to control for this factor in our regressions.

Profit rate. Although the relevant literature provides no evidence or rationale for a relationship between the profit rate and the dividend rate, we thought it desirable, for the cogency of our presentation, to control for this factor. The measure used is the 1964 ratio of net income (after taxes) to invested capital.

Table 3-3. Relationship between the absence of owner control, financial interlocks received, and dividend payout rate

| | Dependent Variable: Dividend Payout Rate | | | |
Independent Variables	Equation 3.1		Equation 3.2	
Growth rate (G)	−.1680[a]	−.0172[b]	−.1753	−.0179
		(6.524)[c]		(7.064)
Debt-asset ratio (D)	−.2700	−.3631	−.2685	−.3610
		(18.840)		(18.601)
Size (S)	.0833	.0345	.0848	.0351
		(1.960)		(2.029)
Profit rate (P)	.0437	.1435	.0422	.0014
		(.491)		(.451)
Financial interlocks received (FIR)	.0390	.0855	−.0844	−.0185
		(.420)		(.616)
Management control dummy (MGR)	.1626	.0556	.0941	.0322
		(6.266)		(1.389)
Possibly family control dummy $(POSS)$	.0773	.0349	.0539	.0243
		(1.423)		(.406)
Interaction: management control and financial interlocks received $(FIR \cdot MGR)$			.1664	.0427
				(2.152)
Interaction: possibly family control and financial interlocks received $(FIR \cdot POSS)$			.0498	.0229
				(.292)
Constant		.4841		.4963
R^2		.1721		.1794
Corrected R^2		.1481		.1487

Note: $N = 250$ (50 cases with incomplete data were excluded).
[a] Standardized regression coefficient
[b] Unstandardized regression coefficient
[c] F-ratio

more effective than managerial insiders in getting corporations to act in their interests.

Finally, the interaction effect predicted by the proprietary control perspective is again positive, as hypothesized, but it is not quite statistically significant at the 5 percent level. Our conclusions are somewhat qualified, but let us first examine the results more closely. The positive regression coefficient for the interaction effect between management control and the number of financial interlocks received shows that the dividend rate increases with the number of such interlocks. An analysis of variance indicated this association to be significant only at the 8 percent level. But in view of the consistent tendency of dividend payout rates to rise with the increasing number of financial interlocks received, we think it is reasonable to tentatively conclude that the effect is genuine. The crudeness of our measure may account for the reduced statistical level of significance, especially because the number of financial interlocks received is highly skewed and has a very small range.[5] Of the 115 management-controlled firms, fully 60 receive *no* interlocks from financial institutions, 40 receive only one such interlock, 11 receive two, 2 receive three interlocks and 2 receive four interlocks. If we had a more sensitive measure of the degree of influence over these corporations exerted by financial institutions than the simple number of interlocks received, we would expect it to show a positive relationship with the dividend payout rate among management-controlled firms (as we find here), and we would expect the relationship to be statistically significant. Until such a measure is constructed, however, we conclude, with some small qualification, that the degree of influence exerted by financial institutions over corporations with no single dominant family control does seem directly related to the proportion of their share of surplus product relinquished to stockholders. This is what the proprietary control perspective predicts, and it is contrary to the expectations derived from the thesis of insider control.

These findings must affect our understanding of both corporate control and the pattern of capital accumulation. If the pattern of interlocks and the dividend payout rate are valid indicators of the locus of control, then our findings surely show that so-called insiders do *not* control these leading industrial corporations. Control is rather exercised by a dominant owning family or, in their absence, by other proprietary interests, often by financial institutions or principal owning families acting through them.

But our findings also show that the category of proprietary control is not all of a piece: A dominant family does not exercise its influence over an industrial corporation in the same manner as do other proprietary interests. Financial institutions apparently induce industrial corporations to pay out a larger proportion of their profits for direct appropriation by their stockholders, whereas dominant owners compel them to retain a larger proportion of their profit for internal accumulation. Which disposition of

[5] The number of financial interlocks received by an industrial firm is only one indicator—and a decidedly imperfect one at that—of the influence exerted on it by financial institutions. Other measures of such influence include the proportion of the firm's stock voted by the trust departments of the financial institutions; the proportion of the firm's debt owed to these institutions; or the degree of cohesion or competition between the financial institutions and *other* extrafirm control interests. Unfortunately, indicators of these other dimensions of financials' influence over industrials were not available for this study.

industrial profits maximizes the overall, societal rate of capital accumulation? The answer to this question is not immediately obvious. On one hand, when a larger proportion of profits is directly appropriated by members of the capitalist class, more is available for individual consumption, which would diminish the overall rate of accumulation. But on the other hand, those receiving the dividends may choose to forego additional consumption and invest the funds in other enterprises that realize a higher return. This would accelerate the overall pace of accumulation. Although the eventual disposition of dividend income is an issue outside the scope of this paper, the locus of control does influence both the pattern and the overall rate of capital accumulation.

What, finally, are the relationships among the proprietary interests that, according to our findings, appear to control most of the leading industrial corporations? Are owning families and financial institutions themselves aligned with and subject to a handful of truly commanding families or institutions, resembling the interest groups that Sweezy described in 1937? The thesis of interest groups was dismissed by Baran and Sweezy when they advanced the notion of insider control, but as our findings contradict the latter, they may also enhance the plausibility of the former, even though our empirical analyses do not bear on it directly. We can therefore do no more here than to emphasize the continued pertinence of the question whether interest groups occupy the commanding heights of today's American economy, what effect they may have on patterns of capital accumulation, and whether they represent important lines of cleavage among the leading echelons of the capitalist class.

References

ALLEN, MICHAEL PATRICK
    1978   "Economic Interest Groups and the Corporate Elite Structure." Social Science Quarterly 58:597–615.
BARAN, PAUL A., and PAUL M. SWEEZY
    1966   Monopoly Capital. New York: Monthly Review Press.
BEARDEN, JAMES, WILLIAM ATWOOD, PETER FREITAG, CAROL HENDRICKS, BETH MINTZ, and MICHAEL SCHWARTZ
    1975   "The Nature and Extent of Bank Centrality in Corporate Networks." Paper delivered at the Annual Meeting of the American Sociological Assocation.
BURCH, PHILIP H., JR.
    1972   The Managerial Revolution Reassessed. Lexington, Mass.: Heath.
DAHRENDORF, RALF
    1959   Class and Class Conflict in Industrial Society. Stanford: Stanford University Press.

ELTON, EDWIN J., and MARTIN J. GRUBER
  1970   "Marginal Stockholder Tax Rates and the Clientele Effect." Review
           of Economics and Statistics 52:68–74.
FITCH, ROBERT, and MARY OPPENHEIMER
  1970   "Who Rules the Corporations?" Socialist Revolution 1(1):73–107;
           1(5):61–114; 1(6):33–94.
HILFERDING, RUDOLPH
  [1910]   Das Finanzkapital. Frankfurt: Europaische Verlagsanstalt (reprinted
           1968).
KOTZ, DAVID M.
  1978   Bank Control of Large Corporations in the United States. Berkeley:
           University of California Press.
KNOWLES, JAMES
  1973   "The Rockefeller Financial Group." Warner Modular Publications,
           Module 343.
LINTNER, JOHN
  1956   "Distribution of Income of Corporations Among Dividends, Re-
           tained Earnings and Taxes." American Economic Review 46:97–113.
  1959   "The Financing of Corporations." pp. 166–201 in E. S. Mason (ed.),
           The Corporation in Modern Society. Cambridge, Mass.: Harvard
           University Press.
MENSHIKOV, S.
  1969   Millionaires and Managers. Moscow: Progress Publishers.
PERLO, VICTOR
  1957   The Empire of High Finance. New York: International Publishers.
PFEFFER, JEFFREY
  1972   "Size and Composition of Corporate Boards of Directors: The Orga-
           nization and its Environment." Administrative Science Quarterly
           17:218–28.
SWEEZY, PAUL M.
  1942   The Theory of Capitalist Development. New York: Oxford Univer-
           sity Press.
  1953   The Present As History. New York: Monthly Review Press.
  1972   "The Resurgence of Financial Control: Fact or Fancy?" Socialist
           Revolution 2(2):157–91.
U.S. CONGRESS, HOUSE BANKING and CURRENCY COMMITTEE
  1913   Report of the Committee Appointed Pursuant to H.R. 429 and 504
           to Investigate the Concentration of Control of Money and Credit.
           62nd Congress, 2nd Session. Washington, D.C.: U.S. Government
           Printing Office.
  1968   Commercial Banks and their Trust Activities: Emerging Influence on
           the American Economy. 90th Congress, 2nd Session. Washington,
           D.C.: U.S. Government Printing Office.
U.S. CONGRESS, SENATE GOVERNMENT OPERATIONS COMMITTEE, SUBCOMMIT-
TEE ON REPORTS, ACCOUNTING AND MANAGEMENT
  1975   Corporate Ownership and Control. 94th Congress, 2nd Session.
           Washington, D.C.: U.S. Government Printing Office.

1976   Institutional Investors' Common Stock: Holdings and Voting
        Rights. 94th Congress, 2nd Session. Washington, D.C.: U.S. Govern-
        ment Printing Office.
1978   Voting Rights in Major Corporations. 95th Congress, 1st Session.
        Washington, D.C.: U.S. Government Printing Office.
U.S. NATIONAL RESOURCES COMMITTEE
1939   The Structure of the American Economy. Washington, D.C.: U.S.
        Government Printing Office.
ZEITLIN, MAURICE
1974   "Corporate Ownership and Control: The Large Corporation and the
        Capitalist Class," American Journal of Sociology 79:1073–1119.
ZEITLIN, MAURICE, and SAMUEL NORICH
1979   "Management Control, Exploitation and Profit Maximization in the
        Large Corporation." Research in Political Economy 2:33–62.
ZEITLIN, MAURICE, RICHARD EARL RATCLIFF, and LYNDA ANN EWEN
1976   "Interlocking Directorates Among the Largest Corporations in
        Chile." Unpublished manuscript.

4 Banks and the Command of Capital Flows: An Analysis of Capitalist Class Structure and Mortgage Disinvestment in a Metropolitan Area

Richard E. Ratcliff
Washington University

The older urban areas of modern American society are, according to observers representing a broad spectrum of viewpoints, engulfed in a fundamental crisis. This crisis metaphor has been applied to a number of different dimensions of contemporary urban distress, including the rapid decline in important urban services; the physical deterioration of both commercial and industrial properties and the housing stock in residential neighborhoods; the fiscal instabilities of city governments; the increase in crime and related threats to public safety; and the emergence of union insurgency among public employees and militancy among dissatisfied citizen groups (Castells 1976; Downs 1973). These problems are even seen by some as so serious that they pose questions about whether older established cities have actually lost their potential as workable social units (Sternlieb 1976).

Although many analyses of the urban crisis have explored the succession of changes that characterize urban decline, relatively little systematic attention has been focused on a principal, though rarely visible, source of these changes: the investment decisions made by the private financial institutions that dominate important sectors of the urban economy. Commercial bank decisions either to invest or to withdraw capital from older urban areas can be affected by the growing ascendancy of groups within the capitalist class with capital investment needs and opportunities increasingly located beyond older cities. The issue that links the problem of the flow of capital out of older urban areas to the internal structure of the capitalist class is whether the process of urban disinvestment is being led and

I would like to thank Kathryn Strother Ratcliff, Donald Strickland, Mary Elizabeth Gallagher, James Wells, Mary Peters, Mark Gallops, Nancy DiTomaso, and Kay Oehler for comments and assistance in completing this paper. This research has been supported by the National Science Foundation under Grant No. SOC77-18036.

dominated by commercial banks that are most closely tied to centers of greatest power and prominence within the capitalist class.

To develop the context for this analysis, I have drawn on three separate sets of studies. First, I review studies of urban disinvestment focusing on the impact of decisions made by financial institutions and related investors. Second, I discuss a number of studies examining factors considered influential in banks' investment decisions. Third, I examine the internal structure of the capitalist class, particularly the relevance that capitalist class structure has to patterns of capital investment. The integration of these diverse concerns will provide us with a basis to consider a set of specific data dealing with the home mortgage loans made by banks in one metropolitan area.

The Crisis of Urban Disinvestment

The home mortgage loans made by banks have become highly controversial in recent years. Both banks and savings and loan associations have been accused of engaging in mortgage loan "red-lining," designating older, low- and moderate-income neighborhoods within the metropolitan areas ineligible for home mortgage loans. Red-lining also means a range of more subtle practices that have the effect of denying mortgage credit to such neighborhoods (Bradford and Marino 1978). These controversies have produced a developed thesis on the process of disinvestment that portrays the withdrawal of mortgage capital by banks and other financial institutions from older urban neighborhoods as a leading cause of the deterioration and decline of such neighborhoods: "the thesis . . . is that these trends [of central city decay and suburban boom] are not inevitable, but are . . . the result of identifiable private and public investment decisions" (Bradford and Rubinowitz 1975:79). Similarly, Harvey argues that "many of the 'urban problems' with which we are familiar . . . [are] tied to the way in which investment is channeled into local housing markets" (1975:140). According to these analyses, housing problems and other symptoms of urban decline are linked directly to the decisions that financial institutions and other institutional investors make to transfer their capital to other geographic and investment sectors.

The major alternative view to the disinvestment thesis is offered by those urban economists who argue that financial institutions which withdraw from lending in certain areas are simply responding to economic realities. Banks and savings and loan associations are seen as avoiding making loans in areas that are deteriorating at a rate that makes long-term mortgage loans too risky. These economists see the deterioration of older neighborhoods as natural because of the "invasion" and "succession" of lower income or minority groups (cf. Downs 1973). Both the disinvestment theorists and those who see natural deterioration agree that urban decline is closely linked to changing patterns of investments.

There is general agreement that two kinds of shifts in the patterns of urban investments have occurred since World War Two. First, investments in housing, industry, and commerce have moved from older central cities to adjacent areas; second, these factors have shifted from metropolitan areas in the Northeast and Midwest to the Sun Belt states of the South and Southwest. The key issue of contention is whether the decisions of those in command of capital to "disinvest" actually stimulate urban decline or whether these decisions merely are prudent reactions to changes that have already begun.

In this analysis I draw heavily on the disinvestment thesis by assuming that decisions made by commercial banks to grant mortgage loans to older urban areas help to stabilize and maintain these areas, and that the transfer of capital into other investments further threatens the economic viability of these same areas. However, no attempt is made here to resolve in any final sense the question of the causal, as opposed to the reactive, character of mortgage lending in regard to the declining urban neighborhoods.

In general, those who have developed the disinvestment thesis have not been concerned with examining and trying to explain differences in the lending behavior among financial institutions or even among different types of financial institutions. Because this analysis is directly concerned with the question of variations in the level of involvement of banks in urban mortgage lending, it is important to consider the available literature on the relationships of banks to mortgage lending.

Banks and Urban Disinvestment

Three different issues are of particular relevance to the involvement of banks in mortgage lending: the role of banks as designated accumulators and redistributors of surplus community capital; the importance of banks, relative to other financial institutions, in the home mortgage market; and the problem of explaining variations in bank mortgage lending behavior according to differences in the characteristics of banks.

The capital controlled by depository institutions such as banks is unique in comparison to that held by large corporations and other large private institutions by being distinctively public. Banks do not own their capital resources. The historically and legally established tradition is that banks, acting as private enterprises, are charged with the responsibility of accumulating the surplus capital available from depositors in their communities and deciding which demands for capital should be met in the form of bank loans. The powers inherent in this role are immense. According to a recent government study, they routinely influence "the allocations of real resources—what is produced, how it is produced, and to whom it is distributed" (Harvey 1975:125).

Given the urban disinvestment thesis, it is important to consider where bank deposits come from and where bank loans go, particularly whether banks draw their deposits from urban neighborhoods. Although supporting data are not available, it seems clear that commercial banks, despite frequent assertions that they primarily receive business deposits, heavily depend on the deposits of individuals. At least one-third and perhaps two-fifths of banks' combined savings and checking deposits come from individuals (Reed and others 1976:74–79). Over half these deposits from individuals are in savings accounts that, because of their relative stability, are considered well suited as a base for mortgage loans.

The clear position of banks as intermediaries between deposits and loans makes it relevant to ask whether the bank's depositors and its borrowers are at all socially or economically similar. The minimal evidence on this point suggests a marked dissimilarity. A study of First National City Bank (Citibank) revealed that many of its branch offices were apparently used overwhelmingly as sources of deposits and provided very few loans. A branch in Brooklyn had generated over $3 million in deposits but had only $36,000 in loans on its books (Leinsdorf and Etra 1974:82). In Boston, the state banking agency found that older neighborhoods received only a small share of their deposits back as mortgage loans while suburban areas often received surpluses. A similar pattern has been found in Chicago (Przybylski 1978:22, 193).

Despite such a low level of bank lending in some local communities, commercial banks, as a result of their orientation to "wholesale" or business lending, are not simply marginally involved in mortgage lending. In fact, according to Reed and others, "residential real estate loans are a growing and important part of the loan portfolio of commercial banks" (1976:276). Depending on the area, the dollar volume of residential mortgage loans held by commercial banks is from one-quarter to one-half the size of the mortgage holdings of savings and loan associations (*Statistical Abstract*, 1974:458). In St. Louis City, banks accounted for over 40 percent of the combined loans of banks and savings and loan associations. However, banks had a considerably lower proportion (20–25 percent) of suburban loans, in large part because of the close economic ties many savings and loan associations have to new home builders (Ratcliff and Gallagher 1978). Even though banks are important as mortgage lenders, residential mortgage loans represent only a relatively small part, about 13 percent, of the total loans of banks. Nevertheless, this amount is still considerable because of the enormous totals involved ($75 billion in 1973). In fact, loans to commercial and industrial borrowers, the other relevant category, were only just over twice as large ($160 billion) (*Statistical Abstract* 1974:453).

Obviously, commercial banks play major roles in the command of a community's capital and in mortgage lending. The remaining question in this section is whether any clear analyses have been developed to explain the differing involvements of banks in mortgage lending.

In fact, two characteristics have been claimed to relate to the lending behavior of banks: the size of banks and their status as either independent banks or as affiliates or branches of a larger banking organization. The basic argument is that large banks tend to do less residential mortgage lending due to their greater access to alternate lending opportunities (Starr 1975:86). According to Eisenbeis (1975), this pattern is not limited just to mortgage loans but also applies to business loans. The largest banks tend to make more of their loans to large corporations that operate in markets beyond the local community. The general pattern of large banks avoiding loans to small local business has also been supported by others (Guttenberg and Herman 1966; Jacobs 1965). Similarly, in the study of Citibank, one of the nation's largest banks, it was found that its business with individuals and small local business provided a net source of capital while the national and multinational corporations were net users of capital (Leinsdorf and Etra 1974:81). These findings are of particular significance in our analysis because they indicate that the notion of urban disinvestment should not just be limited to home mortgage lending. As Leinsdorf and Etra conclude:

> By thus subordinating, if not completely ignoring, unmet community credit needs—such as local economic development and preserving, rehabilitating, and constructing housing—the banking practices operate like a regressive tax, funneling money of communities with declining economies to those of brighter economic prospects (1974:83).

Thus, they see this one very large bank as a siphon that removes the surplus capital of older local communities. Both economists and some more activist-researchers who are critical of banks therefore argue that large banks are not responsive to the credit needs of local communities. The dimension of importance, it is claimed, is size. Similarly, this argument is also expanded to include banks that are included either as affiliates or branches under the control of large banks. Such banks, even when small, are expected to adopt the practices of the large banks that control them.

The emphasis in this literature on the influence of size on lending behavior provides a good point of comparison with the thesis that is central to this analysis. I contend that the attention paid to size is misleading. Even though size might well be related to patterns of lending behavior, I argue that the underlying determinant is not size but rather the position of banks relative to the internal structure of the capitalist class.

Capitalist Class Structure and the Command of Capital Flows

My thesis is drawn from a broader argument concerning the internal structure of the capitalist class and the impact that structure has on the functioning of capitalist enterprises. Unfortunately, most theoretical treatments of the capitalist class have not stressed questions concerning divisions within the class and, correspondingly, have not considered variations in the behavior of capitalist enterprises. In this analysis, these issues are primary.

The guiding assumption is that the leading segments of the capitalist class face an enduring shortage of capital to meet their investment needs and opportunities. Because of this shortage, banks become especially important types of private enterprises precisely because of their role in accumulating the surplus capital available in the broader community. The key analytical issue, then, is whether banks can be seen as capital-accumulating instruments for those capitalist interests to which they are most closely linked and whether the decisions by banks allocating the capital they command will reflect these linkages.

There is considerable evidence of the high level of capital investment demands at the core of the capitalist class. Access to capital is most vital to existing corporations engaged in constant struggles to overcome pressures on their profits. Certainly this pattern has been indicated by the debt structure of the largest corporations. These corporations are the most dependent on external financing, particularly financing obtained from banks (Fitch and Oppenheimer 1970:73). The importance of banks in relation to corporate capital needs is also reflected in the close interconnections between capital-short corporations and banks. For instance, Dooley found that director interlocks between banks and nonfinancial corporations are greatest when they involve corporations with large debt obligations (Dooley 1969). Similarly, the close linkages between banks and the major airline companies became most evident during the period when the airlines were making massive expenditures and going deeply into debt to purchase new fleets of airlines (Fitch and Oppenheimer 1970:89). The close networks of linkages established between these banks and corporations embodies a pattern of shared interests that is most concentrated at the center of the capitalist class (Zeitlin 1976).

The very nature of the interconnections at the core of the capitalist class not only facilitates the flow of loans to meet existing capital needs but also multiplies the access to attractive investment opportunities for those involved in the networks. Because of the structure of capital demands and investment opportunities that surround those in command of capital, the funds in banks most closely related to these networks are constantly being pulled away from other potential borrowers in the community. The effect of this capital absorption is most likely to be directly felt in the mortgage markets by home buyers in older urban neighborhoods, although it ultimately affects the entire mortgage market. As Stone has argued, even the ownership of new homes is becoming increasingly unlikely for young working families "since industrial and financial corporations are trying to capture all available sources of capital" (1978:204).

To the extent that mortgage capital is available, it is likely to come from bankers who are more distant from the close networks at the core of the class and who are, as a result, also likely to be more removed from the capital demands and investment opportunities characteristic of the core. Presumably this relative lack of integration within the capitalist class leaves these bankers more open to a wider range of borrowers with needs for capital. Their willingness to provide capital to meet some of these needs, including those of urban home buyers, thus reflects their class "marginality" rather than any positive attraction to such loans.

Based on this formulation, I argue that urban disinvestment is likely to be most characteristic of those banks that are particularly closely linked to the core groups within the capitalist class. These patterns of disinvestment affect borrowing for a variety of purposes within an urban area, including loans for small local businesses, existing multifamily residences, and various consumer needs. However, this analysis will only consider home mortgage loans, a type of lending directly related to the disinvestment of the existing "built environment" (Harvey 1975) of older neighborhoods.

Because the thesis examined here emphasizes the influence of the bank's position in the capitalist class structure over the flow of bank capital, it follows that it is not sufficient to explain lending patterns according to some "economic logic" supposedly determined by the size of banks and holding companies. In fact, it is likely that the emphasis on size as an explanation for the differing behavior of banks has been to a considerable degree an error reinforced by the empirical pattern for the larger banks to be more closely tied to the center of the class structure. I will attempt to distinguish between these influences.

The internal differentiation of the capitalist class will be examined only in terms of the dimension of class centrality. Although this emphasis can obscure important lines of cleavage within the class, such as those defined by persisting ethnic differences, it does focus our attention on the distinction between those groups clustered at the core of the class and those which are more peripheral. The importance of this distinction has been stressed by a number of observers. Sweezy, for instance, has discussed the "ruling class" in terms of a "core surrounded by fringes which are in varying degrees attached to the core" (1953:124). Similarly, Zeitlin has emphasized the role of "the 'inner group' of interlocking officers and directors, and particularly the finance capitalists, [who] become the leading organizers of [the] system of classwide property" (1976:901; cf. also Useem 1978). The task here has been to develop ways to identify this inner group.

Two different dimensions of class centrality have been employed in this analysis. First, I have sought to distinguish among bankers in terms of their closeness to economic power within the capitalist class. This closeness is measured by the extent of an individual's board of director interlocks with the largest corporations with local headquarters. Second, I have determined the number of ties an individual has to the most exclusive local private clubs and organizations. The indicator of economic power is based on the assumption that interlocking directorates represent positions of power (cf. Zald 1969), while the indicator of upper-class prominence follows Domhoff (1970) and others in assuming that exclusive private organizations embody a level of family integration and enduring social ties that overarch the divisions among capitalist enterprises. Each of these dimensions represents a conceptually distinct aspect of integration at the core of the class. As Sweezy has noted, the capitalist class structure "is not based solely on personal or family relations among the members of the ruling class. On the contrary, it is bulwarked and buttressed by a massive network of institutional relations" (Sweezy 1953).

Given these measures of capitalist class centrality, it is possible to state more clearly the guiding research propositions of this study. I hypothesize that those banks which are most closely tied to the centers of economic power and of upper-class prominence will be least involved in mortgage lending in general and will be particularly uninvolved in lending in older urban areas populated by low- and moderate-income families. Furthermore, concentrations of economic power and upper-class prominence are also expected to pull whatever mortgage lending that does occur in the direction of highly affluent neighborhoods. Correspondingly, the higher levels of involvement in mortgage lending and especially in mortgage lending in older, low- and moderate-income urban areas will be associated with greater marginality within the capitalist class.

The Research Data

The study focuses on the universe of banks based either in St. Louis City or St. Louis County in 1975. Due to Missouri's restrictive law on branch banking, this metropolitan area contains a relatively large number of independently organized banks.[1] Even those banks owned by multibank holding companies are technically independent, each having a separate board of directors and distinct operations. All 890 individuals who served as regular directors of these banks in 1975 have been identified.

I define the dimension of economic power in terms of board of director interlocks between the bank directors and the 100 largest nonbank corporations headquartered in the St. Louis area. The largest corporations were drawn from over 350 area corporations listed in the 1976 *Dun and Bradstreet Million Dollar Directory.* The relative size rankings of these corporations were determined according to their total sales.

To determine closeness of bank directors to centers of upper-class prominence, a group of five country clubs, men's clubs, and other exclusive organizations were identified. These organizations have been found, on the basis of both reputation and correlational criteria, to define the most exclusive patterns of private social interaction.[2]

The extent of ties that each bank has to centers of economic power and upper-class prominence is measured in terms of the aggregate ties represented among its directors. To minimize distortions caused by the contrasting sizes of different bank boards, which range from 6 to 26, the actual measures used here are the proportions of each bank's directors with one or more ties of a particular type.

The extensive data on the mortgage lending practices of the banks have been drawn from information reported under the requirements of the Federal Home Mortgage Disclosure Act of 1975. Under this law, each St. Louis area bank must disclose the number and dollar value of all mortgage loans granted throughout the St. Louis Standard Metropolitan Statistical Area (SMSA) for each fiscal year beginning with 1975. For 1975, these data are available by individual ZIP code areas. The mortgage loans considered here are on either new or existing residential (one- to four-unit) properties with the great majority being for single-family homes.

Given the concern in this analysis with red-lining and disinvestment

---

[1] Seventy-eight banks were identified. Because of the exclusion of banks which had missing data or were formed within the preceding 12 months, only 69 banks are included in this analysis.

[2] The organizations included are the *St. Louis Social Register,* one country club (St. Louis Country Club), two men's clubs (Racquet Club and Noonday Club), and the Veiled Prophet Ball. With the *Social Register* and the three private clubs, the names of the bank directors in the study were checked against complete membership lists. The membership of the Veiled Prophet Ball, the most prestigious and exclusive debutante affair in St. Louis, was not available because the controlling organization is a secret society of prominent men. However, newspaper archives indicate which individuals have had either a wife or a daughter involved in the pageant during any of the last 20 years.

in older low- and moderate-income urban residential neighborhoods, the St. Louis ZIP code areas have been divided into two groups: the average income level of the area and the rate of population growth or decline.[3] The greatest attention is directed to those ZIP code areas that are both stable or declining in population and had median family incomes in 1970 of less than $12,000. Included is all of St. Louis City and most of the older suburbs in St. Louis County that surround the city. These areas, containing 44 percent of the area's population, are neither all "poor" nor predominantly black. In fact, the area is mostly "moderate" income, with median family incomes between $9,000 and $12,000 in 1970, and predominantly white, with an overall white population of 75 percent. It is because this large area contains both white and black areas, and moderate- as well as low-income neighborhoods, that it is well suited to examine the broad implications of the urban disinvestment thesis.

Three different measures of mortgage lending patterns are considered here: (a) *the overall mortgage lending rate,* defined as the volume of the bank's total mortgage lending activity in all geographic areas relative to the size of the bank measured in total deposits[4]; (b) *the mortgage lending rate in stable, low- and moderate-income areas,* defined as the volume of the banks' mortgage

---

[3] The areas were divided into three income groups, depending on the median family income reported in each area for 1970, according to the fifth count U.S. Census tape. These groups included low- and moderate-income areas with median family incomes up to $12,000; upper-middle-income areas with incomes from $12,000 to $17,000; and high-income areas with median family incomes of $17,000 or more. Population figures were also drawn from the census data.

Growth estimates were based on the local electric utility's figures for the number of residential customers from 1970 to 1975 for each ZIP code area. This information relates closely to supplemental information on changes in the number of residential delivery addresses from 1971 to 1976 provided by the U.S. Postal Service. Three areas of population growth for the first half of the 1970s were established: "no-growth" areas that were mostly stable or declining in population but in no case had grown as much as 5 percent; the "medium-growth" areas that had grown between 5 percent and 20 percent; and the "fast-growth" areas that had grown by more than 20 percent.

This research deals only with the five counties in the Missouri portion of the St. Louis SMSA that contain 75 percent of the total population of the SMSA. Few Missouri banks do mortgage lending in the adjacent Illinois counties that are part of the SMSA.

[4] The measure used here is a direct ratio: the percentage that each bank's mortgage lending (in terms of the dollar value of loans) in the St. Louis metropolitan area is of all bank lending in the area divided by the percentage that the one bank's total deposits are to the total of all deposits. Thus a score of 1.0 indicates that the mortgage lending activity of the bank is comparable with its share of deposits; a score between 0 and 1.0 indicates a low level of mortgage activity relative to size; and a score above 1.0 indicates a higher level of mortgage lending. These ratios yield averages among banks that are over 1.0 because ratio measures have a lower limit of zero but no upper limit.

lending in such areas relative to the size of the bank; and (c) *the percentage of the bank's total mortgage lending in high-income areas.*

The first two measures are ratios indicating the level of a bank's mortgage lending activity without being unduly influenced by the vast differences in the banks which range from very large to quite modest (from over $1 billion in assets to less than $10 million). The first measure considers a bank's general involvement in mortgage lending; the second focuses on those older urban areas thought to be most affected by red-lining and disinvestment.

The third measure, the percentage of a bank's mortgage lending that occurs in high-income suburbs regardless of either the volume of mortgage lending or the size of the bank, will be used in the analysis to determine whether class characteristics are associated with a concentration of a bank's lending in affluent areas. The issue here is not how much mortgage lending a bank does but rather whether it diverts the mortgage lending it does do to wealthy borrowers.

Two measures of size are used in this analysis. First, the total deposits of each bank are taken to indicate the resources that the bank directly commands. Second, the resources held by multibank holding companies are measured separately. Each bank in a holding company has been assigned the total deposits of all banks in the holding company. Independent banks are coded once again on this measure in terms of their individual total deposits.

The Internal Class Context of Mortgage Disinvestment

To determine the extent to which differences in the lending practices of banks are a function of the ties that banks have to the centers of power and prominence in the capitalist class, it is necessary to make a careful comparison of the influence of the class structure variables relative to the influence of size of banks. Multiple regression techniques have been used to examine differences in the amount of variance in the mortgage lending measures that is "explained" by different combinations of variables. To make full use of these techniques, I have performed logarithmic (base 10) transformations on those measures with high skewed distributions (the two mortgage lending ratios and the measures of bank and holding company sizes) to establish more normal distributions (cf. Schuessler 1971:408). Before considering the results of the regression analysis, it is necessary to consider the general contours of the allocation of mortgage lending capital within the metropolitan area.

Mortgage lending in the St. Louis metropolitan area

The distribution of mortgage loans made by banks in 1975 is presented in table 4-1. Figures on the 1975 population distribution provide a usable standard of comparison that relates to the likely demand for mortgage loans in each area. Although fast-growth areas do have a high natural demand for mortgage loans, loans on new houses constitute a relatively small minority of all home mortgage loans. Because of the high level of mobility in American society, and the corresponding high rate of house sales in nongrowing areas, the majority of mortgage loans granted each year in the St. Louis area are for existing homes.[5]

The figures in table 4-1 indicate that stable low- and moderate-income areas receive a relatively small share of the total mortgage loan capital made available by St. Louis banks. Although these areas include over two-fifths of the metropolitan population (43.7 percent) they receive only one-fifth of the funds (19.8 percent) granted by banks as mortgage loans. In contrast, the stable high-income areas, with only 1.5 percent of the population, received almost half as much mortgage capital (9.1 percent). The fast-growing high-income areas also received a disproportionately large share of the available bank mortgage funds (23.9 percent while having 4.6 percent of the population).

These figures show the lending distribution that resulted from the combined decisions of all St. Louis banks. But the specific concern in this paper is with differences among banks and the effect of internal class relations on bank lending behavior.

An overview: relationship between mortgage lending and
intraclass structure

Table 4-2 includes the bivariate correlations between the three measures of mortgage lending behavior, the two measures dealing with intracapitalist class relations, and the two measures of the size of banks and holding companies.

Though we cannot compare the strength of one factor relative to another, some suggestive patterns are revealed in this table. First, some reasonably strong relationships occur, particularly that a higher level of corporate interlocks is associated with less involvement in mortgage lending, both in general and in respect to lending in stable low- and moderate-income areas. In contrast, such interlocks are positively associated with a higher percentage of a bank's mortgage total being placed in affluent suburbs. These patterns are consistent with the thesis developed here. A similar

---

[5] Available evidence for St. Louis City and St. Louis County, which contain about 80 percent of population of the counties included, indicates that only 17 percent of the total number of mortgage loans went for newly constructed homes.

Table 4-1. Distribution of bank mortgage loans in five Missouri counties in the St. Louis metropolitan area in 1975

Type of Area[b]	Number of Loans	Value of Loans	Percentage of Total Loan Value	Percentage of Area's Population[a]
Low- and moderate-income areas with no growth	1,124	$17,128,000	19.8	43.7
High-income areas with no growth	146	$ 7,841,000	9.1	1.5
High-income areas with fast growth	489	$20,658,000	23.9	4.6
(All high-income areas)	(635)	($28,499,000)	(33.0)	(6.1)
All other areas	1,899	$40,749,000	47.2	50.2
Total of Missouri SMSA	3,658	$86,376,000	100.0	100.0

[a] Population estimates for 1975 were calculated as part of this study using the 1970 census as a base and rates of increases in electrical utility residential customers between 1970 and 1975 to project population changes. All figures deal with the five Missouri counties in the St. Louis SMSA.

[b] The types of areas are described in the text.

Table 4-2. Zero-order correlations between bank mortgage lending practices, corporate and upper-class ties of bank directors, and the total deposits of banks

	2	3	4	5	6	7
1. Overall mortgage lending rate of bank	.439	−.094	−.407	−.296	−.361	−.008
2. Mortgage lending rate of bank in stable low- and moderate-income areas		−.329	−.371	−.256	−.244	−.123
3. Percentage of bank's mortgage loan value in high-income suburbs			.381	.374	.175	−.080
4. Proportion of bank's directors interlocking with top 100 local corporations				.723	.758	.216
5. Proportion of bank's directors belonging to top upper-class organizations					.565	.226
6. Total deposits of the bank						.257
7. Total deposits of the bank holding company						

(N = 69)

Description of variables:

1. A ratio measure that equals the percentage that each bank's total mortgage lending in 1975 is of all bank mortgage lending divided by the percentage that its total deposits are of the total of all bank deposits (Logarithmic transformation, base 10).
2. A ratio measure that equals the percentage that each bank's mortgage lending value which is located in stable low- and moderate-income areas is of all bank lending in these areas divided by the percentage that its total deposits are of the total of all bank deposits (Logarithmic transformation, base 10).
3. The percentage of each bank's total mortgage lending value (in dollars) loaned in high-income suburban areas.
4. The proportion of each bank's directors with one or more board positions in the 100 largest St. Louis area corporations.
5. The proportion of each bank's directors who belong to one or more of the five leading upper-class organizations in the St. Louis area.
6. The total deposits of the bank as of 12/31/75 (Logarithmic transformation, base 10).
7. The total deposits as of 12/31/75 of the bank holding company to which the bank belongs or, if the bank is independent of any holding company, the total deposits of the bank (logarithmic transformation, base 10).

set of relationships, though slightly weaker, is found between a high level of ties to centers of upper-class prominence and the measures of mortgage lending.

The analysis becomes more complex when the influence of bank size on mortgage lending patterns is examined. The influence of a bank's total size is roughly similar to that of the class variables; that is, larger banks appear to do less mortgage lending and the lending that they do is more likely to be in the direction of high-income suburbs. However, almost no relationship is found between the size of holding companies and the mortgage-lending activities of affiliated banks. Several of these correlations suggest the greater influence of intraclass structure on mortgage practices, but this is best examined by multiple regression analysis.

The impact of class structure on the overall mortgage lending rate

Table 4-3 is the first of three tables that use a similar format to present the results of a multiple regression analysis. The table presents the findings from a series of regression equations that include and exclude the two class structure variables and the two bank size variables in various combinations to reveal their influence in predicting the overall mortgage lending rates of the different banks. The table includes both the standardized regression coefficients associated with each variable in each particular combination and a measure (R^2) of the total variance in the mortgage rate explained by each set of variables. In addition, the lower half of the table presents a comparison between the different equations that allows us to see the additional increment in R^2 resulting from adding a variable or variables to an equation. These comparisons allow us to determine which variables have the greatest independent influence in explaining mortgage patterns.

The data in table 4-3 reveal a mixed pattern of influences. First, there is a high degree of overlap in the effects of class structure and bank size. Thus, the overall R^2 (0.181) drops only slightly when the two bank size measures are left out of the equation (by 0.016 to 0.165) and only slightly more when the bank size measures are retained but the class structure variables are excluded (by 0.043 to 0.138). Even with this general similarity in effects, the greatest effects are associated with the class structure measures, particularly with the measure of corporate interlocks. In fact, these findings indicate that the measure of upper-class ties has no incremental effect on the overall mortgage lending rate in addition to the effect of corporate interlocks.

The impact of class structure on the rate of mortgage lending in
stable low- and moderate-income areas

A much clearer set of distinctions between the class structure and the bank size variables is revealed in table 4-4, which focuses on lending in stable

Table 4-3. Comparisons of the explanatory power of capitalist class connections and total deposit size in determining the overall lending rates of banks

Variables Included in the Regression Equation[a]	Standardized Regression Coefficients (Dependent Variable = Overall Mortgage Lending Rate of Bank)[a]				
	Corporate Interlocks	Upper-Class Ties	Bank Deposits	Holding Company Deposits	R^2
A. All variables	−.309	−.013	−.144	.098	.181
B. Corporate interlocks and upper-class ties	−.404	−.004			.165
C. Bank deposits and holding company deposits			−.384	.090	.138
D. Corporate interlocks, bank deposits, and holding company deposits	−.318		−.144	.097	.181
E. Corporate interlocks, upper-class ties, and bank deposits	−.314	.000	−.123		.172
F. Upper-class ties, bank deposits, and holding company deposits		−.148	−.304	.103	.152
G. Corporate interlocks, upper-class ties, and holding company deposits	−.413	−.016		.085	.172

Table 4-3—Continued

Comparisons of Relative Changes in R^2

	Equations Compared	Interpretation of the Comparison	Increment in R^2
1.	D-C	Corporate interlocks net of bank deposits and holding company deposits	.043
2.	F-C	Upper-class ties net of bank deposits and holding company deposits	.014
3.	E-B	Bank deposits net of corporate interlocks and upper-class ties	.007
4.	G-B	Holding company deposits net of corporate interlocks and upper-class ties	.007
5.	A-F	Corporate interlocks net of upper-class ties, bank deposits, and holding company deposits	.029
6.	A-D	Upper-class ties net of corporate interlocks, bank deposits, and holding company deposits	.000
7.	A-G	Bank deposits net of corporate interlocks, upper-class ties, and holding company deposits	.009
8.	A-E	Holding company deposits net of corporate interlocks, upper-class ties, and bank deposits	.009
9.	A-C	Corporate interlocks and upper-class ties net of bank deposits and holding company deposits	.043
10.	A-B	Bank deposits and holding company deposits net of corporate interlocks and upper-class ties	.016

[a] Variables are described in table 4-2.

Table 4-4. Comparisons of the explanatory power of capitalist class connections and total deposit size in determining the mortgage lending rates of banks in stable low- and moderate-income areas.

Variables Included in the Regression Equation[a]	Standardized Regression Coefficients (Dependent Variable = Mortgage Lending Rate of Bank in Stable Low- and Moderate-Income Areas)[a]				
	Corporate Interlocks	Upper-Class Ties	Bank Deposits	Holding Company Deposits	R^2
A. All variables	−.455	.030	.099	−.057	.144
B. Corporate interlocks and upper-class ties	−.389	.025			.138
C. Bank deposits and holding company deposits			−.227	−.065	.063
D. Corporate interlocks, bank deposits, and holding company deposits	−.434		.100	−.055	.143
E. Corporate interlocks, upper-class ties, and bank deposits	−.452	.022	.087		.141
F. Upper-class ties, bank deposits, and holding company deposits		−.168	−.136	−.050	.082
G. Corporate interlocks, upper-class ties, and holding company deposits	−.383	.032		−.048	.140

Table 4-4—Continued

Comparisons of Relative Changes in R^2

	Equations Compared	Interpretation of the Comparison	Increment in R^2
1.	D-C	Corporate interlocks net of bank deposits and holding company deposits	.080
2.	F-C	Upper-class ties net of bank deposits and holding company deposits	.019
3.	E-B	Bank deposits net of corporate interlocks and upper-class ties	.003
4.	G-B	Holding company deposits net of corporate interlocks and upper-class ties	.002
5.	A-F	Corporate interlocks net of upper-class ties, bank deposits, and holding company deposits	.062
6.	A-D	Upper-class ties net of corporate interlocks, bank deposits, and holding company deposits	.001
7.	A-G	Bank deposits net of corporate interlocks, upper-class ties, and holding company deposits	.004
8.	A-E	Holding company deposits net of corporate interlocks, upper-class ties, and bank deposits	.003
9.	A-C	Corporate interlocks and upper-class ties net of bank deposits and holding company deposits	.081
10.	A-B	Bank deposits and holding company deposits net of corporate interlocks and upper-class ties	.006

[a] Variables are described in table 4-2.

low- and moderate-income areas. The data indicate that class structure, relative to bank size, is much more strongly related to disinvestment practices. The R^2 associated with all four measures (0.144) hardly drops at all when the two measures of bank size are excluded from the regression equation (by 0.006 to 0.138). However, when the two class structure measures are excluded, the R^2 drops considerably (by 0.081 to 0.063). Once again there are great differences in the explanatory power of the corporate interlocks and the upper-class ties measures. The major effect is associated with the level of corporate interlocks; no incremental effect is observed with the level of upper-class ties.

*The impact of class structure on the percentage of mortgage
lending in high-income suburbs*

A notably different pattern emerges when the effects of class structure and size on the distribution of a bank's mortgage capital are considered. The dependent variable in table 4-5 does not consider the level of a bank's mortgage lending volume but simply measures the extent to which the funds allocated to mortgages are concentrated in affluent neighborhoods. The issue is thus changed from whether centrality within the capitalist class structure actually tended to pull capital away from mortgage lending so that it could be invested in other sectors. Rather, the issue is now whether such centrality pulls mortgage funds assumed to be already allocated to mortgages from other geographic areas to mortgage investments in wealthy communities.

The data indicate that higher levels of capitalist class interconnections are associated with a greater concentration of loans in high-income suburbs. Moreover, both class structure measures have independent effects. Although the corporate interlocks measure appears to have somewhat more influence than the measure of upper-class ties, the enduring strength of the latter measure in this instance contrasts with its negligible effects on the previous two mortgage measures. Together the impact of class structure is much greater than that of bank size. Although the four measures together yield a relatively strong model ($R^2 = 0.222$), the effect of the two class structure measures, with the two bank size measures excluded, is not much lower (down 0.057 to 0.165). In clear contrast, the exclusion of the two bank size measures removes most of the strength of the model (down 0.174 to 0.048).

Moreover, the regression equations reveal that the impact of bank size on the relationship is not at all clear. Although the simple relationship between the mortgage measure and bank size is positive in that larger banks appear to place more money in high-income suburbs, when the effects of the class structure measures are controlled, the opposite relationship emerges. This reversal further reinforces the pattern that has emerged throughout this analysis: The capitalist class structure factors are the dominant influence over the flow of bank capital.

Discussion and Conclusion

This analysis began with the question of whether the lending decisions of commercial banks were shaped by the positions of banks within the structure of the capitalist class. The guiding concern has been with the influence of internal class networks on the actual command of capital flows within a metropolitan area. The research has revealed a clear pattern of such influence. The withdrawal of capital from home mortgage lending is most evident in those banks most closely tied to the centers of power within the capitalist class. To a surprising extent, this pattern has been found to be independent of the size of banks. Similarly, the size of the holding company, if any, to which a bank is affiliated has an even weaker influence over the patterns of mortgage lending activity observed in this analysis. These results suggest that it is in fact the class networks that cause capital to be pulled away from urban mortgage lending.

I have argued that the nature of the class networks suggests that the forces behind these patterns of urban disinvestment are the capital needs and investment opportunities at the center of the capitalist class. Within this structure, banks become vital instruments of capital accumulation. The data here do not allow us to determine whether these capital demands are generalized throughout the core of the capitalist class or are concentrated within certain groups or "class segments" (Zeitlin, Neuman, and Ratcliff 1976). However, the distinctions between the core and the fringes of the class are clear.

It should be noted that corporate interlocks have greater explanatory power as a measure of capitalist class centrality than upper-class social ties. These two measures are closely interrelated and therefore difficult to distinguish here in any final sense; however, the primacy of top ranking corporate interlocks has emerged consistently. I suggest that the configurations of capital demands and investment opportunities held by the core of the class are most clearly represented by leading class members who simultaneously direct both banks and large corporations. Because they occupy these positions, they are immediately responsible for the capital needs of large enterprises. Yet upper-class social ties do relate to the concentration of mortgage loans in high-income suburbs. Prominent upper-class directors, even when they are not linked to the largest corporations, seem able to loan money to their "own kind," to preferentially meet the mortgage needs of the wealthy.

The active urban mortgage lenders are those banks outside the net-

Table 4-5. Comparisons of the explanatory power of capitalist class connections and total deposit size in determining the percentage of each bank's mortgage loan value loaned in high-income suburbs

Variables Included in the Regression Equation[a]	Standardized Regression Coefficients (Dependent Variable = Percentage of Mortgage Loans Located in High-Income Suburbs)[a]				
	Corporate Interlocks	Upper-Class Ties	Bank Deposits	Holding Company Deposits	R^2
A. All variables	.425	.239	−.239	−.165	.222
B. Corporate interlocks and upper-class ties	.231	.206			.165
C. Bank deposits and holding company deposits			.210	−.134	.048
D. Corporate interlocks, bank deposits, and holding company deposits	.590		−.234	−.148	.195
E. Corporate interlocks, upper-class ties, and bank deposits	.433	.216	−.275		.197
F. Upper-class ties, bank deposits, and holding company deposits		.424	−.020	−.171	.169
G. Corporate interlocks, upper-class ties, and holding company deposits	.252	.234		−.188	.198

Table 4-5—Continued

Comparisons of Relative Changes in R^2

	Equations Compared	Interpretation of the Comparison	Increment in R^2
1.	D-C	Corporate interlocks net of bank deposits and holding company deposits	.147
2.	F-C	Upper-class ties net of bank deposits and holding company deposits	.121
3.	E-B	Bank deposits net of corporate interlocks and upper-class ties	.032
4.	G-B	Holding company deposits net of corporate interlocks and upper-class ties	.033
5.	A-F	Corporate interlocks net of upper-class ties, bank deposits, and holding company deposits	.053
6.	A-D	Upper-class ties net of corporate interlocks, bank deposits, and holding company deposits	.027
7.	A-G	Bank deposits net of corporate interlocks, upper-class ties, and holding company deposits	.024
8.	A-E	Holding company deposits net of corporate interlocks, upper-class ties, and bank deposits	.025
9.	A-C	Corporate interlocks and upper-class ties net of bank deposits and holding company deposits	.174
10.	A-B	Bank deposits and holding company deposits net of corporate interlocks and upper-class ties	.057

[a] Variables are described in table 4-2.

works of economic power and upper-class social prominence. These "marginal" banks not only allocate more capital to mortgate lending in general, but they are also more likely to make loans in older lower-income urban neighborhoods. One implication of this pattern is thus that banks more deeply involved in urban reinvestment should not be viewed as being "socially conscious" regarding the investment needs of older cities, but rather can be seen as more structurally isolated from the investment opportunities and demands influencing banks more closely tied to the centers of the capitalist class.

The implications of these patterns are certainly serious in regard to the decline of older urban areas. Those banks leading in the disinvestment process are precisely those most closely tied to centers of power within the capitalist class, in particular those most interconnected with the largest corporations. To the extent that these disinvesting banks are also those most actively growing, then the problems caused by the withdrawal of capital from urban areas promise to become worse. Correspondingly, the marginal banks which are involved in urban mortgage lending, and probably also in related commercial and consumer lending, are likely to remain relatively stable in size and, as a group, in command of a decreasing share of metropolitan bank deposits.

This contrast between the investment practices of banks centrally located in the capitalist class and those of marginal banks is particularly striking because it runs directly counter to the patterns of the involvements of bankers in the civic organizations with the most dominant roles in the development and implementation of social and economic policies and in the maintenance of ideological control at the metropolitan level in American society (Ratcliff, Gallagher, and Ratcliff 1979). It is precisely those bankers most closely linked to centers of economic power and upper-class prominence who occupy the leading positions in these organizations. These two patterns, considered simultaneously, reveal the core groups within the capitalist class actively struggling to maintain their social dominance in a declining metropolitan area, while in the economic realm they pursue investment policies that contribute significantly to the continuing decline.

We still have an incomplete picture of the interconnections between the internal structure of the capitalist class and its broader social consequences; but our analysis certainly makes it clear that the origins of the urban crisis in the United States cannot be understood if the relationship between this internal structure and the command of capital flows is ignored.

References

BRADFORD, CALVIN, and DENNIS MARINO
  1978   "Redlining and Disinvestment as a Discriminatory Practice in Residential Mortgage Loans." U.S. Department of Housing and Urban Development.

BRADFORD, CALVIN P., and LEONARD S. RUBINOWITZ
  1975   "The Urban-Suburban Investment-Disinvestment Process: Consequences for Older Neighborhoods," AAPSS Annals 422:77–86.

CASTELLS, MANUEL
  1976   "The Wild City." Kapitalistate 4–5:2–30.

DOMHOFF, G. WILLIAM
  1970   The Higher Circles: The Governing Class in America. New York: Vintage.

DOOLEY, PETER C.
  1969   "The Interlocking Directorate." American Economic Review 59:314–323.

DOWNS, ANTHONY
  1973   Opening Up the Suburbs. New Haven, Conn.: Yale University Press.

EISENBEIS, ROBERT A.
  1975   "The Allocative Effects of Branch Banking Restrictions on Business Loan Markets." Journal of Bank Research 6:43–47.

FITCH, ROBERT, and MARY OPPENHEIMER
  1970   "Who Rules the Corporations?" Socialist Revolution 1:61–114.

GUTTENTAG, JACK M., and EDWARD S. HERMAN
  1966   "Do Large Banks Neglect Small Business?" Journal of Finance 21:535–38.

HARVEY, DAVID
  1975   "The Political Economy of Urbanization in Advanced Capitalist Societies: The Case of the United States." In Gary Gappert and Harold M. Rose, eds., The Social Economy of Cities. Beverly Hills: Sage Publications.

JACOBS, DONALD P.
  1965   "The Interaction Effects of Restrictions on Branching and Other Bank Regulations." Journal of Finance 20:332–48.

LEINSDORF, DAVID, and DONALD ETRA
  1973   Citibank: Ralph Nader's Study Group Report on First National City Bank. New York: Grossman.

PRZYBYLSKI, MICHAEL
  1978   "Perceptions of Risk: The Bankers' Myth." Chicago: National Training and Information Center.

RATCLIFF, RICHARD E., and MARY ELIZABETH GALLAGHER
  1978   "Mortgage Investment and Disinvestment in St. Louis: The Social Impact of Economic Power in a Metropolitan Area." Paper presented at meeting of the Southern Sociological Society, New Orleans, Louisiana.

RATCLIFF, RICHARD E., MARY ELIZABETH GALLAGHER, and KATHRYN STROTHER RATCLIFF
1979   "The Civic Involvement of Business Leaders: An Analysis of the Influence of Economic Power and Social Prominence in the Command of Civic Policy Positions." Social Problems 26.
REED, EDWARD W., RICHARD V. COTTER, EDWARD K. GILL, and RICHARD K. SMITH
1976   Commercial Banking, Englewood Cliffs, N.J.: Prentice-Hall.
SCHUESSLER, KARL
1971   Analyzing Social Data. Boston: Houghton Mifflin.
STARR, ROGER
1975   Housing and the Money Market. New York: Basic Books.
STATISTICAL ABSTRACT OF THE UNITED STATES
1974   Washington, D.C.: U.S. Government Printing Office.
STERNLIEB, GEORGE
1976   "The City as Sandbox." In Stephen M. David and Paul E. Peterson, eds., Urban Politics and Public Policy. New York: Praeger.
STONE, MICHAEL E.
1978   "Housing, Mortgage Lending, and the Contradictions of Capitalism." In William K. Tabb and Larry Sawers, eds., Marxism and the Metropolis. New York: Oxford University Press.
SWEEZY, PAUL M.
1962   "The American Ruling Class." In Paul Sweezy, ed., The Present As History. New York: Monthly Review Press.
USEEM, MICHAEL
1978   "The Inner Group of the American Capitalist Class." Social Problems 25:225–40.
ZALD, MAYER
1969   "The Power and Functions of Boards of Directors: A Theoretical Synthesis." American Journal of Sociology 75:97–111.
ZEITLIN, MAURICE
1976   "On Class Theory of the Large Corporation." American Journal of Sociology 81:894–904
ZEITLIN, MAURICE, W. LAWRENCE NEUMAN, and RICHARD E. RATCLIFF
1976   "Class Segments: Agrarian Property and Political Leadership in the Capitalist Class of Chile." American Sociological Review 41:1006–29.
ZEITLIN, MAURICE, and RICHARD E. RATCLIFF
1975   "Research Methods for the Analysis of the Internal Structure of Dominant Classes: The Case of Landlords and Capitalists in Chile." Latin American Research Review 10:5–61.

Class Conflict
and Political Power

5   Class Politics and Public Bureaucracy: The U.S. Department of Labor

Nancy DiTomaso
Northwestern University

The political demands of subordinate classes under capitalism are defused and isolated by the institutionalization of authority in the state. The struggle underlying the initial organization of the U.S. Department of Labor between 1869 and 1920 and the later reorganization of critical programs between 1957 and 1973 indicates the means by which a specific state agency is limited in its capacity as a "representative" institution of subordinate classes in a capitalist society.

In contrast to many studies which view the Department of Labor as a natural response to the pressure politics of organized labor, within the context of a pluralist analysis of power, I analyze the development of the Department as both a response and a solution to class struggle.[1]

Although these analyses rest on inferences regarding the class nature of events, organizations, and participants involved, the consequences (or "outcomes") of programs and policies are related to three critical issues underlying the relationship between labor and capital: the reproduction costs of labor power (or "the wage bill"), social unrest, and the legitimation process. Although class struggles over these three issues are always present

---

I want to thank Robert Alford, Michael Aiken, John Walton, and Remi Clignet for their assistance with various parts of this manuscript.

[1] This study is based on primary research in government departmental and agency records, official and private correspondence, various biographies, and on personal interviews with government figures. It also incorporates my understanding of various published works on American economic development, political relations, and the history of the labor movement.

within a capitalist society, their intensity varies. Only when the organized actions of the working class are successful in (1) increasing the cost of labor power to capital, (2) rearranging the existing relations of power to the benefit of labor, or (3) making visible the exploitative process of capitalism, will the class struggle reach a crisis and threaten the maintenance and reproduction of the capitalist system itself.

To solve such crises the capitalist class will use strategies incorporating a varying mix of private and public resources. The organization and rearrangement of authority in the state, in this case, in the U.S. Department of Labor, can prevent the rise of real wages, social unrest, or the capitalist system's loss of legitimacy. In other words, as means of administration are expropriated from the workers as a class, their capacity to organize to reappropriate the means of production is weakened. Thus, the effectiveness of subordinate classes in their struggle can be undermined by the structure of authority in which they must operate.

For the capitalist class to use the state for its interests, the organization of agencies within it must help prevent crises, shape them while in process, and end them when they threaten to transform class relations. In short, the capitalist class strives for a form of state organization that embodies their own domination within the structure itself.

The capitalist class is involved at each critical point in the development of those agencies which significantly affect its interests: definition of legitimate goals and the range of legal authority, size and content of the budget, pattern of decisionmaking (who answers to whom), form of accountability, if any, and so on. Whatever organization of authority fits the interests of the capitalist class when the agency is formed will then be institutionalized in the character of the agency at an early point to eliminate the distribution of power from the agenda of class struggle. But all organizations must then be administered, and they must remain flexible at key points to respond to changing conditions. For this reason, the selection of key administrators will also be an issue of concern to the capitalist class. Indeed, the expropriation of the means of administration must take place both at the outset and during the process of policy implementation.

The early stages of the development of the Department of Labor show the means by which the capitalist class tried to block the development of the agency and then acquired control over its administration, while simultaneously preventing workers from doing so. The analysis of the later implementation of key policies in the Department of Labor will show the way expropriation of the means of administration is continued after the development of a specific agency structure which already embodies advantages for the dominant class. Both periods were chosen because they were characterized by significant social unrest, which set the conditions for a renewed struggle over the wage bill and the legitimacy of the system.

Formation of the U.S. Department of Labor

The formation of the capitalist and the working classes occurred between the Civil War and World War One. The development of national markets after the Civil War tied the interests of workers in various regions of the country more closely to each other and subordinated their well-being to the vagaries of the national economic conditions. A series of depressions combined with high inflation increasingly took their toll on the lives of workers. Employers repeatedly tried to improve their competitive advantage by cutting the wages of their workers (even in times of increasing profits), while engaging in rampant speculation that created havoc for the national economy.

In this context, both workers and employers demanded justification for the actions of the others. Several study commissions to investigate the causes of worker unrest (which came to be known as the "labor question") were created at various levels of government during the next few decades. As part of their more general struggle for workers' rights, the leaders of an emerging organized labor movement demanded a department of government to identify the source and the distribution pattern of wealth, so they could determine for themselves whether they were receiving a "fair" price for their own labor (*Congressional Record*, March 10, 1884:1749; Powderly 1890:306). Workers resisted wage cuts, demanded higher wages and shorter hours, and insisted on their right to know how much profit their employers made on their labor power.

The National Labor Union, a shortlived, national organization of workers, first demanded in 1868 an "executive department of government in Washington" to protect the interests of labor "above all others." Although "labor," it claimed, "was the foundation and cause of national prosperity" (Sylvis 1872:293), workers had no government agency to represent them.

Massachusetts was the first state government to respond to the demands of workers for a department of labor. Massachusetts workers were then the most organized in the country (perhaps because of the concentration of craftsmen in the state), and they were translating their union activities into the formation of producers' cooperatives and political strength at the polls. After a particularly bitter strike by shoemakers, who were called by one account the "most powerful labor organization in the world" (Lescohier 1969:8), the political leadership in Massachusetts feared the disaffection of those workers who had lost their demands for shorter working hours, an increase in wages, and union recognition.

To appease the workers, the state established the Bureau of Statistics of Labor, whose function was to "collect statistical details relating to all departments of labor in the Commonwealth, especially in its relations to the commercial, industrial, social, education, and sanitary conditions of the laboring classes" (Wright 1892; Pidgin 1904:7). A former state legislator involved in the active reformist movement in Massachusetts, General Henry K. Oliver, was appointed to head the new agency. He assumed that advocacy for workers was one of the primary responsibilities of the bureau, and he used the summons power of the agency to study depositors in savings banks. The enraged employers in Massachusetts strongly pressured the governor to fire Oliver and to abolish the bureau (Pidgin 1904; Lombardi 1942). Although the governor fired Oliver, the political strength of workers was too strong in the state to abolish the department. Instead, he appointed a new agency chief, Carroll Davidson Wright, a man from a prominent family with no ties to any labor organization who promised to maintain the "neutrality" of the agency.

After other states created their own state bureaus of labor statistics, Wright, who had gained a national reputation for his role in Massachusetts, took the initiative to establish a national organization of chiefs of state bureaus. He used his influence in the organization to frustrate "every effort to commit the chiefs to a program of labor reform" (Lombardi 1942:39). Yet after the severe depression of 1873–1877 culminated in the most violent and extensive strike the country had yet experienced, Wright joined with various leaders of organized labor to recommend a national bureau of labor statistics. He argued before a congressional committee that a national bureau would "harmonize and unify existing divergencies between capital and labor" (Grossman and MacLaury 1975:26).

But the leader of the Knights of Labor, the largest and most important labor organization in the country at the time, argued such a bureau should rigidly scrutinize "the means by which employers or moneyed men acquire wealth" and "put a stop to illegitimate profit-taking" (Powderly 1890:158–60). In effect, Wright assumed that the centralization of a national bureau of labor statistics would neutralize the political demands of organized labor, but only if it did not have cabinet status. In contrast, the leaders of organized labor wanted an autonomous agency with full cabinet status to strengthen their demands to employers.

Wright's preferences were more influential. A Bureau of Labor Statistics was created, at Wright's suggestion, in the Department of the Interior in 1884. After seven months of lobbying by a number of union leaders for the position of Commissioner of Labor, President Arthur appointed Wright to the position. Wright gained increasing favor among government leaders; among other tasks, he was given responsibility for conducting the national census. He became for all intents and purposes the adviser to the president on labor matters. In 1888, after the extensive 1886 strikes and subsequent congressional hearings, the Bureau of Labor Statistics was made into an independent, noncabinet department with Wright at the head. The lines of authority went directly from the new Department of Labor to the president and Congress, but it was denied cabinet status, with Wright's full approval, to prevent it from becoming a "political" agency.

Organized labor, however, continued to pressure for a cabinet agency. In some of the many government hearings on labor unrest, the creation of a cabinet-level department of labor was looked on as a panacea for the problems of workers. However, despite several forms of reorganization, the Department of Labor never determined "the source and distribution of wealth," the primary and continuing goal that organized labor envisioned for the agency (Powderly 1890:324–25). Indeed, each successive reorganization of the department made it possible to direct its statistical talents toward studying workers rather than employers. In the earliest days, employers even resisted the collection of information on workers, and many fired workers who cooperated with the state bureaus. Under the strong and predictable leadership of Wright, however, the federal agency gained national and international legitimacy by the turn of the century. But Wright's impending retirement worried members of the dominant class.

Hearings began in 1901 on the creation of a Department of Commerce that would incorporate the independent Department of Labor as a bureau. Such major industrialists as Senator Mark Hanna, who had organized the presidential campaign of William McKinley, were centrally involved in pushing for the new legislation. Senator Knute Nelson of Minnesota, a former state governor and board of regents member of the state university, introduced the Department of Commerce bill. Nelson said of Wright, "He is a very able man, but he will not always be with us." Arguing that the future head of the Department of Labor "may not be so able and so good as he," Nelson said, "it is altogether safer for the public service to have a division or a bureau of this kind under some responsible executive department" (U.S. Department of Commerce and Labor 1904:491). Beyond the uncertainty created by Wright's retirement, members of the dominant class also expressed a strong need for more predictable information so they could expand U.S. business abroad. Hanna said in the hearings on the bill:

> We are on the eve of a condition in this country where we are forced to expand our trade and commerce. Already our productive capacity is far beyond our capacity for consumption, and either one of two things must result. We must either find a market for that surplus or we must restrict our production to our home wants (U.S. Department of Commerce and Labor 1904:500).

A Department of Commerce that could control the collection of labor statistics, as well as collect other information of importance to business, was so important to the dominant class that Hanna could argue:

> There is no interest in the United States today that demands the attention of Congress to help and further our development more than this very question of having an established department of the Government, acting in concert like departments all over Europe and the civilized world; for a department of commerce established and acting along these lines in every nation that competes with us in the markets of the world (U.S. Department of Commerce and Labor 1904:498).

The need of the dominant class to both control and to use the information collected by the Department of Labor led to exactly the opposite logic than had been used 15 years earlier. In 1888 the government denied cabinet status to the Department of Labor so that it would not become "political"—that is, preventing organized labor from gaining too much influence in the government. In 1902 the dominant class, working directly through their supporters in the legislature, insisted on placing the Department of Labor in a cabinet office, but only as a subordinate bureau to a Department of Commerce. Among others, Hanna argued that the Department of Labor should be joined to the new Department of Commerce because "a close, effective organization, with one able executive head, is always the best way to accomplish a result" (U.S. Department of Commerce and Labor 1904:499). Hanna reasoned that the interests of labor and capital are "identical and mutual," and that any presumed difference in their interests was "sentimental." Although the supporters of the bill kept insisting that a Department of Commerce by definition incorporated the interests of labor, they yielded to the pressure from organized labor and added "Labor" to the title of the new department. But the budget of the new agency indicated the real political inequality of business and labor within it. Of the total Department budget of \$8,363,032, labor was allocated only \$184,020.

After a decade of political turmoil in which organized labor increasingly gained strength, the joint Department of Commerce and Labor was separated into two independent cabinet agencies. The Progressive reform movement, the growth of a socialist consciousness and the Socialist Party and the entry of organized labor into party politics each contributed in some important way to the creation of the new cabinet-level Department of Labor in 1913. The legislation creating the department said it would:

> go far to allay jealousy, establish harmony, promote the general welfare, make the employer and employee better friends, prevent strikes and lockouts, stop boycotts and business paralysis, and every year save millions and millions of dollars of losses which result necessarily therefrom (U.S. House of Representatives, Hearings before Committee on Labor, 1912:5).

Nevertheless, once the Department of Labor was separated from the control of business, the dominant class again tried to limit its jurisdiction and continually treated it with suspicion. For 50 years after, it remained one of the smallest of cabinet offices, and in the 1940s the dominant class tried to have it abolished.

Even so, the Department of Labor was not, as Senator Bacon of Georgia testified, "an ornamental bureau" (U.S. Department of Commerce and Labor 1904:494). The information needs of employers increased with the tremendous expansion of industry around the turn of the century. Mark Hanna had argued that "furnishing statistics" was "absolutely important, aye, . . . absolutely a necessity" for economic development (U.S. Department of Commerce and Labor 1904:501). But the dominant class wanted to control themselves the collection and distribution of labor statistics and to prevent organized labor from having an independent political leverage. The dominant class wanted a centralized organization structure as long as they were in control of it, but a decentralized structure whenever labor might gain control. Because of the potential for organized labor's gaining control over an agency specialized in labor issues, the dominant class continually tried to limit the responsibility of "labor's" agency. They strongly preferred their own data needs on labor issues to be provided through the Bureau of Statistics in the Department of Treasury, which was later the base for the Department of Commerce. Although some businessmen supported the creation of a Department of Labor, the intent was to appease workers by letting them collect data on themselves. Under no circumstances did members of the dominant class support the Department of Labor's collecting data on employers.

The process underlying the creation of the Department of Labor indicates a major contradiction for the state in a capitalist society. Like employers, the state is often in the position of giving with one hand and taking away with the other. Thus, the Department of Labor was given as a response to social unrest, but then carefully stripped of any radical content. The political demands of organized labor, reinforced by social unrest, gradually led to an improvement in the status of the department, but its jurisdiction was always carefully limited. From 1913 on, the Department of Labor has remained a highly decentralized, fragmented, and ineffectual agency. The few powerful bureaus within it by the late 1950s would not even allow their telephone calls to go through a central switchboard (Ruttenberg 1970). Therefore, the issue of reorganizing the Department of Labor in any way that would centralize power under the Secretary of Labor has been strongly resisted by business; the decentralization of the Department of Labor and insulation of major bureaus within it was strongly supported by business interests in order to prevent an independent power base for organized labor. Thus, when the introduction of federal manpower training programs in the 1960s greatly expanded the scope of the Department of Labor, it occasioned a renewed political battle over control and reorganization of the agency.

Reorganization of the Department of Labor: Federal Manpower Training

In the 1960s, the Department of Labor became involved in a welter of social conflicts that threatened its internal organization of authority. Whether the capitalist class prefers centralization or decentralization of authority in government departments depends on its relative access to and control over a given agency, compared to labor and other subordinate classes. The Department of Labor and the Department of Health, Education and Welfare (HEW) have been relatively accessible to organized labor and other popular pressure groups. For this reason, both agencies have been decentralized at the federal level, and the primary business access to these departments has come at the local and state level. At the state level, business has fairly well controlled the Department of Labor's Bureau of Employment Security and, through it, unemployment insurance programs that affect its labor costs; and in HEW, Vocational Education has been largely influenced by business interests. Because it was not assured of control at the national level, the "business community" has preferred decentralization of both agencies, in contrast to increased centralization, for example, in the White house staff organization.

The conflicts within business, between small and large capital, were complicated by the conflict between business and labor, and in the 1960s, between business and the poor. The manpower training programs were created as an alternative to organized labor's aggressive demands for guaranteed incomes. In this context, the dominant class preferred Vocational Education, and hence HEW, to the Department of Labor. Although Employment Security enrolled trainees in the manpower programs, Vocational Education actually implemented them. Because both agencies were decentralized and because their primary decisionmaking took place at the state level, big business could manipulate small business to agree to this arrangement. During the 1960s, however, when the skill shortage created by the Vietnam war enabled big business to gain significant control within the Department of Labor, big business preferred a more centralized Department of Labor to Vocational Education, despite objections from small business. When the poor were making demands that threatened the legitimacy of the system and when big business had control over the Department of Labor, business also preferred a more centralized Department of Labor to the autonomous Office of Economic Opportunity (OEO), because the demands being made by the poor then had more far-reaching consequences than those of organized labor. Indeed, during the 1960s, although their intentions never fully materialized, the dominant class appeared to support a centralized Department of Labor. Then Employment Security would take over programs from the Community Action Agencies of OEO.

Although the more conservative craft unions have settled for a decentralized input to the Department of Labor in the Bureau of Apprenticeship and Training, organized labor as a whole favors a centralization of most programs in the Department of Labor. The American Federation of Labor–Congress of Industrial Organizations (AFL–CIO) has made continual demands for the "federalization" of the Bureau of Employment Security, especially unemployment insurance. Nevertheless, organized labor preferred Employment Security in the Department of Labor to Vocational Education in HEW because of their easier potential access to the former. For the same reason, organized labor preferred the Department of Labor to OEO. There has always been an uneasy relationship between unions and minority workers and hence between unions and the poor. In fact, the conservative craft unions have been a major target of criticism of minority groups. Thus, during the War on Poverty years of the 1960s, a conflict developed between organized labor and the poor, which was fought through as a conflict between the Department of Labor and OEO. It appears that the dominant class used organized labor's desire to gain control over Employment Security to encourage their conflict with the Community Action Agencies in OEO. And they used minority group suspicion of craft unions to strengthen the attack on the Bureau of Apprenticeship and Training. At the end of the decade, both organized labor and the poor lost out to the dominant class. These several conflicts were in the background of the proposals to reorganize the Department of Labor.

The crisis in class relations that eventually led to the development of federal manpower programs was twofold. At the end of the 1950s and the beginning of the 1960s, workers and employers had distinctive but convergent concerns over employment problems. A plethora of books and articles on automation and the supposed effects of technological change appeared at that time. One account suggests that "anxiety almost amounting to panic" developed "over the reported loss of jobs and escalation of skill demands due to automation" (Crossman and Larner 1969:176). Workers feared the effects of automation on the elimination of jobs (termed "structural unemployment" by policymakers). Capitalists worried that the skill level of the U.S. labor force prevented the technological changes necessary to compensate for their competitive disadvantage with European economic organizations (hence their concern about the activities of Apprenticeship and Training). These competing concerns were complicated by a close election, a changing administration which had made elaborate campaign promises, and a growing and militant civil rights movement, which was yet to blossom to its full potential. This combination of factors induced policymakers to define federal manpower training programs as a solution.

Despite the demands by organized labor that business compensate workers displaced by automation (including guaranteed annual income proposals), the current economic problems probably had more direct influence on the selection of manpower training programs as a solution to the crisis: an unprecedented high unemployment rate during a period of expansion, a second recession before the first one was over (1960–1961 and 1957–1958), pockets of depression in the midst of overall prosperity, increasing mobility of both plants and workers, as well as the declining competitive position of the United States compared to Western Europe. In this context a controversy among political factions of the dominant class developed within the Kennedy and later within the Johnson administrations. William McChesney Martin, head of the Federal Reserve under Kennedy, supported the use of more traditional and conservative economic policies, but Walter Heller, Kennedy's chairman of the Council of Economic Advisors, supported the use of Keynesian fiscal and monetary policies. The two positions were reconciled by the Manpower Development and Training Act of 1962:

> Those who favored an expansionary fiscal policy looked upon retraining as a necessary *supplement*. Those who opposed strong fiscal measures tended to seize upon retraining as a *substitute*. If the economy did not need stimulation to absorb the unemployed, they found themselves reasoning, then jobs for all must in fact exist or would exist if only the unemployed were competent to fill them. If the shortcomings were not in the economy, they could only be in the people (Sundquist 1968:85–86).

The representatives of organized labor were dismayed with their initial experience with federal manpower training programs. President Kennedy delegated responsibility for the first programs under the Area Redevelopment Act of 1961 to the Department of Commerce. At first Commerce did not implement them at all, and when it did, money was given to nonunion, runaway shops in the South. Under the Manpower Act of 1962, responsibility was jointly delegated to Vocational Education in HEW and to the Bureau of Employment Security in the Department of Labor.

Organized labor leaders preferred that such programs be administered through a new agency because there was no bureau within the Department of Labor acceptable to them. Union leaders had no desire to expand the power of Employment Security because of its ties to business. Nor did they want Apprenticeship and Training to administer the programs because this would necessitate an expansion of the number of skilled workers, and the high wages of the skilled in part depended on limited recruitment. A new agency, the Office of Manpower, Automation, and Training (OMAT), was created in the Department of Labor to officially administer the Manpower Act, but the programs were actually implemented through Employment Security (in conjunction with Vocational

Education) and Apprenticeship and Training. The Manpower Administration (as OMAT was later called) consequently became the arena for working out a new institutionalization of class interests within the Department of Labor. It was at the center of the several controversial attempts to reorganize the Labor Department in the 1960s.

The pressure that organized labor exerted on the Department of Labor declined soon after the passage of MDTA, because the most immediate cause for its support—high (white, male) unemployment—disappeared. Yet a new crisis in class relations erupted as a result of the development of the civil rights movement, the two major goals of which were jobs and freedom. The marches in Birmingham in the spring and the March on Washington in August 1963 marked a turning point for the movement. By the end of the year urban riots began in a number of cities, and then expanded with fury during the next few years. The Johnson administration responded with several critical pieces of legislation in 1964, including the Civil Rights Act and the Economic Opportunity Act. Again, job training programs provided a solution.

Conflict among Employment Security, Apprenticeship and Training, and the Manpower Administration developed immediately after the passage of the 1962 Manpower Act. The first attempt to reorganize the responsibilities among the bureaus occurred soon after the Birmingham events in 1963. Secretary of Labor Wirtz appointed a Manpower administrator, John C. Donovan, to coordinate the activities of the three bureaus, and Donovan hired an outside consulting agency. Its recommendations satisfied neither Employment Security nor Apprenticeship and Training, however; the consultants recommended the dissolution of the field offices of both and a reintegration of their functions into a new centralized agency. Such centralization would have placed the unemployment insurance program under the direct authority of the Secretary of Labor, and it would have placed the activities of the conservative craft unions under the closer scrutiny of the federal administrators. As the director of Employment Security remarked, "The proposed reorganization would disrupt [existing] relationships and require the development of an entirely new fabric" (memo from Robert C. Goodwin, director, BES, to Secretary of Labor Wirtz, February 1, 1965).

In other words, centralizing authority within the Department of Labor would decrease the power of those groups who had purposely created decentralization earlier. In this situation, the conservative building trades department of the AFL–CIO joined with the Interstate Conference of Employment Security Agencies, the government-funded, business-controlled lobbying group for Employment Security, to prevent any reorganization. Donovan resigned and former AFL–CIO research director, Stanley Ruttenberg, took his place—on the condition that he would not support any reorganization of the Department of Labor (see Ruttenberg 1970: 76–78).

As the urban riots increased, the agency Johnson had created to solve the problems of unrest, the Office of Economic Opportunity, began to create problems of its own. As early as 1965, OEO was charged with "trying to wreck local government by setting the poor against city hall" and with being a "nightmare of bureaucratic bungling" (U.S. Code, Congress and Administration News, 1st Session, 89th Congress, 1965, pp. 3525–26). Of most concern to the dominant class, however, were the political activities of OEO personnel. The Hatch Act was extended to OEO to make political organizing by its employees illegal, but this did not end the social movement to which OEO provided an organization base.

Johnson had made OEO a "staff agency" in the White House, rather than a cabinet office, ostensibly to protect it, but his real intent was probably better control. When it was evident that even direct White House control was not enough to curtail OEO's political influence, other means had to be found. The proliferation of riots made it politically impossible to eliminate the War on Poverty programs; instead, the dominant class began taking steps to transfer the programs out of OEO into the more predictable and more easily controlled cabinet offices. To maintain the legitimacy of such an action, those agencies with liberal images, like the Department of Labor, had to be used, but they had liberal images precisely because the subordinate classes potentially had access. This strategy, therefore, was a risk in a precarious political climate.

The Department of Labor had apparently been slated to receive the job programs of the War on Poverty. The president's administrative agency, the Bureau of the Budget, began working behind the scenes with the Labor Department, and President Johnson himself began making statements favorable to an expanded Department of Labor. With the prospect of the Department of Labor's gaining more power in the federal government, organized labor then renewed their efforts to gain more control over "their" agency. Apparently organized labor was encouraged at this point by representatives of the dominant class to strengthen the Labor Department's challenge to OEO.

Two reorganization plans on the agenda for the Department of Labor at this time would have had opposite effects. The first, supported by Secretary of Labor Wirtz and Assistant Secretary Ruttenberg, would have centralized all of the manpower training programs from OEO, HEW (the classroom training of Vocational Education), and Labor (including on-the-job training from Apprenticeship and Training) into a reorganized Manpower Administration. This proposal was similar to Donovan's approach, and it was strongly supported by organized labor, even though the craft unions were not anxious to jeopardize their control over on-the-job training.

The second proposal was articulated by a 1965 Task Force, headed by George Shultz, dean of the School of Business at the University of Chicago and later Nixon's Secretary of Labor. This Task Force proposal recommended separating the U.S. Employment Service from Unemployment Insurance in the Bureau of Employment Security and increasing Employment Service funding from the Department of Labor's general budget. The Employment Service normally is funded by the Unemployment Insurance tax on employers. This proposal would have insulated unemployment insurance even more from the access of organized labor and prevented business-provided funds from being tapped for the War on Poverty manpower programs. Secretary of Labor Wirtz took no immediate action, but the proposal later surfaced as the accepted reorganization plan.

Wirtz and Ruttenberg were encouraged behind the scenes by the Bureau of the Budget staff to pursue their own goals of reorganization in the spring of 1967. Ruttenberg held secret meetings in which he was assured of White House support. Wirtz announced a "realignment" of the Department of Labor later in the year. The primary change in the department was to expand the on-the-job training program and to remove the administration of the new positions from Apprenticeship and Training and consequently from the craft unions. Although the Interstate Conference of Employment Security Agencies and some unions opposed the change, their opposition was to no avail in the context of President Johnson's support for it.

By removing Apprenticeship and Training's control over on-the-job training, the programs could be used to channel unemployed blacks into "accelerated" (meaning shorter time and less training) apprenticeship programs with big business, when it was facing tremendous pressure from the urban uprising (symbolized by the summer of 1967 in Detroit) and from the shortage of skilled labor during the Vietnam war. The realignment also prepared the way for President Johnson to launch a $350 million on-the-job training program, sponsored by the newly formed National Alliance of Businessmen (NAB). The NAB-JOBS program not only benefited big business, it did so at government expense, because the federal government paid the training costs for industry to hire the disadvantaged (see U.S. Code, Congress and Administration News, 90th Congress, 1st Session, 1967, p. 2576; Ball 1972:175; Perry and others 1975:187).

Just as important, however, this realignment was another step along the way to the Department of Labor's taking over OEO's programs. Three "job creation" programs had been moved from OEO to the Department of Labor in 1966, and the placement of the NAB-JOBS program in Labor instead of OEO was significant. The Community Action Agencies fought Labor's claims to the War on Poverty job programs, but their only support in the late 1960s was from public opinion. Organized labor was willing to acquiesce on the issue of Apprenticeship and Training, because they thought they were going to gain some control over Employment Security. Their cooperation in the realignment was a means to demonstrate their commitment to minorities and to quell the suspicions of the "poverty" people.

Wirtz and Ruttenberg interpreted their success in the 1967 realignment as a coup and began to make plans for a more extensive reorganization soon thereafter. They were especially encouraged by the preferential support the Department of Labor was getting—in contrast to OEO which was coming under increasingly hostile attacks—from the Bureau of the Budget and the White House staff (Ball 1972:146). They began secret meetings again in 1968 with the same people who had planned the realignment. Their intent was to implement a reorganization plan similar to the aborted 1965 Donovan plan. Assuming the Interstate Conference of Employment Security Agencies was the primary obstacle to implementing their reorganization, they felt confident because they were assured of White House support. Much to their surprise, though, President Johnson rejected their plan to centralize the Department of Labor. In fact, Johnson threatened to fire Wirtz when he announced the reorganization anyway, even though the 1968 presidential elections were only two weeks away. A compromise was finally reached between Wirtz and Johnson that the reorganization order which Wirtz had announced would remain in effect, but not be implemented before the elections.

After being elected, Nixon appointed George Shultz, the former Task Force head, as Secretary of Labor. Shultz recommended implementing the Wirtz-Ruttenberg reorganization plan on an interim basis, but the reorganization carried out was actually his own earlier plan. The 1969 reorganization further decentralized the Department of Labor, with greater input from business and less from organized labor. In addition, Nixon moved the Job Corps, the last of the War on Poverty job programs, from OEO to the Department of Labor. Nixon gave his full support to the NAB–JOBS program and to the Job Corps, because both were organized to provide monetary benefits to cooperating private industry—"for profit" service delivery—but all other programs were cut back. Within six months, Shultz left the Department of Labor to become head of the Office of Management and Budget (formerly the Bureau of the Budget).

After the Shultz reorganization, the Department of Labor was said to have "fresh appeal" to employers. The president of the National Association of Manufacturers said that it was "one of the most accessible agencies in this town" (Cooney and Silverman 1970:140) and a representative of the Chamber of Commerce said "the business community is pleased with the change of administrations in the Labor Department" (Cooney and Silverman 1970:140). Nixon then embarked on his revenue-sharing campaign, in which the Manpower Revenue Sharing Bill was to be the first implemented. Organizationally, this legislation meant complete decentralization of federal programs. For all federal agencies in which subordinate classes had some influence, Nixon attempted to reduce their power through decentralization of the agencies to the state level, where business had more predictable control.

Nixon's own OEO director said, "I know of no way in which the Comprehensive Manpower Bill can be proposed by the President without it being viewed by large segments of the public as a conscious and systematic diminution of the role of OEO" (Letter from Donald Rumsfeld, secretary of OEO to Robert Mayo, director of the Bureau of the Budget, August 7, 1969). Despite opposition from organized labor and from some "pro-poverty" legislators, the Comprehensive Employment and Training Act (CETA) was passed in 1973. It was supposed to be a compromise bill that balanced centralization of federal oversight and decentralization of program choice, but the Nixon administration screened out all of organized labor's input from the federal guidelines used to implement legislation. Rather than a balance, the new legislation completely decentralized federal job programs. What in effect was a doublecross of the Office of Economic Opportunity by organized labor, turned out to be a "double-doublecross" of organized labor by the dominant class.

Conclusions

For the capitalist class to maintain control over the working class while simultaneously gaining their cooperation in capital accumulation, it has to prevent the effective use of the state by the working class. At a critical point in the formation of the working class in the United States, workers assumed that a department of labor would help them determine the extent of their exploitation and thus strengthen their demands against employers for higher wages, but the dominant class first tried to prevent the development of a department of labor altogether and then to shape its organization to their own advantage. Even so, they acquiesced only when workers' unrest threatened the legitimacy of the system as a whole.

The dominant class used various strategies to ensure their control. Generally, it has used centralization of authority in those agencies where its control is predictable, and decentralization (or fragmentation) of authority in those agencies in which subordinate classes have potential access. The choice of strategy depends on its interpretation of the power of subordinate classes (big and small labor, the poor, and even small business). The strategies have not always been consistent because of the internal contradictions of each class, and the dominant class is not married to any one form of organization. It uses whatever is necessary to maintain its control. It has also actively tried to control the appointment of key personnel, the content and size of budgets, and limitations on legal authority, especially in those agencies where subordinate classes are likely to have access. The result is the creation of an organizational structure to which subordinate classes have limited access, thereby preventing the state from becoming a resource for their own political organization.

References

BABSON, ROGER W.
  1919   W. B. Wilson and the Department of Labor. New York: Brentano's.
BALL, JOSEPH H.
  1972   "The Implementation of Federal Manpower Policy, 1961–1971." Ph.D. dissertation. Columbia University.
COONEY, ROBERT B., and MARCIA SILVERMAN
  1970   "CPR Department Study/The Labor Department." National Journal 2:130–41.
CULHANE, CHARLES
  1974   "Manpower Report/Revenue Sharing Shift Set for Worker Training Programs." National Journal 6:51–58.
DULLES, FOSTER RHEA
  1966   Labor in America, 3d ed. New York: Crowell.
FEAGIN, JOE R., and HARLAN HAHN
  1973   Ghetto Revolts: The Politics of Violence in American Cities. New York: Macmillan.
GOLDBERG, ARTHUR J.
  1961–   Correspondence. National Archives.
  1962
GREENSTONE, J. DAVID
  1969   Labor in American Politics. New York: Vintage.
GROSSMAN, JONATHAN
  1945   William Sylvis, Pioneer of American Labor. New York: Columbia University Press.
  1973   The Department of Labor. New York: Praeger.
HODGSON, JAMES D.
  1970–   Correspondence. National Archives.
  1973
JOHNSON, MIRIAM
  1973   Counter Point, the Changing Employment Service. Salt Lake City: Olympus.
KIPNIS, IRA
  1968   The American Socialist Movement, 1897–1912. New York: Greenwood.
LESCOHIER, DON D.
  1969   The Knights of St. Crispin, 1867–1874. New York: Anno and the New York Times.

LEVITAN, SAR A.
   1964   Federal Aid to Depressed Areas. Baltimore: Johns Hopkins.
   1969   Programs in Aid of the Poor for the 1970s. Baltimore: Johns
            Hopkins.
LEVITAN, SAR A., and GARTH L. MANGUM
   1967   Making Sense of Federal Manpower Policy. Washington, D.C.: Na-
            tional Manpower Policy Task Force.
LOMBARDI, JOHN
   1942   Labor's Voice in the Cabinet. New York: Columbia.
MACLAURY, JUDSON
   1975   "The Selection of the First U.S. Commissioner of Labor." Monthly
            Labor Review 16–19.
MANGUM, GARTH L.
   1968   MDTA: Foundation of Federal Manpower Policy. Baltimore: Johns
            Hopkins.
METCALF, EVAN B.
   1972   "Economic Stabilization by American Business in the Twentieth
            Century." Ph.D. dissertation, University of Wisconsin.
MITCHELL, JAMES P.
   1953–   Correspondence. National Archives.
   1961
PERRY, CHARLES R., BERNARD E. ANDERSON, RICHARD L. ROWAN, and HER-
BERT R. NORTHRUP
   1975   The Impact of Government Manpower Programs in General and on
            Minorities and Women. Philadelphia: Wharton School of Finance.
PHILIPSON, MORRIS (ed.)
   1962   Automation, Implications for the Future. New York: Vintage.
PIDGIN, CHARLES F.
   1904   Massachusetts Bureau of Statistics of Labor. Boston: Wright and
            Potter.
POWDERLY, TERENCE V.
   1890   Thirty Years of Labor, 1859–1889, rev. ed. Philadelphia: T. V.
            Powderly.
RUTTENBERG, STANLEY
   1970   Manpower Challenge of the 1970s. Baltimore: Johns Hopkins.
SHULTZ, GEORGE P.
   1969–   Correspondence. National Archives.
   1970
SUNDQUIST, JAMES L.
   1968   Politics and Policy. Washington, D.C.: Brookings Institute.
SYLVIS, JAMES C.
   1872   The Life, Speeches, Labors, and Essays of William H. Sylvis. Phila-
            delphia: Claxton, Remsen, and Haffelfinger.
TODES, CHARLOTTE
   1942   William H. Sylvis and the National Labor Union. New York: Inter-
            national Publishers.

U.S. Code, Congressional and Administrative News, Legislative History
  1963–   88th through 93rd Congress, for Vocational Education Act, Man-
  1974   power Development and Training Act, Revenue Act, Civil Rights
          Act, Economic Opportunity Act, Social Security Act, Emergency
          Employment Act, and Comprehensive Employment and Training
          Act. Washington, D.C.: Government Printing Office.
U.S. Congress, House of Representatives, Committee on Education and Labor
  1912   Hearings. H. R. 22913 To Establish a Department of Labor. Wash-
          ington, D.C.: Government Printing Office.
U.S. Department of Commerce and Labor
  1904   Organization and Law of the Department of Commerce and Labor.
          Washington, D.C.: Government Printing Office.
Wilson, William B.
  1913–   Correspondence. National Archives.
  1921
Wirtz, W. Willard
  1962–   Correspondence. National Archives.
  1969
Wright, Carroll D.
  1892   "The Workings of the Department of Labor." Cosmopolitan.

6 Class Politics and School Reform in Chicago

Julia Wrigley
University of California–Los Angeles

The United States is distinctive among capitalist nations both for the range of its industrial power and its lack of a strongly rooted socialist or left tradition. Although social scientists have offered many explanations for the distinctive quality of American political life, the social upheavals of the 1960s gave rise to a new interpretation of the perceived lack of radical change or even of radical challenge. A group of historians contended that throughout the twentieth century sophisticated corporate leaders had been able to forestall challenges from below by implementing strategic reforms. The corporate liberal theorists presented an image of a relatively cohesive set of major businessmen who possessed a high level of consciousness that allowed for the planning and implementation of long-range strategies of social control. The unifying thread in the work of writers analyzing the Progressive era (Kolko 1963; Weinstein 1968), the role of the labor movement (Radosh 1969), and the growth of policy research bureaus (Eakins 1966) was this emphasis on the relative sophistication of the corporate elite. While small businessmen had characteristically been vehemently antiunion and opposed to government regulation, business leaders at the highest reaches of the U.S. corporate world were portrayed as having had the confidence and political insight to promote the integration of the corporate sphere with the state sector.

The development of corporate liberal theory was paralleled during the 1960s by the emergence of a revisionist interpretation of the origins and expansion of the American public school system. The revisionist historians contested a previous consensus view that the public school system in the

---

I would like to thank Eric Chester, Nora Hamilton, and Maynard Seider for their helpful comments on an earlier draft of this paper.

United States is the product of enlightened social policy and, instead, have focused attention on its ideological functions. Although the revisionists comprise a very diverse set of writers, the thrust of their argument has been that the schools reinforce class inequalities in the society and have been used by the dominant class as a means of instilling docility in the children of workers and immigrants (Katz 1968, 1971; Carnoy 1972; Spring 1972; Bowles 1972; Bowles and Gintis 1976; Field 1974; Karier, Violas, and Spring 1973). Just as to the corporate liberal theorists the supposed liberal reforms of the Progressive era actually represented a solidification of corporate power, so to the revisionists the extension of education had a similarly paradoxical quality, appearing to be a popular victory while in fact stabilizing control.

The most influential of the revisionist historians, Michael Katz, advanced a bold interpretation of the growth of the schools as agencies of social control in his book, *The Irony of Early School Reform* (1968). He asserted that the conventional interpretation of a labor movement fighting for free public schools is a myth and that, on the contrary, schooling was imposed on a reluctant and hostile working class. The corporate liberal emphasis on the sophistication of the dominant elite is entirely in accord with the main thrust of Katz's work on the schools in Massachusetts. The industrialists and their intellectual spokesmen were increasingly concerned with the growing restlessness of the workers in the rapidly expanding factories of New England, and they were appalled by the "depravity" that met their eyes in the urban slums. They saw state-provided compulsory schooling as a means of socializing workers into a proper acceptance of their lot, and thus they "mounted an ideological and noisy campaign to sell education to an often skeptical, sometimes hostile, and usually uncomprehending working class" (Katz 1968:214). In this interpretation, the creation of a public school system was simply another attempt to ensure the continuance of the ideological hegemony of the upper class in the face of the dwindling ability of religion or of communities to serve as agencies of social control.

The revisionist educational writers and the corporate liberal theorists share a distinctive outlook in that they analyze the United States as being a class society, yet they do not believe that conflicts between classes have been dynamic forces in historical change. Working-class groups have seldom mounted effective or even audible challenges to upper-class domination. Public schools and other agencies of socialization operate in a way that helps make the prospect of ideological divergence unlikely. The revisionist authors do not describe deliberate popular efforts to influence social policy; rather, the adherents of popular protest movements are more usually described as reacting blindly against forces they do not fully comprehend. In Katz's analysis of schooling in Massachusetts, for example, he ascribes working-class resistance to the spread of public education largely to vague but deeply felt anxieties about the new industrial order (1968). Workers resisted "innovation" because it appeared potentially threatening; they lashed out at the closest institutions to hand, the public schools, although without a clear sense of the nature of their grievances. Most important, they did not organize to take focused and effective actions. In the revisionist and corporate liberal analyses, initiative and ideological awareness belong almost exclusively to the elite.

The work of the leading figure in developing the theory of corporate liberalism, Gabriel Kolko, strongly reflects the tendency to focus almost exclusively on the actions and beliefs of members of the corporate class. Kolko is a writer of bolder sweep than many authors with roughly the same viewpoint, and in his work he explicates many of the ideas implicit in the work of the other theorists. Kolko contends that the ideological hegemony of the corporate class was so complete as to be effectively beyond challenge. In his reinterpretation of the Progressive era, he argues that the industrialists conceded nothing as federal regulatory programs were initiated. Indeed, they gained from federal regulation, according to Kolko, and radicals and reformers were deluded into thinking that they had won a victory (1967). They failed to understand the dynamics of corporate capitalism; their failure "reflected the consensual and voluntarily accepted total domination of American political ideology" (1972:464). Kolko does not identify any mechanisms that potentially could have disrupted this voluntary consensus; indeed, he maintains that "a static class structure . . . might be frozen into American society" (p. 464) and that pre–World War One dissenters were negligent for not having entertained "Defeat as a possibility of long-term, even permanent duration" (p. 457).

The parallels between the educational revisionists and the corporate liberal theorists cut across the differences in the specific institutions they analyze. Kolko has argued not that business accommodated itself to increased regulation, a demand that clearly could easily be absorbed within a capitalist framework, but that business *wanted* government regulation (1967:4–5). Similarly, the revisionist educational historians have argued not that business leaders accommodated themselves to rising educational demands, but that business leaders *promoted* increased schooling. In each case, the assumption has been that business control of the institutions of government and of socialization was so assured, so beyond challenge, that there was no hesitation to strengthen public agencies.

Neither set of theorists is sensitive to the potentially contradictory effects of changes such as the expansion of schooling. The revisionist educational writers do not consider the possibility that expanded education could potentially increase people's dissatisfaction with the existing order; rather, with few exceptions, as in Bowles and Gintis's more recent work (1976), they describe the schools only as agencies of social control. To the corporate liberal theorists, class conflicts occur only over relatively trivial issues and have little or no potential for generating genuine social transformations. The hegemony of the corporate class is reinforced through a range of public and private institutions, from public schools to trade unions, that ultimately incorporate the major elements of the population into the framework of the society.

The methodology of the revisionist educational writers reflects their perspective on the mechanisms of social change. The working-class population seldom appears in these studies except as an object of manipulation and socialization; the revisionist writers have paid almost no attention to organized political or economic groups in the working class. The domination of the upper class is perceived as being so complete that popular resistance to the imposition of schooling is described as occurring only through such individualistic actions as simply not sending their children to school or by expressing sporadic and undirected opposition to school programs. Despite more than a decade of debates about the class nature of the school system, there have been few efforts to trace the actual pattern of class interactions around the schools.

The revisionist writers have contributed to making the sociology of education more relevant to political and social realities by giving historical grounding to a critique of American education. They have, however, operated according to a simplified political model and have relied on a sketchy body of historical evidence. To contribute to the development of an alternative theoretical explanation of the role of education, I have carried out a case study of conflicts in the Chicago public school system. My intent is to provide a clearer understanding of the pattern of class interactions surrounding the expansion and development of public education.

Social Conflicts and the Chicago Public Schools

Clearly, many factors influence the growth and development of the public school system at the local and national level. These factors include the size and age-structure of the population, the economic climate, the existence of private religious schools, the desire for technically trained personnel, pressures from educators and the educational establishment, and the immediate political considerations of elected officials. The analysis of Chicago school politics, although not denying the influence of these factors, centers on two questions: under what conditions did public education become a focus of class conflict? Were there consistent class perspectives on the value and nature of the school system?

Chicago was selected for this study because it is a major industrial city that has long had a sizable working-class population while serving as a center of powerful business institutions. Any city presents a unique history that limits the generalizability of findings. Yet through analyzing Chicago school politics and the roles of labor, business, political, and middle-class civic groups over a relatively long period—from the early 1900s to the World War Two era—it is possible to explore the effects of changing political contexts and to hazard hypotheses about the conditions under which the nature of the educational system is perceived as a class-related issue.

Although the concept of class clearly encompasses far more than is expressed in the notions of "the labor movement" or "business organizations," class interests must find some political or organizational expression. The organized labor movement in Chicago was the primary vehicle for the expression of working class interests in political terms. As E. J. Hobsbawm has noted, "working class consciousness . . . implies formal organization" because, unlike employers, the working class does not possess political strength except through collective action (1971:15). Business leaders, because their interests are favored by the logic of capitalist development (for example, the level of employment depends on the prosperity of business firms) and because they are fewer in number and thus more able to develop informal means of cohesion, have a somewhat different range of available political strategies. I will consider different modes of political involvement employed by the organized labor movement, by business leaders and by reform-oriented civic associations with largely professional memberships.

Chicago's history during the first decades of the 1900s was marked by extensive and bitter conflicts over the control, funding, and curriculum of the public schools. During this early period, the debates frequently took on a class character. After the entrenchment of the Democratic Party machine during the 1930s, conflicts between competing groups were mediated through the machine, often in closed-door bargaining in the mayor's office. The labor movement was essentially absorbed as a junior partner of the machine and ceased to struggle over broad social issues such as the control and direction of public education. However, the labor movement never opposed the expansion and development of public schooling, although the intensity of its involvement with social issues varied markedly with its social reform orientation.

The conflicts that occurred over educational policy during the first decades of the 1900s are particularly striking because they reveal the ability of the labor movement to generate an independent educational perspective. The Chicago Federation of Labor fought for educational policies which differed both from those of Chicago's business leaders and those of the city's middle-class progressives, although on certain specific, important instances the labor movement found common educational ground with the progressives. The labor federation developed a distinctive educational ideology during sustained battles over the control of the schools, their funding, the content of the curriculum, and the rights of unionized teachers. Two of these struggles are particularly significant for what they reveal of class interactions and the schools. These disputes specifically concern the scope of education to be offered working-class children and the introduction of social efficiency measures into the schools.

During the early period, the most bitter and far-reaching educational controversy occurred over the scope of the education to be offered working-class children. The organized labor movement consistently argued for a broad liberal education, while business groups developed plans for "moral education" and vocational training that involved extremely limited academic schooling for the bulk of the working-class population. Moral education did not necessarily reflect a strong business desire for intensive socialization of working-class children; such plans could also limit the genuine academic education received by students drawn from industrial backgrounds, and they were in fact perceived in this light by the organized labor movement.

The Scope of Education for Working-Class Children

In Chicago the initial debate over the breadth of the curriculum began as early as the 1890s. As the schools began to fill with the children of immigrants, there were increasing calls for the elimination of "fads and frills" from the curriculum of the public schools (Clark 1897:77). The *Chicago Tribune* published 30 vituperative editorials in one year critical of the waste of public money on such subjects as singing, drawing, and foreign languages. The Trades and Labor Assembly, the forerunner of the Chicago Federation of Labor, defended all of the special subjects and said that if they were considered desirable for the children of the rich, they should also be taught in the public schools (Herrick 1971:33).

Businessmen who had earlier privately funded vocational schools in Chicago began to turn their attention to the reorientation of the public schools in a more practical direction. In 1901 the Merchants' Club sponsored a discussion on the need for business-oriented high school training. John G. Shedd, the first president of the Chicago Association of Commerce, returned to the "fads and frills" debate, telling the club that, "I don't think that fads are objected to, so long as they do not interfere with the ordinary education of the masses." The problem arose, he continued, when fads such as classes in artistic subjects were applied to the "ninety-five percent of those who are neither prepared for them nor desire them" (Merchants Club 1901:125).

The campaign against frivolous subjects in the schools evoked from the Chicago Federation of Labor its earliest full statement on educational questions (CFL 1902). The Federation unanimously approved and distributed 10,000 copies of a report calling for retention of a broad liberal curriculum in the schools.

The controversy over fads and frills in the schools proved to be only the forerunner of a more far-ranging and intense controversy between 1912 and 1917. The Commercial Club of Chicago, backed by most of the city's other business organizations (Commercial Club 1915:275; 1912:278), developed a plan for the establishment of two separate school systems in the upper grades, one academic and one vocational, each with its own separate school board (Commercial Club, undated). The Commercial Club was the most powerful and selective of Chicago's business organizations (London 1968). It was also the business organization that was best-equipped for pursuing long-range goals. Its criterion for membership was "conspicuous success in one's private business" and membership was limited to the 60 or so most important merchants, industrialists, and financiers of the city. Club members were confident that they could successfully undertake the reorganization of the school system and that their plan would become a national model (Commercial Club 1912:277; 1915:274).

What led the Commercial Club to throw its energies behind the reorganization of the public school system, and why was it able to persuade other business organizations to join in the effort? The Commercial Club's reorganization plan held out a number of potential benefits. First, a minority of children would have received fairly extensive full-time trade training. A 1912 survey of 346 major employers in Chicago found that 74.7 percent reported that they faced a shortage of skilled labor (City Club 1912a:46). The club's plan offered a potential means of alleviating this shortage. Second, the provision for separate school boards enabled and legitimated a direct business role in the management of the vocational schools. And third, the plan for a dual school system would have enabled children to receive the form of education considered most appropriate and useful for their varying stations in life. In the case of the great majority of working-class children, the form of education required seemed plainly to be vocational rather than academic.

The limited nature of the education that was slated for most of the students in the vocational school system was in keeping with a tradition of business emphasis on the importance of moral rather than intellectual training for the bulk of working-class children. The Commercial Club's educational spokesman, Edwin G. Cooley, a former superintendent of the Chicago public schools, was particularly forthright in counterposing moral to intellectual education: "We must realize from the start in our educational efforts that the moral reformation of the child is of more importance than the sharpening of his intellect" (1906:16) The child had to be taught the three chief virtues—industry, obedience, and punctuality—which formed "the basis of good moral character," although Cooley acknowledged that moralists might rank other traits rather more highly (1906:4).

It is not surprising that businessmen should have found a close connection between work-related values and moral virtue. This theme received blunt expression from H. E. Miles, the president of the Wisconsin State Board of Industrial Education and the chairman of the Committee on Industrial Education of the National Association of Manufacturers. Miles explained the benefits of the type of continuation schools proposed by the Commercial Club. He suggested that "the businessman's solution to the school problem" was "to organize education so that good vocational teaching costs less than $10 per year per child" (1913:667). He reported that in some areas vocational schooling in fact cost only $7 per child per year; continuation schools combined efficient functioning with a program geared to the intellects of the great mass of "hand-minded" working-class children. Those interested in industrial education should demand that it be extremely practical, he insisted: "They want it to bear upon its face the grime of the factory and the stress of the store and the counting room. It must be free of any slightest touch of sentimentality. Work is real; work is hard" (1911:6).

Although the high goal of moral education was counterposed to that of intellectual education, the actual content of the proposed education bore a close relation to simple hard work at industrial jobs, along with several hours a week of work-related (and inexpensive) schooling. With their conception that most working-class children would enter jobs requiring little skill, many businessmen could think of academic education above the level of basic literacy as a fad and frill.

The Labor Movement and Liberal Education

The Illinois State Federation of Labor joined the Chicago Federation in denouncing the Cooley Bill, which it termed "the *notorious* Cooley Industrial Training Bill," and the issue assumed a statewide importance (ISFL *Weekly News Letter,* May 8, 1915). As early as November 1912, when the Cooley Bill was first introduced, labor groups charged that the bill was intended to turn the public schools into a supply house for docile workers (*Chicago Record Herald,* November 10, 1912). The unionists argued that the "dual system" would create class distinctions in the public schools and that working class children would be shunted into the vocational program, while middle class students remained in the academic division. Rather than create a stratified school system, they maintained that all children should remain in school through age 16. The provision for a separate vocational board of education, composed of "practical men and women," struck the labor federations as an obvious attempt at employer control (ISFL 1915:73).

While business leaders stressed that schools should teach subjects that would be relevant to children's ultimate job needs, labor representatives turned this argument on its head. Factory jobs had been specialized to the point where they required very little skill or education of any sort, the Illinois State Federation of Labor asserted in a 1914 report. The labor movement had to work toward the goal of altering industrial conditions that led to many workers performing repetitive tasks. In the meantime, vocational education could only become a travesty if students were to be trained to become cogs in a machine. "What good will come from giving vocational training in the public schools if we continue to permit our children to be chained to machines which require but the repetition of a few muscular motions?" (ISFL 1914:46)

During this and later disputes labor representatives charged that employers did not want working-class children to receive extensive schooling because of their fear that education would make them less tractable in the shop or factory. An editorial in the CFL's newspaper declared that employers wanted children ground out at the end of the schooling "as perfect parts of an industrial machine, calculated to work automatically, smoothly and continuously for a short period and then go on the scrap heap, to be replaced by other cheap, simple parts exactly like them" (*New Majority*, Dec. 29, 1923:4) Employers were not averse to schools being crowded and hurried as it would "accustom the children to the nerve-destroying pace-making of industry" (p. 4); they were primarily interested in seeing that children taught in the public schools would, in the words of John Fitzpatrick, president of the CFL, "jump when the string is pulled and . . . be splendid material to draw upon for employees in stores, offices, shops, factories, or elsewhere" (Fitzpatrick 1913).

The Commercial Club had so framed the issue of reorganizing the school system that it isolated itself even from sectors of opinion that were often responsive to business-supported proposals. The plan for separate control of vocational schools led Chicago's leading middle-class civic organizations to oppose the Cooley Bill. The City Club, a largely professional organization that was the voice of Chicago's leading progressives, spoke out against the Cooley Bill and joined the labor groups in calling for an extension of compulsory schooling to age 16. The City Club prepared legislation opposing the Cooley Bill (City Club 1912b) and lobbied energetically against the business-sponsored plan at the state legislature. John Dewey also entered the fray with several articles critical of the Cooley Bill which were extensively quoted by the labor groups (1915). In reply to Dewey's claim that the schools would be class-stratified, Cooley wrote that the only segregation in the schools would be of the sort that segregated art students from music students, "purely for the sake of special study and increased efficiency" (undated:7).

The Commercial Club responded to the widespread opposition to the plan by intensifying its lobbying in the state legislature, with club members chartering a train to Springfield to present their case to the legislators (Commercial Club, 1915:254). Despite these personal lobbying efforts, however, the Cooley Bill failed in three successive sessions of the legislature. Labor groups claimed credit for having spearheaded the victory and announced that they trusted that in the future business interests would not seek to tamper with the public schools.

During the struggle over the Cooley Bill, trade unionists had been able to make common cause with the city's liberal civic reformers. Their goals differed in some respects, however, as a key element in the reform ideology stressed the need for control by experts rather than by lay people or politicians (Wrigley 1977). The differing goals of the civic reformers and the trade unionists were thrown into relief during a series of conflicts over the superintendency of William McAndrew. McAndrew had been hired in 1923 to clean up the corrupt administration of the schools and bring new standards of public efficiency. He was a fervent advocate of the social engineering version of Taylorism, declaring that the aim of the school system was "to produce a human, social unit, trained in accordance with his capabilities to the nearest approach to complete social efficiency possible in the time allotted" (McAndrew 1926).

Once in office, McAndrew introduced plans for abolishing teachers' councils, tighter centralization of the school system, new forms of differentiated schooling, and the increased use of IQ tests. These plans were attacked by the Chicago Federation of Labor as more sophisticated versions of the earlier business proposals for differentiated schooling and school system reorganization. On these grounds, the labor federations opposed the introduction of IQ tests, the development of "platoon schools" (which would, among other things, have allowed for greater differentiation of school programs at the elementary level), and were highly dubious about vocational guidance.

The Chicago Federation of Labor and the state federation were particularly scathing in their hostility toward the use of IQ tests to sort children into differentiated programs. Such tests, the federations argued, were inherently inhumane and resulted in the treatment of children as numbers, the favorite goal of the efficiency engineer. As one labor editorial remarked, "It is a monstrous thing to do to a child, to label him as less bright than another. . . . It smacks too of the quackery of the efficiency engineer. And certainly it is the reverse of democratic to group kids in a caste system of intelligence" (*New Majority,* April 26, 1924:4).

The labor representatives viewed the tests as transparently reflecting class position, and they rejected the idea that the tests rested on any "scientific" principle. The labor movement had fought the Cooley Bill because it was intended to separate children into vocational or academic programs, and the intelligence tests seemed merely a new way of achieving the same goal. The labor federations did not find support from the civic associations in this conflict, however. Nearly all of Chicago's middle-class civic leaders had agreed that the Cooley Bill was undemocratic, but the intelligence tests struck many of these professionals as being, in fact, genuinely scientific, and McAndrew's efficiency goals held a special appeal to them. As a result, they were much less ready to desert the embattled superintendent and stand with the labor federations in opposition than they had been willing to oppose the earlier Cooley Bill (Wrigley 1977).

During the disputes over McAndrew's proposals and over the earlier Cooley Bill, the labor movement displayed a willingness to generalize a range of educational issues into class questions. The unionists also developed an educational ideology that was distinctive from the views predominantly held by the city's progressive leaders and from those of the business leaders. By the 1930s, however, the organized labor movement had altered its independent political posture and increasingly moved into the orbit of the Democratic Party political machine. This alteration in the political context did not result in the abandonment of labor support for the development of the school system, but it did sharply affect the willingness of the union movement to throw its resources into battles over educational or other broad social reform issues. There were specific historical reasons for the labor movement's absorption into the dominant political process. They exemplify the variability of political relationships and their bearing on public policy conflicts.

School Crisis and Machine Politics

During the early 1900s, the Chicago Federation of Labor's militant and progressive stance led it to challenge both the national American Federation of Labor leadership and the dominant political powers of Chicago. The president of the CFL, John Fitzpatrick, was not a socialist but believed in the creation of a broad working class movement on the model of the British Labour Party (Fitzpatrick 1928). The labor federation attempted to organize unskilled workers, initiating major organizing drives in meat packing and in steel. And in the political arena, the CFL ignored Samuel Gompers' grim warnings of protest and founded the Cook County Labor Party in 1918 (*New Majority*, March 27, 1920:2).

The founding of the Labor Party was not propitious, however, as the

1920s marked a time of labor retrenchment both nationally and locally. A wave of government repression directed by Attorney General Mitchell Palmer created a climate of intimidation and resulted in the arrest and jailing of scores of dissidents. Under employers' offensives and in a generally conservative climate, membership in the AFL fell from 4.1 million in 1920 to 2.8 million in 1926 (Keiser 1965:v). In the "era of normalcy," the labor movement in Chicago began shifting toward a policy of political accommodation that was to have decisive consequences for the union movement's engagement with social issues.

The accommodation with the newly entrenched Democratic Party machine during the early 1930s was hastened by a range of factors both internal and external to the labor movement. Internally, the CFL was weakened by the failure of the organizing drive in steel in 1919, by the continued hostility of Samuel Gompers and the AFL bureaucracy, and by faction fighting with the Communist-controlled Workers Party, which disrupted the independent labor party founded by the CFL (Keiser 1965). The Depression made the CFL all the more a beleaguered organization; nearly half Chicago's work force was unemployed (Gottfried 1962:241). The massive unemployment had a devastating effect on many of the unions which composed the CFL's core (Newell 1961:34). Further, despite historic ties between the leaders of the CFL and those who tried to organize the mass production industries, ultimately bitter organizational and political rivalries developed between the Chicago Federation of Labor and the CIO unions (Fitzpatrick 1939; March 1970:93).

The essence of machine politics is the welding together of a diverse coalition within a centralized framework; it is essential to the smooth workings of the machine that the different groups incorporated within it make limited and narrow demands upon the political system (Greenstone 1970). In the new constellation, the schools once again became a focus of controversy, but the conflicts were muted because most of the contending elements were embraced within the Democratic Party. The key disputes centered on educational funding and political manipulation of the school system.

In the 1930s businessmen in Chicago used their ties with the machine and with the banks to mount a sustained drive to force slashing cutbacks in the educational budget. Although in the Depression cutbacks were inevitable in the absence of federal support, no other major agency of government in Chicago suffered cuts as sustained and drastic as the schools (Herrick 1971:218–19). The school cutbacks were effected through direct business intervention. In 1932, about 100 of Chicago's most prominent businessmen formed a body called the Committee on Public Expenditures to force reductions in public spending. The committee's chairman, Fred W. Sargent, president of the Chicago and Northwestern Railroad, was frank in stating that "the extralegal body" gained its power because the banks "have shown that they positively will not lend money for any municipal function that does not have our active support" (1933:78). The Committee on Public Expenditures forced the reluctant board of education to make a series of sweeping cutbacks to meet the goal of "retrenchment, and then more and more retrenchment" (Sargent 1933:74). Later, however, such a direct business role became unnecessary as Mayor Edward Kelly appointed an "economy-minded" board that carried out its own very deep expenditure reductions (Hancock, undated).

Over the next 13 years, Chicago's middle-class civic associations and the unionized teachers bore the brunt of the resistance to the school board's "economy" measures (Levit 1947). The city's reform leadership was not constrained by support for the local Democratic machine and did not hesitate to point out that the instructional budget had been drastically pared while the graft-inflated administrative budget survived relatively unscathed.

The civic associations were joined in their campaign against the cutbacks by the Chicago Federation of Labor, but the CFL was so intimately tied to the Chicago Democracy that it did not back its pronouncements with effective political actions. The CFL declared that Fred Sargent was "Public Enemy No. 1," and John Fitzpatrick told a rally of 25,000 people who had jammed into the Chicago stadium to protest the cuts that the labor movement intended "to hold Mayor Edward J. Kelly responsible until such time as this action is rescinded by the Board of Education" (*Federation News*, July 29, 1933:1). The threat carried little conviction, however; the CFL, far from withdrawing support from the mayor, was moving into an increasingly close alliance with the party politicians. In 1935, the CFL unhesitatingly endorsed Kelly; the secretary of the CFL wrote a letter of support hailing him as the "People's Friend" (Nockels, 1935).

Although gradually over the next decade some school programs were reinstituted, the reformers' campaign against the general decline in educational services and the flagrant political/business manipulation of the schools proved unavailing. When help finally came, it was from the outside. In 1945, the National Education Association issued a report criticizing the maladministration and corruption of the Chicago schools (1945); the North Central Association of Colleges and Secondary Schools threatened to withdraw accreditation from the schools unless major reforms were made. As a groundswell of public protest began, the board president and superintendent resigned, the mayor declined to seek an additional term of office, and administrative reforms were instituted (Hancock, undated).

During the era when the labor movement had engaged actively in struggles over educational policy, the civic associations and the labor organizations had been able to affect the direction of the school system. The labor movement's activism was tied to a broader social reform ideology. During the 1930s the CFL's educational goals underwent little change in terms of support for public schooling on a general level, but in the specific political and economic circumstances of the city the organized labor movement demonstrated far less willingness to commit its resources to broad political battles.

Conclusions

The revisionist writers created intensified interest in the history of public education because they advanced a notion of the expansion of schooling that ran directly counter to the conventional view: Education was not expanded in response to popular demand and it was not intended to serve as a democratizing institution. They argued that members of social elites, either upper class or capitalist, depending on the particular theorist, pushed schooling on a reluctant working-class population, which was sullenly suspicious of their motives but unwilling or unable to take concerted, effective action to challenge the proposed mode of schooling. In its specifics, this interpretation does not correspond to the facts of educational development in Chicago. Although the labor movement varied greatly in its commitment to reforming the schools, there was never a pattern of hostility to public education. Further, businessmen were often reluctant to promote increased schooling. Clearly, expanded education did not pose any essential challenges to the stability of the capitalist order, but it could potentially lead to a gap between expectations and reality that could heighten discontent. In addition, businessmen were highly cost-conscious and were hesitant to see education or other social services expand because of the resulting increased tax burden.

What are the implications of the fact that the Chicago pattern was different from the one that, if the revisionist theory has general significance, we would have expected to find? Identifying who supported the schools and why is crucial to the revisionists' analysis because it is their views on these points that strikingly distinguish them from the earlier, more orthodox historians of education. Katz's book, *The Irony of Early School Reform*, was original and provocative because of his assertion that "one dynamic of educational controversy was the attempt of social leaders to impose innovation on a reluctant working class" (1969:86). The revisionists and the corporate liberal theorists describe the upper class as holding decisive power on a practical, but more importantly, also on an ideological level. Working-class restiveness served only to spur the intensified development of agencies of social control, such as the public schools. Only in this very limited sense do the revisionists describe the schools as being the products of popular struggles. The schools were not a *goal* of the working class, but they were an *outcome* of social disruption, however undirected that disruption might have been.

The Chicago experience indicates the working out of a very different process of historical change on several levels. On the first level, the conflicts over the control and content of schooling demonstrate that working-class groups were able to generate an ideology that was in significant respects counter to that held by the dominant elements of the society. The labor movement in Chicago developed a well worked-out set of educational demands that differed both from the educational policy goals of businessmen and from those of many of Chicago's middle-class progressive leaders. The image of a disordered mass of people on the bottom rungs of the society who were basically confused and uncomprehending, and lacked any sense of collective consciousness or clarity about their political strategies, is not borne out by the record of educational controversies in Chicago. The generation of this alternative educational ideology, during periods of working class militancy, was one aspect of building a broad social reform movement that contested business control in a number of arenas and on a number of levels.

Second, Chicago's experience points to the one-sidedness of the revisionists' stress on the ability of the upper class to unilaterally shape social institutions. Not only did the Chicago Federation of Labor enunciate a different educational ideology from that propounded by businessmen in the city, but the labor organization was able to take, in some specific historical circumstances, effective and focused action to support its educational demands. Further, and equally critically, the outcome of struggles was not always a foregone conclusion: The successful mobilization against the Cooley Bill and the platoon schools proposed by Superintendent McAndrew were examples of labor victories. They were very limited and partial victories, as the labor movement at no time possessed the strength to win implementation of its own view of schooling. They do demonstrate, however, that it was far from being the case that even the most powerful of Chicago's businessmen were able to simply mold the schools or other public institutions to their desires; rather, they were forced to take into account the possibility of determined working-class resistance, a resistance that was based on an awareness of the class implications of different policies. The history of educational development in Chicago is a history of struggle, accommodation, compromise and resistance, not of simple elite domination.

Business groups in Chicago were constrained in part because the officially sponsored ideology of the society imposed a framework that could limit their freedom of maneuverability. Chicago's middle-class civic leaders joined the organized labor movement in denouncing the Cooley Bill because it violated elementary precepts of equality in schooling. Thus, although revisionist writers have stressed the ways in which the propagation of elite-sponsored values has undermined any prospects of working-class resistance, there are instances in which striving to put content and meaning into the official ideology has in itself contributed to the generation of popular protests. This process is similar to the one that E. P. Thompson describes in England, when artisans justified their claims to political rights on the grounds of being "free-born Englishmen" and tried to give this notion a political content (1966). A societal emphasis on schooling does not inevitably limit popular struggles; whether it does or not is, broadly speaking, a function of the political context and of factors outside the immediate educational situation.

A third point of difference with the revisionist authors concerns the impact of education itself on people's consciousness. Their analysis is deterministic in assuming that expanded schooling necessarily is effective in fostering elite control; from the capitalists' perspective, increased schooling is at least more problematic than this. Businessmen in Chicago acted in ways that show they were aware of a potential double-edged character to increased schooling. They supported the development of a highly stratified school system that would not have led to the "overeducation" of the children of the working population; further, the stress on moral rather than academic education could serve as a powerful rationale for limiting the actual education received by the majority of working class children. During the Depression, a period of general social turbulence, businessmen responded not by increasing education, but by taking the opportunity to make massive cutbacks in public expenditures. It is hard to find a pattern of business eagerness for increased education, with its presumed socializing power; but there is a pattern of business efforts to control and orient the nature of the education provided in such a way that most children did not receive education beyond that which would be necessary for their likely station in life. Certainly, labor spokespeople argued that businessmen believed that too much education was a dangerous thing.

There is a final level on which I believe that the revisionist or corporate liberal perspective does not allow full exploration of the dynamics of social controversies. Because the social control theorists usually dismiss, implicitly or explicitly, popular protest movements as ineffective and irrelevant, they are precluded from analyzing the conditions under which movements were able to make an impact or under which they reached accommodation and were absorbed into the dominant political process. To assume in advance a pattern of no significant variability is to foreclose the possibility of addressing the question of why social movements arise or decline. In Chicago there were marked changes in the labor movement's social orientation over time; these changes sprang from different political and economic situations, but there is no simple set of reasons for the development of different ideological perspectives in different periods. The question of what historical conditions evoke class-related challenges deserves full exploration, with an awareness that social movements do not grow in a linear fashion but through a series of partial defeats and victories that in turn sometimes spur further conflicts. Rather than assuming the existence of a social system that operates without major cracks or fault lines, researchers should consider the potentially contradictory quality of institutions such as the public schools and should try to specify the varying historical conditions that give rise to passivity or movements for change.

References

BOWLES, SAMUEL
    1972   "Unequal Education and the Reproduction of the Social Divison of Labor." Pp. 36–64, in Martin Carnoy (ed.), Schooling in a Corporate Society. New York: McKay.

BOWLES, SAMUEL, and HERBERT GINTIS
    1976   Schooling in Capitalist America. New York: Basic Books.

CARNOY, MARTIN
    1972   "Introduction." Pp. 1–17, in M. Carnoy (ed.), Schooling in a Corporate Society. New York: McKay.

CHICAGO FEDERATION OF LABOR
    1902   A Report on Public School Fads. An Investigation Made by the Legislative Committee of the CFL. Chicago: Chicago Federation of Labor.

CITY CLUB OF CHICAGO
    1912a   A Report on Vocational Training in Chicago and in Other Cities. Chicago: City Club.
    1912b   "A Report of the Public Education Committee." Bulletin (Dec. 4): 373–83.

CLARK, HANNAH BELLE
    1897   The Public Schools of Chicago. Chicago: University of Chicago.

COMMERCIAL CLUB OF CHICAGO
    1912   Yearbook, 1911–1912. Chicago: Commercial Club.
    1915   Yearbook, 1914–1915. Chicago: Commercial Club.
    Undated   Vocational Schools for Illinois. Chicago: Commercial Club.

COOLEY, EDWIN G.
    Undated   "In Reply to Dr. John Dewey's 'Some Dangers in the Present Movement for Industrial Education.' " Chicago.
    1906   "Public School Education in Morals." Address delivered before the Chicago Principals' Association (September 8).

DEWEY, JOHN
    1915   "Splitting up the School System." New Republic 2:283–84.

EAKINS, DAVID W.
1966   "The Development of Corporate Liberal Policy Research in the United States, 1885–1965." Ph.D. dissertation. Madison: University of Wisconsin.

FIELD, ALEXANDER J.
1974   "Educational Reform and Manufacturing Development in Mid-Nineteenth Century Massachusetts." Ph.D. dissertation. Berkeley: University of California.

FITZPATRICK, JOHN
1923   Letter to William McAndrew. Reprinted in *Federation News*, June 12, 1926.
1928   Speech delivered at meeting of Chicago Teachers Unions, March 2. Chicago: Chicago Teachers Union Papers, Chicago Historical Society.

GOTTFRIED, ALEX
1962   Boss Cermak of Chicago. Seattle: University of Washington.

GREENSTONE, J. DAVID
1970   Labor in American Politics. New York: Vintage.

HANCOCK, MARGARET CAMPBELL
Un-   Interview by Elizabeth Murray. Transcript in possession of Robert J.
dated   Havighurst, University of Chicago.

HERRICK, MARY J.
1971   The Chicago Schools. Beverly Hills: Sage Foundation.

HOBSBAWM, ERIC J.
1971   "Class Consciousness in History." Pp. 5–21 in I. Meszaros (ed.), Aspects of History and Class Consciousness. London: Routledge and Kegan Paul.

ILLINOIS STATE FEDERATION OF LABOR
1914   Report of the Committee on Vocational Education to the Illinois State Federation of Labor. Thirty-Second Annual Proceedings: 45–54.
1915   Thirty-Third Annual Proceedings.

KARIER, CLARENCE J., PAUL VIOLAS, and JOEL SPRING (eds.)
1973   Roots of Crisis. Chicago: Rand-McNally.

KATZ, MICHAEL B.
1968   The Irony of Early School Reform. Cambridge: Harvard University.
1971   Class, Bureaucracy and School. New York: Praeger.

KEISER, JOHN HOWARD
1965   "John Fitzpatrick and Progressive Unionism, 1915–1925." Ph.D. dissertation. Evanson, Ill.: Northwestern University.

KOLKO, GABRIEL
1963   The Triumph of Conservatism: A Reinterpretation of American History, 1900–1916. New York: Macmillan.
1972   "The Decline of American Radicalism in the Twentieth Century." Pp. 457–70, in Milton Mankoff (ed.), The Poverty of Progress. New York: Holt, Rinehart and Winston.

LEVIT, MARTIN
   1947   "The Chicago Citizens Schools Committee." Ph.D. dissertation. Chicago: University of Chicago.
LONDON, STEPHEN D.
   1968   "Business and the Chicago Public School System, 1890–1966." Ph.D. dissertation. Chicago: University of Chicago.
MCANDREW, WILLIAM
   1926   "What Public Schools Are For." Woman's City Club Bulletin. 15:197–200.
MARCH, HERBERT
   1970   Interview by Elizabeth Balanoff (November 16). Roosevelt University Oral History Project. Chicago: Roosevelt University.
MERCHANTS CLUB OF CHICAGO
   1901   "Commercial High Schools." Pp. 99–130, in Season of 1900–1901. (Meeting of February 9). Chicago: Merchants Club.
MILES, H. E.
   1911   "How the Obligation to Provide Industrial Education Shall be Met." Extracts of Addresses delivered at Fifth Annual Convention of the National Society for the Promotion of Industrial Education. Chicago: Victor Olander Papers, Chicago Historical Society.
   1913   "What I Am Trying to Do." World's Work. 26:667–73.
NATIONAL EDUCATION ASSOCIATION
   1945   Certain Personnel Practices in the Chicago Public Schools. Washington, D.C.: National Education Association.
NEWELL, BARBARA
   1961   Chicago and the Labor Movement. Urbana: University of Illinois.
NOCKELS, EDWARD N.
   1935   Letter to Edward Kelly (March 23). Chicago: John Fitzpatrick Papers, Chicago Historical Society.
RADOSH, RONALD
   1969   American Labor and United States Foreign Policy. New York: Random House.
SARGENT, FRED W.
   1933   "The Taxpayer Takes Charge." Saturday Evening Post. 205–21.
SPRING, JOEL
   1972   Education and the Rise of the Corporate State. Boston: Beacon.
THOMPSON, E. P.
   1966   The Making of the English Working Class. New York: Vintage.
WEINSTEIN, JAMES
   1968   The Corporate Ideal in the Liberal State, 1900–1918. Boston: Beacon.
WRIGLEY, JULIA
   1977   "Social Conflicts and the Public Schools: The Politics of Education in Chicago." Ph.D. dissertation. Madison: University of Wisconsin.

7 The Emergence of Socialist Political Culture Among Finnish Immigrants in Minnesota Mining Communities

Kathleen M. Blee
Al Gedicks
University of Wisconsin–Madison

*The historical materialist leaves it to others to be
drained by the whore called "Once upon a time" in
historicism's bordello. He remains in control of his
powers, man enough to blast open the continuum of
history.*—Walter Benjamin, "Theses on the
Philosophy of History, XVI"

The goal of the Finnish socialist movement in America was "to awaken ourselves to the task before us—through word of mouth and writings, to promote the liberation of the working class" (Pinola 1957). Through the development of socialist halls, consumer cooperatives, the Work People's College, immigrant newspapers, and numerous other working class political institutions, Finnish-American radicals projected "miniature, if incomplete, models of the commonwealth toward which so many immigrant eyes were turned" (Kolehmainen 1947:66). Under what conditions does a working-class political culture provide an organizing framework for class consciousness and a challenge to capitalist class hegemony?

The associations and institutions of Finnish working class culture forged in the temperance movement, socialist halls, cooperative societies, and mutual aid societies represented a socialist political culture able both to shield the working class from the degradation of industrial capitalism and to pose an alternative vision of human relations within a socialist society. By tracing the creation and reproduction of the major institutional vehicles of working-class culture within the Finnish immigrant communities, we can analyze the contradictory dynamics that caused one of the most significant socialist political cultures to emerge and decline in the industrial United States.

Antonio Gramsci, the Italian communist and political theorist, was

This article is a collaborative effort that draws on the research of the authors' separate dissertations on immigrant families and Finnish radicalism. Members of the Social Organization Training Program at the University of Wisconsin made invaluable comments and criticisms on earlier drafts of this paper. Partial support for this research came from the NIMH-funded Center for Social Organization Studies, the Graduate School fellowship of the University of Wisconsin, and the Small Grants Awards of the Sociology Department at the University of Wisconsin.

one of the first to suggest that the establishment of socialist political culture has the most far-reaching consequences for any social movement which attempts to overturn one social order and replace it with an opposing one. Gramsci built on the emphasis that Lenin gave to the political class struggle and argued that the struggle for "hegemony" was a critical aspect of the class struggle in advanced capitalist societies (Boggs 1972:30–31). Although revolutionary upsurges might weaken the power of the state, this weakness is but momentary, for behind the state stands "a robust structure of civil society" that maintains capitalist class hegemony much more through consent than coercion (Gramsci 1971). For revolutionary movements to succeed under such circumstances, workers must not only see the internal contradictions of capitalism. They must simultaneously understand their own strength, responsibility, value, and creativity—which is the critical role of socialist political culture in the Gramscian revolutionary strategy.

To probe the meanings and values of a working-class culture it is more valuable to scrutinize elements of concrete existence such as the organization of family life, the structure of leisure time, and the organization of political beliefs than to analyze proletarian art or language (Williams 1961; 1966). In this sense, working-class culture reflects not only its collective understandings but also the organization of the collective awareness necessary to resist the social relations of capitalist society. This aspect of working-class culture—the cultural organization of human experience both to resist the intrusion of the social relations of capitalism and to provide a vehicle for challenging the institutions and social relations of capitalist society—has been labeled the "proletarian public sphere" by Negt and Kluge (Knödler-Bunte 1975); we call it a "socialist political culture."

The restoration of our historical consciousness about Finnish-American cultural politics provides a vantage point to assess the present and future. Rather than viewing Finnish-American radicals as having "adapted" or becoming moderate,

> one must view the Finnish-American radical movement in all its factions and phases . . . as a set of shifting strategies by which a sizeable element of the Finnish immigrant population believed it could, in cooperation with other groups, alter the basic character of the American political and industrial system, to make those systems conform to the expectations the immigrants had when they left Finland for America (Karni 1975:383–84).

Anticlericalism and the Rise of Labor Radicalism

During the formative period of Finnish-American socialism (1904–1914), a Finnish church and temperance movement leader observed that the ideas of socialism:

sank into us like hot grease into dry leather. Before long the whole Finnish immigrant population from East to West had gotten such powerful impressions from this doctrine that a great many of us had our heads literally swimming (cited in Kangas 1962:160).

Why had so many Finnish immigrants turned from organized religion to socialism after they arrived in America? Hoglund (1977) has suggested that the Finnish Lutheran State Church, bound by a puritanical theology, failed to develop viable auxiliary social policies that could inspire an allegiance to the church among landless rural workers. During most of the nineteenth century, Finnish Lutheran clergy wielded enormous authority, power, and influence in rural areas. As representatives of the official state church, the clergy had ultimate authority over marriage through its confirmation schools. To obtain a passport, a positive character reference was necessary from the local pastor. To maintain this oppressive establishment, the church exacted taxes from the peasantry.

The influence of the Finnish Lutheran State Church began to diminish in the 1860s when Finnish nationalists demanded that control of the educational system be removed from the church. Although church schools gave instruction in the Finnish language, nationalist leaders argued that a modern social order required instruction beyond religious subjects. By the middle of the 1880s most clergymen declared that socialism was a "godless heresy" and stayed aloof from the social concerns of the Finnish labor movement. The refusal of the church to support popular opposition to the oppressive actions of the Russian government in Finland between 1899 and 1905 further alienated the church from most workers (Hoglund 1977:26). Anticlericalism became especially strong among the rural emigrants when the church condemned emigration as a sign of moral weakness and injurious to the "moral health" of the nation (Hoglund 1975:41).

These anticlerical attitudes persisted among immigrants as the Suomi Synod became established in the United States and regarded itself as the American daughter of the Finnish church (Ollila 1963). The relative weakness of organized religion created a vacuum in the social life of Finnish immigrants that was filled by community centers such as saloons, boarding houses, and, later, the temperance movement.

Saloon Culture and the Temperance Movement

Until the early twentieth century, many iron mining towns in the Mesabi range were populated by male immigrants whose families remained in Europe. In 1895, for example, 655 men and 109 women lived in Eveleth. In the same year, Hibbing had 896 men and 189 women; Virginia had 2664 men and 983 women. Smaller villages and towns on the Minnesota mining frontier had even more extreme imbalances in the ratio of men to women (Minnesota Bureau of the Census 1895).

The settlement of large numbers of immigrant men without families in the Mesabi range towns created a social milieu based on transiency, boarding houses, and the saloon. Many early immigrants intended either to return to Finland with savings amassed in the mines or to send for their families and establish permanent residence in the United States. In fact, more than one-third of the Finnish emigrants returned to Finland (Hoglund 1960:8). Few had the means or inclination to purchase houses or to make organizational commitments in the mining communities. The alienation of large numbers of Finns from organized religion as well as the severance of family life during emigration left a social and cultural void in the associational life of immigrants.

Finnish boarding houses and saloons were critical in the preservation of an ethnic identity among immigrants because they provided a common meeting ground for working-class Finns from geographically dispersed mines. Without the social network and community of church or family life, the boarding houses and saloons served as important, if fragile, carriers of a working-class ethnic culture. Although organized religion tried to forge alliances between working-class and middle-class Finns, the saloons and boarding houses brought together immigrants of a similar class, ethnic background, and, often, family situation.

As Finnish immigrant communities were gradually transformed from transient frontier towns with single male workers to more stable communities with family units, the ethnic community entered a new stage of organization. The immigration of the wives and children of the Finns meant the decline of ethnic boarding houses and the increase of distinct family dwellings, and provoked a clash between the associational life of the saloon and the ties of family and kinship. As the conflict between the saloon culture and the ties of family deepened, newly arrived Finnish women became increasingly concerned with the problem of alcoholism in the Finnish community and a temperance movement gained momentum. Women represented a large proportion, and sometimes the majority, of members in local temperance societies.

From the beginning, these temperance societies reflected a wide variation of political and social values. Many Lutheran clergy seized on the temperance issue as a way to control the social behavior of immigrants who had left the church. Business leaders and the middle class championed temperance to curb the unruly behavior of the working class. Immigrant workers, building on the fledging notions of collectivism and ethnic solidarity established in the saloons and boarding houses, entered into the temperance movement to seek the transformation of those social conditions which produced alcoholism. Socialists were advised by their leaders to remain within the temperance clubs and gain control of them (Ross 1977:71).

The temperance movement in Finnish immigrant communities of the Mesabi range represented less a coherent antisaloon ideology than a formative stage in the development of an organizational locus for Finnish immigrant culture. The working-class cultural life of the saloons could not survive the complexities of family life and the emergence of a middle class of shopkeepers, managers, and professionals in the mining communities; saloons were incapable of providing a stable forum for working-class political action or of integrating women and children into community life. Temperance societies, however, provided an institutional framework within which ethnic working-class culture and values could be preserved. Some of the earliest victories of Finnish labor organizations were made possible through union organizing under the umbrella of temperance societies since only a highly developed labor union could be exposed to the repression of the mining corporations (Ross 1977:97).

The temperance societies not only protected labor organizers against company repression, but frequently furnished the infrastructure for the preservation of ethnic identity in the "Finn halls" (Kolehmainen 1942). The Finn halls became the center of the cultural, associational and political life of Finnish immigrants. The halls were meeting places for a variety of clubs, religious associations, and mutual aid groups as well as a center for dances, bands, choirs, speakers clubs, drama groups, and festivals. By 1900 over 150 temperance societies embraced a membership estimated at from 6,500 to 10,000.

While the temperance movement provided both a strong sense of ethnic and community identification and experience in organization and collective action among working-class Finns, the lack of a coherent political ideology and the amorphous organizational structure of temperance societies meant that they were not able to organize the community around the concerns of an increasingly sophisticated working class. Within a year after the 1906 founding convention of the Finnish Socialist Federation, the president of the National Temperance Brotherhood reported that numerous chapters of the temperance movement were feuding internally over the issue of socialism. In fact, many new socialist chapters were simply old temperance societies in which socialists had gained a majority. Many other socialist chapters were formed by splinter groups of dissatisfied working-class temperance supporters. Although socialism did not cause a direct schism within the temperance movement, the temperance societies gradually were transformed into socialist "workers' clubs" or, to a lesser extent, into organizations of the Lutheran church.

The development of temperance societies among Finnish immigrants to the Mesabi range can be understood as a stage in the development of a stable class-conscious working-class movement. Just as the temperance societies reflected a need for ethnic organization no longer possible through saloons and boarding houses, the socialist movement reflected the need for an organizational structure that would address the concerns of an ethnic working class. The development of a Finnish middle class with little sympathy for the goals of the working-class Finns meant that ethnic solidarity and ethnic cultural institutions could not alone sustain the immigrant working class. The political skills and understanding of organized action that were developed by the working class in the temperance movement were later transferred to socialist organizations. It is in this sense that Hoglund comments, "the conversion [to socialism] via the temperance arena, was indeed common" (1977:36).

Mutual Aid Societies

The intense debate within the temperance movement between church people and the more social reform–oriented workers was reflected in yet another process of development of Finnish associational life. In 1890 several Finnish workers met in Brooklyn, New York, to form the Imatra Aid Society. The Imatra society defined its purpose as "advancing the material and spiritual position of Finns" and promoting among members "civilized conduct and avoiding drunkenness" (Sulkanen 1951:56, cited in Ross 1977:30). To achieve its goals the Imatra society set up a modest health insurance program, helped immigrants to find employment, and taught classes on various subjects. Membership in these societies was open to workers, tradespeople, and businesspeople. These clubs, which promoted ethnic solidarity more than interethnic socialist consciousness, soon spread throughout the Finnish immigrant communities of the Mesabi range of northern Minnesota. Paradoxically, despite their initial intentions, the mutual aid clubs encouraged a collective definition of ethnic culture and social life and awakened an interest in labor issues and social reform. The social practice of coming together as equals to achieve collectively defined goals was a tremendous barrier against the bourgeois ideology of individualism which sought to keep workers separated from each other and incapable of forming combinations.

By 1903 at a meeting in Gardner, Massachusetts, a league of socialist workers' clubs, known as the Imatra Worker's League was founded. The new Imatra League represented a transition between mutual aid associations and purely socialist organizations. The leftist orientation of the new Imatra Worker's League soon found favor among the more class-conscious elements within the mutual aid societies. Supporters of the Imatra Worker's League organized a meeting in 1904 to establish a national organization affirming social democratic principles.[1] Although no national organization emerged from this meeting, a resolution was passed that urged Finnish workers' societies to join the American Socialist Party through state organizations as a means of gaining importance and influence in the American labor movement. By 1908 there were 23,697 members of the Imatra movement and almost all of these had become Marxian in orientation (Ollila 1975:29).

The leftward shift of the mutal aid societies set in motion a similar shift among members of temperance societies. By the turn of the century, Finnish immigrant workers had established a network of ethnic institutions that provided members with educational resources, leadership training, and collective support for efforts to improve the situation of Finnish working people. At the same time, many of these efforts brought Finnish immigrants into contact with the larger American working class and thus helped to break down their ethnic exclusiveness.

The Finnish Socialist Federation and the 1907 Strike

The culmination of the first phase in the self-emancipatory activity of the Finnish-American socialist movement came at the socialist federating convention in Hibbing, Minnesota, in August 1906. The Finnish Socialist Federation (FSF) that emerged from this convention was the first, and soon the largest, of the foreign-language federations in the American Socialist Party. The first major campaign of the Finnish-American socialists took place the following year when Finnish socialists in the Western Federation of Miners led a multiethnic organizing drive among striking miners on the Mesabi range.

The decisive split between the conservative Finnish nationalists and the radical Finnish internationalists came during this important strike when Finnish merchants on the Mesabi range, bowing to pressure from the mining companies, refused credit to striking miners. Conservative Finnish-American church leaders soon joined the Finnish-American business community and the mining companies in condemning the role of Finnish socialists in the strike.

In the aftermath of the 1907 strike, the Oliver Mining Company de-

---

[1] Following the example of the German Marxists at the Erfurt Congress in 1891, the Finnish Labor Party changed its name to the Finnish Social Democratic Party in 1903. The orientation of Finnish-American social democratic leaders was toward working within existing conservative unions such as the American Federation of Labor and through participation in electoral politics through the American Socialist Party.

veloped the infamous blacklist and systematically denied Finns reemployment, regardless of political affiliation. Oliver's repression forced over 1,200 Finnish workers out of their major source of employment in northern Minnesota. According to an Oliver historian, the strike created not only the blacklist, but also an extensive labor espionage system. This espionage system employed spies from all ethnic groups who reported regularly the names of workers who advocated unionism or who supported radical Finnish, Slavic, or Italian newspapers (Karni 1977:78).

As in many of the earlier Finnish-led strikes in the mining areas, women and children were active in support demonstrations and picket duty (Karni 1977). The repression directed against the Finns was therefore also directed against their families and the community in general. The 1907 strike marks a turning point in the development of a socialist political culture among Finnish immigrant workers. In the eyes of the Finnish-American working class, the conservative Finnish community had betrayed the cause of the workers by ignoring the gross injustices in the mining towns and siding with the mine owners. After the 1907 strike the conflict between Finnish nationalism and socialism within the temperance and mutual aid societies was superseded by the conflict over whether to support or oppose the American cultural, economic, and political status quo.

Socialist Halls, Newspapers, Educational Institutions, and the Creation of a Socialist Political Culture

The repression following the 1907 strike did not slow the growth of radicalism among the Finns. On the contrary, the leadership provided by Finnish radicals succeeded in enlisting for the first time many Finnish-American workers into the ranks of American labor radicalism. Socialist strength on the Mesabi range increased dramatically between 1908 and 1910.

How could the blacklisted Finns not only survive the repression, but actually increase their political influence in the community? The answer must be sought in the network of Finnish cultural institutions that shielded the radicals from repression while providing them with a means to deepen and affirm their implacable opposition to capitalist society. One historian of the immigrant communities on the Mesabi range described these halls as "a total way of life" for the Finnish radicals (Berman 1964:22–3):

> At the clubs they read their literature, discussed their problems, heard lectures, put on plays, sang, danced, flirted, romanced, were married, celebrated the birth of their children, had parties, became ill, died and began the procession to the cemetery. At the halls the miner was able, for a while,

to forget his back-breaking toil and his problems of loneliness in what seemed to him a hostile world. He met his own people, reminisced about the homeland, spoke of aspirations and vented his hostility against a system which he thought prematurely robbed him of his manhood.

Finnish-American radicals were successful in their attempt to create this total way of life, or socialist political culture, because the socialist halls "became the effective promoters of a transference to the American scene of a cultural tradition that originated in Finland and took root in America" (Ross 1977:70). Another participant who grew up in the Finnish socialist halls summarizes the legacy that the radical Finns gave to their children and grandchildren (Lee 1978:49):

> It was a legacy rich in culture—in appreciation of what the human spirit can accomplish under the umbrella of a group, a group that believes in socialism and also of individual responsibility. It was a legacy that culture was not for the rich only—that workers are entitled to have beauty around them as well as better wages and working conditions. It was, if you will, a legacy of the renaissance man with a socialist or communist base—the ability to mentally, spiritually, and physically understand the politics of socialism and its hope for the future.

The hegemonic position of this socialist political culture was maintained through the chapters of the FSF and through the socialist press, which grew to three daily newspapers with a combined circulation of over 25,000. Educational institutions also played an important role in the creation and reproduction of this socialist political culture. According to Ollila, "socialist children attended their own Sunday School and summer schools where they memorized A. B. Makela's primer which included a 'Socialist Child's Ten Commandments'" (1977:88). Within four months after the founding of the FSF in 1906, socialists decided to found a "Work People's College" in Minnesota because "lack of knowledge is our worst enemy" (Ollila 1977:98).

The Work People's College became an ethnic institution that continually created the conditions for Finnish workers to adapt Finnish traditions to the American political context. Although a primary task of Work People's College was to teach Finnish immigrants English, it was also an institution that nurtured a future generation of socialist newspaper editors, teachers, and agitators. Seen from this perspective, it can be argued that the very success of the Finnish-American radical movement in creating institutions that simultaneously preserved Old World values and challenged the hegemony of the social relations of capitalist society created the conditions for the erosion of a specifically ethnic radicalism.

The commitment of Finnish-American radicals to the vision of a communal society required that they abandon their ethnic exclusivity and join with other ethnic groups to create a socialist society on an international scale. Finnish socialists were active in spreading the Slavic socialist newspaper among their Slavic fellow-miners and helped the Slavs establish a few Slavic socialist clubs on the Mesabi range. Finnish and Slavic socialist immigrants used the same Finnish socialist halls for their meetings, celebrated May Day together, and cooperated in electoral campaigns in many range towns.

Once Finnish socialists joined with other workers for their mutual benefit, they had to overcome the resistance of the Socialist Party to allow the FSF to affiliate as a national federation. The reluctance of the Socialist Party to accept the Finns on their own terms resulted from a view that was shared by the leadership of both the AFL and the American Socialist Party. Both thought that the recent immigrants were backward, passive, and poor material for either trade union or socialist organization (Leinenweber 1968:3). The first national convention of the FSF had emphasized that "our movement can only become significant and influence the development of socialism in this country by affiliation with the Socialist Party," and advised that no obstacles set up by the party should be allowed to stand in the way (Wasastjerna 1957:225). In 1906 the National Executive Committee of the American Socialist Party allowed the FSF to affiliate in exchange for dues to the national with no voting privileges. The Finnish locals then joined their respective state socialist parties to gain the vote indirectly, while maintaining their distinctive national organization.

The inability of Finnish-American radicals to reproduce this socialist political culture at the level of the entire society should not detract from the success of their culture in challenging the hegemony of capitalist society. The success of this socialist political culture in capturing the imagination and loyalty of Finnish immigrant workers was nowhere more apparent than in Finnish-American opposition to World War One.

Americanization, Repression, and Finnish Opposition to the War

In June 1916, a strike swept the 75-mile length of the Mesabi Iron Range. The strikers' major demand was the elimination of the contract system in which miners were paid for the amount of ore produced rather than for their labor time. This piecework penalized miners who worked hard on lean veins of ore. Under the contract system, miners were forced to pay bribes to the mining captains for choice mining locations and were often subject to arbitrary reductions in wages when their production increased. The system of contracted wages was particularly devastating to miners with families to support; they could not compete with the bribes of single miners and were often forced to offer their wives and daughters to mining captains in exchange for choice locations in the mines. In addition, the arbitrary fluctuations in contract rates and wage deductions made it difficult to support a wife and children on a miner's pay.

When miners walked off their jobs in protest against the low pay, the Finnish socialist halls became strike headquarters for many local communities, although, unlike during the 1907 strike, the Finns were not the largest ethnic group. A network of institutions representing the various ethnic groups had grown up since 1907 around the principles of labor unionism. These ethnic institutions became the vehicle for labor organizing after the mining companies had smashed the regional union movement during the 1907 strike and blacklisted its leaders and supporters. Despite the defeat of the miners after the 1907 strike, at least one newspaper was forced to admit that the Western Federation of Miners was still alive on the range in 1910 and that "a substantial number of the miners had maintained their membership since 1907, paying dues to the International Office" (Pinola 1957:72). In addition, the AFL's refusal to organize miners on the Mesabi and the failure of the WFM in the Michigan Copper Country strike of 1913 led the Finnish socialists to enlist the support of the Industrial Workers of the World (IWW or "Wobblies") after the miners had shut down all mines (Foner 1965:493).

In contrast to the pro–mining company stance of small businessmen during the 1907 strike, by 1916 the inequitable tax burden borne by small businessmen had made them openly antagonistic toward the mining companies (Berman 1964:52). Moreover, the small businessman depended on the miners for political support and profits (Sofchalk 1971:230). The growth of the immigrant communities on the Mesabi range had enabled some immigrants to become storekeepers while retaining their allegiance to the miners.[2] These storekeepers extended credit to the strikers until the Oliver Mining Company pressured wholesale houses in Duluth to stop the flow of credit to the range retailers (*The Virginian Daily* 1916:1). The mayors and local officials of Hibbing, Chisolm, Virginia, and Aurora also sympathized with the strikers (Berman 1964:52).

In the face of widespread public support for the strike, the right-wing Finnish newspaper of Duluth (*Paivalehti*) blamed the strike on "black"

---

[2] Robert Michels notes that this process of the "embourgeoisement of certain strata of the working class party" is "a necessary characteristic of every movement towards emancipation," and is paralleled "by the constitution of a petty bourgeoisie of strongly proletarian characteristics, itself also developed from below upwards, itself also an accessory phenomenon of the struggle of the organized workers for social emancipation, but which takes place outside the various forms of socialist organization" (1962:266).

(*mustat*) southern and eastern European immigrants who in their ignorance had been seduced by the IWW (Ollila 1977:47). The Oliver Mining Company refused to bargain with the miners and brought in 1,000 deputized armed guards to terrorize the immigrant communities. The U.S. Commission of Industrial Relations depicted the importation of deputized thugs to break the strike and stated that "the miners of Minnesota and their families face want and suffering and endure the abuse and violence of a private army of gunmen."

The repression against miners and their families during the 1916 strike provided the spark for the IWW lumberjacks' strike in Virginia, Minnesota, from late December 1916 through January 1917. Many striking lumberjacks were blacklisted iron miners from the Mesabi range; over half of the 4,000 workers were Finns. The organizing activities of the IWW and their support among the various ethnic groups prompted the introduction of an IWW control bill in the Minnesota state legislature in March 1917.[3] Although the bill failed to pass, it was clear that public officials considered continued labor agitation by the IWW as treason. The political stage was being set for the use of a variety of legal and illegal means, from outright repression to the well-organized "loyalty" movement, to crush the labor movement of northern Minnesota and its institutional supports in various ethnic communities.

Although opposition to the war had been widespread in the "isolationist" Midwest, "among the Finns opposition to the war was exceptionally widespread, and persisted after the U. S. declaration of war on Germany" (Ross 1977:145). After the break with Social Democrats within the FSF over the issue of industrial versus craft unionism, Finnish radicals in Minnesota promoted industrial unionism through the Duluth Work People's College and through the newspaper *Socialisti*. By 1916 the supporters of the IWW succeeded in taking control of the paper and renamed it *Industrialisti*. This new voice of the IWW was "strongly opposed to the war and was a militant voice of labor unrest for the thousands of Finns working in Mesabi mines and the northern Minnesota logging industry" (Ross 1977:146).

Shortly after America entered World War One in April 1917, Minnesota established a Commission of Public Safety (MCPS). Its principal objective was to smash the IWW movement in northern Minnesota. When many IWW Finns decided not to register for the draft and to call another strike in the iron mines, over 200 were arrested by U.S. Attorney Alfred Jaques during the summer of 1917. The MCPS went even further in their

---

[3] For a detailed discussion of the repression of the Industrial Workers of the World (IWW) and the Americanization movement after the 1916 Mesabi Range strike, see Berman (1964), Ollila (1976), and Ross (1977).

crackdown on the IWW and successfully pressured the federal Department of Justice to raid the IWW headquarters throughout the United States, arrest and indict the leaders, and bring them to trial for violating the criminal conspiracy code (Dowell 1936:186). Among the 166 IWW leaders who were convicted of sabotage and conspiracy to obstruct the war were the two Finnish-American editors of *Industrialisti.*

By encouraging a wave of unofficial "red-baiting" by "patriots," the MPSC made an example out of the Finnish supporters of the IWW. The MPSC even went so far as to justify the invasion and destruction of the Finnish socialist halls on the grounds of public sentiment, noting that:

> The temper and sentiment of the people is good. The wiping out of the IWW headquarters ... while theoretically a lawless act, is generally approved of and is more in line with public sentiment than the course pursued with reference to such headquarters by municipal officials (Prince 1917; cited in Berman 1964:59).

Support for continued labor militance among the southern and eastern European ethnic groups was considerably weakened as a result of the repression and the "industrial Americanization" drive of the Committee for Immigrants in America, which encouraged employers to recognize "the need for a better understanding of and an improvement in the conditions of the immigrants" (Hartmann 1948:165). When the Oliver Mining Company announced a 10 percent wage increase after the 1916 strike and set up an improved labor spy system, most of the foreign-born mine workers refrained from participating in further labor agitation for the duration of the war. Within a year after the 1916 strike, a special agent for the MPSC could report that two prominent Slav leaders "of the big Slav lodge can keep the Slavonian people of the state in line" (cited in Ollila 1977:42). While the combination of these carrot-and-stick measures effectively secured labor peace in northern Minnesota, it was not the end of the state's efforts to deal with widespread opposition to the draft.

At the request of the Wilson administration, a number of prominent Finnish-Americans were asked to develop a "loyalty movement" among Finnish-Americans (Ross 1977:145). In contrast to the open repression of the MPSC, the leaders of the Finnish-American Loyalty League favored indoctrinating prowar sentiments within the ranks of the Finnish-American community. This approach was in accord with the method devised by George Creel, director of the National Committee on Public Information. The assumption behind the committee's work was that support for the war and the capitalist system was not likely to be spontaneous among immigrants and labor union members.

These loyalty campaigns were carried out among 14 nationalities in northern Minnesota. Far from being a spontaneous outburst of enthusiasm for the war effort, as Clarke Chambers (1963) has suggested, the loyalty movement was a well-orchestrated effort that was initiated at the highest levels of government as part of the U.S. mobilization for war. With the effective suppression of immigrant radicals in northern Minnesota, the Finnish-American Loyalty League concentrated its efforts on securing loyalty pledges from the church conservatives and the temperance movement.

The combination of the repression of the IWW Finns and the Americanization campaigns devastated the revolutionary industrial unionist movement of northern Minnesota. The arrests of Finnish IWW leaders and the vigilante raids on Finnish socialist halls frightened many potential IWW supporters among southern and eastern European immigrants. Slovenian socialists who had been IWW supporters during the 1916 strike did not participate in antiwar agitation because they hoped that the war would create a South-Slavic Federation in Europe (Berman 1964:60). The interethnic labor solidarity forged in the heat of the 1916 strike collapsed as immigrant miners concluded that "trade union activity of any kind would bring down the wrath of the government as well as the mining companies on their heads" (Berman 1964:59). With their political allies in the immigrant community either repressed or coopted, Finnish radicals exhausted their energies and resources defending themselves from the repression. According to Ollila, "the movement became orthodox in its industrial union ideology, but its life style and class morality better reflected typical non-revolutionary working class values and practice" (1977:50).

The Finnish Cooperative Movement

With the repression of the interethnic labor movement and the migration of blacklisted Finns to the interior farmlands of northern Minnesota, the arena of socialist political culture shifted from socialist halls to the cooperative movement. The period of wartime repression forced the Finnish radical movement to insulate its cultural institutions from state intervention. This insulation, in turn, precluded the constant exchange between the interethnic labor politics and cultural organizations that had been the lifeblood of Finnish socialist political culture. The radical political culture of the Finns turned inward—toward intraethnic solidarity and the creation of cooperatives that could shield the Finns from the vagaries of the capitalist marketplace and the capitalist state. The decline of Finnish-American socialist culture as a significant force in American labor politics can be seen in the dynamics of the cooperative movement of the 1920s and 1930s.

The Finnish cooperative movement grew out of a need to protect Finns on farms and in mining communities from overcharging by retail merchants and agricultural middlemen and from retaliation by local shop-keepers during industrial conflicts. The 1916 strike and the movement of Finns from mining towns to agricultural communities before and after the strike was a major impetus to the formation of a broad Finnish cooperative system. By 1917 there were 65 cooperatives in the Minnesota–Wisconsin–Michigan region; of these, 19 coops organized a joint buying circle, the Cooperative Central Exchange (CCE) in July 1917. The formation of the CCE was primarily guided by the ideology of the FSF and the Tyomies Society to promote "production for use, instead of for profit" (Jokinen 1953:118). Although many of the more conservative or nonpolitical cooperatives were initially leary of the CCE's radical philosophy, they turned to the CCE for management assistance during the severe crisis of deflation in 1920–1922. By 1926, the CCE had 74 member organizations, annual sales in excess of $1 million, and a monthly magazine, the *Co-operative Pyramid Builder*.

The success of the CCE in offering financial assistance and managerial expertise to nonsocialist cooperatives throughout the 1920s broadened the base of the organized cooperative movement in the Finnish communities of the Mesabi range, but left the political allegiances of "cooperators" unresolved. With the triumph of the Bolshevik Revolution in Russia and the defeat of a proletarian revolution in Finland the debate over tactics in the working-class movement raged within the FSF (Kostiainen 1977:232). In 1920 the FSF withdrew from the American Socialist Party and in 1922 joined the Worker's Party of America (WPA), a united front of the Communist International. By 1924, the Finns represented 40 percent of the membership of the WPA.

Although the FSF controlled much of the organized cooperative movement in Minnesota by the mid-1920s, the political ideology of co-operatism and the place of cooperatives in the Finnish working-class movement had not been resolved. Sections of the Finnish community, particularly church groups, remained aloof or even hostile to the idea of co-operatives; squabbles between radicals and conservatives within individual stores mounted; and CCE leaders fought over the question of neutrality versus political affiliation.

Throughout the latter half of the 1920s, relations between communists and politically neutral "cooperators" within the cooperative movement continued to deteriorate. By 1925 the Communist International's policy of "Bolshevization"—the abolition of all communist clubs and organizations—had forced the FSF to withdraw as a foreign-language affiliate of the WPA, over the opposition of many radical Finns who feared the loss of control over newspapers, halls, theaters, and cooperatives run by the FSF (Karni, 1975). The Sixth Congress of the Communist International in 1928 dealt another blow to the radical Finns in the cooperative movement by arguing that "working class co-operative organizations under capitalism are doomed to play a minor role and in the general environment of the capitalist system not infrequently degenerate into mere appendages of capitalism" unless strictly controlled by party members (Karni 1975:292–93).

The anti-WPA sentiment generated among both radical and conservative Finns by the policies of the Communist International culminated in 1929 when the WPA requested a $5,000 loan from the CCE and a stipend of 1 percent of annual sales of the CCE to be arranged through the WPA faction of the CCE. Although the CCE had donated funds to political and labor causes in the past, the WPA request touched off an intense debate over the political allegiances of the cooperatives and the relationship of radical working-class Finns to the WPA. This debate resulted in a split between the WPA and the CCE. The remaining Finnish members of the WPA set up a shortlived competing wholesale cooperative, the Worker's and Farmer's Unity Alliance, while the CCE moved in an increasingly conservative direction. Throughout the 1930s, the cooperatives established cultural clubs, youth leagues, and courses to compete with the Communists' cultural organizations (Karni 1975). In fact, Karni suggests that "the cooperative goal [of the 1930s] which by and large was realized, was to wean the Finns of the Great Lakes region away from communism . . . in effect [the cooperative movement] 'de-radicalized' most of the Finnish-American working class" (1975:4). By 1936 most of the cooperative clubs were housed in the old socialist halls, replacing the socialist perspective of early Finnish culture with the consumer-oriented view of the cooperatives. The cooperative movement no longer preached the message of class struggle and labor agitation; the enemy was now seen as middlemen and price gougers who could be defeated with quality merchandise and consumer control over the economic process.

The isolation of the Finnish socialist culture within the ethnic culture of the cooperative movement, the lack of continual interaction between rural cooperatives and the working-class movement of the mines and camps, and the internal struggles within the radical Finnish community all contributed to the depoliticization of the cooperatives and the decline of Finnish socialist political culture. As the Finns became increasingly isolated from the multiethnic working-class movement, the cultural institutions of Finnish society were used less to promote a socialist vision than to preserve ethnic identity and associational life, an ethnic culture that was quickly eroded by the assimilation pressures of the post-Depression era.

Summary and Conclusions

Our major concern has been to determine the extent to which the associations and institutions of Finnish working-class culture represented the emergence of a socialist political culture that could resist the intrusion of the social relations of capitalism while providing a weapon with which to challenge the hegemony of capitalist society. One of the major dilemmas of revolutionary movements arises whenever people are called upon to destroy one set of institutional arrangements in society before the new institutions become a source of support and further revolutionary transformation. Finnish-American radicals saw the importance of preserving Finnish cultural traditions at the same time that they transformed this culture into a weapon in the struggle for hegemony in capitalist America.

While Finnish radicals preserved their ethnic identity, they continually came in contact with the larger American working-class movement through the development of a variety of Finnish cultural and political institutions. Finnish participation in labor struggles and radical politics ruled out the possibility of developing an exclusively ethnic radicalism. On the other hand, as the foundations of Finnish socialist political culture in the ethnic institutions came under increasing attack from both the right and the left, Finnish radicals retreated from the cutting edge of American labor radicalism.

The right wing aimed its attack at the socialist dimension of Finnish culture while the left wing attacked the ethnic dimension of Finnish socialist culture. The right-wing attacks on the Finnish socialists came in open repression by the Minnesota Public Safety Commission, the Oliver Mining Company, and the various Americanization campaigns during and after the war. The combination of these measures helped to polarize the Finnish immigrant community. The left-wing attacks on the Finnish socialists were aimed at the attempt to maintain Finnish cultural traditions and ethnic identity while joining with workers of other nationalities for mutual benefit. Neither the American Socialist Party nor the Communist International could tolerate the existence of autonomous ethnic federations capable of opposing party discipline.

As Finnish radicals retreated from the vanguard of American labor radicalism they suffered from what Guenther Roth has called a "negative integration"; that is, when a political system permits a hostile mass movement to exist legally, but prevents it from gaining access to the centers of power:

> A radical mass movement constitutes at least a potential source of instability, but if it can be legalized without sharing in governmental power it may contribute to the stability of the dominant system by leaving intact the latter's basic structure and by developing vested interests in its own legal status. From the viewpoint of the historical participants in this phenomenon it may appear as a matter of purposive isolation or of self-containment, but from the viewpoint of the observer it can be regarded as a form of integration (1963:7–8).

This form of negative integration can be seen in the emphasis given to the social and recreational side of the Finnish working-class movement following the repression of the 1907 strike. Finnish-American supporters of radical industrial unionism and the IWW first called attention to the dialectical nature of Finnish socialist political culture when they criticized the phenomenon of "hall socialism." The radicals charged that the heavy emphasis on cultural activities centered around the Finn halls promoted an acceptance of the status quo rather than revolutionary class struggle. The more moderate social democrats, who supported the American Socialist Party and the Western Federation of Miners, were wary of direct confrontations with the state that would expose Finnish socialist political culture to repression. Many Minnesota Finnish socialists had painful memories of the 1907 blacklist and sympathized with the sentiment expressed by the editors of the Social Democratic newspaper, *Raivaaja:*

> We have built fortifications during the past years, but they are still insufficient if we, while being militant, are not also cautious. In any event we are foreigners. If we were to undertake strange assignments, the most unscrupulous wrongs could be visited upon our newspapers, our organizations, and our ranks without our voices being heard beyond our own corners (Kolehmainen 1951:128).

The dialectic of Finnish socialist political culture as both supporting and challenging capitalist hegemony was most dramatically illustrated during the great Mesabi strike in Minnesota in 1916. Although many veterans of the 1907 strike were reluctant to pursue another direct confrontation with the power of the state and the giant steel corporations, a substantial number of Finnish radical industrial unionists became heavily involved in the strike during the summer of 1916 and viewed the strike as the prelude to the final destruction of American capitalism itself. These radicals were able to unite their fellow workers around the struggle for substantive vital interests and to arouse a collective enthusiasm for industrial unionism at a time when this form of labor organization was only a dream among the masses of immigrant workers. Although Finnish radical industrial unionists criticized "hall socialism," it was precisely these ethnic socialist institutions which had kept alive the spirit of rebellion among large numbers of immigrant workers between 1907 and 1916.

Finnish radicals could not sustain the momentum of this challenge to industrial capitalism, however. Divisions within the Finnish working-class community and the overwhelming repression directed against other ethnic working-class communities made it clear to the Finnish radicals that nothing could be accomplished by heroic effort alone. Unable to withstand the repression of the state and unable to garner sufficient support from their working-class allies, the radical Finns were forced to retreat from the cutting edge of American labor radicalism to the rural cooperatives. Many Finnish radicals continued to play a role in the organizing drive of the timber workers and the Mine, Mill, and Smelter Workers in the 1930s, but Finnish political culture became increasingly isolated within the ethnic culture of the cooperative movement. Once the cooperative movement ceased to be an integral component of working-class labor struggles, the movement developed vested interests in its own legal status and contributed to the depoliticization of Finnish culture.

The emergence and decline of one of the most successful socialist political cultures in the United States can be placed in a broader political and theoretical context. In the first place, the Finnish-American experience reminds us of the critical importance of ethnicity to the development of a radical–working class movement in the United States. Second, the dialectical character of ethnicity permitted a working-class socialist political culture simultaneously to oppose and yet to become integrated into capitalist society. Any analysis of Finnish socialist political culture, however, that concludes with the failure of Finnish-American radicals to achieve their socialist dream is in danger of overemphasizing the absorption of this culture into American society. We must also remember that historic moment when radical Finnish-Americans resisted the onslaught of industrial capitalism and projected a concrete vision of their socialist dream in their daily lives. Let the recovery of our many-sided ethnic history serve as our contemporary conscience, "reminding us that world Socialism (if it ever arrives) will presumably uproot the present notion of Time and progress, collapse stages of history into each other, and resurrect the experiences and traits that humanity has devised at every point in its odyssey" (Buhle 1978:7).

References

BERMAN, HYMAN
    1964   "Education for Work and Labor Solidarity: The Immigrant Miners and Radicalism on the Mesabi Range." Unpublished paper, Minnesota State Historical Society.

BOGGS, CARL
    1972   "Gramsci's 'Prison Notebooks' Part 2." Socialist Revolution 2:29–56.

BUHLE, PAUL
    1978   "Introductory Note to The Origins of Left-Culture in the U.S., 1880–1940." Cultural Correspondence 6–7:3–10.

CHAMBERS, CLARKE A.
    1963   "Social Welfare Policies and Programs on the Minnesota Iron Range, 1880–1930." Unpublished paper, Minnesota State Historical Society.

DOWELL, ELDRIDGE FOSTER
    1936   "A History of the Enactment of Criminal Syndicalism Legislation in the United States." Ph.D. dissertation, John Hopkins University.

FONER, PHILIP S.
   1965   The Industrial Workers of the World, 1905–1917. New York: International.
GRAMSCI, ANTONIO
   1971   Selections from the Prison Notebooks. New York: International.
HARTMANN, EDWARD GEORGE
   1948   The Movement to Americanize the Immigrant. New York: Columbia University Press.
HOGLUND, A. WILLIAM
   1960   Finnish Immigrants in America: 1880–1920. Madison: University of Wisconsin Press.
   1975   "No Land for Finns: Critics and Reformers View the Rural Exodus from Finland to America Between the 1880s and World War I." Pp. 36–54, in Michael G. Karni, Matti E. Kaups, and Douglas J. Ollila, Jr. (eds.), The Finnish Experience in the Western Great Lakes Region: New Perspectives. Turku, Finland: Institute for Migration.
   1977   "Breaking with Religious Tradition: Finnish Lutheran Workers and the Church, 1890–1915." Pp. 23–64, in Michael G. Karni and Douglas J. Ollila (eds.), For the Common Good: Finnish Immigrants and the Radical Response to Industrial America. Superior, Wis.: Tyomies Society.
JOKINEN, WALFRID J.
   1953   "The Finns in Minnesota: A Sociological Survey." Master's thesis: University of Minnesota.
KANGAS, HENRY R.
   1962   "Blades, Ears and Corn." Unpublished paper, Suomi Synod.
KARNI, MICHAEL G.
   1975   "Yhteishyvä-Or, For the Common Good: Finnish Radicalism in the Western Great Lakes." Ph.D. dissertation, University of Minnesota.
   1977   "The Founding of the Finnish Socialist Federation and the Minnesota Strike of 1907." Pp. 65–86, in Michael G. Karni and Douglas J. Ollila, Jr. (eds.), For the Common Good: Finnish Immigrants and the Radical Response to Industrial America. Superior, Wis.: Tyomies Society.
KNÖDLER-BUNTE, EBERHARD
   1975   "The Proletarian Public Sphere and Political Organization: An Analysis of Oskar Negt and Alexander Kluge's 'The Public Sphere and Experience.'" New German Critique 4:51–75.
KOLEHMAINEN, JOHN I.
   1942   "Finnish Temperance Societies in Minnesota." Minnesota History 22:391–402.
   1947   The Finns in America: A Bibliographic Guide to Their History. Hancock, Mich.: Finnish Lutheran Book Concern.
KOLEHMAINEN, JOHN I., and GEORGE HILL
   1951   Haven in the Woods: The Story of the Finns in Wisconsin. Madison, Wis.: State Historical Society of Wisconsin.
KOSTIAINEN, AUVO
   1977   "The Tragic Crisis: Finnish American Workers and the Civil War in

Finland." Pp. 217–35, in Michael G. Karni and Douglas J. Ollila, Jr. (eds.), For the Common Good: Finnish Immigrants and the Radical Response to Industrial America. Superior, Wis.: Tyomies Society.

LEE, SIRKKA TUOMI
1978   "The 'New Immigrants' and the I.W.W." Cultural Correspondence 6–7:41–49.

LEINENWEBER, CHARLES
1968   "The American Socialist Party and the 'New Immigrants.'" Science and Society 32:1–25.

MICHELS, ROBERT
1962   Political Parties. New York: Macmillan.

MINNESOTA BUREAU OF THE CENSUS
1895   Fourth Decennial Census of the State of Minnesota. St. Paul: Pioneer Press.

OLLILA, DOUGLAS J., JR.
1963   "The Formative Period of the Finnish-Evangelical Lutheran Church in America or Suomi Synod." Ph.D. dissertation, Department of Religion, Boston University.
1975   "The Emergence of Radical Industrial Unionism in the Finnish Socialist Movement." Publications of the Institute of General History (Turku, Finland) 7:25–54.
1976   "Defects in the Melting Pot: Finnish-American Response to the Loyalty Issue, 1917–1920." Turun Historiallinen Arkisto (Turku, Finland) 31:397–413.
1977   "A Time of Glory: Finnish-American Radical Industrial Unionism, 1914–1917." Publications of the Institute of History (Turku, Finland) 9:31–53.

PINOLA, RUDOLPH
1957   "Labor and Politics on the Iron Range of Northern Minnesota." Ph.D. dissertation, Department of History, University of Wisconsin.

ROSS, CARL
1977   The Finn Factor in American Labor, Culture and Society. New York Mills, Minn.: Parta Printers.

ROTH, GUENTHER
1963   The Social Democrats in Imperial Germany: A Study in Working Class Isolation and National Integration. Totowa, New Jersey: Bedminister Press.

SOFCHALK, DONALD G.
1971   "Organized Labor and the Iron Ore Mines of Northern Minnesota, 1907–1936." Labor History 12:214–42.

VIRGINIA DAILY
1916   "Wholesalers Will Demand Cash for Goods."

WASASTJERNA, HANS R. (ed.)
1957   History of the Finns in Minnesota. Duluth, Minn.: Minnesota Finnish-American Historical Society.

WILLIAMS, RAYMOND
1961   The Long Revolution. Middlesex, England: Penguin.
1966   Culture and Society, 1780–1950. New York: Harper & Row.

8   Class, Power, and Social Control: The War on Poverty

Roger Friedland
University of California–Santa Barbara

After World War Two, major corporations and labor unions increasingly united to forge new central city political coalitions. Organized around policies to maintain the city's economic growth and fiscal viability, these coalitions pushed forward with costly urban renewal projects, intrametropolitan transportation, industrial parks, development corporations, zoning variances, underassessments, subsidized water and power, and similar programs. For the corporations, such policies promised subsidized profits; for the labor unions, unionized employment. The political coalitions were often centered in strong Democratic mayors who had the partisan identification, if not the political machine, necessary to deliver the central city vote (Mollenkopf 1976).

Political challenge by the poor, especially by the nonwhite poor, threatened the dominance of the corporations and labor unions and the growth policies they pursued. It was the poorest communities that were displaced by urban renewal and highway construction, whose housing stock was depleted by clearance, whose employment opportunities were often reduced by the expansion of office employment stimulated by central business district growth and restrictive unionization on large construction projects and municipal jobs, and whose social services were constrained by the enormous fiscal costs of the growth programs (Friedland 1980, forthcoming).

Yet without the support of the central city nonwhite and poor communities, many of the Democratic mayors—the political focal point of

This paper has benefited from critical readings from many friends: Mike Aiken, Robert Alford, Ira Katznelson, John Mollenkopf, and Erik Wright. I am particularly indebted to my writing group, which pushed me toward clarity. Included are Eric Wright, James Jackson, Barbara Heyns, Ann Steuve, and Rob Mayer.

[193]

these progrowth coalitions—could not long remain in office. Thus the policies of the coalition were inconsistent with its electoral base. Although the electoral base of the coalition included the central city poor and nonwhite populations, their political mobilization was inevitably directed against the policies on which corporate and labor union support was contingent. Mollenkopf writes.

> Most of the community turbulence of the 1960s was firmly directed against urban renewal, highway construction, the declining availability of decent, inexpensive housing, expansion of dominant institutions, and city bureaucracies tightly dominated by ethnic groups being displaced in the urban population by minority newcomers (1976:22).

In her study of 91 northern cities, Morlock (1972) found that reputational influence based on successful rejection of major city programs was highest for nonwhite social groups. The most frequently rejected program was urban renewal.

Labor unions, in particular, occupy an ambivalent position in relationship to central city poor and nonwhite communities. Labor's political power depends on its position within the Democratic Party. Without a cohesive, centralized national party system in the United States, this dependence means that urban political organizations are the elemental building blocks of national Democratic victories, victories that labor unions consider essential to pass prolabor legislation. Labor unions have traditionally played an important role in organizing and assuring the Democratic vote of the nonunionized working class and dependent populations.

On the local level, Greenstone's study of three American cities describes the limitations on the union role in building a political coalition that includes the central city poor. Nonetheless, labor unions in Chicago, Detroit, and Los Angeles have a common aggregating role:

> In the three cities . . . organized labor in varying degrees assumed . . . an aggregating posture toward relatively new groups of urban immigrants who felt excluded from American political life in the generation after the New Deal, notably blacks and Spanish-speaking Puerto Ricans and Mexicans. At a minimum the labor movement helped these groups to organize and vote so that they could begin to articulate their own demands, which labor as a party faction then helped aggregate into programs and slates of candidates (1969:249).

In Morlock's 91-city study, labor union and nonwhite reputational influence were highly correlated.

At a national level, labor unions have been quite effective in securing broad redistributive legislation benefiting the entire working class, relative to their effectiveness in securing regulatory changes that benefit the particularistic concerns of the union (Lowi 1967). National labor union leaders are as ideologically supportive of national programs for welfare expansion and income equalization as national corporate officials are opposed (Barton 1975). Support for welfare and social service expansion flows both from their desire to maintain the electoral base of the Democratic party and from their objective interests in increasing the floor under union wages (Greenstone 1969).

Beyond their support of the central city growth program, labor union market interests conflict with those of the central city's nonwhite and poor populations. Continued labor union market power depends on the maintenance of highly dualistic and sometimes racist labor markets. That central city industrial jobs are increasingly occupied by suburban union workers only exacerbates the political visibility of the problem. A large body of nonunionized, low-wage labor willing to occupy unskilled, but relatively high-paying jobs threatens the union's monopoly of access to such positions. Further, as a result of declining central city industrial employment, access to the city payrolls became exceedingly important for the expanding nonwhite population.

Judicious dispersal of patronage positions had historically been a means of absorbing ethnic political leadership and assuring ethnic loyalties of established political leadership. Civil service reforms and municipal employee unions consolidated white-ethnic control over city jobs in the public bureaucracies. Frances Fox Piven writes of the municipal unions:

> when blacks entered the cities, they were confronted by a relatively new development in city politics: large associations of public employees, whether teachers, policemen, sanitation men, and the like. These groups had become numerous, organized and independent enough to wield substantial control over most matters affecting their jobs and their agencies: entrance requirements, tenure guarantees, working conditions, job prerogatives, promotion criteria, retirement benefits. When blacks arrived in the cities, local political leaders did not control the jobs—and in cases where job prerogatives had been precisely specified by regulation, did not even control the services—which might have been given as concessions to the newcomers (Piven 1972; see Hill 1976).

As a result of this economic relationship between labor unions and the central city poor, their political relationship was increasingly strained. At a local level, the growing numerical strength and political militancy of the poor challenged the political dominance of the labor unions in the Democratic party apparatus. In a study of five, mostly nonwhite communities, Greenberg found:

The association of the poor with working class organizations is ambiguous in all these neighborhoods, sometimes reflected in open hostility, sometimes in indifference, and increasingly in an uneasy participation (1974:193).

Urban black support for the national Democratic party began to slip in the late 1950s, dropping from 79 percent in 1952 to 61 percent in 1956 (Piven 1972:18).

To finance a significant material response to the demands of the poor without cutting into growth programs or raising taxes, and thus further reducing the competitive advantage of the central city as a location for plant or office investment, the city had to look beyond its strained treasury.

The War on Poverty: A Contradictory Strategy of Social Control

As the causes of political challenge deepened and protest intensified, the War on Poverty, formally legislated during the Johnson administration, attempted to institute entirely new mechanisms of social and political control. The War on Poverty was a co-optive reform. It attempted to incorporate politically threatening nonwhite and poor communities within new bureaucratic structures without increasing their political power. If by co-opting them, it prevented a more comprehensive repudiation of the structure of urban power, it also brought them within the political system and thus exposed dominant institutions to more direct attack.

The War on Poverty created new local agencies whose direct links to Washington gave them potential independence from local government and long-established private community organizations. The poverty agencies' intended purpose was to provide direct social services for the poor; refer problems to other health, welfare, and employment agencies; and serve as a forum for the articulation and organization of community demands (Moynihan 1969; Piven and Cloward 1971). The War on Poverty could be used to mobilize the poor communities both for political participation in the poverty agencies themselves (Cole 1974; Greenstone and Peterson 1973) and as pressure groups in the city's electoral and bureaucratic politics (Piven and Cloward 1971).

Within the city, poverty funds were directed at those communities which had been hardest hit by city-growth policies. The design of the War on Poverty's precursor, the Grey Areas project, clearly targets those inner areas which had been the special victim of the renewal and highway bulldozers (Ford Foundation 1963). However, the War on Poverty was neither designed nor empowered to alter those growth programs; nor could it stem their deleterious effects on the housing and employment opportunities of the central city poor.

Incorporation into the new bureaucratic structures was not conducive to challenging the city's power structure. In a study of five California cities between 1964 and 1968, Kramer found

> the effects on city politics of resident participation were . . . minimal. Although a new center of minority influence was established in each community, the CAP (Community Action Program) did not appear to disrupt the prevailing structure and balance of power in any significant way (1969:257).

Community groups were embroiled in particularistic bureaucratic urban politics and recruited as constituents for poverty agencies (Kramer 1969; Bachrach and Baratz 1970), rather than mobilized to challenge the dominant interests and policies that actually created poverty.

Within the city, the poverty agencies represented new bureaucratic targets for political action. Community groups were absorbed with strategies for controlling the new bureaucracies, rather than transforming the existent ones. As Piven and Cloward note

> The creation of separate citywide coordinating structures (e.g., antipoverty councils) also deflected white antagonism; blacks were to be conciliated with a measure of influence over entirely new structures rather than given greater control over traditional municipal agencies dominated by whites (1971:276).

Just as the central city was increasingly composed of poor, especially black poor, with electoral clout, these federal project grants located the origins and thus the limits of reform policy outside the city. This structure of urban policy formation favors those interests best able to organize at the national level of government. At the national level, the poor and nonwhite populations were not well organized. Black groups, for example, were loose, ineffectual federations of local groups, whose efforts were confined to legislative lobbying once the limits of policy variation had already been set and reactive politics to local implementation of those policies (Wolman and Thomas 1970). Central city policy formation and control over the use of limited city fiscal resources became even less accessible to the poor.

The War on Poverty encouraged citizen participation at the city level. Yet the interests that control economic processes which cause poverty are highly dependent on federal and state legislation and bureaucracies. Both corporations and labor unions depend on federal and state legislation and bureaucracies that actually cause many of the problems experienced in the city and thus limit the efficacy of local community participation.

Corporations and labor unions are critical constituents for the state and federal agencies that originate and implement such policies as taxation, highway and mass transportation development, industrial location, land-use planning, lending rates, and housing finance. All these policies affect central city employment, tax revenues for social services, and decent low-income housing. By encouraging participation at the city level in response to problems caused by economic processes and policies outside the city, the War on Poverty insulated very important centers of power from political challenge. Programs such as the War on Poverty sever the politics of poverty from the politics of wealth.

The War on Poverty was a new bureaucratic strategy of social control. However, rather than diffuse urban conflict, the War on Poverty could also be used by poor people to intensify their struggles for power, social services, and income.

The War on Poverty was both a major innovation in the structure of city politics and a new departure in federal urban intervention through project grants. It created direct relationships between poor communities and the federal level of bureaucracy, thereby potentially undercutting the control of traditional city bureaucracies and party organizations (Piven and Cloward 1971:261–62). Further, under the banner of "maximum feasible participation," the War on Poverty organized poor communities to demand procedural rights, better-quality service, and improved benefits from traditional city bureaucracies (Piven and Cloward 1971; Moynihan 1970).

If the War on Poverty was a co-optive social control strategy, it was not without danger. Politically mobilized communities might break the back of bureaucratic politics, contesting not only poverty fund allocations but also the distribution of municipal employment, wealth, and political power. The political mobilization achieved by the War on Poverty, combined with its largely symbolic consequences, probably helped to catalyze and intensify the ghetto rebellions of the late 1960s (Friedland 1980, forthcoming). Further, the agencies created by the War on Poverty were often able to achieve considerable bureaucratic autonomy, especially within a reformed city structure where the dominant political coalitions were less able to determine agency recruitment patterns or policy implementation (Greenstone and Peterson 1973:203–225).

Piven and Cloward argue that poverty agency leadership often secured city elective office and established independent electoral organization at the city level (1971:275; Urquhart 1974:36). Such penetration could only exacerbate the growing tensions between the social groups that formed the social base of the Democratic party. As Piven and Cloward note:

In one city after another, racial strife led to polarization and division within the Democratic ranks. Local Democratic leaders in some cities became so threatened by cleavages in their constituencies that, to avoid further trouble, they simply ignored controversial national candidates and worked mainly to win local contests (1971:254; see also Greenberg 1974).

Although such tension hampered the national Democratic party's efforts to win the presidency in 1968, it also threatened the local Democratic progrowth coalitions operative in congressional and municipal politics. Many political activists who were organizing communities to oppose growth policies were employed in poverty program agencies (Mollenkopf 1973:6, 11). Such community resistance was often effective enough to delay, halt, and change urban renewal and highway developments, thereby raising their fiscal and political costs. As the National Housing and Economic Development Law Center reported

> Nationally, in large part due to administrative complaints and lawsuits filed by Legal Services attorneys (a War on Poverty component), poor and minority residents have increasingly been able to halt and delay urban renewal projects which would displace large numbers of people without providing adequate relocation and replacement housing, and change redevelopment plans to provide for the inclusion of more low and moderate income housing, including rehabilitation. This is reflected in the fact that HUD now reports that of the urban renewal residential re-use projects, 69 percent will be for occupancy by low and moderate income tenants (Law Center 1972; cited in Mollenkopf 1973:13).

Local programs also pushed up welfare rolls through political organization, litigation, and improved referral and case-finding (Piven and Cloward 1971).

On one hand, the new poverty agencies coopted community activists through new forms of patronage, embroiled community organizations in interbureaucratic rivalries, and increased competition between lower-income ethnic groups for poverty program spoils. Such cooptation politically insulted those agencies which controlled the economic processes that caused poverty.

On the other hand, the War on Poverty opened channels of access for poor, nonwhite leaders, legitimated their emerging political organizations, and provided a new bureaucratic base for continued political mobilization. This thaw exposed the central city's social service agencies, its schools, and its growth programs to attack from within the city's political system. If the War on Poverty offered political benefits as a potent mechanism of social control, it also had political costs as a potential bureaucratic base for further political challenge.

The Intercity Distribution of War on Poverty Funds: A Hypothesis

I suggest that federal War on Poverty funds were not distributed among cities according to the local level of poverty, but rather according to the local power of national corporations and labor unions and the extent to which their political dominance was at stake. The War on Poverty provided a strategy for political control over poor and nonwhite communities that were growing in electoral and organizational strength and challenging corporate and labor union political power and the policies they pursued.

In those cities with powerful national corporations and labor unions, the level of funding by the War on Poverty will vary directly with the political challenge posed by the poor and nonwhite populations. In cities with less powerful national corporations and labor unions, the level of poverty funding will not be responsive to such political challenge. The point is that it is the local combination of powerful corporations and labor unions, and the social conditions that threaten their political dominance, that leads to a high level of co-optive response. Co-optation is the result of the coincidence of corporate and labor union *power* and corporate and labor union *interest* in containing political conflict. Without both, co-optive public policy is less likely.

National corporations and labor unions are *potential* organizational bases of urban political power. Because political conditions vary across central cities, national corporate and labor union interests in the adoption of local programs for social control are not constant across all cities. Consequently, the impact of corporate labor union power on public policy is likely to be contingent on the extent to which local conditions threaten their political or material interests. Put another way, the impact of local social conditions affecting corporate or labor union interests on public policy is likely to depend on the level of corporate or labor union power. The local power of national corporations or labor unions selectively filters the potential impact of local social conditions.

Piven and Cloward (1971, 1975) have argued that the War on Poverty and the welfare explosion it engendered originated nationally as a Democratic presidential response to nonwhite disruption and the changing strategic value of the nonwhite vote. However, I am concerned not with the origins of the War on Poverty but with the intercity distribution of War on Poverty funds. The local presence of powerful national corporations and labor unions increase a city's co-optive responsiveness to local political challenge. Local political challenge may be a singularly ineffective determinant of poverty funding when a central city's class structure fails to provide sufficient interest or power to secure War on Poverty funds. In cities with more powerful corporations and labor unions, the level of political

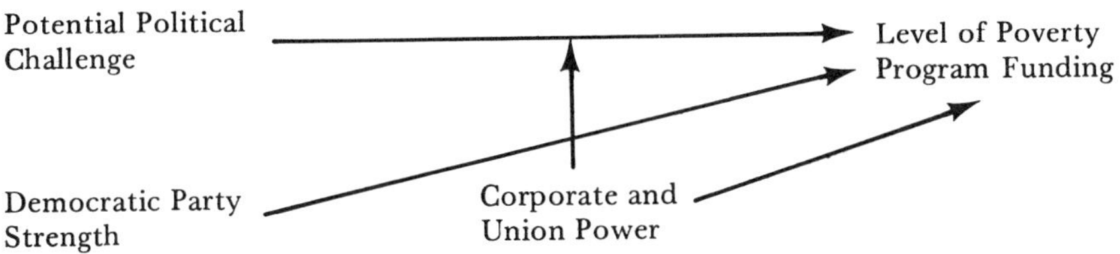

*Figure 8-1. Class power and poverty program funding:
a conceptual model*

challenge posed by the poor and nonwhite population will be a more important determinant of poverty funding levels. In cities with less powerful corporations and labor unions, only national electoral factors will make a difference.

In the conceptual model (figures 8-1 and 8-2), the effect of potential political challenge on the level of poverty program funding depends on the local power of national corporations and labor unions. Although corporate and union power may have additive net effects on the level of poverty funding, the effects of most theoretical interest are the interaction of corporate or labor union power and potential political challenge.

Operationalization

Potential political challenge is operationalized by the extent of poverty in the city, the numerical strength of the nonwhite population, the extent of nonwhite population increase, and the number of urban renewal projects.

1. *Poverty* is operationalized as the percentage of the city's families with annual incomes under $3,000 in 1959. The level of poverty not only indicates the political significance of the central city poor, but their need for a substantive response. A large percentage of poor people indicates a large social base with the *potential* for mobilizing an electoral challenge to established political elites. Aiken and Alford (1970) found that poverty was related to federal War on Poverty funding in cities with populations over 25,000.

2. The numerical strength of the nonwhite population is operationalized as the percentage of the central city population that was nonwhite in 1960. A study of 15 major central cities shows that industrial executive, banker, and Chamber of Commerce influence in city politics is *negatively* related to the influence of black groups (Rossi, Berk, and Edison 1974:38). Further, Morlock (1972) found that business influence, measured by reputational scores for downtown merchants, local industrialists, and bankers,

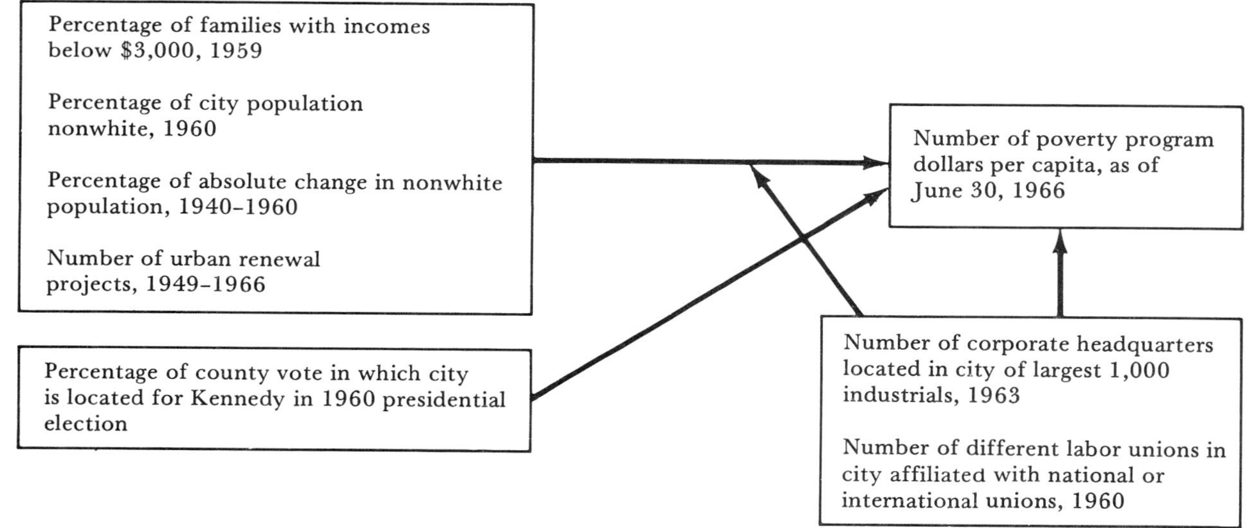

Figure 8-2. *Class power and poverty program funding: an empirical model*

was negatively correlated with both the percentage and absolute number of nonwhites.

3. The extent of nonwhite population increase is operationalized as the absolute percentage increase (or decrease) in the size of the city's non-white population between 1940 and 1960. The percentage change is measured against the base of the size of the nonwhite population in 1940. This taps the strain on the capacities of political organizations and city bureaucracies to exercise political and social control.

4. The number of urban renewal projects between 1949 and 1966 is the measure of the number of communities that were razed (although not necessarily reconstructed) by urban renewal. This ratio indicates the number of neighborhoods in which political protest and organization might have emerged to challenge central city growth policies.

5. Democratic party strength is operationalized as the percentage of the county vote in which the city is located that voted Democratic in the 1960 presidential election. When a city was in more than one county, the county in which the majority of the city's population resides is used. The 1960 presidential contest between Kennedy and Nixon was a normal election, that is, the Democratic and Republican candidates took ideologically divergent stands on domestic social programs. The percentage voting for Kennedy is an approximation of the electoral support for a liberal, expanded federal role in urban welfare, social services, and civil rights (Hamilton 1972). Because the city and county are not coterminous, this measure probably underestimates the central city's Democratic vote because of the concentration of nonwhite, low-income individuals likely to vote Democratic in the central city and the concentration of white, higher-income individuals likely to vote Republican in the suburbs.

6. Corporate and union power is operationalized by the number of different corporate headquarters of the largest 1,000 industrial corporations and the number of national or international unions with at least one local union in the city as of 1960. Each different affiliated union is counted only once, regardless of how many locals it has in the city. In the additive models, the continuous variables will be used. In the split sample covariance models, the variables will be dichotomized so that cities with between 6 and 49 different unions will be characterized as low union-power cities and cities with between 50 and 120 unions will be characterized as high union-power cities. This measure of labor union power refers to the presence of national unions, not to union membership.

The localized power of national corporations is operationalized as the number of national corporate headquarters of the largest 1,000 industrial corporations as ranked by sales in the city. In the covariance models, the variable will be dichotomized so that cities with 0 to 1 corporate headquarters will be characterized as low corporate-power cities and cities with between 2 and 215 corporate headquarters will be characterized as high corporate-power cities.

This measure of corporate power refers to the presence of corporate ownership–management organizations, not to all plants owned by national corporations. However, corporations with headquarters in a city also tend to own plants in that same city (see Friedland 1980, forthcoming).

The presence of national corporations and labor unions indicates several attributes of the organizational basis of class power in the city. First, it indicates the presence of national capitalists and national working-class leaders within the city who are available for local political participation. Second, it indicates the presence of critical organizational actors and organizational units of political representation in local politics. Third, it indicates the size and diversity of the organizational base for local political action by either class, if it occurs. Fourth, it indicates the presence of organizations in control of enormous political and economic resources, which, by their very presence, structure the range of feasible political coalitions and public policies. National corporations and labor unions are powerful actors and units of representation in urban politics. However, corporate and labor union power is not necessarily mediated through instrumental participation in local policy formation. National corporations situated in the city control the economic processes that determine the viability of the urban economy and tax base. Locally situated national labor unions control the mass political organizations that can be a powerful force in the determination of electoral outcomes.

In many ways, the visible political participation of corporate and labor union officials only communicates the economic and political resources these national class organizations control. Their political participation is often a consequence and not a cause of their political power.

Fifth, the presence of corporations and unions indicates the extent to which the city is integrated into national networks of urban policy formation and diffusion. As the federal government has increasingly formulated and financed urban policy, locally situated national corporations and labor unions have become important bases of integration into national networks of urban policy formation and diffusion. Corporations and labor unions provide the city with information and influence helpful in securing federal project grants (such as the War on Poverty, Model Cities, urban renewal; see Friedland forthcoming). Although the evidence is sketchy, corporations and unions did participate in the policy networks that originated and diffused the War on Poverty. The War on Poverty evolved out of a series of urban programs sponsored by the Ford Foundation, dating back to the Great Cities program of 1960, the Grey Areas projects of 1961, and the federally supported Mobilization for Youth launched in 1962 (Urquhart 1974; Moynihan 1969). Moynihan's interpretation of the poverty program

Table 8-1. Descriptive statistics for War on Poverty analysis

Variable	Indicator	Mean	Standard Deviation
	1. Percentage of families under $3,000	0.18	0.06
	2. Percentage of nonwhite, 1959	0.16	0.13
Potential political challenge	3. Percentage of absolute change nonwhite population	2138	1996
	4. Number of urban renewal projects	5.13	6.50
Democratic party strength	5. Percentage of Democratic vote	0.51	0.08
Corporate power	6. Number of corporate headquarters	5.45	20.22
Labor union power	National labor unions	51.93	23.54
Level of War on Poverty funding	7. Number of poverty cents per capita, 1966	835.6	851.09

evolution can be used to show how the structure and content of the Economic Opportunity Act of 1964 were identical to the 1961 proposal for the Ford Foundation Mobilization for Youth (Urquhart 1974). Both corporate capital and labor unions are represented in the cities chosen for Grey Area Ford grants.

7. The level of poverty program funding is operationalized as the number of dollars standardized by the 1960 population in June 30, 1966. This measure taps both the city's ability to secure federal funds and the extent of its material response to federal poverty program opportunities. Although it does not indicate how poverty funds were used to deliver services or politically organize poor communities, per capita funding for CAP was found to be significantly associated with overall institutional change in the study of target areas in cities with 50,000 or more population (Barss, Reitzel, and associates 1970). A city with no poverty program is coded as zero. Only four of the 130 cities studied here lacked poverty programs in 1966.

The descriptive statistics for these indicators and the zero order correlations among them are presented in tables 8-1 and 8-2.

Table 8-2. Bivariate correlations for War on Poverty analysis

	1	2	3	4	5	6	7	8	9
1. Percentage of poor	1.0								
2. Percentage of nonwhite	0.522	1.0							
3. Percentage of nonwhite population change	−0.456	−0.370	1.0						
4. Renewal projects	−0.002	0.235	−0.168	1.0					
5. Percentage of Democratic	−0.028	0.046	−0.166	0.431	1.0				
6. Labor unions	0.069	0.216	−0.153	0.617	0.224	1.0			
7. Corporate headquarters	−0.084	0.038	−0.040	0.612	0.271	0.438	1.0		
8. Poverty dollars	0.124	0.254	−0.117	0.259	0.313	0.243	0.063	1.0	

Data Analysis

The level of corporate and labor union power will be used as dichotomies to split the population of cities into two groups: high corporate (or union) power, and low corporate (or union) power. This model describes the interactive effect corporate or union power has on the relationship between political challenge and poverty funding. Cities with more powerful corporations or labor unions are hypothesized to be more responsive to potential political challenge than cities with less powerful organizational structures. The effect of political challenge is hypothesized to be contingent on the level of corporate or union power (t-tests were done on the difference in the unstandardized regression coefficients when either one or both coefficients were significant).

Split Sample Covariance Analysis

I have argued that the effect of political challenge on poverty funding levels is contingent on the local level of corporate and union power. My question here is: Does the effect of political challenge on poverty funding depend on the level of corporate or union power? If so, to what extent? To answer these questions, the level of poverty funding was regressed on the political variables within high and low corporate-power cities and within high and low union-power cities. First, the differential size and significance of effects in the two samples can be used to argue whether corporate or union power is necessary for political challenge to have an effect. Second, a t-test on the difference between two regression coefficients can be used to argue whether the effect of political challenge on poverty funding is significantly greater in high as opposed to low corporate (or union) power cities (see table 8-3).

Three variables have different effects in high as opposed to low corporate-power cities: percentage poor, percentage nonwhite, and number of urban renewal projects. In high corporate-power cities, the percentage of poor and nonwhite has stronger positive effects on poverty funding levels than in low corporate-power cities. In high corporate-power cities, the number of urban renewal projects has an insignificant negative effect on poverty funding, but in low corporate-power cities it has a significant positive effect. However, none of these differences were strictly significant, although the difference in the unstandardized beta for percentage of poor and number of urban renewal projects fell just short of significance. Two variables have similar effects in high and low corporate-power cities: percentage of nonwhite population change and percentage of Democrats. Nonwhite population change has an insignificant positive effect in both high and low corporate-power cities, whereas percentage Democratic has a strong positive effect in both high and low corporate-power cities.

Table 8-3. Corporate power and poverty funding levels: a split sample covariance analysis

Variable	High			Low			
	b_1	Standard Error	F	b_2	Standard Error	F	t-Test $(b_1 - b_2)$
Percentage of poor	4300	2980	2.08*	17.3	1704	0.000	1.247
Percentage of nonwhite	1416	986	2.06*	377	918	0.17	0.77
Percentage nonwhite population change	0.0238	0.101	0.05	0.0238	.042	0.31	
Renewal projects	−2.207	17.51	0.016	44.4	31.5	1.97*	1.29
Percentage of Democratic	3823	1765	4.69*	2825	1236	5.225*	0.46
Constant	−1980.5			−1001			

$n = 58$ $r^2 = 0.230$ $n = 71$ $r^2 = 0.124$
Adjusted $r^2 = 0.172$ Adjusted $r^2 = 0.072$
$F = 3.109$ $F = 1.85$

* = significant at 0.10 level, one-tail

These results suggest that a strong corporate presence changes the city's power structure to be more responsive to the numerical strength of the nonwhite and poor populations. In the 1960s the electoral strength of the poor and nonwhite populations threatened to topple the powerful mayors who had engineered the city's growth programs. The impact of partisan national electoral pressures on poverty funding appears to be impervious to the level of corporate power.

That the number of urban renewal projects executed only has a positive impact in low corporate-power cities is contrary to my original prediction. I suggested that the number of renewal projects indicates the number of disrupted poor and nonwhite communities and thus the level of political mobilization which required cooling out by War on Poverty dollars.

An alternative interpretation of this indicator, which is consistent with the empirical findings, is that the number of renewal projects indicates the city's political and administrative experience in acquiring project grant funds from the federal government. Although urban renewal was under the jurisdiction of different congressional committees and lodged in other federal agencies than the War on Poverty, urban renewal probably provided the city with critical experience preparing grant applications and developing administrative and political linkages with Washington. In cities with powerful corporations, these administrative and political linkages may have been less important because the corporations themselves provided many informational and influential linkages to national centers of power and decisionmaking.

Turning to the split sample covariance analysis in which labor union power is the factor (table 8-4), two variables have different effects in high as opposed to low union-power cities. The percentage of nonwhites has a strong positive effect in high union-power cities, as opposed to an insignificant negative effect in low union-power cities. The number of urban renewal projects has an insignificant negative effect in high union-power cities, compared to a significant positive effect in low union-power cities. The differences in the effects of the percentage of nonwhites and of the number of urban renewal projects are significant. The three other variables—percentage of poor, nonwhite population change, and percentage Democratic—have similar effects in both groups of cities. Percentage Democratic has a strong positive effect in both high and low union-power cities, whereas percentage nonwhite population change and percentage of poor have insignificant effects in both.

Because labor unions lack systemic power (the ability to control the economic growth of the central city), they are particularly sensitive to the social forces that might endanger their electoral or coalitional political influence. Although the white poor were ethnically fragmented and relatively unorganized, blacks had become increasingly politicized in the postwar

Table 8-4. *Union power and poverty funding levels:*
a split sample covariance analysis

Variable	High			Low			*t*-Test $(b_1 - b_2)$
	b_1	Standard Error	F	b_2	Standard Error	F	
Percentage of poor	−494.9	2750	0.03	−4.67	1592	0.00	
Percentage of nonwhite	2981	1147	6.75*	−325.8	735.6	0.19	2.43
Percentage nonwhite population change	0.013	0.095	0.02	0.026	0.039	0.42	
Renewal projects	−1.52	17.1	0.008	90.12	34.6	6.76*	2.37
Percentage of Democratic	3361	1632	4.24*	3359	1210	7.7*	. . .
Constant	−1253			−1247			
	$n = 69$ $r^2 = .199$ Adjusted $r^2 = 0.149$ $F = 3.13$			$n = 60$ $r^2 = 0.230$ Adjusted $r^2 = 0.174$ $F = 3.23$			

* = significant at 0.10 level, one-tail

period. The central city black population was particularly threatening to the political dominance of the labor unions. In mayoral electoral politics, labor unions were likely to be key coalitional partners with the nonwhite communities (Greenstone 1970). Securing the support of the nonwhite political community for liberal, Democratic candidates while maintaining restrictive craft, industrial, and municipal unions was a difficult balancing act. The continuity of a coalitional alliance between unions and blacks was contingent on the survival of a relatively moderate, if independent, black leadership. Co-optation through incorporation in the new poverty bureaucracies was a means of containing the militancy of emerging nonwhite political organizations.

These results suggest that a strong labor union presence did not cause the city power structure to be more responsive to the potential power of the central city poor, nor to the growth in the nonwhite population. The impact of Democratic electoral strength is equally strong in high and low union-power cities, suggesting the independence of partisan electoral determination of poverty funding from the level of labor union power within the city. And finally, high union power significantly depresses the positive effect of urban renewal projects on the level of poverty funding. This again suggests that the number of renewal projects indicates the city's development of administrative and political linkages with the federal government which substitute for the national connections of the labor unions.

Summary and Conclusion

The results suggest that poverty funds were not distributed according to the level of poverty but according to the national significance of local constituencies: blacks who were pressing their demands into national issues, Democratic voters who had elected both a Democratic president and Congress, and labor unions and corporations who formed a major organizational basis for urban and national class politics in the United States.

In the interactive, split sample models, some of these results held in both high and low corporate- and union-power cities, whereas others were entirely contingent on the level of corporate or union power. Table 8-5 summarizes the significant results.

The magnitude of nonwhite population increase was singularly ineffective in all groups of high and low corporate- and union-power cities. While straining the central city's system of social control, a rapid influx of nonwhite population may have unsettled patterns of political leadership within the nonwhite community. Because of the instability of a rapidly changing political community, the community's need for large poverty programs may have been offset by their diminished capacity to organize demands for new programs.

Table 8-5. *Significant variables in poverty funding: split sample analysis*

High corporate power	Percentage poor (+)	Renewal projects (+)	Low corporate power
	Percentage non-white (+)	Percentage Democratic (+)	
	Percentage Democratic		
High union power	Percentage non-white (+)	Renewal projects (+)	Low union power
	Percentage Democratic (+)	Percentage Democratic (+)	

Democratic party strength had a strong positive effect on poverty funding in all groups of cities. The city's position in the national political system with respect to the dominant political party is an important determinant of the city's ability to secure War on Poverty funds. The effect of urban partisan pressures on poverty funding is independent of the city's position in the national structure of corporations and labor unions. As a result, the political system does affect the level of poverty funding, but this is independent of the city's location in the national class structure.

The positive effect of the percentage of nonwhite, unlike the effect of Democratic, *depends* on the level of corporate and union power. The positive effect of the percentage of poor is contingent on the level of corporate power, but not on union power. The results suggest that cities in which corporations and labor unions were powerful were more responsive to the potential political challenge posed by the poor and nonwhite central city populations. Where national corporations and labor unions were organizationally weak, cities lacked both internal political leadership and class base and the external political linkages necessary to develop a preemptive policy in response to the *potential* power of exploited groups.

Furthermore, in cities where national corporations and unions were weak, blacks probably faced more conservative political groupings dominated by smaller, more localized capitalists. Because local competitive capital was more vulnerable to city decisions and thus more dependent on the outcomes of city political conflict, local capital was more likely to be oriented to and dominant in city politics. Because of their dependency on low-wage, nonunionized labor (and the depressing effect racism had both on wages and unionization) (Reich 1973; Hill 1973), and their low margins of profitability and their consequent vulnerability to tax increases or city subsidy cutbacks, local capital resisted political concessions to popular interests.

A political alliance between white and nonwhite poor and the organized working class was especially threatening. Without a strong union presence as a base for the Democratic party or coalition partner, or a politically sophisticated corporate leadership, nonwhite communities lacked the political leverage necessary to secure even co-optive, symbolic benefits. In such cities, police guns may have been a substitute for welfare.

Finally, the positive effect of the number of urban renewal programs executed on poverty funding is also contingent, but on the absence of corporate or labor union power. Urban renewal projects represented the development of city experience in grant application and cultivation of administrative and political contacts with Washington, D.C. Where corporations and labor unions integrated the central city into national networks of urban policy formation and diffusion, these administrative and political linkages were less important in determining the city's success in securing War on Poverty funds.

The local presence of national corporations and labor unions indicates a set of locally and nationally powerful political forces. Where corporations and labor unions are locally powerful, they integrate the central city into a structure of national classes and thus provide mechanisms by which urban policies are diffused to the central cities. They also transform the framework of central city politics, providing enormous political capabilities, highly influential coalition partners, and very sophisticated political leadership. When potentially powerful nonwhite or poor populations threaten their political dominance, they provide both the political base, interest, and capability necessary to assure a co-optive policy response. Where they are absent, the city's electoral and administrative linkages to the federal government become all-important in determining the city's ability to secure poverty funds.

It is necessary to go beyond mass electoral studies in which acts of individual political participation are aggregated into party or programmatic victories, as well as elite studies in which political and bureaucratic elites merely respond to potential demands latent in different social groups or objective technocratic needs of the system. The power of national class organizations—such as corporations and labor unions—intervenes between the city's potentially disruptive popular base and the city's public policy designed for that social base.

The War on Poverty was more than the outcome of manifest mass political pressure in the central city. And it was not merely the result of powerful political leaders or administrative officials responding to the obvious failures of central city public services and private economy. National class power intervened to manage the potential disruption of mass politicization, which moved with increasing force at the ballot box and with increasing violence in the streets.

References

AIKEN, MICHAEL
1970   "The Distribution of Community Power: Structural Bases and Social Consequences," in Michael Aiken and Paul Mott (eds.), The Structure of Community Power. New York: Random House.

AIKEN, MICHAEL, and ROBERT ALFORD
1970   "Comparative Urban Research and Community Decision-making," *The New Atlantis* 1:85–110.

ALYEA, P. E.
1969   "Property-tax Inducements to Attract Industry." Pp. 139–58, in R. W. Lindholm (ed.), Property Taxation—U.S.A. Madison: University of Wisconsin Press.

BACHRACH, PETER, and MORTON BARATZ
1970   Power and Poverty. New York: Oxford.

BARSS, REITZEL, and ASSOCIATES
1969   Community Action and Institutional Change. Cambridge, Mass.
1970   Community Action and Urban Institutional Change. Cambridge, Mass.

BARTON, ALLEN.
1975   "Consensus and Conflict among American Leaders," *Public Opinion Quarterly* 38:507–30.

BOOMS, B. H., and J. R. HALLDORSON
1973   "The Politics of Redistribution: A Reformulation," *American Political Science Review* 67:924–33.

CLOWARD, RICHARD A., and FRANCES F. PIVEN.
1974   The Politics of Turmoil. New York: Pantheon Books.

COLE, R. L.
1974   Citizen Participation and the Urban Policy Process. Lexington, Mass.: Lexington Books.

FORD FOUNDATION
1963   "American Community Development. Preliminary reports by directors of projects assisted by the Ford Foundation in four cities and a state," presented at the 29th Annual Conference of National Association of Housing and Redevelopment Officials, Denver, Colorado.

FRIEDLAND, ROGER
1980   Power, Crisis and the Central City. London: Macmillan.
Forth-
coming
1975   "Big Apple and the Urban Orchard." Unpublished paper.

FRY, B. R., and R. F. WINTERS
1970   "The Politics of Redistribution," *American Political Science Review* 64:508–522.

GREENBERG, STANLEY
1974   Politics and Poverty. New York: Wiley Interscience.
GREENSTONE, J. DAVID
1969   Labor in American Politics. New York: Vintage.
GREENSTONE, J. DAVID, and PAUL PETERSON
1970   "Reformers, Machines, and the War on Poverty." Pp. 267–91, in
        James Q. Wilson (ed.), City Politics and Public Policy. New York:
        Wiley.
HAMILTON, RICHARD
1972   Class and Politics in the United States. New York: Wiley.
HICKS, ALEXANDER, ROGER FRIEDLAND, and EDWIN JOHNSON
1975   "The Political Economy of Redistribution: The Case of the Ameri-
        can States," presented at the American Sociological Association
        meetings, San Francisco.
HILL, RICHARD CHILD
1976   "Black Struggle and the Urban Fiscal Crisis," *Kapitalistate* 4.
1973   "Urban Income Inequality," Ph.D. dissertation, Department of Soci-
        ology, University of Wisconsin, Madison.
KATZNELSON, IRA
1975   "The Crisis of the Capitalist City: Urban Politics and Social Con-
        trol," in W. Hawley and M. Lipsky (eds.), Theoretical Perspectives
        on Urban Politics. Englewood Cliffs, N.J.: Prentice-Hall.
KRAMER, R. M.
1969   Participation of the Poor: Comparative Community Case Studies in
        the War on Poverty. Englewood Cliffs, N.J.: Prentice-Hall.
LOWI, THEODORE
1967a   "The Public Philosophy: Interest-Group Liberalism," *American Politi-
        cal Science Review* 61:5–24.
1967b   "Machine Politics Old and New," *The Public Interest* 9:83–92.
MOLLENKOPF, JOHN
1975   "The Postwar Politics of Urban Development," *Politics and Society*
        5:247–95.
1973   "On the Causes and Consequences of Neighborhood Mobilization."
        Paper delivered at the 1973 American Political Science Association
        meetings, New Orleans.
MORLOCK, LAURA
1972   "Business Interests, Countervailing Groups and the Balance of Influ-
        ence in 91 Cities." Unpublished paper, John Hopkins University.
MOYNIHAN, DANIEL P.
1969   Maximum Feasible Misunderstanding. New York: Free Press.
PIVEN, FRANCES FOX
1972   "Cutting up the City Pie," *The New Republic* (February 5):17–22.
PIVEN, FRANCES FOX, and RICHARD CLOWARD
1971   Regulating the Poor. New York: Vintage.
REICH, MICHAEL
1973   "Racial Discrimination and the White Income Distribution," Ph.D.
        dissertation, Department of Economics, Harvard University.
ROSSI, PETER, RICHARD BERK, and BETTYE EDISON
1974   The Roots of Urban Discontent. New York: Wiley Interscience.

Urquhart, Heather J.
  1974   "The Ford Foundation and the Origins of the War on Poverty," senior essay for Sociology, University of California, Santa Cruz.
Wolman, H. L., and N. C. Thomas
  1970   "Black Interests, Black Groups and Black Influence in the Federal Policy Process: The Cases of Housing and Education," *Journal of Politics* 32:875–97.

 The Political Economy of
Redistribution in the American States

Alexander Hicks
Northwestern University

What have been the effects of class, class structure, and class political practices on state action in the United States in the twentieth century, and how have these effects changed with varying conditions? In particular, what have been the effects of class on redistributive policies in the United States from the economic crisis of the 1930s up to the advent of the new crises of the 1960s?[1]

A broad array of class forces is most likely to affect state action in the context of threats from system contradictions and subordinate classes to the state's reproduction of capitalist social relations. Contradictions and class practices have yet to manifest themselves in direct and unequivocal challenges to capitalist relations of production in the United States. They have been felt instead in threats to sustained capital accumulation, transformations of the distribution of goods produced (circulation relations), and hindrances to the use of repressive measures in the reproduction of international capitalism.

The second of these factors—the transformation of circulation relations—has taken two principal forms: first, the institutionalized involvement of unions in the determination of labor costs (that is, collective bargaining); and second, state intervention in the distribution of income. In the United States, where employment policies have been limited compared to other advanced capitalist nations, welfare policies have consisted princi-

---

The author is indebted to Michael Aiken, Charles N. Halaby, and Erik Olin Wright for helpful criticisms, comments, and suggestions.

[1] A less theoretically elaborate, operationally developed, and historically complete attempt to treat the same question is Hicks and others (1978:302–315).

pally of the progressive redistribution of income through government expenditure and tax programs.[2] Such redistribution provides the state side in the relation of class to state. State governments have played a significant role in government redistribution in the United States. By examining state government, we can analyze redistribution in both comparative-historical and quantitative terms.

Theory: Classes, State Policy, and Governmental Redistribution

Class

Classes are social aggregates delineated by their positions within social relations of production. These positions are defined, following Wright (1977:32–55), in terms of their possession or nonpossession of effective control over money, physical capital, and the organization and disciplining of employees. I identify four major classes: (1) the capitalist class, those who have effective control over each of these variables; (2) the petite bourgeoisie, those in positions with control over money and physical capital, but without control over more than a handful of full-time, nonfamily employees; (3) the middle class, those having some but not all dimensions of control (excluding the petite bourgeoisie); and (4) the working class, those with control of none of these variables. Unlike Wright, I exclude, as criteria of class, positions in the formal institutions of government.

To relate classes to state policy, classes are subdivided into *class segments* (see Zeitlin and others 1976:1009–10). The capitalist class is divided into monopoly and competitive capitalists on the basis of the size, pricing power, and other highly interrelated characteristics of capital-accumulating units (see O'Connor [1973:13–39] and Poulantzas [1975]). The focus on the working class is confined to unionized labor, on the premises that union organization integrates the perceived economic interests of the workers whom it organizes, and served as an important condition for the capacity of workers to affect policy during the 1929–1961 period. The petite bourgeoisie is divided into farm and nonfarm sectors on the assumption that differing political-economic interests coincide with this distinction, which is made yet more consequential by the different political voluntary associations of these two petite bourgeois groups.

Such factors as classwide or class-segmentwide ideological and organizational integration are not regarded here as prerequisites for the exis-

---

[2] The conceptualization and measurement of redistribution are discussed in following sections and the appendix.

tence of classes, but rather as determinants of the extent to which classes are likely to be influential.

The state and the determinants of state policy

The state is conceptualized as a structure which reinforces the basic social relations of capitalist society. This activity of the state is the result of a number of causes, constraints, and mechanisms that operate on it both from the outside and from within. These may be categorized as three types of determinants: "influence," "systemic" and "state-structural."

Influence determinants. Influences are the *effects* of a social aggregate's political *resources* on outcomes in line with the aggregate's outcome-related *interests*. Influences may be of two sorts, depending on the kinds of conscious activities involved in affecting their outcomes. They may be intentional; that is, they may be consciously pursued by the influential aggregate by means of its intentional exercise of its political resources. Influences may also be unintentional. That is, an influencing aggregate may be granted its interests without ever using its resources. This granting of interests will be done by some party, such as a legislature, to obviate the costs that it would incur if the influencing party fully mobilized its resources. *Influence determinants* of state policy are simply those influences which have state policies as their outcomes.

As effects of resources, influence effects would be prohibitively difficult to identify and measure if every conceivable kind of resource that a group might use to realize its ends had to be considered. Therefore, our focus here is mainly on "organizational capacities," the political resources involved in, or closely associated with, organization. These capacities take such diverse forms as specialized lobbying and propaganda personnel, control over jobs or other resources, influence over organizational members' votes, and money. To determine governmental redistribution, I systematically considered organizational capacities. However, other political resources, such as an aggregate's potential electoral weight or its degree of support by prevailing ideological orientations, are considered where relevant.

I not only focus on the effects of the political resources of social aggregates and classes, but also on *class struggles* over state policy, where the classes are interdependent in their efforts to exert conflicting pressures on the state. That is, how do classes, in their state-oriented political practices, attend to each other's practices, and affect the impact of other classes on state action?

Systemic determinants. Systemic determinants are the imperatives, constraints, and opportunities (aside from influence determinants) that, because of the state's location within the social formation, determine state functioning (Poulantzas 1973:245). For example, the constraining effects of sustained capital accumulation on the state's tax base solvency, and consequently its actions, are a principal systemic determinant. Similarly, the constraining effects of individualistic anti-statist definitions of economic problems and solutions to the state's economic policies represent a second major systemic determinant.

State-structural determinants. The characteristics of the internal structure of the state that partially determine its functioning are the state-structural determinants. Such determinants may be symbolic, such as neo-Keynesian demand management paradigms, or organizational, such as the functional differentiation of state administration. They may be unitary attributes of state structure, such as its aggregate organization of policy-making routines in ways which select problems and solutions that repress anticapitalist interests and to emphasize and integrate procapitalist interests (Offe 1973). They may be attributes of particular agencies and policy precedents that differentially favor one class or the other (Poulantzas 1973:255).

Governmental Redistribution

Governments may redistribute income in a variety of ways. They may redistribute income among various *social units,* such as households or corporations, geographic regions or economic sectors. Governments may also use various means to redistribute income. They may redistribute income *fiscally,* by means of their own expenditure and revenue flows; or they may do so *legalistically,* by means of the preponderantly legal rather than fiscal regulation of those in the private sector. They may do so *directly,* by means of the net give-and-take of expenditure benefits and revenue burdens for specific populations such as the poor; or they may do so *indirectly,* by employing fiscal measures to stimulate businesses disproportionately likely to employ the poor.

These four means of governmental redistribution of income—fiscal and legalistic, direct and indirect (or market-mediated)—can be used to generate a typology of governmental redistribution. Four types of government redistribution result: (1) fiscal-direct redistribution, exemplified by such policy means as public assistance payments and income taxes; (2) fiscal-market redistribution, exemplified by such policy means as tax subsidies to labor-intensive industries; (3) legalistic-market redistribution, exemplified by such policy means as minimum wage, open shop, and affirmative action legislation; and (4) legalistic-direct redistribution, currently an almost nonexistent category that might be exemplified by non-fiscally related legislation governing the operation of private charities.

A substantial degree of fiscal-direct governmental distribution is now documented for the United States and a number of other political democracies (Reynolds and Smolensky 1977; Nicolson 1974: chap. 3; Franzen 1975:31–35). For example, Reynolds and Smolensky find that fiscal-direct redistribution augments the incomes of the poor by nearly 100 percent and yields a roughly 25 percent reduction in U.S. Gini indices of household income inequality. Other types of governmental redistribution are less well-documented and appear, on the basis of existing documentation, to be less, if not negligible (Hicks 1979).

Focusing on fiscal-direct governmental redistribution to poor households is a good starting point for developing theory and research on governmental redistribution, in light of the relief character of U.S. welfare programs, a key overall component of redistributive state policies. The centrality of welfare policies to many discussions of the economic, political, and ideological stabilization of capitalist political democracies during the latter part of the 1929–1961 period provides a complementary reason for this focus (see Shonfield 1966: chap. 1; O'Connor 1973:137–68). So does the centrality of such policies for subsequent destabilizations (Esping-Andersen and others 1976:186).

A focus on state governments is pertinent to a concern with fiscal-direct governmental redistribution during the 1929–1961 period for several reasons. During this period, states raised about a fifth of total government revenues and spent about a third of total government expenditure. They had primary jurisdiction over most welfare programs other than the massive social security retirement ones (such as general public assistance, unemployment, and workmen's compensation). A focus on poor households is central because of the relief character of most U.S. welfare programs and because of the urgency of redistribution for the poorest.

My 1929 starting point allows for the study of governmental redistribution from its advent. In 1929, government expenditures as a percentage of GNP and welfare expenditures as a percentage of governmental expenditures were too small for governmental redistribution to be very notable. My own estimates of state fiscal-directed redistribution show close to zero dollars per poor household in 1929, as opposed to $250 in 1962.

The determination of state fiscal-direct governmental redistribution

The economic crisis of the great depression and the political practices it stimulated and portended gave rise to fiscal-direct governmental redistribution in the United States. Although state redistributive policies preceded these federal initiatives and later developed within the context of the policy precedents and incentives established by such major federal legislation as the Social Security Act of 1935, they developed within this context with considerable variation and independence. What influence, systemic, state-structural, and other determinants generated this development?

Class influence. The organizational capacities of monopoly capitalists for influencing policy extend to at least several decades before the 1929–1961 period. The organizational capacities of large corporations and their heads include control over state manufacturer's associations, well-financed lobbyists, monopolies over expertise required by government, control over career trajectories out of the public sector, and discretionary control over investment decisions on which governmental effectiveness depends (Hicks and others 1978:303). The antiredistributive interests guiding the resources of monopoly capital have been dominant throughout the post-1929 period (Lowi 1964; Hicks and others 1978). Consequently, I hypothesized antiredistributive effects of the monopoly capital class segment and its organizational capacities for all portions of the 1929–1961 period.

Competitive capital has had similar, if weaker, organizational capacities and even stronger and more pervasive antiredistributional interests (see O'Connor 1973). Consequently, I hypothesized that competitive capital had negative effects on governmental redistribution throughout the period studied.

By the late 1930s, organized labor had surely acquired the organizational capacities for influencing governmental policies, if it had not had them earlier. Among its political resources since that time have been numerous, broadly dispersed, well-financed, and rationally coordinated public relations and lobbying specialists, plus a considerable degree of organization (and an even more considerable reputation) for mobilizing the typically substantial union vote (Hicks and others 1978:303). Union support for redistributive policies is equivocal until the late 1930s because of a union commitment to protecting the scope of collective bargaining goals from curtailment by competing government functions (Sander 1973). However, its support is strong from then on (Sander 1973; Hicks 1979). Because the redistributive interests of unions during the 1930s might well have been sufficiently redistributive for intentional influence or perceived as sufficiently redistributive for unintentional influence, I tentatively hypothesized redistributive effects for organized labor during the 1930s. Given the combined interests and capacities of organized labor thereafter, I hypothesized redistributive union effects for the 1940s and 1950s.

By the 1940s, the hypothesized conflicting redistributive effects of monopoly capitalists and organized workers were expected to have taken place in a context of mutual attention, antagonism, and adjustment in which monopoly capital and organized labor each employed its resources to mitigate the undesired policy effects of the other. Consequently, I hypothesized redistributive effects of class struggles between monopoly capital and unionized labor for the 1940s and 1950s.

The organization, interests, or circumstance of a number of additional class or class-related groups were also expected to influence governmental redistribution. First, the militancy and organization of the depression's unemployed, coupled with the sheer magnitude of unemployment as a real and perceived dimension of the depression, suggested the following hypothesis: the proportion of unemployed positively affected governmental redistribution during the 1930s (see Karsh and Garman 1961). The disorganization and reduced ranks of the postdepression unemployed does not suggest any redistributive influences by them during the 1940s and the 1950s. However, because of the simple fact that the unemployed constitute at all times a pool of persons disproportionately likely to meet and to utilize the eligibility requirements of transfer payment programs, I tentatively hypothesized that unemployment rates positively affected governmental redistribution during the 1940s and 1950s.

Second, the militancy and extensive membership of farmers' voluntary organizations during the 1930s, coupled with the gravity of the 1930s agricultural depression, suggested the hypothesis that the agricultural petite bourgeoisie positively influenced governmental redistribution during the 1930s (Benedict 1953:299; Schlesinger 1957:174–76). Conversely, the conservatism of most farm organizations during the postdepression period suggested the hypothesis that the agricultural petite bourgeoisie negatively influenced state fiscal-direct redistribution during the subsequent two decades (see Benedict 1953).

Finally, I hypothesized that the poor would positively affect governmental redistribution during all portions of the 1929–1961 period. I reasoned that the poor would exert unintentional positive influences upon governmental redistribution as politicians sought to mobilize their votes with redistributive policies and programs. They would also positively affect governmental redistribution for technical reasons resembling those for expecting that the unemployed of the 1930s and 1940s would positively affect redistribution during the same time.[3]

Systemic determinants

Relatively high income levels are commonly required to expand the pool of potential revenues that can be raised for redistributive uses without causing

---

[3] The main technical reason for expecting the poor (operationally, their number as a proportion of state population) to positively affect governmental redistribution is that the proportion of poor in a state can be expected to be related to the proportion of the *very* poor in a state. The poorer a state's poor, the more likely they will be eligible for welfare and tax relief forms of redistribution. Hence the greater the proportion of poor the greater the extent of per poor household redistribution.

zero-sum conflicts abhorred by state policy-makers. This argument is plausible and has garnered considerable empirical support (see Wilensky 1975). Consequently, I hypothesize that per capita income levels positively affected governmental redistribution during all of the decades studied.

Urbanization as an indication of proletarianization reflects declines in petite bourgeois laissez-faire ideologies, and declines in kinship-based welfare systems. As a source of population density it provides otherwise unorganized workers with a facilitating condition for redistributive collective action. Accordingly, I hypothesized that levels of urbanization would positively affect governmental redistribution during all of the decades studied.

Wilensky (1975) has argued that the incidence of relatively visible direct taxes upon middle-income strata generates a "welfare backlash" among them and an electorally influential opposition to governmental redistribution to the poor. However, such middle-strata direct tax burdens are more likely to generate opposition to redistributive policies during periods of relatively high economic growth and prosperity. During such periods, humanitarian and "public interest" ideologies have less extensive and salient appeal and are less likely to offset the resentment of tax burdens that redistributive policies aggravate. Consequently, I hypothesized that the middle-strata direct tax burden negatively affected governmental redistribution during the relatively prosperous 1940s and 1950s.

Commitments to individualistic, careerist, anticollectivist, laissez-faire components of bourgeois ideology have been hypothesized to vary with rising consumption levels, occupational upgrading, and structural upward mobility. These vary positively with long-term economic growth. Accordingly, I hypothesize that laissez-faire individualism negatively affects governmental redistribution. Unfortunately, I have not been able to construct a direct measure of laissez-faire individualism. However, economic growth, net of controls for measures of poverty, unemployment, income level, urbanization, and middle-strata tax burdens—all consequences of economic growth—can be assumed to be a major source of laissez-faire individualism via the consumption and mobility mechanisms. Accordingly, in operational terms, controlling for the variables just enumerated, economic growth should negatively affect governmental redistribution during all three decades.

Income levels, urbanization, middle-strata direct tax burdens, and laissez-faire individualism, together with poverty and unemployment, are all consequences of *capital accumulation processes.*[4] As such, the four systemic determinants discussed in this section together with poverty and unemployment link these fundamental processes of capitalist economic structures and objects of state functioning to governmental redistribution.

---

[4] For arguments and evidence supporting this point see Hicks (1979).

State-structural determinants

Two aspects of state structure seem to merit special consideration as determinants of government policies; (1) any structural characteristics of the state which, as results of past concessions to anticapitalist redistributive interests, may prove structurally conducive to further governmental redistribution; and (2) mechanisms of the state's selection and regulation of state outputs in line with capitalist interests. These emphases are derived from certain formulations of the possibility of anticapitalist enclaves within the state and the characteristic procapitalist functioning of the state as a whole (Poulantzas 1973:255).

Program precedents of particular types—their number and cumulative age—have been found to be strongly related to aggregate outputs of the same types. For example, Cutwright's "Social Insurance Program Experience" is a strong predictor of welfare expenditures (see Cutwright 1964:537–50; Wilensky 1975). Hicks (1979) argues that Walker's "progressive" innovations index (1970) is effectively an index of the number and cumulative age of progressive program precedents that are structurally conducive to governmental redistribution. Accordingly, I hypothesized that progressive innovations positively affected governmental redistribution in the 1930s, the 1940s, and the 1950s.

The so-called incrementalist hypothesis that the scales and compositions of budgets at one time are principal determinants of later budget characteristics has received strong empirical support (see Sharkansky 1970). The impact of governmental redistribution at one time on later governmental redistribution (that is, $FDR_t = b[FDR_{t-1}]$) can, it turns out, be examined concurrently with a more interesting relation. This is the impact of governmental redistribution at one point in time on changes in governmental redistribution during a subsequent period (that is, $FDR_t - FDR_{t-1} = b[FDR_{t-1}]$). Study of the latter technically incorporates study of the former.[5] It also provides information not only on whether relatively high levels of redistribution at one time tend to be followed by relatively high subsequent *levels*, but also on whether relatively high redistributive levels tend to be followed by increases or decreases in governmental redistribution. If high levels at one point are followed by decreases, or redistributive cutbacks, in a subsequent period, a regulative process favoring capitalist interest can be identified (see Hicks 1979). I expect that such a process does dampen redistributive outputs, at least partially offsetting the expansionary impact of redistributive program precedents or progressive innovations.

---

[5] The essence of this statement is that the b^* coefficients that test the incrementalism hypothesis can be algebraically derived from the b^* coefficients that test the cutbacks hypothesis. Only the equation containing b^* must be estimated. (See Hicks 1979, for details.) FDR = fiscal-direct redistribution.

Accordingly, I hypothesize that levels of governmental redistribution at the beginning of a decade negatively affected subsequent decennial changes in governmental redistribution for the 1930s, the 1940s and the 1950s. To test the related incrementalist hypothesis, which can be tested simultaneously, I tentatively hypothesized that earlier levels of governmental redistribution positively affected subsequent levels of governmental redistribution. (I describe the logic underlying the state-structural hypothesis of this section in my dissertation. [Hicks 1979].)

Conjuncture: Louisiana

Besides the relatively systematic structural determinants of phenomena, other determinants are relatively coincidental, unsystematic, and conjunctural. One potential conjunctural source of governmental redistribution is the political movement headed by Huey Long during the 1928–1935 period. A second, related one is the Long legacy, particularly as championed by Governor Earl Long during the late 1940s. Although the origins and redistributive consequences of these two related reform periods are complex (see Williams 1969; Howard 1971:211–94), Louisiana's changes in governmental redistribution seem to be significantly higher than redistributive changes elsewhere during the 1930s and 1940s.

Residual determinants

Five hypotheses were tentatively made in deference to existing empirical findings and to other theoretical formulations. The first four may be summarized as Democratic competitive mobilization, Democratic party strength, interparty strength, interparty competition, and state population size, *tentatively* hypothesized to *positively* affect governmental redistribution. Hypotheses concerning Democratic competitive mobilization are not made for the 1930s and 1940s because no measures are available; all other "residual" hypotheses apply to all three decades. This constraint applies to the following, second hypothesis: membership in the "Southern" regional category negatively affects governmental redistribution. These hypotheses (see table 9-1) are primarily made as grounds for including the independent variables involved as control variables in analyses.

Governmental Redistribution in the American States, 1929–1961

The hypotheses outlined in columns 1, 3, and 5 of table 9-1 were tested by means of multiple regression analyses of decennial changes in state governmental redistribution together with relevant statistical tests (see section 3 of

Table 9-1. The determination of governmental redistribution: hypotheses and findings

Variables: Models:	1930s		1940s		1950s	
	Hypotheses (1)	Findings (2)	Hypotheses (3)	Findings (4)	Hypotheses (5)	Findings (6)
Monopoly capital	−	=	−	−	−	−
Organized labor	+Q		+	++	+	
Class struggle			−	≡	−	
Competitive capital	−		−		−	−
Agrarian petty bourgeoisie	+	+	−	+	−	−
Unemployment	+	+++	+Q		+Q	
Poverty/poor	+		+	++	+	+++
Middle-strata tax burden			−		−	−
Economic growth/laissez-faire	−	≡	−		−	−
Income level	+	+++	+		+	+
Urbanization	+	=	+		+	+
Cumulative innovations	+	++	+		+	+++
Lagged redistribution (cutbacks)	−	=	−	=	−	≡
Incrementalism	+Q		+Q	++	+Q	+++
Louisiana–Long's	+	+	+Q	++		
Democratic cumulative mobilization	+Q		+Q		+Q	
Democratic strength	+Q		+Q		+Q	
Interparty competition	+Q		+Q		+Q	
Population	+Q		+Q		+Q	
South	−Q		−Q		−Q	−

+   Significant at 0.10 level; $B < 0.25$, $B > 0$
++   Significant at 0.10 level; $B \geq 0.25$, $B < 0.50$
+++   Significant at 0.10 level; $B \geq 0.50$
−   Significant at 0.10 level; $B \geq -0.25$, $B < 0$
=   Significant at 0.10 level; $B \leq -0.25$, $B > -0.50$
≡   Significant at 0.10 level; $B < -0.50$
Q   hypothesis was weak or otherwise qualified.

the appendix; Hicks 1979). The principal dependent variables are decennial *changes* in redistribution. Hypotheses are considered supported if regression slope coefficients for pertinent variables have hypothesized signs and are statistically significant at the 0.10 level.

For cases of supported hypotheses, I talk about effects of varying strengths. Variables with standardized regression coefficients greater than or equal to 0.50 in absolute value are considered to have strong effects. Those with standardized coefficients less than 0.50 but greater than or equal to 0.25 in absolute value are regarded as having moderate effects. Those with standardized coefficients less than 0.25 in absolute value are said to have weak effects.

The 1930s

The three determinants closely linked to characteristic depression phenomena are the only determinants with *strong* effects on governmental redistribution: (1) the unemployment rate, presumably an indicator of influence efforts by the period's numerous organized and militant unemployed; (2) the economic growth rate, which is intended in context to indicate commitments to laissez-faire individualism; and (3) per capita income levels, a conventional indicator of relatively disposable resources for financing redistributive policies.

The organizational capacities of monopoly capitalists had a moderate negative effect on governmental redistribution. However, contrary to my hypothesis, the organizational capacities of competitive capitalists had no significant antiredistributive effect. Lagged levels of governmental redistribution moderately affected decennial changes in governmental redistribution, in support of the cutback hypothesis. Interestingly, the incrementalism hypothesis linking earlier and later levels of governmental redistribution is not supported, which is consistent with speculations that the incrementalist hypothesis applies poorly to periods of precipitous policy change. Progressive innovations had a moderate, positive redistributive effect. A fourth and final moderate effect goes against predictions. This is the negative effect of urbanization, which I earlier imputed to the relative severity of the depression in agricultural areas.

Support for the hypotheses concerning the influence of the agricultural petite bourgeoisie and the redistributive impacts of forces associated with Huey Long emerged from the 1930s analysis, although the estimated agricultural petite bourgeoisie and Long effects are weak.

None of the tentative hypotheses received support. In addition, two of the unqualified hypotheses failed to garner support. The hypothesis involving competitive capitalist influence has already been noted. The other involves the proportion of poor in a state. The lack of a redistributive effect during the great depression is very unexpected and may be attributed to two factors. First, the poor frequently were unemployed farmers, frequently belonged to farm organizations and organizations of the unemployed, and had few organizations to deal with their poverty. Consequently, the poor as such may indeed have exercised no redistributive influence; or whatever influence they may have had may have been picked up in my analyses by the unemployed and farmer variables. Second, poverty was so pervasive during the depression that all states may have had more poverty than they could respond to with redistributive measures. That is, for the depression era, poverty may be better regarded as a pervasive and invariant condition for redistributive policy rather than as a variable useful for explaining redistributive policy variations.

In summary, business-cycle related phenomena—that is, income levels and growth rates and unemployment rates—dominate the determination of depression-era government redistribution. The multiple coefficient of determination for the 1930s analysis is a substantial 0.416.

The 1940s

The 1940s analysis reveals only one strong effect, that of class struggle. (This entails interdependent effects of monopoly capitalist and organized labor resources.)[6] This analysis also reveals several moderate effects: cutback *and* incrementalism effects, a poverty effect, and an Earl Long or Huey Long legacy effect. The last of these is striking and deserves some exposition. Briefly put, during a decade in which the change in per-poor-household net redistributive transfers was only (a positive) $23 for an average state, the increase in such transfers in Louisiana that is attributable to being in Louisiana was $243. This remarkable increase is consistent with descriptive information on the welfare and tax reforms of Governor Earl Long about 1948 (see Howard 1971:211–294). Finally, contrary to prediction, the agricultural petty commodity producers had a weak *positive* effect on redistribution. This suggests that farm organizations maintained reformist stands during the 1940s, or that they were perceived by governmental personnel as doing so.

Hypotheses linking competitive capital, the middle-strata direct tax burden, economic growth and laissez-faire ideology, income levels, progressive innovations, and urbanization to governmental redistribution are not supported. Neither are any of the qualified hypotheses linking the unemployed and the residual variables to governmental redistribution.

Class struggle dominates the determination of 1940s changes in gov-

---

[6] For more on the implications of class struggle effects on "separate" class effects, see Hicks (1979).

ernmental redistribution. The multiple coefficient of determination for the 1940s was a relatively low 0.324, perhaps because of period idiosyncracies associated with World War Two.

The 1950s

The determination of governmental redistribution is dominated by state structure during the 1950s. Three of the period's four strong effects are state-structural—cutback, incrementalism, and progressive innovations effects. Incrementalism effects are algebraically derived from cutback coefficients, as described earlier. Because the former, unlike the latter, predicts levels of governmental redistribution rather than changes in governmental redistribution, the 1950s models may be said to have only two state-structural effects. These are in conflict. The progressive innovations effect, as interpreted here, reflects the expansionary pressure of progressive program precedents and associated state structures (such as agencies, goals, and personnel) on governmental redistribution. The cutback effect reflects a more general state process, rooted in state selective mechanisms and acting to reduce governmental redistribution.

The fourth strong effect is a poverty effect. This effect is interpreted in terms of both unintentional influences of poor mobilized by state personnel in their search for electoral support, and technical relations between the proportion of poor in a state and for poor-household transfers to the poor. In brief, the higher the proportion of poor the higher the proportion of the very poor and those relatively eligible for welfare benefits. This poverty effect involves initiatives by state personnel and attributes of the eligibility structures of state programs. As such, this final strong effect is also partially a state-structural effect.

There are no moderate effects for the 1950s. Weak effects were estimated for monopoly capital, competitive capital, the agricultural petite bourgeoisie, middle-strata direct tax burdens, economic growth and laissez-faire individualism, and the regional category South, all in hypothesized directions. None of the tentatively proposed hypotheses except the incrementalist and Southern ones were supported.

Significantly, the 1950s analysis provides no support for the class struggle hypothesis. Neither does it provide any evidence of an independent redistributive impact of organized labor. Two explanations for the absence of a 1950s organized labor effect are possible. First, in the 1950s, most labor unions had relegated such shared interests with the poor (see Hicks and others 1978:302–315) to a very low level of salience, at least at the state level. Concentration on the 1950s union goal of productivity-tied wage increases may have influenced such a downgrading of union perceived interests in redistribution because of the imperative of business-labor cooperation entailed by the quest for productivity-tied wage increases (see O'Connor 1973). The second explanation for the lack of a 1950s union effect is the ideological conservatism of public opinion and political officeholders in the 1950s relative to the 1940s. The multiple coefficient of determination for the 1950s analysis is 0.55.[7]

The overall determination of governmental redistribution is marked by a substantial shift from the depression-related systemic and influence factors of the 1930s and the class struggle of the 1940s toward a determination by state-structural factors.

Conclusions

The theory of governmental redistribution elaborated here stands up well to empirical testing. The magnitude of the changes in governmental redistribution predicted and observed fit closely enough to be acceptable for each of the three decades studied, despite the unavoidable crudity of certain measures of redistribution, especially the ones for the period before 1960. All but two of the determinants that are central to my theory have significant effects on governmental redistribution in at least half the decades hypothesized. (The two exceptions are the organizational capacities of competitive capitalists and urbanization, whose hypothesized effects appear only in the 1950s.) Most hypotheses are supported. Two crucial sets of hypotheses are persistently supported, the monopoly capitalist hypotheses and the cutback hypotheses. Thus, in line with the present theorizing on monopoly capitalist influence and the so-called instrumentalist (or "class practices") positions, monopoly capital appears consistently able to influence state policy in line with its interests. Consistent with the position taken here and elsewhere (for example, Esping-Andersen and others 1976:186–220), the state fulfills the antiredistributive interests of capital (see Hicks and others 1978:302–315).[8]

---

[7] A final note on method: the coefficients for lagged values of redistribution are, for technical reasons, liable to be biased; however, tests for biases in these coefficients reveal no significant biases at even the 0.40 level! (See Johnston 1971:305–313, and Hicks 1979.)

[8] The objective (as well as the perceived) interests of capital oppose high levels of governmental redistribution during the period studied, even though capital may have a general objective interest in some minimal redistributive level or in high redistributive levels when working class quiescence clearly requires them.

Empirically, my theory requires investigation with better measures and new subject matter for replication, refinement, and extension. For example, better measures of competitive capital's organization capacities might reveal stronger and more persistent competitive capitalist influences; and evidence from governmental units and time periods other than those treated here would be illuminating. At present, my formulation of the theory of general state functions and of its role in redistribution, in particular, is still quite crude because it can address historical shifts in the relative importance of determinants only with considerable ad hoc amendments. Considerable theoretical elaboration and historical specification are needed to remedy this shortcoming (see Hicks 1979, for a step in this direction). I hope that my efforts will provoke others to try to employ the tools of class theory—emphasizing both structure and conjuncture—to explain some of the issues raised here. For example, do redistributive union influences in fact emerge with class struggle in the 1940s only to vanish with it in the 1950s? If so, why?

Whatever the outcome of such future inquiries, it is clear that state policy in the United States cannot be understood without considering the impact of classes and class struggles.[9]

References

BENEDICT, MURRY R.
    1953   Farm Policies of the United States, 1790–1950. New York: Twentieth Century Foundation.

BOOMS, BERNARD, and JAMES R. HALLDORSON
    1973   "The Politics of Redistribution: A Reformulation," *American Sociological Review* 77:920–923.

CUTWRIGHT, PHILLIPS
    1964   "Political Structure, Economic Development and National Social Security Programs," *American Sociological Review* 70:537–50.

ESPING-ANDERSEN, GÖSTA, ROGER FRIEDLAND, and ERIK OLIN WRIGHT
    1976   "Modes of Class Struggle and the Capitalist State," *Kapitalistate* 4–5:186–220.

FRANZEN, THOMAS, LOVGREN KERSTEIN, and IRENE ROSENBERG
    1975   "Redistributional Effects of Taxes and Public Expenditures," *Swedish Journal of Economics* 77:31–55.

---

[9] The preliminary findings in this chapter may differ slightly from the final results of the analysis presented in Hicks (1979).

HICKS, ALEXANDER, ROGER FRIEDLAND, and EDWIN JOHNSON
1978   "Class Power and State Policy: The Case of Large Business Corporations, Labor Unions and Governmental Redistribution in the American States," *American Sociological Review* 43:302–315.

HICKS, ALEXANDER
1979   "The Political Economy of Redistribution: The Case of the American States, 1929–1961," Ph.D. thesis, University of Wisconsin, Madison.

HODSON, RANDY
1977   "Labor Force Participation and Earnings in the Core, Periphery, and State Sectors of Production," M.S. thesis, University of Wisconsin, Madison.

HOWARD, PERRY H.
1971   Political Tendencies in Louisiana, rev. ed. Baton Rouge, Louisiana: State University Press.

JOHNSTON, J.
1971   Econometric Methods, 2d ed. New York: McGraw-Hill

KARSH, BERNARD, and PHILLIPS L. GARMAN
1961   "The Political Left." Chap. 3 in Milton Derber and Edwin Young (eds.), Labor and the New Deal. Madison: University of Wisconsin Press.

LOWI, THEODORE
1964   "American Business and Public Policy," *World Politics* 16:677–719.

NICOLSON, J. L.
1974   "The Distribution and Redistribution of Income in the United Kingdom." Chap. 3 in Dorothy Wederburn (ed.), Poverty, Inequality and Class Structure. Cambridge: Cambridge University Press.

O'CONNOR, JAMES
1973   The Fiscal Crisis of the State. New York: St. Martin's.

POULANTZAS, NICOS
1973   Political Power and Social Class. London: New Left Books.
1975   Classes in Contemporary Capitalist Society. London: New Left Books.

REYNOLD, MORGAN, and EUGENE SMOLENSKY
1977   Public Expenses, Taxes and the Distribution of Income: the U.S.: 1950, 1961, and 1970. New York: Academic Press.

SANDER, DANIEL S.
1973   The Impact of the Reform Movements on Social Policy Change: The Case of Social Insurance. Fair Lawn: R. E. Burdick.

SCHLESINGER, ARTHUR
1957   The Age of Roosevelt: The Crisis of the Old Order. Boston: Houghton-Mifflin.

SHONFIELD, S. ANDREW
1966   Modern Capitalism. London: Oxford University Press.

WALKER, JACK L.
1970   "The Diffusion of Innovations among American States," *American Political Science Review* 3:880–89.

WILENSKY, HAROLD
1975   The Welfare State and Equality. New York: Wiley.

WILLIAMS, T. HARRY
1969   Huey Long. New York: Knopf.

WRIGHT, ERIK O., and LUCA PERRONE
   1977   "Marxist Class Categories and Income Inequality," *American Sociological Review* 73:673–81.
ZEITLIN, MAURICE, W. LAWRENCE NEUMAN, and RICHARD EARL RATCLIFF
   1976   "Class Segments: Agrarian Property and Political Leadership in the Capitalist Class of Chile," *American Sociological Review* 41(6):1006–29.

Appendix

The measurement of fiscal-direct redistribution

Fiscal-direct redistribution to poor households (or FDR) is operationalized by some modifications of the redistribution index used by Booms and Halldorson (1973:920–33) in their study of state redistribution. Fiscal-direct redistribution is defined for operational purposes as the dollar value of net transfers per poor household. More specifically, fiscal-direct redistribution equals $(BN - BR)/h$, where BN is an estimate of net expenditure benefits for all poor households in a state, BR is one of net revenue burdens, and h is an estimate of the number of poor households per state.

This net transfer definition of *FDR* differs from the original Booms and Halldorson measure in two respects. First, the Booms and Halldorson measure was a ratio measure equaling BN/BR. Such ratio measures only measure rates of return to tax payments in expenditure benefits. They are not sensitive to magnitudes of expenditure and revenue flows to and from the poor. For example, if Massachusetts' $BN/h = \$600$ and $BR/h = \$300$, Massachusetts' net transfer measure would equal $300, while its ratio measure would equal 2. Similarly, if South Dakota's $BN/h = \$240$ and its $BR/h = \$60$, South Dakota's net transfer measure would equal $180, but its ratio measure would equal 4. These two states would rank differently on the two scales. The essence of my argument for choosing a net transfer measure is that a measure that denotes Massachusetts as the more redistributive of the two states in the above example has more face validity for the extent to which taxes and expenditures redistribute income to the poor than a measure that denotes South Dakota as the more redistributive.

My net transfer measure of fiscal-direct redistribution also differs from Booms and Halldorson's because I modified some of the data they used to allocate state insurance trust benefits and burdens among income strata. First, I purged the data used to allocate the state insurance trust expenditure and benefit programs of information of *federal* social security pension programs. I also added detailed information on the three state insurance trust programs, namely, unemployment compensation, workmen's compensation, and state government retirement pensions. Second, I used suggestions from a number of studies of agricultural expenditures to change the data used to allocate state agricultural expenditures (see Hicks 1979).

Measures of government redistribution for 1951, 1941, and 1929 were constructed without certain data used to construct 1961 measures. In particular, data on the progressiveness or regressiveness of particular expenditure and revenue categories were not available prior to 1961. Pre-1961 measures of governmental redistribution were constructed on the assumption that the progressiveness or regressiveness of given categories of expenditures and revenues is sufficiently stable across time so that the differences in governmental redistribution across time are predominantly functions of the presences or absences, magnitudes, and mixes of given expenditure and revenue programs, not of changes in the progressiveness or regressiveness of such programs. A number of quantitative checks on the accuracy of this assumption made in Hicks (1979) support this assumption.

Measurement of independent variables

Measurement of monopoly capital's organizational capacities is based on the natural logarithm of the "corporate presence" principal component scores described in Hicks and others (1978:305–312). The varied information on corporate headquarters, assets, and so on used to construct that criterion measure are not available for most time points of interest preceding 1961. Hence, a proxy is used for 1929, 1941, 1951 and, for comparability, 1961. This is the natural logarithm of total assets of private commercial banks in the state; this correlated very strongly with the principal factor criterion in 1961 ($r = 0.92$). Competitive capital's organizational capacities are measured with an index of the per capita number of "managers, officials and proprietors in nonagricultural competitive industries," as defined by Hodson (1977). The presence of the agricultural petite bourgeoisie in a state is measured as the per capita number of self-employed persons in a state. Organized labor's organizational capacities are measured as the per capita number of union members in a state in 1939, 1953, and 1961. Class struggle is measured as the ratio of monopoly capital's capacities to organized labor's capacities.

Poverty is measured as the proportion of families with incomes of less than \$3,000 in 1960, \$2,500 in 1950, and \$600 in 1940. Unemployment is measured as the proportion of the labor forces unemployed. The 1940 measure is an average of 1940 and 1930 percentages to tap depression employment more accurately than with 1940 data alone.

The 1941 income level is measured as the 1940 per capita income; the 1951 income level is measured with the 1950 median personal income; and the 1961 income level with a 1960 index of socioeconomic development described with 1960 median income ($r = 0.91$).

The 1961 urbanization measure is the "urbanization-industrialization" index described in Hicks and others (1978:302–312). The 1951 and 1941 urbanization measures are measures of total urban population as percentages of total state population.

Capital accumulation rates are measured with long-term changes in personal income—that is, 1929–1960 changes for 1961 analyses, 1929–1950 changes for 1951 analyses, and 1920–1940 changes for 1941 analyses.

The middle-strata direct tax burden is measured as the estimated per capita total of federal and state income taxes and state and local property taxes paid out by middle-income households. These middle strata are defined for 1961 in terms of households with incomes of $4,000 to $10,000. They are defined for similar percentiles of households for earlier time points. (See Hicks 1979, for further details.)

Walker's innovations index (1970:880–89) is used to measure structural redistributive policy precedents or cumulative innovations; and 1951, 1941, and 1929 estimates of *FDR* are used as lagged values of *FDR* in the estimations of cutback coefficients for 1961, 1951, and 1941 analyses, respectively.

The three-party variables are measured for 1961 as described in Hicks and others (1978:305–312) for 1961, and descriptions of the measures of Democratic strength and interparty competition for 1951 and 1941 analyses (which measures are similar to those used in 1961 analyses) are available in Hicks (1979).

"Long-Louisiana" was measured as a dummy variable equal to one for Louisiana and otherwise zero.

All variables were measured for 1929 or 1930, 1940 or 1941, and 1950 or 1951 unless otherwise noted. Detailed sources of the more than 50 measures and 100 items are reported in Hicks (1979).

10 The Great Anti-Injunction Strike of 1976

Mary Lou Worth

The United Mine Workers of America (UMWA) went on contract strike in December of 1977. Without strike benefits, and facing one of the harshest winters in recent history, the miners forced their bargaining council to reject one contract offer, themselves voted down a second contract offer, and finally accepted a contract only after the strike had dragged on for 15 bitter weeks. Toward the end of the strike, the miners received widespread publicity and although much of the media attempted to blame the miners for a so-called energy shortage, it was clear that organized labor in the United States and the vast majority of working Americans understood that their interests lay with the miners.

Typically, however, the media or journalists analyzing the strike provided little historical background and tended, instead, to deal with the miner and the UMWA in romanticized, stereotyped terms. Few people outside the coalfields knew of or understood the recent history of strikes in the UMWA and how the legal contract strike of the union was an integral part of a developing motion within the miners' union, in particular, and the American working class in general.

This study focuses on the most important of the "illegal" strikes leading up to the contract strike—the injunction strike of 1976. In this unauthorized work stoppage (or wildcat strike), over 120,000 working coal miners in Appalachia and the West walked off their jobs in the late summer of 1976 in protest against repeated company violations of their contract (the National Bituminous Coal Wage Agreement of 1974) and the misuse by the companies of federal court injunctions as a tool of labor relations. The walk out, which lasted several weeks and never received international union endorsement, was the largest and most militant wildcat carried out by an industrial union in this country in several decades. Lacking international union approval, the miners articulated their grievances and organized their tactics in a manner that bypassed the union bureaucracy. As a result of the strike, several injunctions were halted and, for a period of time, companies ceased their misuse of the federal court injunctions.

This wildcat strike by the United Mine Workers of America is a social phenomenon with its own internal contradictions, responding to the forces within its environment. But these contradictions also develop in the context of the larger contradiction between the interests of the miners and the owners of the mines—the classic labor-capital contradiction, so to speak. For the union is not a mechanical reflection of some idealistic notion of the major contradiction; the union itself shapes and affects the principal contradiction as its own contradiction develops. Likewise, the state cannot be simplistically categorized as the "tool of the capitalists." The role of the state is part of the process of change and development and must be seen as reacting to and reflecting the challenge posed to it by the miners' movement.

The United Mine Workers of America fought for their right to life as a militant, fighting trade union, and many bled and died in the 1920s and 30s for that right. Now, 50 years later, they may have to do it over again. Unless the energy of the fight is used to lay the basis for a long-term change, the spontaneous anger of the workers leads only in circles.

The Context of the Strike

The history of the Appalachian coal fields and the struggle to win and keep a coal miners' union have been well documented (Roy 1905; Coleman 1943; Boyer and Morais 1971; Lee 1969; Hume 1971; Finley 1972). Several material and social conditions distinguish the Appalachian coal industry from other industries and give the United Mine Workers of America a somewhat distinctive character.

Coal mining has always been a particularly dangerous and dirty occupation. The coal companies were forced to utilize a number of mechanisms to trap their labor force and ensure that trained and disciplined cohorts of workers were available. The Appalachian people, prior to the development of the coal industry, were small farmers noted for individualism and independence; they were not easily won to the notion of spending long hours underground for poor wages. Over several decades the coal companies overcame the problem of labor shortage by importing labor from abroad (Welsh miners, Italians, and some Poles) and poor blacks from the South. They also developed social mechanisms by which native Appalachians, as well as the importees, were locked into an area with few options other than to enter the industry. Once that labor force had been established, the infamous company town held people in through debt, fear, and in some cases overt physical force. These towns were a way of life for generations of coal miners and their families (Dreiser and others 1932; Tams 1962; Lee 1969).

The miners faced desperate conditions. Nine- and 10-year-old children worked under slavelike conditions in the mines. Employers made no secret of the fact that they considered the lives of their mules to be more important than the lives of men. The wages were poor and employment fluctuated. Working conditions were often extremely bad and death and maiming injuries expected. These conditions led to a cultural fatalism and hopelessness among the people (Ross 1971; Althouse 1974). But these same conditions called forth their opposite—a fierce pride among the people of themselves as coal miners, intense loyalty to community and to one another—and ultimately laid the basis for the strength that allowed the union to be built. The mine workers' union was organized despite large-scale military operations carried out by the companies, subversion by company spies and provocateurs from within, and a workforce that was widely dispersed. The motto "United We Stand, Divided We Fall" came to be deeply understood as a life-or-death practicality and the ability to organize under hard repression became a fine art (Lee 1969).

The union was a distinctive reflection of these conditions and, at the same time, of the fact that some capitalists themselves desired and encouraged a single union. J. P. Morgan, for one, clearly understood that it was to his benefit to bargain with a single organized entity rather than continuously cope with small, dissident groups of miners. At the same time, big capital could pass along the increased costs of union wages while its smaller competition could not (Coleman 1943:72). The United Mine Workers of America, then, were eventually recognized by the largest companies and charged with keeping labor peace in the coal fields.

For several decades in this century the job of running the union fell to a strong man—John L. Lewis. Lewis was a leader who was properly militant and successfully controlled the internal life of the organization. His leadership had both positive and negative effects.[1] On the positive side, he was able to build the union into a militant fighting force and successfully used the strike, slowdowns, and the force of his authority to gain substantial benefits for miners and a serious respect for the union. He used his position to initiate and then support the organizing efforts of the fledgling Congress of Industrial Organizations (CIO), which was initially built with the coal miners' dues (Boyer and Morais 1971).

On the negative side, Lewis accomplished his goals by eliminating de-

---

[1] Too often, discussions of John L. Lewis have degenerated into polemics between his ardent supporters and his bitter enemies. Such an approach is static, for it fails to place the man in the context of history and in the context of what the American trade union movement was. Three different interpretations of Lewis's role in the UMWA can be found in Carnes (1936), Alinsky (1949), and Finley (1972).

mocracy in the union and by setting the union on the path to "business unionism." At the end of his tenure, the UMWA was in itself a business, with major investments in coal companies, real estate, and an inherent inability to fight for the working and retired coal miner. Lewis's death left the union caught in shady financial deals, devastated in membership by the onslaught of mechanization in the industry, and wracked from within by factions manipulating to gain power (Bethel 1971; Finley 1972). The membership had been locked out of democratic participation and Lewis's policies had become increasingly less responsive to the needs of the members. Lewis's eventual successor, Tony Boyle, was no more than a henchman and the contradictions planted during Lewis's tenure came to fruition during Boyle's reign. Anarchy in the coal fields and murder in the internal hierarchy brought forth a new burst of energy from both the rank and file and local and district level leaders who sought reform in their union. On the heels of the murder of the presidential, reform candidate Jock Yablonski and the growing demand for reform, Arnold Miller rode into union leadership.

But personalities are not the key to this analysis. Rather, the question is what roles a union leader is expected to play, and by whom, and what expectations the miners have of the union itself. The Bituminous Coal Operators' Association also has expectations of the union—not its ability to deliver benefits to its members but its ability to discipline and control the workforce. The ultimate question, of course, is whether an organization devoted to the protection of workers' interests, under capitalism, can reconcile that function with that of the interests of profit. The smaller strikes of 1975 and the mass injunction strike of 1976 must be analyzed in this context.

Background of the Strike

Mining in the United States is an exceedingly dangerous occupation (Hume 1971; David 1972).[2] Demands for increased productivity in coal mining, perhaps more than in any other industry, conflict with the safety concerns of the coal miner. The very fact that men go into a mine with the consistent dread of death, maiming injury, and black lung disease underlies the essential consciousness of the coal miner (Ross 1971). Appalachian miners have also understood that the union holds out their principal hope for protection against the relentless drive for profits. Coal miners become angry then, in a very contradictory fashion. They become angry at the company for its exploitation and oppression and they become angry at

---

[2] In 1977, in the state of West Virginia alone, 30 coal miners were killed and 5,357 disabling injuries occurred.

their union if it fails to protect them from the company. At times, the relationships between the enemy and their own representative becomes blurred and confused. And at times that confusion is real—for it is questionable as to whose interests the union genuinely represents (Harvey 1975:267–70).

Under the system of business unionism in this country, the contract is binding between contract periods.[3] Thus, the union, once it signs the contract is, with rare exception, legally bound to ensure that the workers carry on work until all legal remedies have been pursued. The problem with this process lies in the very nature of negotiating the original terms of the contract. Labor relations theory asserts that at the bargaining table all parties are equal—each having powers analogous to sovereign states (Beal 1972: 248). But the two parties in a contract negotiation do not approach the tables as equals in some community of interest. Industry approaches the table given its legal right to own the mines and the machinery, its right to take profit from the labor of the workers, and the tremendous influences it can bring to bear, through these rights, on Congress, the presidency and the courts (Miliband 1969:81).

The union approaches contract negotiations defensively. Its major weapon is a strike, and with the UMWA, a contract stike is a strike without benefits. A strike is by its very nature defensive for it does not increase labor's control over the means of production. It is maximally a threat to the companies in that if they do not agree to a somewhat more beneficial term for the sale of miners' labor power, the union will temporarily withhold that labor power, at great hardship for the union members.[4]

This essential inequality is exacerbated once the contract is ratified and set in force. Miners are forced to go through a difficult and long grievance procedure in which they may be harassed, intimidated, and even fired

---

[3] The ability of the state to enforce the union contract as legally binding was a change in American labor relations wrought by the reactionary Taft-Hartley legislation of 1947. Radicals from the left often denounce the sellout policies of trade unions, but fail to do anything toward mobilizing organized labor and the public to repeal the law that so essentially cripples the militancy of the trade-union movement. Likewise, the business union bureaucrats who have become comfortable with the existing situation also tolerate the Taft-Hartley law and have in recent years only carried on token education campaigns among their membership regarding Taft-Hartley. They have relied only on lobbyists to try to defeat Taft-Hartley—an effort that has consistently failed. The inability of the government to enforce the Taft-Hartley provision ordering the miners back to work in the contract strike of 1977 is ample proof that an organized and militant membership can easily do what the paid professional lobbyists of George Meany cannot.

[4] Industry clearly understands the limitations of a strike and can calculate and plan for its effect. Dean Witter & Company, stock analysts, accurately predicted the nature and outcome of the UMWA contract strike in the fall of 1974 in their March 1974, bulletin (Price 1974:19–21).

at every step for attempting to exert their union rights. Continual company refusal to abide by the contract forces the union into long and difficult negotiations and legalistic proceedings that drain union resources and stretch scarce personnel.[5] The end result is that the companies have, in general, extremely poor records of keeping good faith; instead, they flagrantly and openly violate the terms of the contract, knowing full well that the chances are good that they will not get caught and if they are, that they will only be minimally punished.[6]

At the same time, the companies loudly preach to the miners that they must abide by the contract. When the miners resort to their most successful defensive tactic, a strike—through disillusionment with the grievance procedure, ignorance as to how to proceed legally, or goaded into a strike by the arbitrary and capricious policy of the company—the company turns to the courts to get the miners back to work.

This general process—company violations of the contract, miners' anger and frustration, and miner violation of the contract through the wildcat strike—has been played out repeatedly in the coal fields in the past several years. The companies have increasingly turned to the courts—the allegedly neutral arm of the justice system—to carry on their labor relations (Miliband 1969:138–45). By 1974 many companies had even ceased any attempt to resolve disputes at the mine site and simply filed for injunctions at the first sign of worker distress and strike. Even one of the judges involved felt it necessary to acknowledge this situation, as in the following statement by District Federal Judge K. K. Hall:

> I want to, someplace along the line—this may be a good place. I've just about reached the conclusion that the Court—this Court is being used in a

---

[5] The grievance procedure is a five-step procedure beginning at the mine level, proceding through various meetings between union representatives and management officials, to arbitration, and finally to the Arbitration Review Board. There are technical procedural requirements at each step, and therefore almost unlimited opportunity for delay at each step. Setting up an arbitration, for example, requires at least two months and then at least one to four months for decision. An arbitrator's fee for a single arbitration is $750, split by company and union. The local union also must pay lost time to its committeemen for the numerous meetings prior to arbitration. Repeated violations of the same provision of the contract by the same company is very common. This is especially infuriating because they impose unrecoverable costs on union locals, in what is literally a process of "plowing the same ground" time after time (UMW *Journal* 1975c:8–13).

[6] There are differences between companies in this area, with some of the larger and more financially secure companies more willing to observe the essential parameters of the contract. The coal industry is still relatively competitive, however, and the smaller, more marginal companies are under greater pressure to increase their profits. The current economic crisis, the increased drive for profit maximization, and the consolidation of the energy monopolies within the industry, however, all decrease the difference between companies.

manner that was not anticipated at all, that the way to settle strikes has just come to be by going to the Federal Court and getting him to issue a temporary restraining order without the parties doing something about it. . . . *The Court finds it distasteful being placed in the position of being the policeman or disciplinarian for the coal companies all the time* (Amherst Coal Company 1975:5, emphasis added).

Although this process characterized general company policy throughout the Appalachian coal fields, it achieved its finest form in District 17, the largest district of the UMWA and the home district of Arnold Miller, a stronghold of the Miners for Democracy movement.[7]

The spiral of events that occurred was predictable. Although miners hauled into court were initially respectful of the legal process and anxious to be law-abiding citizens, the unevenness of the justice meted out, the obvious biases of the judges, and the continued violations of the contract on the part of the companies began to undercut the effectiveness of the "judge as labor relations manager for coal company X." Soon the judges were no more effective in ordering miners back to work than the mine boss had been. The judges then escalated the conflict by increasing the severity of the fines levied, by fining individual miners, and finally, in late summer of 1975, jailing the president of one of the largest locals in Logan County.

The legal issues and arguments were complex—but the social forces at work were more fundamental and more powerful than any legal questions. With the jailing of Sim Howze, president of Local 8454, pickets fanned out across the coal fields and mines were shut down in several districts. Sim Howze was placed on the stand and asked, under penalty of remaining in jail, whether he would demand that his men cross the picket lines to return to work. Sim Howze said "No," he could not tell his men to do that (Buffalo Mining Company 1975). Sim Howze went back to jail, mass demonstrations were held at the court house, and no coal was mined.

It is not important what legal nicety the judge used to back off and let Sim Howze out of jail, nor what legal explanation the judge gave the coal companies for laying back temporarily on injunctions. The fact remains that a large-scale walkout had exerted the political pressure necessary for the temporary resolution of the mounting conflict between the legal system and the coal miners.

The international union could do little, legally, to resolve the problem. Authorizing the strikes as legitimate would have opened the union to potential lawsuits that might have bankrupted it. International leadership would have had to be willing to go outside the law to exercise the political

---

[7] Certain large law firms for the companies have become rich by promoting the legal response to labor disputes. These lawyers literally live off both the companies and the courts.

and economic muscle of the union—a risk that the leadership of President Miller was unwilling to take.

The companies counterattacked. Appalachian Power Company, Carbon Fuel Company, U.S. Steel, and Amherst Industries filed multimillion dollar lawsuits against District 17 and the international as a result of the wildcat strikes; all the companies increased their pressure on the courts to punish work stoppages. Several locals in District 17 were literally bankrupted by the size of the fines levied on them as individual locals. And the miners watched as the price of coal went up and the companies increasingly cut corners on health, safety, and benefits whenever possible—continuing to violate the contract with relative impunity.

District 17, the largest district, responded with an attempt to rechannel and make miners' frustration more effective by carrying on an intensive internal education program of miners. It spent $210,000 to train key union members who in turn were asked to educate local leadership in more effective processing of grievances and more careful monitoring of company activity. The district's legal staff planned a counteroffensive strategy to bring the companies into court, demanding injunctions against the companies for violation of the contract.

Although this strategy had merits, in reality the objective basis for carrying out a genuinely effective response did not exist. The education program was enthusiastically received, but was clearly going to be far more expensive than could easily be absorbed by the limited budget of the district.[8] The same limited budget could not increase the size of the legal staff, so that although the potential for countersuits by the unions against the company existed by the dozens, only a few of the most important suits could be brought. Meanwhile, the companies pursued their policy of using the courts as a mechanism of labor mediation and continued to exacerbate the situation.

The Injunction Strike of 1976

By spring of 1976, rank-and-file union leaders generally agreed that they were sitting on a powderkeg. The arbitrary use of injunctions by the companies had been publicly exposed during that winter in a series of public hearings held by District 17. In these hearings, covered extensively by the

---

[8] Perhaps the best example of these difficulties was the fact that after choosing some of the best local-level leadership to receive intensive training, hiring top-notch instructors, and paying expenses and lost work time, two of the best graduates of this training were subsequently approached by the companies and given lucrative offers to "go company." When one trainee accepted this offer, a union official bitterly remarked: "Well, we found out what his price was."

press, witnesses and documents showed conclusively the nature of company violations of the contract and the one-sided role of the federal courts. Company representatives were invited to the hearings to present countertestimony, but only one company appeared. Nonetheless, the judges continued their general policy of disciplining the miners for the companies, assuming the miners to be guilty unless proven otherwise.

In March 1976 the frustrated courts, unable to stem the rising tide of workers' anger, jailed 17 miners from the Carbon Fuel Company who had struck for one shift in sympathy with pickets from the Lightfoot mine of Eastern Associates Coal Company. The lesson was not lost on the miners. Richard Nixon and Spiro Agnew could break the law with impudence and impunity, the coal companies could willfully violate the contract, but the state would physically incarcerate the miners for protecting their economic rights. Frustration and anger brewed in the Appalachian coal fields.

In June, one more of many incidents occurred; however, this incident became the spark that ignited the fuse. The miners at Cedar Coal Local 1759 had had a grievance against the company for the company's refusal to fill a job by the rules of the contract. Urged by the district leadership to avoid more costly strikes, the men undertook the lengthy grievance procedure to redress a flagrant violation of the contract.[9] The arbitrator sided with the union, but in an effort to concede something to the company, agreed that, contrary to the contract, the job did not have to be posted.[10]

Again the union was forced into attempting to overrule an arbitrator's decision that clearly violated the given contract. The district legal staff filed a suit in court, this time seeking an injunction against the company and hoping that a strike could be avoided. In other words, the union was attempting to do what the companies had been doing all along—obtain a federal injunction to force the company to obey the contract. The judge, sensing the political undercurrents at work, sought to avoid a decision and claimed that he did not have time to hear the case, revealing what

[9] The company simply refused to follow the contract and thereby forced the union into the expensive grievance procedure, merely to get what the companies had promised when they signed.

[10] The position of arbitrator is extremely rewarding financially. Because an arbitrator has to be mutually agreed on by both the BCOA and the union, the arbitrators tend to make vacillating decisions to keep both parties satisfied and therefore protect their fees and retainers. In the case under discussion, the arbitrator, in an attempt to pacify the company, ruled that a job did not have to be filled by job posting. But the coal wage contract sets forth a detailed procedure by which the miners may advance to different and better jobs: it states that "filling of all permanent vacancies and new jobs created during the term of this agreement will be made on the basis of mine seniority, as set forth in the . . . [job bidding] procedure." The reason for such a contractual provision, from the miners' standpoint, is to prevent the bosses from using promotion to reward their pets.

the miners had gradually come to understand—that the federal courts functioned as an apparatus of the capitalist class to enforce coal production, not to serve justice. In subsequent courtroom proceedings the judge again revealed his class bias. The following interchange is between the federal judge and the chairman of the mine committee of the striking local (Cedar Coal 1976:11–13):

> *Mr. Forms:* Judge Knapp, could I say something, please? Judge Knapp, it disturbs me that through my education as a child I always understood that there would be equal justice, and before vacation we came to this Court, appealed to this Court twice so that we may obtain a temporary restraining order against Cedar Coal Company. Twice we could not be heard in court. Now we still don't get to hear our side of it. The Court still won't hear it.
>
> *The Court:* There isn't any side.
>
> *Mr. Forms:* Yes, there is a side. There certainly is a side.
>
> *The Court:* All right. There isn't any side to it. The only issue before the Court at this time is failure of you to obey the Court order. If you don't want to obey it, I can accommodate you.
>
> *Mr. Forms:* If you had heard us in the first place, we would have shown that the company would have been in contempt.
>
> *The Court:* You're bordering on contempt. I want to inform you of that. If you want to spend the night in jail, why you continue and I'll give you that opportunity. You're not telling this court what this Court ought to do, see. That's a matter for the Court to determine.
>
> Now, if you have any idea that you're going to think you may be needed in certain government circles, if you feel that you are better equipped to run the country and run the government than the people who are running it now, then I think there might be certain people interested in your services.
>
> *Mr. Forms:* Well, I don't think I stated in any way that I was better equipped—
>
> *The Court:* Well, I don't know, but you're trying to tell this Court what this Court should have done and, of course—
>
> *Mr. Forms:* We asked you to hear us.
>
> *The Court:* —nobody tells this Court what this Court is going to do, not even you.
>
> *Mr. Forms:* Okay. Thank you for your—
>
> *The Court:* If you—just one more remark out of you and you'll be headed for jail. All right.

The men understood from that trial that there was no legal recourse for justice. And a major strike was on. By this time the issue of the federal injunctions had come to be widely understood and the strike had general support throughout the coal fields. The pickets from Cedar Coal fanned out across District 17 and from there the strike spread throughout Appalachia and into the West.

The companies, of course, immediately went to court, demanding fines and punishment for the striking miners. The international union leadership, again caught in a legal box, implored the men to return to work, but those pleadings fell on deaf ears. The intensity of the strike clearly threatened the federal judges who, under mounting attacks by the miners, began to back down, even to the point of offering personal apologies to the men who had been degraded in the courtroom. But the local leadership of Cedar Coal now realized that their case was merely one example and that simply settling for a redress of their own particular grievance would not affect the general policy of the companies. The strike now became a political strike, and the general demand became that the federal courts cease using the injunction as a tool of labor relations for the companies.

The main strike lasted approximately one month. It was a well-organized mass movement, with clearly defined objectives and conscious leadership from individuals within the union who had a fairly developed understanding of the forces at work. At the same time, the objective constraints acting on the leadership limited the overall effectiveness of the strike. By bypassing the legitimate legal representative, the international, the local leadership was denied both the full force of union power and access to union resources. Likewise, the lack of strong leadership from the top office opened the door for those union bureaucrats and rank and file who placed the interests of their own careers or political caucuses above the overall interests of the union movement. As the strike lengthened these internal divisions deepened.

The question of when to end the strike was an obvious point of struggle. Conservatives within the union, frightened by the unleashing of rank-and-file militancy, wanted the strike ended as soon as it began. Adventurists and careerists within the union, on the other hand, wanted to raise the goal of the strike to the reopening of the contract—a demand that could not possibly be won. The main body of local leadership agreed to end the strike when it became obvious that the miners' actions had had a significant impact on the court and that the principal objective of the strike—to halt or slow the use of federal injunctions—had been reached at some level. It was agreed that lengthening the strike beyond that point would only undercut what the month of striking had accomplished. The miners went back to work, having won limited gains. No written agreements were published, but a clear understanding had been reached between judges and miners—the judges now understood that their obeisance to the companies could and would be exposed by the miners.[11]

---

[11] Except for a few sensitive reporters, the press coverage of miners' activities in the coal fields is overwhelmingly procompany. The press often promotes an image of the miner as irrational, superstitious, and violent. During the wildcat strikes, the com-

Analysis

The mass injunction strike of 1976 exemplifies the form that class struggle is taking in the country today. The elected legal leadership of the UMWA can, of course, be criticized by miners for being unwilling to act and protect the interests of the members, regardless of the legal costs. But, at the same time, the UMWA is one of the few unions left in the United States that often defends the unauthorized strikes of its members in court. In other words, although the international leadership failed to act positively, neither did it act as repressively as other major unions in this country have done in similar circumstances. The point is obvious: in industries where the unions act to discipline the workforce, the companies generally have not needed to use the force of the state (the courts) to protect their interests (Hall 1972; Weir 1977).[12]

It is here, then, that the critical nature of the miners' struggle becomes clear. The coal industry is a key component of the so-called energy crisis and a large proportion of the coal industry is now controlled by the giant multinational corporations, including EXXON, Continental Oil, and IT&T. Capital can only temporarily overcome the current economic crisis by enforcing increased worker productivity and, at the same time, lowering the standard of living of the working class (otherwise known as "inflation"). But even a semiautonomous workforce, such as the miners, are a major threat, especially when their product is critical to the profit-making process.[13] The mass injunction strike of 1976 has called forth its op-

---

panies attempted to heighten the pressures on the press by forcing two reporters into court as witnesses against the miners. The two reporters, sympathetic to the miners, refused to divulge sources or identify miners and pleaded the freedom of the press. They were convicted but their convictions were overturned on appeal.

[12] Even in those unions which have traditionally functioned to enforce the contract against the pressure of rank and file, recent productivity demands and worker unrest have led to a new level of struggle. An example of such a case was the Trenton Plant of Chrysler Corporation, where the UAW machinery became totally ineffective in halting a wildcat. In July 1977, several workers were fired for leading a walkout when the temperature in the plant rose to over 120°. Eventually, Chrysler was forced into the courts because the union could no longer perform its expected function. Unlike the case of the UMWA, however, the UAW legal staff either worked with the corporation lawyers or were nowhere to be found. The workers were compelled to hire their own legal defense.

[13] The profitability of both coal and oil have been well documented. What is less well known is the extent to which the industries defined primarily in terms of oil production have purchased coal properties and begun production. A minimum of 13 of the 50 largest industrial corporations on *Fortune*'s list (1977) own coal mines—not one of which is identified as a coal corporation: Exxon, IT&T, Shell Oil, U.S. Steel, Atlantic Richfield, Continental Oil, Tenneco, Union Carbide, Occidental Petroleum, International Harvester, Sun Oil, Bethlehem Steel, and W. R. Grace. The profitability of the

posite—an increased and more vicious assault on the union and the miners.

The assault on the union is clearly a reflection of the fact that the energy conglomerates desire to develop Western coal and scab (nonunion) coal. Because Western coal is found primarily in states with laws forbidding union shops (under 14-b of the Taft-Hartley Act), union organizing is extremely difficult (Greene 1977). At the same time, Western operators have arranged their full arsenal of attack against serious union efforts. They have cultivated and encouraged the antiunion sentiments of the ranch owners seeking employment in the mines by telling them that unions are collectivist and violate principles of American individualism. They have encouraged other, more docile unions to organize when it appears that the UMWA may be gaining a foothold. Where propaganda has failed, they have used the police and military forces to break up pickets and harass prounion miners. (UMW *Journal* 1975a:6–14; 1975b:9–11). The result has been that as Western coal production has expanded, the percentage of coal mined by UMWA miners dropped from 70 percent to less than half.

The coal operators understand, however, that such repressive tactics were applied in the Appalachian coal fields in the early 1900s and a strong and united union, liquidating its treasury to carry on an uphill battle to "organize the unorganized," literally fought a military campaign to organize Paint Creek, Cabin Creek, and eventually all of West Virginia. Thus, external resistance to the union is clearly not enough. The union must be attacked from within and divided to ensure the success of the operators' Western coal strategy. Thus, in July 1977 the BCOA announced their intention to punish the miners for their wildcat strike by withholding a transfer of funds from the 1974 pension and welfare fund to the nearly bankrupt 1950 fund. The 1974 fund had an excess of $14 million coming in per month. Legally, such a transfer of funds was permissible with the mutual consent of the UMW and the BCOA, but the BCOA withheld consent; the BCOA effectively blackmailed the union, by hurting the old and disabled. Another result was that the medical card of the union—one of the best health plans in existence—had now become nearly worthless. Disabled miners, retirees, and widows on extremely limited benefits were cut off from health care. At the same time, the loss of the medical card seriously undercut organizing efforts in the West. Western miners, lacking a history of union struggle or union consciousness, were often won to the UMWA on the basis of its economic benefits and job and health protection. Without

---

coal industry is reflected in the fact that in 1975 *Fortune* listed coal mining as first among all industries in return on stockholders' equity; mining and crude oil production was second in 1976 and again in 1977 (UMW *Journal,* 1974a:7–25; 1974b:8–20; U.S. Government 1978).

the medical card as a selling point, the Western organizing campaign lost a key asset.

The attack on the medical benefits also had internal consequences. The greatly weakened leadership of Arnold Miller could not, and did not, effectively cope with the crisis. Without effective international leadership, factions within the union jockeyed to use the crisis for their own benefit. Arnold Miller reacted to the crisis by leading a campaign against Reds in the union, further dividing the union by calling all critics and militants Communists. The objective result of disarray within the union was an almost complete halt to the UMWA's efforts to organize miners in the West.

The mass social movement of miners in the summer of 1976 did not occur as an isolated phenomenon that can be separated analytically from its historical context and dissected from within. Nor can analysis be separated from the question of interests—in whose class interests were forces applied? Rather, the injunction strike was a culmination of a series of smaller struggles between the two contending classes and the continued use by the companies of the judiciary as a means to enforce their interests against the workers.

The miners' response was spontaneous in the sense that it focused on the immediate issues and did not transcend union consciousness. At the same time, the miners' response was a serious rebuff to the company attacks. The companies did not cease their attacks and, as the analysis suggests, the attacks have shifted to another level. The companies clearly operate from a strategy based on their class interests. This strategy allows the companies (in this case, the large energy conglomerates) full utilization of their class resources—including the courts, the press, and presidential and congressional influence.[14] The spontaneous response by the miners, on the other hand, is carried on within the limits of fighting for union rights; they still have no clear understanding of the links between their union and their interests as a segment of the working *class*. Lacking such an understanding, the union struggle, no matter how valiant, remains limited to just that, rather than taking on explicit form as class struggle. The growing miners' awareness that the courts form a part of a system of class justice is a beginning of class consciousness. And, as miners come to understand that the cutbacks in their medical benefits are linked to a general medical crisis in this country, which in turn is part of an assault on the standards of living

---

[14] Events during the 1977 contract strike clearly demonstrated how the coal operators were able to use the Department of Labor, the Department of Energy, and the Office of the President to represent their own interests. A quick reading of the testimony offered by the union representatives and a simple rendering of the facts of the events that led to the rolling back of the Taft-Hartley injunction clearly reveals the complete complicity of the state with the companies in imposing the injunction. As John L. Lewis remarked, during his fight against it—"Taft-Hartley is a slave labor law!"

of all working people, their consciousness can begin to go beyond trade-union consciousness and can become class consciousness.

But even with such analysis, growing class consciousness must be organized and directed to unite the working class and focus its energies and resources in an effective response to the growing economic crisis. The trade-union movement, by itself, is incapable of organizing that response. The leadership of any single individual, no matter how well intentioned, is limited by personal and career considerations. The historical interests of the working class as a class can only be ultimately defended and advanced by linking the unions to a party that combines real working class leadership, both within and outside the union organization, with a concrete program of realistic and pragmatic reform demands. But at the same time, these demands and the reforms themselves should be based on an understanding of the socialist alternative, while concretely revealing the source of the crisis in the exploitative class relations of capitalism.

References

ALINSKY, SAUL D.
:   1949 John L. Lewis: An Unauthorized Biography. New York: Random House.

ALTHOUSE, C.
:   1974 "Work Safety and Lifestyle Among Southern Appalachian Coal Miners," *West Virginia University Bulletin* 74 (11–9).

AMHERST COAL COMPANY
:   1975 Amherst Coal Company versus United Mine Workers of America, Civil Action No. 75-0510-CH, Federal District Court for the Southern District of West Virginia.

BEAL, EDWIN F., EDWARD D. WICKERSHAM, and PHILIP KIENAST
:   1972 The Practice of Collective Bargaining. Homewood, Ill.: Irwin.

BETHEL, TOM
:   1971 Conspiracy in Coal. Huntington, W.V.: Appalachian Movement Press.

BOYER, RICHARD O., and HERBERT M. MORAIS
:   1971 Labor's Untold Story. New York: United Electrical, Radio and Machine Workers of America.

BUFFALO MINING COMPANY
:   1975 Buffalo Mining Company versus United Mine Workers of America, Civil Action No. 75-0523-CH, Federal District Court for the Southern District of West Virginia.

CARNES, CECIL
:   1936 John L. Lewis: Leader of Labor. New York: Robert Speller. Cedar Coal Company

CEDAR COAL COMPANY
1976   Cedar Coal Company versus United Mine Workers of America, Civil Action No. 76-54440-CH, Federal District Court for the Southern District of West Virginia.

COLEMAN, MCALISTER
1943   Men and Coal. New York: Arno Press Reprint (1969).

DAVID, JOHN P.
1972   "Earnings, Health, Safety and Welfare of Bituminous Coal Miners since the Encouragement of Mechanization," Ph.D. dissertation, University of West Virginia.

DREISER, THEODORE
1932   Harlan Miners Speak. New York: DeCapo Press reprint.

FINLEY, JOSEPH E.
1972   The Corrupt Kingdom: The Rise and Fall of the United Mine Workers. New York: Simon & Schuster.

FALTERMAYER, EDMUND
1974   "Clearing the Way for the Age of Coal," *Fortune* (May): 215–20.

FORTUNE
1975,   "The Fortune Directory of the 500 Largest Industrial Corporations,"
1976,   May.
1977

GREENE, DAVID
1977   The Threat of Western Coal. Box 13, Racine, W.V.: Hall.

HALL, BURTON, ed.
1972   Autocracy and Insurgency in Organized Labor. New Brunswick, N.J.: Transaction.

HARVEY, EDWARD B.
1975   Industrial Society: Structure, Roles, and Relations. Homewood, Ill.: Dorsey.

HUME, BRIT
1971   Death and the Mines: Rebellion and Murder in the United Mine Workers. New York: Grossman.

LEE, HOWARD B.
1969   Bloodletting in Appalachia. Parson, W.V.: McClain.

MILIBAND, RALPH
1969   The State in Capitalist Society. New York: Basic.

PRICE, JOEL
1974   The Renaissance of Coal. New York: Dean Witter (March).

ROSS, M. H.
1971   "Lifestyle of the Coal Miner," *Appalachian Medicine* (March): 3–9.

ROY, ANDREW
1905   A History of the Coal Miners of the U.S. Westport, Conn.: Greenwood Press Reprint (1970).

TAMS, W. P.
1963   The Smokeless Coal Fields of W.V. Parsons, W.V.: McClain.

United Mine Workers *Journal*
  1975a   May 16–31
  1975b   June 16–30
  1975c   November 1–15
  1974a   March 16–31
  1974b   April 1–15
  1974c   July 15–31
United States Government
  1978   Competition in the Coal Industry: Report of the U.S. Dept. of Justice Pursuant to Section 8 of the Federal Coal Leasing Amendments Act of 1975. Washington, D.C.: Government Printing Office.
Weir, Stanley
  1977   "U.S.A.: The Labor Revolt." Pp. 487–524 in M. Zeitlin (ed.), American Society, Inc., 2nd ed. Chicago: Rand McNally.

II Class and State in Comparative Perspective

11 The Political Limits of Social Democracy: State Policy and Party Decomposition in Denmark and Sweden

Gösta Esping-Andersen
Harvard University

"Revisionist Marxism," or social democracy, contrary to its orthodox Marxist forebears, or to its later Leninist opponents, believed that it was possible—even imperative—to conduct the struggle for socialism within the framework of the bourgeois democratic state.

During the past decades social democratic parties have indeed held office in a number of advanced capitalist states. In fact, it had appeared virtually impossible to oust the Swedish Social Democrats via the ballot until the 1976 election. In most other cases, socialist rule has been more interrupted and occasional. But whether in office or not, social democracy has achieved considerable political influence in postwar capitalism. It has not only become a dominant mode of working-class politics, but has moved even the staunchest bourgeois parties to sanction social reformism. Although bourgeois parties rarely win elections by promising to roll back social democratic reforms, no social democratic regime has yet introduced socialism.

In contemporary Western capitalisms there appear, however, to be signs of social democratic stagnation, or even decline. Politically, the traditional social reformist formula appears close to exhaustion; electorally, they never seem capable of winning absolute majorities.

Several alternative perspectives seek to explain the limits of social democracy. First, liberal sociologists have argued that modern capitalism has eroded the bases of class cleavages, which, in turn, has diminished the relevance of ideological confrontation. It has been argued that the working class has become "bourgeois" (Mayer 1955; Zweig 1961); that full political

---

This research is based on a larger project funded by a grant from the Danish Social Science Research Council. I would also like to express gratitude for the generous support and criticism given by Aage Sorensen and Erik Wright.

and social citizenship rights have eliminated essential class differences (Marshall 1964). Such developments have been associated with a decline in ideology (Lipset 1967) and the "waning of oppositions" (Kirschheimer 1968). In view of the recent tax revolts and anti–welfare state protests, it has also been argued that the upper ranks of the working class have joined with the middle classes in a middle-mass backlash against the welfare state (Wilensky 1975). In this milieu, socialist parties would logically lose support were they to retain a platform based on socialist ideology.

Second, whereas liberals tend to claim that class differences are decomposing, Marxists frequently see the limitations of social democracy in its commitment to bourgeois parliamentarism (for a recent discussion, see Miliband 1977). In this perspective the barriers to socialist advances lie in the constraints of the bourgeois state, not the working class.

Third, Social Democrats themselves have quite obviously been aware of the dilemmas confronting a democratic reformist road to socialism. They have seen the necessity of forming political alliances with other classes in the pursuit of reforms, admitting to the more limited horizons for change that are thus imposed. From Bernstein (1961) and Kautsky (1971) to the present, Social Democrats have held that immediate reforms were important as a first step toward consolidating a more unified mass movement, because they would reduce the cleavages between the poorer and the more privileged segments of the working class.

On this point there seems to be little which divides social democratic theory from Marshall's theory of social citizenship. Both see the attainment of full citizenship rights as a major objective for the working class. Indeed, such Social Democrats as Crosland (1963) have claimed that genuine socialism may be achieved through a blend of welfare state reforms, taxation policies, and sophisticated use of Keynesean economic management techniques. Yet, as a number of Swedish Social Democrats have argued, political and social citizenship rights are only meaningful forms of working-class participation if they are supplemented with full economic citizenship, which essentially implies a democratic form of control over the means of production (that is, a total redistribution of economic power) (Adler-Karlsson 1967; Wigforss 1971; Johansson, 1974). Swedish Social Democratic theorists, in other words, reject Crosland's assumption that private capital today is controlled by impartial managers rather than a capitalist class, and therefore the goal of democratic control over capital must remain on the agenda.

A comparison of the two most advanced Social Democratic regimes, Denmark and Sweden, is theoretically relevant because the Danish Social Democratic party has declined rapidly in recent years and may be actually decomposing; the Swedish party, in contrast, has retained its basic position (despite being ousted from office). Differences in the two parties' state policies have played a decisive role in shaping the present politics of the working classes and in determining the fate of the parties themselves. My thesis is that the long-term strength and cohesion of social democracy is contingent on its ability to shift from what I term "circulation level redistribution politics" to "production politics" (see also Esping-Andersen, Friedland, and Wright 1976). Whereas circulation politics refer to policies that seek to improve the welfare of the working class via the redistribution of incomes, production politics imply attempts to take increasing control over the flow of capital to maximize the collective welfare of the working class. Typical examples of circulation politics are income transfers or welfare services; an example of production politics would be effective public steering of capital investments.

In other words, the social democratic parties' failure to establish more public control over capital via production politics may stimulate party decline and even decomposition. However, the Swedish Social Democrats, in contrast to the Danish, have succeeded in shifting towards production politics, thereby securing a substantial degree of state control over private capitalist investments. This shift has had a cohesive rather than divisive effect on Swedish working-class politics and has strengthened the Social Democratic party. The Danish Social Democrats have been unable to expand control over the sphere of production and have thus been confined to conventional circulation politics in their struggle for more equality. This has had a fragmenting and even polarizing effect on working-class politics and has severely weakened working-class loyalty to social democracy in Denmark.

In summary, the form of social democratic state policy has a decisive impact on working-class politics. Yet, ultimately we can only understand variations in state policy if we take into account the peculiar configuration of class relations of the two countries. Thus I seek to demonstrate the relationships between class structure, class politics, and state policy, as illustrated in the causal model in figure 11-1.

This model posits that class structure affects the nature of class politics; that class politics have an effect on the form of state policy; and that, in

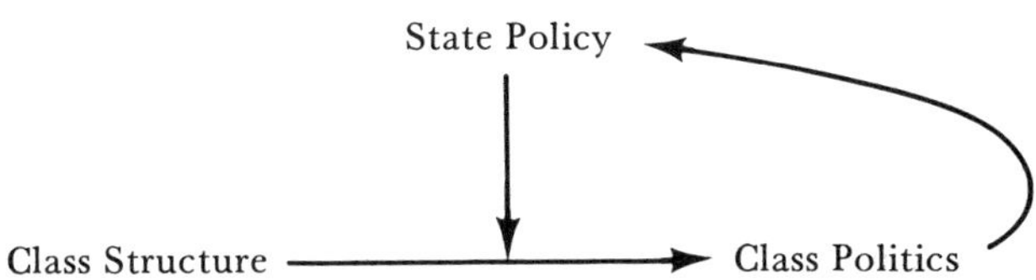

Figure 11-1. A causal model of the relationships among class structure, class politics, and state policy

turn, state policy itself affects the political behavior of classes. That is, class politics are both contingent on the nature of the class structure and also on the social and economic impact of state intervention. In view of this model, the Danish-Swedish comparison will begin with an examination of class politics, particularly the concept of party decomposition, then move to an analysis of Social Democratic state policies—especially social welfare, economic, and housing policies—and finally I shall examine how differences in Social Democratic state politics and party power can be explained by variations in class structure.

The Problem of Social Democratic Party Decomposition

The concept of party decomposition is borrowed from W. D. Burnham's landmark study of American politics (1970). In his study, party decomposition, briefly, refers to a growing incapacity of parties to mobilize the electorate and forge viable coalitions of various interest groups. Because Denmark and Sweden have a different form of electoral system as well as a very high rate of class-based voting, Burnham's measure must be substantially revised to take into account three dimensions of party decomposition: aggregate levels of voter support, the class distinctiveness of party support, and changes in the organizational strength and cohesion of the party.

Until the early 1960s, the stability of both Danish and Swedish politics was astounding. The Social Democrats dominated the left and faced essentially three bourgeois parties. The share of the electorate accruing to each of these two blocks remained virtually fixed and, moreover, no significant shifts in support occurred among the individual parties. In Denmark, the Social Democrats' share of the total vote typically hovered around 40 percent; in Sweden, around 45 percent. The patterns of political alignments were similarly stable. In both countries, the Social Democrats tended to govern with support from a center-leaning liberal party representing largely rural and urban petite bourgeois strata. But, in Sweden following the big struggle over pension reforms in the late 1950s, this political alliance was effectively broken. Until 1976, the Swedish Social Democrats held office alone, occasionally with tacit support from the small Left Communist party. Since the late 1950s, the pattern of Social Democratic support in Sweden has been rather cyclical. The party peaked in 1968 with 50.1 percent of the vote; in 1973, its share was 46 percent; and in 1976, 43 percent.[1]

In contrast, the fate of the Danish Social Democrats since 1960 has

---

[1] The Swedish Social Democrats' loss in the 1976 election was only 0.9 percent compared to the 1973 election.

been tumultuous. In comparison, the Danish party did not have sufficient strength to break off their necessary collaboration with the bourgeois parties and seeking compromises to the right. Moreover, aggregate voter support for the Social Democrats began to decline during the 1960s, culminating with the 1973 election in which they only received 25 percent. During the 1960s their electoral losses coincided with a strong growth of left-wing parties, especially the new Socialist Peoples party. In the 1970s, however, the Social Democrats have lost fairly heavily to the right as well; in particular to the newly founded Progress party, which advocates a total dismantling of the welfare state apparatus, elimination of taxing, and most other features that have come to identify social democracy. Although the Social Democrats recaptured some of their losses in the 1975 and 1977 elections, Danish politics are still subject to a high measure of electoral volatility and polarization. The extreme right, represented by the neo-Poujadism of the Progress party, has retained its strength, as have the left-wing parties. But the Socialist Peoples party vote has shifted toward the Left Socialists and Communists.

The second dimension of party decomposition is the degree of class distinctiveness of Social Democratic support and the political distinctiveness of the working class's voting behavior. The former concept refers to the extent to which the Social Democratic party's base is composed of one single class; the latter refers to the degree to which one social class is unified behind one party (Alford 1963). In countries with a historical pattern of very high class voting, the importance of these two phenomena is obviously great, and the strength of the Social Democrats will largely depend on their success in mobilizing a united working class. When we compare recent trends in Denmark and Sweden on these dimensions, the differences are clear.[2] In 1960, about 80 percent of all Danish manual workers supported the Social Democrats compared to 77 percent in Sweden. But after 1960, the convergence ends. In Denmark, the proportion had declined to 60 percent by 1971, and by 1975 to 45 percent. In short, barely half the Danish manual workers support social democracy today. For Sweden, manual worker support for the Social Democrats has declined very slowly, with the lowest rate reached in 1976 (68 percent). To a large extent, these losses have been offset by gains among the new white-collar working class.

The fall in manual-worker support for the Danish Social Democrats has coincided with a sharp working-class shift toward the left socialist par-

[2] The findings reported here, as well as in subsequent analyses, are based on data from three data sets: for Denmark, Gallup surveys 1960 through 1975, and the Electoral Surveys for 1971, 1973 and 1975 of political scientists Ole Borre and others; for Sweden, the data are derived from Sveriges Statitstik's election surveys, Almanna Valen, 1960 through 1976. I would like to thank the Danish Data Archive for use of the electoral surveys.

ties and, to some extent, also to the Progress party after 1973. Indeed, the survey data show that almost 25 percent of Danish manual workers supported the left in 1975, while perhaps 10 percent supported the Progress party. In Sweden manual working-class support has gradually shifted toward the bourgeois parties, but not in any sense of comparable magnitude to Denmark. Swedish workers do not appear to have moved to the left of the Social Democrats.

Of particular significance are differences in the age distribution of the two parties' electoral base. In the Danish case the party's age distribution has become extremely skewed; the older being vastly overrepresented, the younger being highly underrepresented. Indeed, the Danish Social Democrats appear to have become a pensioner's party. By 1975 pensioners accounted for 32 percent of their voters as opposed to 24 percent in 1968. The younger generation workers in Denmark not only show a very weak loyalty toward social democracy; they are also the most polarized. In Sweden, there is no important variation in Social Democratic support by age groups. These differences suggest that the Danish Social Democrats' electoral demise may be more than temporary given their growing incapacity to attract new generations of the working class.

The third dimension of party decomposition is the organizational apparatus of the party. Historically, the Social Democratic parties have conformed closely to Duverger's notion of the modern mass party, or the "Soziale Ghettopartei" (1954). They built vast organizational spheres, including cooperatives, sports clubs, boy scout movements, schools, and newspapers, designed to integrate the working class, educate it politically, and insulate it from bourgeois society. Party organization is obviously also of critical importance in the recruitment and training of leadership, the mobilization of votes, and the consolidation of loyalty and class solidarity. In the Danish case, party membership grew steadily until the mid-1950s but has declined steadily ever since. The drop, in fact, has been even more rapid than the party's decline in votes. In the mid-1950s, membership as a percentage of the party votes was about 33; today it is about 15.

Membership in the Swedish party has actually increased steadily, and recently reached the 1 million mark (in a country of 8 million). As a percentage of party votes, membership has remained rather permanent at about 42 percent. However, in Sweden the Social Democrats promote a system of collective membership, like the British, whereby a union local may elect to join the party as a collective, which obviously explains much of the increase in Sweden even if individuals are free to opt out. Nevertheless, in contrast to Denmark, membership has increased despite the party's electoral decline in the 1970s.

Regardless of how membership actually is recruited, the Swedish Social Democratic party may have a far superior ability to function organizationally, and thereby a stronger potential for retaining its dominant position in the working class. The Danish party, in comparison, appears to be disintegrating and decomposing.

On all three indices of decomposition the evidence seems to point in the same direction. The Danish Social Democrats may not have reached the point of paralysis, but they are suffering from major party decomposition, which, moreover, shows signs of being chronic rather than temporary. Along with this trend is the substantial decline in working-class political unity. Not only have working-class politics become more volatile and fragmented; the working class is actually internally polarized between the neo-Poujadist anti–welfare state party on the right and the left socialist parties. Although the Social Democrats have decomposed, working-class politics have polarized.

The survey data suggest that the most loyal supporters of the Social Democrats are becoming the lowest paid, economically most vulnerable workers; the workers who drift either toward the left or right tend to be skilled and higher paid. One may tentatively argue that the Danish Social Democrats are becoming a party of those most dependent on the welfare state. The Swedish Social Democrats have lost some support, but in comparison the party does not appear to be decomposing. Similarly, a greater degree of continuity and stability has characterized class politics in Sweden. In particular, the longstanding political unity of the Swedish working class seems intact.

The difference in party decomposition in Denmark and Sweden can be located in terms of Burnham's theory of political realignment. Burnham's basic hypothesis is that party decomposition is a symptom of an overdue realignment of the electorate and the party system. I shall later argue that the decomposition of the Danish Social Democrats is associated with their inability to break with alliances to the political right and with the strong petite bourgeois influence on Social Democratic state policy. The absence of decomposition in Sweden may be ascribed to the Social Democrats' break with a petite bourgeois coalition and the move toward state policies that attempt to stimulate a coalition between blue-collar and white-collar wage earners. In other words, the Swedish Social Democrats initiated a critical political realignment in the late 1950s and early 1960s, whereas the Danish Social Democrats did not. This difference, as I shall indicate in the next section, has had critical implications for the nature of Social Democratic state policy in the two countries.

Social Democratic State Policy in Denmark and Sweden

The extent of differences in Danish and Swedish state policy may help explain the rather opposite fates of the two Social Democratic movements.

Given that the growing literature on government overload (King 1975) and welfare state backlash (Wilensky 1975) has gained substantial popularity, I shall begin with an examination of the two countries' welfare state spending and taxing, and thereafter analyze specific state policies.

Whereas King primarily focuses on the spending side, Wilensky's focus is mainly on the revenue dimension. According to Wilensky, a welfare state backlash is more likely where welfare financing rests on highly visible forms of taxing, such as the direct income tax. At first glance these theses seem to offer a good explanation for the demise of the Danish Social Democrats. The sudden collapse of electoral support in the 1970s has coincided with a powerful anti–welfare state movement that has mobilized support from a large element of the working class. Survey data indicate that a full 86 percent of the Danish electorate, compared to only 41 percent in Sweden, express the opinion that the state is too lavish with taxpayers' money.

But, if we compare Denmark and Sweden with respect to levels of public spending, we find that, as a proportion of GNP, the Swedish percentage was higher in the past and was about the same in 1973 (43 percent in Sweden compared to 44 percent in Denmark). Thus, aggregate spending levels are poor predictors of electoral backlash. Similarly, with respect to Wilensky's argument, the role of taxing must also be dismissed. As a proportion of all tax revenues in 1971, the direct income tax in Denmark and Sweden was, respectively, 45 and 46 percent. Neither is there much variation in total tax revenue as a percent of GNP.

However, disaggregated overall figures reveal marked differences. On the spending side it is obvious that the Danish state is more heavily burdened with unproductive expenditures. Social welfare spending (social assistance, sickness, and pensions) account for 34 percent of all state expenditures in Denmark, as compared to only 11 percent in Sweden. Yet per capita social expenditure is actually somewhat higher in Sweden. This apparent contradiction can be explained by differences in the two systems' mode of financing. In Denmark the lion's share of pension and social assistance spending is central government responsibility, financed via direct taxes. In Sweden, the Social Democrats have managed to shift a major burden for financing these expenses onto private employers, thus reducing fiscal pressures on the state and on taxpayers. Whereas the Danish state budget is heavily burdened with directly unproductive expenditures, the Swedish is relatively more weighted toward productive goods and services—that is, services which enhance the productive performance of the economy. Thus, Sweden spends significantly more, relatively, on education, on health care delivery, and on labor market activities. Thus, taxpayer resentment is voiced against the largely unproductive allocation of tax monies.

If the system of taxing and spending is a critical variable in explaining the decomposition of social democracy, it is necessary to analyze the structural links between taxing and spending, and how they affect various social strata and classes. To explain changes in working-class politics, we must pay more attention to how the typical worker is affected by the system of state intervention. One approach would be to study its redistributive effects; another would be to study the impact of specific important programs on working-class welfare.

The most meaningful way to gauge the impact of the fiscal incident for working-class living standards is to study the tax-benefit ratio over time, controlling for inflation. Inflation raises taxable income levels and tends to reduce eligibility for various public benefits. First, although nominal wage increases over the past 10 to 15 years have been higher in Denmark, Swedish governments have been more successful in controlling inflation. Second, in the 1970s the net negative impact of inflation and taxes on the development of workers' real disposable income has been different in the two countries. In Sweden, the net increase of real income between 1964 and 1972 is an estimated 10 percent; in Denmark, only 5 or 6 percent. The higher Danish inflation rates, of course, account for the discrepancy, but the Danish state also imposes a somewhat higher rate of taxing on the average industrial worker's income. Because, finally, typical public benefits (such as sickness compensation, rent subsidies, and pensions) are relatively more generous in Sweden, it is not surprising that the net improvements in Danish workers' disposable income are inferior. To illustrate the combined effect of taxes and benefits, we may compare a tax-benefit ratio for typical worker incomes with a similar ratio for a typical higher-income manager in the private sector. As one would expect, the tax-benefit ratio (16:10) for Swedish workers is considerably better than that (27:10) for Danish workers. The Swedish system is more progressive, as can be seen from the much heavier tax-to-benefit burden imposed on higher-income managers in Sweden (204:10 in Sweden compared to 147:10 in Denmark).[3]

Danish working-class income earners appear to be shouldering a considerable burden of the welfare system in comparison to their Swedish brethren. The real issue, however, is what permitted the Swedish Social Democrats to establish a less burdensome, more redistributive welfare state, which can only be explained by a closer examination of the interplay of social and economic policy legislation. The problematic nature of state taxing and spending must be gauged on the basis of a full assessment of the reforms that underpin them.

---

[3] The ratios for Denmark refer to 1971. The ratios for Swedish managers refer to 1970, but those for workers refer to 1976. Taxes include all direct taxes and levies; benefits include typical direct transfers to households, such as family and child allowances and rent subsidies.

Social Democratic Social and Economic Policy: The Problem of State Control over the Sphere of Production

Despite the proclivity of liberal thinkers to believe that the "good society" had arrived with the attainment of the welfare state, it was clear to socialists that social welfare did little more than compensate for the negative by-products of industrial capitalism (Offe 1972). Democratic collective control over the means of production remained a necessary goal. Indeed, such authors as Wigforss (1971), Martin (1975), and even Keynes (1936:378) have noted that the continued stability of the welfare state and the long-run guarantee of full employment will require substantial state control over private production. A major reason for Social Democratic party stability in Sweden is its superior ability to control politically private-capitalist investments. Such achievements have both helped avert a crisis of the welfare state and boosted the party's electoral image.

Perhaps the single most burdensome welfare provision is social security. Although pension benefits in Sweden are considerably more generous than in Denmark, the Danish state spends much more because most pensions in Denmark are financed directly from income taxes. In Sweden, in contrast, employers carry a very large part of the pension burden (38 percent in 1972). This fundamental difference can only be explained by historical variations in the two Social Democratic regimes' struggle for social reforms.

In the late 1950s, the Swedish Social Democrats launched a major campaign to reform the existing pension system, which was modeled after the British Beveridge plan with universal flat-rate pensions. Not only was inflation a factor in eroding pensions, but with general income improvements among active workers, pensioners tended to fall behind. To counter the growing burden on the public budget that an indexation solution would have incurred, the Social Democrats instead sought to introduce a superannuation system financed by employers and, to a lesser extent, employees. The most important—at any rate most controversial—aspect of the proposal was that pension contributions were to be paid into a state-administered central fund. To the Social Democrats the pension fund system would be a means whereby governments could exercise a more active role in steering investments and control the overall economy.

Predictably, the bourgeois parties and employers flatly refused to sanction the bill. Most important, the Social Democrats' parliamentary coalition partner, the Center party, broke completely off on the question, and thus, severed the longstanding working class–petite bourgeois coalition. The Social Democrats instead sought to mobilize white-collar support, and after two years of intense campaigning in a highly politicized and ideologically polarized atmosphere, they succeeded in squeezing through the reform. In the ensuing local and national elections it was clear that the Social Democrats had capitalized electorally on the reform.

During the following years, as the pension funds began to accumulate, it was clear that the state was presiding over a major source of economic influence. First taking a cautious stance toward their use, in the late 1960s the Social Democrats began to pursue a more active and direct policy of employing these capital funds for steering the private economy. Given their magnitude—today they account for about 50 percent of all domestic savings (Lindbeck 1975)—the funds will obviously have a critical impact. Initially, they were primarily used as a source of investment capital within the housing sector, but lately have come to play a role in industrial development. Thus, the state has invested in steel production and has bought shares in a number of corporations. A major shift had already occurred in 1967 when, after considerable pressure from the union apparatus, the Social Democrats went to elections with a proposal for establishing a centralized state investment bank based on pension capital to further facilitate public control over investments, in particular to strengthen the export sector and stimulate a thorough structural rationalization of the economy. This political program seems to have had quite an appeal in the electorate. In the 1968 election, the Social Democrats' share of the vote jumped to a full 50.1 percent.

A complete understanding of the Swedish Social Democrats' struggle to amass more power over private investment flows is only possible in the context of the union's and the party's overall strategy. Following the war, the Swedish union federation (LO) pursued a set of policies that sought both genuine wage improvements and a more egalitarian distribution of incomes among workers, and between workers and other groups, without stimulating inflation. The formula, known as the Rehn model, was the system of solidaristic wage bargaining, whereby collective labor market agreements would stipulate equal pay increases for workers across the board; that is, whether or not individual companies were able to afford them. Less-efficient, low-productivity firms would consequently be driven out unless they could enhance their productivity to offset the fall in profits.

The labor movement's attempt to weed out the weaker elements in the economy, according to the Rehn model, would put a damper on inflationary developments; but, of course, with the cost of massive layoffs. It was thus also necessary to establish the active labor market policy, according to which a centralized labor market board (AMS) effectively steers the laid-off labor into growth sectors and absorbs labor from stagnant unproductive sectors by manpower retraining programs. The increased role of government in steering investments via the pension funds must be viewed as a complement to the labor market policy.

Postwar developments in Swedish Social Democratic state policy thus mark a fundamental shift from traditional social welfare–oriented reforms to a much more direct attack on the mobility of labor power and the mobility of capital. (For a theoretical treatment, see Esping-Andersen, Friedland, and Wright 1976.)

The profile of Social Democratic state policy in postwar Denmark stands in sharp contrast to the Swedish. Parallel problems that began to affect the pension system of Sweden in the 1950s also beset the Danish Beveridge system. In the early 1960s, inspired by the Swedish example, the Danish Social Democrats sought to introduce a major reform modeled after the centralized fund principle. But it became obvious that a parliamentary majority was not attainable. A watered-down version was passed in which employer contributions were minuscule, and in which there could not occur any substantial accumulation of state-controlled capital funds. Pension financing, increasingly becoming a substantial financial burden, remained the principal responsibility of the central government. Pressed from the Danish LO and from the growing left-socialist opposition, the Social Democrats attempted again in the late 1960s to legislate a centralized fund system in combination with a state investment bank. But the proposal never even got beyond its first parliamentary debate.

Thus, on one hand, the Danish welfare state's burden of unproductive spending has grown exponentially and, on the other hand, the Social Democrats lack the means for effectively using what state power they possess to influence the private economy. Danish governments have, consequently, had to rely on more conventional fiscal and monetary policy measures to redress economic imbalances, solve recurrent balance-of-payments crises, and dampen high inflation rates. With a weak grip on capital markets, governments have, on occasion, been forced to introduce incomes policies which, in turn, have tended to antagonize the working class. To offset the negative consequences that tightened economic policy has for the income distribution, the Social Democrats have typically answered with compensations in the form of traditional social welfare measures. Thus, the irony is that the tremendous growth of the Danish welfare state may be taken as a sign of the Social Democrats' political impotence. Although the Social Democrats have moved toward a more planned effort at managing the economy, the overall pattern of state intervention reflects attempts to stem off crises more than deliberate attacks on the origins of economic problems.

Social democratic regimes that struggle to represent working-class interests under capitalism are faced with the dilemma of both having to generate more equality and having to administer the economy effectively. To summarize the major differences between Danish and Swedish social democracy, the Swedes have sought to solve the dilemma by seeking more state control over capital flows. The Danes, lacking the power to do so, have been forced to rely more heavily on redistribution via the public budget. Thus, it should now be more clear why indicators such as aggregate tax and spending levels alone are rather poor predictors of electoral revolts. We must look at both the fiscal incident and at the government's success in steering the vital variables in the economy: unemployment levels, growth rates, and inflation levels. The data indicate a better fiscal incident in Sweden from the point of view of the working class. If we turn to the state's ability to steer the economy, we must conclude that the Swedish Social Democrats' steering efforts have had some success.

First, we may look at GNP growth rates since 1957. In both countries the average annual rate of GNP growth has been declining. In the 1971–1973 period, Sweden experienced a moderate recession but pulled out of it around 1974 and maintained a real GNP growth rate with only 2 percent unemployment during the worldwide recession. Denmark's resistance to that recession was, however, very poor, with stagnation of growth and as much as 10 percent unemployment.

Second, Denmark's level of unemployment between 1956 and 1974 was consistently higher than Sweden's. Thus, during the most dynamic years from 1966 to 1970, Denmark had an average of 3.2 as opposed to Sweden's 1.7 percent unemployment.

Third, considering the close relationships between employment levels and inflation, higher levels of inflation would be expected in Sweden; yet, the opposite is the case. Although both countries have been victimized by the Phillips curve dilemma (the trade-off between inflation and full employment), average inflation levels have been substantially higher in Denmark throughout the past 20 years. Sweden's export position in world markets is stronger than Denmark's, but this difference itself is partially the product of active Social Democratic production politics. As economist Assar Lindbeck (1975) suggests, there is reason to believe that the aggressive attempts at economic steering in Sweden have had positive results.

State Policies and Class Politics

Earlier I suggested the problems of explaining Denmark's higher levels of anti–welfare state sentiment by a straightforward application of Wilensky's backlash theory. If anti–welfare state attitudes are compared with levels of attitudinal support for more state control over the economy, the evidence is quite puzzling. In Denmark, where the Social Democrats have had least success in promoting production politics, overall electoral support for more state control was a full 57 percent in 1971, rising to 63 percent in 1973—almost the same proportion which favors less welfare spending. For Swedish voters, the level of support for more state control in 1969 was only 21 percent.

Support for more state control in both Denmark and Sweden is exceptionally strong among manual workers and among Left Socialist and Social Democratic voters. Among Swedish manual workers who vote Social Democratic or Communist, 75 percent agree that the state should have more control, as opposed to 40 percent among manual workers in general. Among nonmanual workers, the comparable percentages are 52 and 28 percent. In Sweden, workers tend to be much less resentful of welfare spending than favorable to more state control of investments, particularly Socialist and Communist party voters.

Universally, Danish workers show much higher support for more state control. In 1973, a full 96 percent among Left Socialists, 77 percent among Social Democrats, and even 85 percent among workers who voted for the Progress party favored increased state control. This support suggests an extremely important qualification to the welfare backlash theory. The same workers who protest excessive welfare spending and taxing may also protest the lack of production politics. The same workers who in 1973 shifted to the neo-Poujadism of the Progress party seem also to embrace fairly radical socialist state policies. It is therefore possible that electoral polarization in combination with Social Democratic party decomposition reflects both electoral frustration with the shortcomings of the social welfare–circulation politics formula and the absence of more socialistic political achievements.

The Case Study of Social Democratic Housing Policy

That failure to intervene effectively in production and investments may stimulate Social Democratic party decomposition is perhaps best illustrated by contrasts in housing policy. The Swedish Social Democrats have had most success in this sector in gaining control over production, whereas in Denmark the Social Democrats have pursued a policy that has led to a gradual decline of state control over the housing market.

Denmark and Sweden faced similar housing shortages during the late 1950s, and housing reform became one of the single most pressing issues. In Sweden, the Social Democrats launched a very ambitious program of building 1 million new units within 10 years. But to control strong inflationary trends in real estate and to assure the realization of the promise, they adopted a strategy of forcing private credit out of the housing sector by holding interest rates at artificially low levels. To fill the vacuum, government supplied capital from the pension funds and the state budget. As a result, today more than 90 percent of all housing construction is financed with the aid of public capital. Moreover, the state sought to diminish the role of private builders by favoring cooperative, semipublic, and local government construction. The proportion of private construction declined from 90 percent in 1945 to 35 percent in the late 1960s.

As a consequence the Swedish state has gained virtual control of, first, the volume, type, and location of residential building; and second, with its power to determine interest rates and rents, the state enjoys a substantial amount of control over the pricing of housing. Recently, the Social Democrats have begun to shift to an expansion of the system of tax-free rent allowances to low-income households in answer to demands for a more equitable distribution of quality housing.

In Denmark, the housing sector was crisis-ridden in the late 1950s. But, in contrast to the Swedes, the Danish Social Democrats promoted, as a compromise with the bourgeois parties, a housing reform that overwhelmingly favored a solution based on single-family homeownership, backed by generous tax deductions and mortgage loan guarantees. At the same time, the 1965 housing reform gradually abolished rent controls and diminished public control over the housing market in general. The reform had serious economic consequences. It stimulated an explosion of homeownership so that, for example, the proportion of working-class homeowners jumped from 30 to 50 percent in 10 years. This, in turn, pushed up interest rates and stimulated a heavy flow of speculative capital into the housing sector. With rampant inflation, homeownership actually became a means whereby wage earners could defend themselves against erosion of their incomes.

For the Danish Social Democrats, housing policy has had severe political consequences, and housing policy clearly became one of the most controversial and politicized issues in postwar Denmark. First, the strong homeowner bias of the reform created a strong cleavage between renters and homeowners. Following the 1965 reform, renters moved heavily to the left in the 1966 election. The Socialist Peoples' party, which campaigned hard against the reform, attracted a large share of renter voters from the Social Democrats; but the Social Democrats did not lose support among their homeowner constitutents.

As the housing sector was gradually liberalized, the status of renters deteriorated notably and there was mounting political pressure on the Social Democrats to reverse the inequities. In the late 1960s they responded with a package of rent-allowance compensations, but these allowances generally failed to keep abreast with inflation and growing tax burdens. Indeed, a large population began to experience an erosion in their allowances despite no genuine income gains. Thus, the remedy tended to produce even deeper resentments and did little to boost the Social Democrats' image among renters. Increasingly, government was attacked on the issue of homeowners' generous tax allowances, because they were viewed as a highly regressive form of income redistribution.

Pressed from the left, the Social Democrats proposed a bill in the early 1970s to diminish these allowances. But, given the large proportion of workers who had purchased homes and were heavily dependent on favorable tax breaks, homeowners rebelled. First, a group from within the Social Democratic party's parliamentary group broke off, refused to sanction the bill and, instead, formed the new Center Democrat party. In both 1973 and 1975, homeowners reacted by moving heavily to the right. Homeowner support for the Social Democrats declined from 73 percent in 1966 to 46 percent in 1975. Thus, housing policy appears to have had a significant impact on Danish Social Democratic party decomposition in a two-step sequence, alienating first renters, later homeowners; losing first to the left, later to the right. In short, Social Democratic housing policy seems to have exacerbated inequities within the housing sector in a highly politicized way. Rather than having a unifying effect on the working-class electorate, Danish Social Democratic policy has introduced new dimensions of stratification.

To estimate the extent to which housing status, as opposed to social-class membership, explains changes in Social Democratic support over time, I entered the two as independent variables, and party choice as dependent variable in a regression equation for the years 1960 through 1975.[4] As expected, the importance of housing status for party choice—controlling for class—increased dramatically after the 1965 reform. The unstandardized regression coefficient jumped from 0.136 in 1960 to 0.326 in 1966. Yet the coefficient for social class remained stable—1.122 and 1.059, respectively ($R^2 = 0.376$, significant at 0.001 level). This pattern then remained basically stable until the early 1970s, when a new major wave of politicization occurred. In the 1973–1975 period, the coefficient for housing status leaps dramatically (in 1975 to 0.800) whereas class voting declines sharply to 0.762 ($R^2 = 0.246$, significant at the 0.001 level).

A parallel analysis for Sweden cannot be undertaken because time-series data are not available. Yet, a comparison of the distribution of renters and homeowners among political parties in the two countries for 1975–1976 shows that Swedish renters and homeowners have much stronger support for the Social Democrats and housing status is not polarized as it is in Denmark. Among renters, for example, 24 percent support

---

[4] The variables were coded as follows: Social class was dichotomized as working class (manual and nonmanual) = 1; nonworking class = 2. Housing status was coded with renters = 0; homeowners = 1. Party choice was coded along a left-right continuum with Left Socialist parties = 0; Socialists = 1; Social Democrats = 2; liberal center parties = 3; and bourgeois parties (after 1973, including the Progress party) = 4.

parties to the left of the Social Democrats in Denmark, as opposed to only 6 percent in Sweden; among homeowners, 72 percent support the right in Denmark, as opposed to 58 percent in Sweden. Therefore, the nature of housing policy can have a significant differential effect on party support.

Conclusion

I have tried to demonstrate that differences in the degree of party decomposition in Danish and Swedish social democracy must be traced to variations in state policy. What is detrimental to Social Democratic party strength is not necessarily circulation type politics as such—redistributive welfare-state politics—but the political inability to match such policies with more effective state control over the production process, capital flows, and investment decisions in particular. The political capacity to shift from pure circulation level to production politics is critical, because the former has the potential effect of creating new cleavages within the working class, and because efforts to increase equality via redistributive politics tend to incur heavy fiscal burdens, especially on the economically active and better-off workers.

What allowed the Swedish, but not the Danish, Social Democrats the opportunity to pursue production politics and avoid party decomposition? It has been, I suggest, the differences in the two parties' political alliances. In turn, these differences in Social Democratic alliances can be traced to differences in the two nations' class structures.

As mentioned, the struggle over pension reform in Sweden was a critical historical juncture in terms of political realignment. The Social Democrats broke completely with their traditional petite bourgeois coalition and sought, instead, to build a new wage earner coalition by mobilizing the growing white-collar strata. Preceding this historical realignment was a period of immense capital concentration in the Swedish economy, in the wake of which the size of the petite bourgeoisie was sharply reduced and the size of white-collar strata sharply increased. Changes in the class structure thus facilitated, if not fueled, the Social Democratic realignment. The internal unity of the Swedish working class has also been of critical importance for Social Democratic policy. In Sweden, virtually all manual and the majority of white-collar workers are unionized. The unions, especially the LO federation of manual workers, is unitary and organized on industrial rather than skill lines. In the context of a highly monopolistic capitalist economy, the powerful union movement has sought to ally with white-collar unions in direct confrontations with large capital. The alliance of the unions has, furthermore, facilitated the Social Democrats' ability to broaden the state's control over investments and pursue production politics.

The Danish class structure has evolved quite differently. The Danish economy has, until very recently, been dominated by a powerful class of independent farmers and a large urban petite bourgeoisie. In contrast to Sweden, capital is not very concentrated. Equally important, the Danish working class is somewhat less organized and the union movement has historically been divided between the skilled and the unskilled workers. As in Sweden, the Danish Social Democrats have historically forged an alliance with petite bourgeois forces, but capitalist development did not lead to a sharp decline of the petite bourgeoisie, and it has retained a decisive veto power over Social Democratic attempts to emulate the more radical politics of the Swedes. The Danish Social Democrats did have the power to expand the welfare state, but they could not initiate a major political realignment designed to unite wage earners behind production politics. The presently fragmented and polarized nature of the Danish working class can be viewed as one consequence of this failure. The other consequence, of course, is the decomposing trend in the Social Democratic party itself. If production politics are deemed a necessary condition for Social Democratic power and unity in advanced capitalism, the essential precondition seems to be the existence of a centralized, unified, and highly organized working class, and the relative weakness of small capitalists and petite bourgeois strata.

References

ADLER-KARLSSON, GUNNAR
    1967   Funktionssocialism. Lund: Prisma.
ALFORD, ROBERT
    1963   Party and Society. Chicago: Rand McNally.
BERNSTEIN, EDWARD
    1961   Evolutionary Socialism. New York: Schocken.
BURNHAM, W. D.
    1970   Critical Elections and the Mainsprings of American Politics. New
             York: Norton.
CROSLAND, C. A. R.
    1963   The Future of Socialism. New York: Schocken.
DUVERGER, MAURICE
    1954   Political Parties. London: Methuen.
ESPING-ANDERSEN, G., R. FRIEDLAND, and E. OLIN WRIGHT
    1976   "Class Conflict and the Capitalist State," *Kapitalistate* 4/5:186–220.
JOHANSSON, STEN
    1974   Nar er Tiden Mogen? Karlskrona: Tidens Forlag.
KAUTSY, KARL
    1971   The Class Struggle. New York: Norton.
KEYNES, J. M.
    1936   The General Theory of Employment, Interest, and Money. London:
             Macmillan.

KING, ANTHONY
   1975   "Overload: Problems of Government in the 1970s," *Political Studies*
           23:290–95.
KIRCHEIMER, OTTO
   1968   "The Transformation of the Western European Party Systems," in
           J. Lapalombara and M. Weiner (eds.), Political Parties and Political
           Development. Princeton: Princeton University Press.
LINDBECK, ASSAR
   1975   Svensk Ekonomisk Politik. Malmö: Aldus.
LIPSET, S. M.
   1967   "The Changing Class Structure and Contemporary European Poli-
           tics," in S. Graubard (ed.), A New Europe? Boston: Beacon Press.
MARSHALL, T. H.
   1964   Class, Citizenship, and Social Development. Garden City, N.Y.:
           Doubleday.
MARTIN, ANDREW
   1975   "Is Democratic Control of Capitalist Economies Possible?" in
           L. Lindberg and others (eds.), Stress and Contradiction in Modern
           Capitalism. Lexington, Mass.: D. C. Heath.
MAYER, KURT
   1955   Class and Society. New York: Random House.
MILIBAND, RALPH
   1977   Marxism and Politics. Oxford: Oxford University Press.
OFFE, CLAUS
   1972   "Advanced Capitalism and the Welfare State," *Politics and Society* 4.
WIGFORSS, ERNST
   1971   Vision och Verklighet. Stockholm: Tidens Forlag.
WILENSKY, HAROLD
   1975   The Welfare State and Equality. Berkeley: University of California
           Press.
ZWEIG, FERDINAND
   1961   The Worker in an Affluent Society. Glencoe, Ill.: Free Press.

12 Workers' Views on Self-Management: A Comparative Study of the United States and Sweden

Ain Haas
Indiana University–Purdue University at Indianapolis

There is currently a great deal of interest in the idea of self-management, workers' control, or industrial democracy. Some people envision it in the form of general assemblies of all the employees voting on decisions, while others have in mind a council of representatives elected by and accountable to the mass of employees. The details of the vision vary, but the basic idea is that ordinary workers would ultimately control their workplaces, instead of being subservient to investors, government planners, or some other set of officials that can unilaterally make policy for an enterprise and compel the workers to go along.

Until recently, the idea of workers' self-management was usually dismissed as a quaint notion from the nineteenth century when the labor movement was immature and led by naive anarchosyndicalists, or it was considered a utopian vision that could not be implemented until a distant future when the economy would be fully developed and the labor force would be trained enough to work without imposed supervision. In the last two decades, however, a growing interest in the idea has been sparked by spontaneous protests where workers have openly questioned the rights of management to make decisions unilaterally on all sorts of matters. These

An earlier version of this paper was presented at the Ninth World Congress of Sociology in August 1978 at Uppsala, Sweden. The research reported herein would not have been possible without the assistance of numerous people whom I cannot thank individually here due to limitations of space and promises of anonymity. I do want to express special thanks, however, to Russell Middleton, Linda Haas, Leif Kanderhag, and Karin Ratas for many helpful suggestions. Financial support and other resources were provided by the National Institute of Mental Health Training Program in Social Organization at the University of Wisconsin, by the American-Scandinavian Foundation, and by the Fulbright Commission for Swedish-American Educational Exchange.

[276]

protests have often taken the form of wildcat strikes, where a local group of workers stages a sitdown or walkout demonstration to contest an unpopular decision handed down by an autocratic management. Sometimes such scattered protests by workers demanding democracy in the workplace have evolved into general strikes that immobilized an entire country, as in Hungary (1956), Poland (1956, 1970), France (1968), and Sweden (1970).

What are the attitudes that underlie such protests? How do some people come to believe in a revolutionary idea like workers' control while others remain committed to the established order and see no reason to advocate changes in it?

The Setting

To study workers' views on self-management, I have polled workers in the United States and Sweden. These are both advanced industrial nations, with a common cultural heritage in many respects. Yet the extent to which their labor movements have fought for industrial democracy is far different.

In the United States, employees have occasionally bought a controlling share of a company's stock and become their own bosses, and managers in many firms have sought to increase productivity and morale through experiments in employee participation in management (Jenkins 1974). Public opinion polls have revealed widespread displeasure with incumbent corporate bosses and approval of workers having a greater voice in decisionmaking (Rifkin 1977:173–77; Yankelovich 1974:19). Nevertheless, no major American labor union or political party has made industrial democracy part of its platform or felt compelled to court public support on this issue.

In Sweden, as recently as a decade ago, there was also a great reluctance among labor leaders and politicians to take the issue of industrial democracy seriously, even as opinion polls were revealing a readiness of the populace to challenge autocratic management (Andersson 1969:67–71; Oskarsson 1971:84; Jenkins 1974:262). The mood of rank-and-file workers became harder to ignore, however, as the frequency of wildcat strikes increased through the 1960s, culminating in a general strike of miners, dockworkers, and others in 1970. Labor union leaders joined the bandwagon and moved to the forefront to articulate the demands of their restless members (Martin 1977:51). Through their influence on the Social Democratic party, the dominant force in Parliament for nearly half a century, the Swedish unions succeeded in obtaining several important reforms in the 1970s that gave employees and their representatives an expanded role in decisionmaking. The most important of these reforms was the 1977 law on codetermination. It requires employers to postpone any decisions that involve and are contested by the employees (including policies on wages, production methods, or relocation), until negotiations with the employees' local representatives have produced a mutually agreeable solution or until the issue of contention has been settled through bargaining with union-federation officials or through adjudication in the labor court (Ministry of Labour 1977). As the next step, the blue-collar union federation LO has suggested a plan that would turn a certain percentage of a company's pretax profits over to a collectively administered wage earners' fund in the form of new issues of stock, gradually giving workers the controlling share of corporate stock (Meidner 1978). The Social Democratic party included no such proposal in its 1979 election platform, but is expected to do so in the 1982 campaign.

Most of my research on American workers' views on self-management was done in Indianapolis, a manufacturing, food processing, and state government center with about 1 million people. After some exploratory interviews with 25 workers, I made a series of random-digit telephone calls in the summer of 1976 to locate full-time adult workers (those 18 or older who usually work for someone else 20 hours or more per week). Averaging 15 minutes, interviews were conducted over the phone with 203 such workers, the response rate being around 80 percent. A subsample of the more articulate and interested respondents were asked to participate in a second round of hour-long interviews conducted in person and recorded on tape. The 41 workers who took part in this follow-up round were generally representative of the original phone respondents, in terms of the characteristics and opinions measured in the telephone interview.

Some additional U.S. data come from Madison, the state capital of Wisconsin, a city of 300,000 that includes a large university. Using random-digit dialing, a series of 15-minute telephone interviews was carried out with 125 Madison-area residents (including 80 workers) in the winter of 1976, with a response rate of about 75 percent. More extensive treatment of the procedures and results of the research in Madison and Indianapolis appears in Haas (1977).

The research on Swedish workers was done in Göteborg (Gothenburg), a center of industry and shipping with 500,000 people. In the winter of 1976–1977, intensive in-person pretest interviews were conducted with 65 workers whom I knew or were contacted through local labor union offices. In the spring of 1977, a four-page questionnaire in Swedish was mailed to 500 people aged 20 to 64 who were picked randomly from the government register of residents in the metropolitan area. After four waves of questionnaires or reminders and a final appeal by telephone, 64 percent of the original sample answered.

The 252 respondents who were full-time workers (i.e., employees averaging 20 hours or more per week) seem to have answered more readily than other types in the sample. Using local census figures to estimate the number of full-time workers who should have been in the original sample, it appears that their response rate was around 80 percent.

Quantitative comparisons are probably most valid when the sample of workers in the Indianapolis telephone survey is matched against the subsample of workers in the Göteborg mail survey. In both cases, the respondents were full-time workers in a large industrial city, a random method of sample selection was used, the sample size was over 200, and the response rate was a respectable figure around 80 percent. Madison is atypical in several important respects. It has more liberal college students and academics, fewer factories and blue-collar jobs, and less racial diversity than most American cities. The Indianapolis follow-up and Göteborg pretest groups will be used as sources of quotes to illustrate people's opinions in their own words, but quantitative results from these groups will be used only when they provide data that was not gathered in the larger, random surveys. Though the questionnaires varied from sample to sample in terms of the items included and the method of interrogation used (in person, by phone, by mail), the conclusions drawn from the different studies are basically similar.

"Workers" in this analysis means employees, people who hire themselves out to earn a living. This category includes not only those who do manual labor or factory work but also those who have nonmanual and even supervisory tasks. The latter types are sometimes considered in the dominant class rather than the subordinate working class or considered to occupy an intermediate position between the capitalist class and the working class. However, I think that the objective position that people occupy in relation to means of production, in terms of being owners or hirelings, is the crucial consideration. Some employees may be closer than others to their employers in terms of their style of consumption, the nature of their tasks, or the allocation of their loyalties, but I prefer to consider these dimensions as forms of variation within the ranks of workers rather than as aspects which define some as nonworkers.

The Appeal of Self-Management

The idea of workers' self-management has great appeal in both the United States and Sweden. In response to an item which read, "Regardless of the kind of job you have now, I'd like you to tell me which of these three kinds of companies you think you would like to work for if you had the choice," most workers polled in both countries indicated that they would rather work in "a company in which the stock is owned by the employees, who appoint their own management to run the company's operations" than in a firm run by private investors or by the government. This item was used in the Madison phone survey, the Indianapolis follow-up interview, and the Göteborg mail survey. In each case, the employee-run company was the most popular (chosen by 74 percent, 53 percent, and 56 percent of the workers in these three samples, respectively), followed by the company controlled by private investors (chosen by 19 percent, 39 percent, and 22 percent, respectively) and the government-run company (chosen by 5 percent, 9 percent, and 13 percent, respectively). When this item was originally used in a 1975 Hart Poll, 66 percent of a nationwide sample of Americans preferred employee control, 20 percent favored investor control, and 8 percent preferred government control (Rifkin 1977).

Few workers in either country thought it would be detrimental to the economy if "the people who worked in companies selected the management, set policies, and shared in the profits." When the workers in the Madison phone survey, Indianapolis follow-up interview, and Göteborg mail survey were asked what such an arrangement would do to the condition of the economy, only a minority (12 percent, 37 percent, and 11 percent in the three samples, respectively) thought it would make the economy worse. Most thought it would either improve the economy (60 percent, 39 percent, and 36 percent, respectively) or make no difference (28 percent, 24 percent, and 42 percent, respectively). When this item was originally used in the Hart Poll, half of a nationwide American sample expected an improvement, while only 14 percent anticipated a worsening of the economy (Rifkin 1977).

In both countries, many respondents explained their preference for self-management on the grounds that it would increase workers' morale and loyalty to the company. There would be more team spirit, more conscientious work, and lower supervisory costs, according to respondents who made such comments as:

> *Secretary:* "They'd work harder for themselves than someone else, when they don't know where [the profit] is going." (Indianapolis follow-up interview.)
> *Auto mechanic:* "They could save a lot of money, especially on salaries. . . . There are so many directors and supervisors and sales managers . . . who don't do anything productive. They only furnish paperwork for each other." (Göteborg pretest.)

Another reason that both Americans and Swedes frequently offered for favoring self-management was the belief that workers have information and skills that are not fully used in the existing system of hierarchic decisionmaking. The quality of decisions would improve as the power to make policy is transferred to the mass of ordinary employees who are familiar with local conditions and have firsthand practical knowledge of the production process:

> *Welfare caseworker:* "The administrators, they're too far away from it. They don't have any personal contact with the clients. They don't know what sort of reactions to expect." (Indianapolis follow-up interview.)
> *Cement finisher:* "A worker stands on the shop floor and knows about a lot of things. . . . If a board member came from the workers, he could suggest things . . . that would expand and improve production." (Göteborg pretest.)

A third reason that workers in both countries gave for favoring self-management was that it would bring less greedy and more public-spirited people to the fore as shapers of company policy:

> *Machine repairman:* "The employees . . . should have some say 'cause [the bosses] try to get one guy to do the work of three if they can." (Indianapolis phone survey.)
> *Machine repairman:* "The profit that is [now] plucked out of the company could be used for reinvestments in the company, for raising our wages, for training people—instead of having the money put into a luxurious villa." (Göteborg pretest.)

In both countries, such a basic feature of the social order as the system of ownership and control of enterprises fails to elicit the loyal support of the majority. In both countries, most of the press is owned by people who believe in capitalism, the schools teach the workings of this system without criticism, the churches accept the basic features of the existing order, and so on. Apparently the amount of indoctrination that can be done is limited. Workers have an independent source of information in their day-to-day experiences. As they work or shop, they discover that industrialists, merchants, and other businessmen have no monopoly on intelligence or virtue, and they become receptive to suggestions that the power to make corporate policy should be more evenly distributed.

Workers' Commitment to Self-Management

Despite the appeal that self-management has for most workers, there were indications that it was only a dream-wish for many who were intrigued by the idea. Many who expressed interest in it at one point also expressed doubts at another point about its workability or about the propriety of various actions to implement it.

This ambivalence was much more common among Americans than

Table 12-1. Respondents' views on the ideal distribution of final say over company policy areas (by percentages)

	Private Employer	Public Authority	Workers in Company	Other	Not Sure, No Answer
	US/Sw*	US/Sw	US/Sw	US/Sw	US/Sw
a. Hiring and firing	73/31	4/15	22/42	—	1/12
b. Assigning people to work tasks	73/29	3/8	22/49	1/0	1/13
c. Prices of products or services	66/22	16/41	9/17	5/2	4/18
d. What kinds of products to make or what kinds of services to provide	80/35	8/20	6/25	4/2	1/19
e. How to make the products or how to provide the services	72/22	8/8	17/55	2/0	1/15
f. How fast work should be done or how much work should be done	65/22	4/8	29/53	1/0	1/16
g. Amount of wages to be given for different jobs	67/25	8/14	23/44	1/0	0/17
h. Scheduling of work times (hours, vacations, etc.)	65/20	4/10	30/57	1/0	0/14
i. Spending on equipment or facilities	87/31	4/9	8/44	—	1/16
j. Choosing foremen and supervisors	79/27	2/8	17/48	1/0	1/18
k. Improving physical surroundings at the workplace	53/16	6/12	40/60	1/0	1/12
l. Choosing top management	88/31	2/11	9/37	—	1/20

* US = 203 workers in Indianapolis; Sw = 252 workers in Göteborg survey.

Note: The survey question was "For each area, I'd like to know who you think should ideally have the final say in making decisions about such matters in a typical company. In deciding about [a, b, c, etc.], should the final say ideally belong to a private employer, to a public authority (such as the government or community representatives), or to the workers in the company?" Multiple choices were apportioned evenly to the parties named.

Swedes. For example, only 37 percent of the workers in the Indianapolis follow-up group answered yes when asked: "Where you work, would it make sense to give workers a bigger role in decisions?" In the Göteborg mail survey, on the other hand, 74 percent of the workers said yes. Another question asked who should ideally have the final say over each of a dozen different policy areas. As table 12-1 shows, the majority of workers in the Indianapolis phone survey invariably delegated the final say to a private employer, while the modal response in Göteborg was to delegate it to the workers.

Why did workers, especially those in the United States, hesitate to support self-management here when they favored it in responding to the items discussed in the previous section? The answer may lie in the different versions of self-management that different phrasings of items suggested to respondents. The items that elicited the most support were phrased in general terms, without specifying the situation in which workers would manage themselves or the types of decisions they would have to make. The general items presented a package deal in which several aspects of self-management were included, and respondents may have been tempted to approve of the whole package even though only part of it really appealed to them. When different aspects of self-management were specified, the level of support may have dropped because respondents were forced to give separate opinions about options that did not appeal to them.

Profit-sharing appeared to be the most attractive feature of self-management for American workers. Items that mentioned employees owning company stock or sharing in the profits elicited majority approval for worker-controlled companies, whereas items that focused on the division of decisionmaking responsibility without touching on the division of profits failed to reveal majority support. It is easy for American workers to support profit-sharing because it would give them a piece of the action under capitalism without requiring a total break with economic traditions that they have learned to accept as conducive to productivity and efficiency, such as private property, competition, the profit motive, and unequal distribution of the fruits of production.

In contrast, Swedish workers were just as interested in changing the structure of decisionmaking as the distribution of profits. A union official in a ball-bearing factory explained:

> It is meaningless if the workers own a company and only a handful are interested in the company's operations, for then there might as well be another owner.

When contemplating an expansion of the ordinary worker's role in making company policy, Americans had more reservations about workers' qualifications:

> *Stockbroker/office manager:* "Workers don't have all the facts and you don't
> have time to feed them all the facts, or there'd be no production." (India-
> napolis phone survey.)
> *Dishwasher:* "If workers would decide, everything would be messed up. . . .
> They'd be having their friends in eating for free. . . . They wouldn't show
> up for work. They'd raise wages to $400–500 a week." (Indianapolis phone
> survey and follow-up.)

Some American workers also had reservations about the efficiency of democratic decisionmaking by the mass of employees:

> *Priest:* "You can't have all chiefs and no Indians. Someone has to accept all
> the responsibility." (Indianapolis phone survey.)
> *Customs inspector:* "There'd be too much division. . . . You can't run a com-
> pany by committee." (Indianapolis phone survey.)

Among the Swedish respondents, such comments were much rarer.

The greater ambivalence of the American workers was also evident
when questions were posed about taking specific actions to bring about
workers' control. The majority of workers in both countries (65 percent in
the Indianapolis phone survey and 66 percent in the Göteborg pretest) said
they would support the purchase of a bankrupt company by municipal
government for the purpose of leasing it back to the employees to run as a
self-managed company. Half of both samples (48 percent and 53 percent,
respectively) said they would be willing to join other workers in buying a
firm and setting up a worker-run company. A plurality (49 percent) of the
workers in the Indianapolis phone survey were willing to join a labor union
that tries to get workers a voice in management, but nearly all (88 percent)
in the Göteborg pretest were willing to do so. Only 38 percent of the former
indicated willingness to vote for candidates who support workers' control,
as opposed to 53 percent of the latter. Most (54 percent) of the Indianapolis
follow-up group had primarily negative reactions to a description of the
new Swedish codetermination law that makes all aspects of the workplace
negotiable issues in the collective bargaining system, but only 14 percent of
the workers in the Göteborg mail survey thought the law went too far.

Extremely militant actions were generally disliked in both countries.
Only a small minority (19 percent in the Indianapolis phone survey and 20
percent in the Göteborg pretest) were willing to go on strike to demand
workers' control, and few were willing to take over a company without the
owner's permission and run it as a worker-managed company (6 percent
and 9 percent, respectively). Many were ready to approve such actions as a
tactic of last resort in desperate situations, however. Reacting to a description of a forcible takeover by workers trying to prevent profiteering owners

from closing a plant in a small town, 39 percent in the Indianapolis follow-up and 41 percent in the Göteborg pretest approved of the workers' attempt to keep the plant going on their own.

The general pattern in the responses to items on actions to implement self-management was that there was little difference between Americans and Swedes in their readiness to support reforms that could be accomplished within the framework of existing laws, or in their general unwillingness to support illegal or violent methods to introduce workers' control. Between these two extremes, the Swedes were more willing to change the existing structure through conventional methods such as passing new laws and negotiating new agreements with employers.

American workers' reluctance to demand changes in the status quo was based to a great extent on the acceptance of employers' traditional property rights as legitimate. The suggestion that some of the investor's decisionmaking prerogatives should be abrogated was rejected as a threat not only to the capitalist but also to the worker who aspires to own a business, a home, or some other form of private property.

> *Truckdriver:* "If I started a business and worked my ass off, I wouldn't want a guy I hired to do dishes to tell me what to do." (Indianapolis phone survey.)
> *Battery repairer:* "I wouldn't want the workers to tell the boss what to do, because it would be like someone coming into my house and telling me what color to paint the walls." (Indianapolis follow-up interview.)

American workers sometimes defended hierarchy on principle, without specifying the benefits expected from it:

> *Gear-factory worker:* "It's like your children telling you how to run your family . . . ordering you around. They're not the head!" (Indianapolis follow-up interview.)

In contrast to American workers, Swedes tended to affirm the worth of labor instead of private property:

> *Clerk:* "[Employers] just sit and take in money. . . . It's the workers who keep companies going with their manpower. . . . We're the ones who actually wear ourselves out." (Göteborg pretest.)
> *Longshoreman:* "We're the ones who do the work . . . who are exposed to bad weather and wind and . . . accidents." (Göteborg pretest.)

Swedish workers also tended to affirm the worth of equality or democracy on principle, rather than hierarchy:

> *Hospital union steward:* "I prefer the collective idea—that this society will be based on the conditions set by the absolute majority of the people and not by those few who have the economic power." (Göteborg pretest.)
> *Training director:* "It would give people a bigger chance to influence their own work situation. . . . Everyone would consider others as equal, equally worthy." (Göteborg pretest.)

The Origin of Support for Self-Management

The comparisons of American and Swedish workers' views on self-management are based on the typical responses in each country, but opinions within each country varied a great deal and some views overlapped between the countries. Several factors may explain the variation in opinions within, as well as between, these countries. In both the Indianapolis phone survey and the Göteborg mail survey, the extent of support for workers' control was measured by how many of a dozen areas of corporate policy (see table 12-1) the respondent wanted workers to have final say on.

In deciding why some workers favor self-management while others do not, one of the first factors that comes to mind is the extent of job satisfaction. Those who are dissatisfied with their jobs should be more favorable to a reform that would allow them to shape workplace arrangements more to their liking; those who have no grievances about their work should be less interested in such a change. The workers in the Indianapolis and Göteborg surveys were asked:

> In general, how well would you say that your job measures up to the sort of job you really want? Would you say it is exactly like the job you really want, very much like it, somewhat like it, not very much like it, or not at all like the job you really want?

This measure was significantly ($p = 0.05$) correlated in the expected direction with support for workers' self-management, both in Indianapolis ($r = -0.23$) and in Göteborg ($r = -0.13$). About half the workers in each country said their jobs were exactly or very much like what they really wanted, and most of the rest had jobs that were at least somewhat like what they wanted.

The distributions of responses in the two countries were also remarkably similar when the Indianapolis follow-up group and the Göteborg mail sample were asked about specific features of their jobs. Swedish workers were no more likely than Americans to report specific grievances such as low pay, uncomfortable surroundings, safety hazards, exhausting pace, lack of variety, or lack of opportunity to use one's ideas and skills on the job. So the Swedish workers' tendency to be more favorable to self-management than American workers cannot be attributed to any greater discontent with working conditions in Sweden.

Another factor that may explain some of the variance in support for self-management is the worker's opinion of incumbent bosses. Respondents in the Indianapolis and Göteborg surveys were asked to react to this statement:

> Most bosses who run companies nowadays care so little about what happens to their workers or to the public that they don't deserve to keep their positions. (Very true, somewhat true, not too true, not at all true.)

As expected, those who agreed with this statement were significantly more favorable toward self-management ($r = 0.27$ in both surveys), but there was not much difference between the two countries in the extent of criticism of those who run companies. A majority of the workers in both countries did not express the extremely disaffected view that the incumbent bosses deserve to be ousted, though sizable minorities of nearly 40 percent in each survey did.

Not many differences were found, either, when the workers in the Madison phone survey and the Göteborg pretest were asked to rate businesses in their respective countries on more specific criteria. Majorities in both cases gave corporations unfavorable ("only fair" or "poor") ratings for their performance in keeping down the cost of living, keeping profits from being excessively high, preventing unemployment and economic recessions, and enabling people to make full use of their abilities. Swedish corporations were given favorable ("excellent" or "pretty good") ratings by the majority in the Göteborg pretest only on the matters of providing good quality products and paying good wages, while the Madison workers gave American businesses favorable ratings only for paying good wages and for safeguarding the health of workers and consumers.

Swedish and American workers differed in their orientations toward incumbent policymakers in one respect. American workers were more likely to aspire to join the ranks of businessmen. In the Indianapolis follow-up, 44 percent of the workers expected to go into business for themselves, as opposed to only 13 percent of the workers in the Göteborg mail survey. American folklore is full of stories about entrepreneurs who rose from rags to riches, and such success is still held out as a realistic goal for the ambitious and resourceful commoner. Aspirants to self-employment may be more interested in making individualistic efforts to find a more comfortable niche in the status quo than in casting their lot with the collective movements that are necessary for any wholesale improvement in the existing system (Chinoy 1970).

Another factor seems conducive to support for self-management: a sense of solidarity with other workers. Those who are critical of the status quo but unwilling to trust the working masses would probably be cynical about changing the existing order or want to replace the incumbent bosses with government planners, revolutionary leaders, or some other group of enlightened experts. Several indicators were used to measure faith in workers' dependability as decisionmakers. One of these called for respondents to react to this statement:

> You can't count on other workers to look out for you because most of them are too wrapped up in looking out for themselves. (Very true, somewhat true, not too true, not at all true.)

Answers to this item were not associated with support for self-management in either survey, but the item did reveal a dramatic difference in American and Swedish workers' views of their colleagues. Most (58 percent) of the American respondents agreed that workers are selfish and unreliable, while only 30 percent of the Swedes did so. Responses to this item did not correlate with support for self-management because, perhaps, the reference is to workers as they are at present rather than to workers as they would be if they had control of companies.

To measure views about workers' potential rather than current character, an item in the Göteborg mail survey and the Indianapolis follow-up interview asked whether workers with a chance to decide things for themselves would work harder than usual. Most (62 percent) of the workers in the Göteborg survey expected more diligence rather than more laziness under self-management; the Indianapolis follow-up group was evenly split. In both studies, faith in workers' industriousness was associated with support for workers' control ($r = 0.25$ and 0.44, respectively). Respondents in both studies were also asked whether workers know more than they're generally given credit for. Large majorities of the workers in both the Göteborg mail survey (75 percent) and the Indianapolis follow-up group (66 percent) thought so, and the responses to this item were correlated with support for self-management in the expected direction ($r = 0.20$ and 0.36, respectively). About 95 percent of the workers in both studies indicated agreement with the statement, "My co-workers are friendly and helpful," so the Swedes' higher opinion of workers in general did not appear to be based on having more workmates of good character. Apparently it was the impressions formed about the workers seen only in passing or heard about second-hand that made the difference in Americans' and Swedes' views on workers.

As a mechanism for increasing communication between workers in scattered workplaces and coordinating their actions, the labor union can play a major role in developing a sense of solidarity with workers outside the immediate workplace. Swedish unions have served this function more successfully than their American counterparts in several important respects. For one thing, Swedish unions are much more inclusive in their membership: 83 percent of the workers in the Göteborg mail survey were union members, as opposed to only 30 percent in the Indianapolis survey. (These figures represent the national averages in both countries.) As a result, Swedish unions are in a better position to claim that they represent the public interest. In addition, nearly all Swedish unions are subsumed under either the blue-collar union federation (LO) or the white-collar union federation (TCO). LO and TCO negotiate general agreements at the national level with the employers' representatives, thus minimizing jurisdictional disputes. The Swedish unions, particularly those in the blue-collar LO federation, have made a concerted effort in recent years to even out wage differences by winning higher raises for the lowest-paid workers than for the traditionally best-paid workers, thus reducing wage competition. The Swedish unions have also played a very active role in economic planning since the Social Democratic party came into power in 1932. By having a direct hand in getting the Swedish economy out of a depression and keeping it prosperous, the unions have demonstrated that workers' representatives have a great deal to contribute for the common good. Finally, Swedish unions have lobbied for social welfare benefits and full employment policies that have cushioned workers from the worst effects of corporate competition, retooling, and rationalization. As a result, workers do not become rivals for scarce jobs or proponents of such practices as feather-bedding that, in the public's view, obstruct technical progress.

The differences between the labor movements in these countries may result from American unions' difficulties in organizing a workforce that is many times larger than Sweden's and is much more heterogeneous in terms of racial, ethnic, regional, and religious divisions. American unions have also had to contend with a stronger class of opponents that has been able to accumulate wealth in larger amounts than Swedish capitalists. American unions face further difficulties in trying to lobby for favorable legislation in a country where political parties are loose confederations rather than cohesive organizations on which pressure can be focused and where the government consists of so many units, levels, and branches that pressure must be applied simultaneously to many points before results are obtained. Whatever the reason, Swedish unions have a public image of integrity, public-spiritedness, and progressiveness, whereas American unions are plagued by a reputation for corruption, selfishness, and complacency. In the Madison phone survey, 48 percent of the workers gave labor unions some or most of the blame in answering a question about the source of the nation's economic problems, but only 27 percent of the workers in the Göteborg mail survey did so. If the unions' image suggests that labor leaders do not work for the common good, people will naturally be less likely to favor an expansion of the influence of employees and their representatives on company policies.

Swedish labor unions have made workers receptive to the idea of self-management not only by developing a sense of solidarity within the working class but also by directly promoting the ideas of democracy and equality. For a century, Swedish labor leaders have been exponents of socialist ideology. Some possible reasons for the greater frequency of such idealists in the Swedish labor movement were suggested earlier, but whatever the reason for their presence, they have been in an excellent position to publicize their critiques of the status quo and their proposals for change. Their influence is reflected in the popularity of the socialist vision of making companies a property held in common and serving the common good.

A plurality of 45 percent of the workers in the Göteborg mail survey thought it would be rather good or very good to promote a transition from privately owned companies to publicly owned ones, whereas only 7 percent of the Indianapolis follow-up group favored such a change. To reach their goal, socialist leaders in Sweden have been willing to compromise with capitalists through collective bargaining and piecemeal reforms, but they have also pointed out limitations of this approach.

The appeal of democratic and egalitarian ideas may also be stronger in Sweden because the struggle for limiting the king's powers and enfranchising the masses is a fresher memory there than in the United States. Sweden did not have universal suffrage until after World War One, and the right to vote was still an issue when the labor movement was formed. In contrast to American unions, Swedish unions were actively involved in winning their members the right to vote and affect government policy, so it is easy for labor leaders to invoke democratic principles in the struggle to win their members' influence over corporate policy as well.

The Social Location of Advocates of Self-Management

The experiences that increase interest in self-management are not distributed evenly through the population of workers. In this section, advocates of self-management are identified by their location in the social structure, in terms of membership in various categories that are commonly used to classify and compare people. Certain categories of workers are unusually favorable to self-management, as I suggest in the following sections.

Race/ethnicity

In both countries, minority groups did not differ significantly from the rest of the working population in their views on self-management. Making up

12 percent of the workers in the Indianapolis phone survey, blacks were no more or less likely ($p = .05$) than whites to favor self-management. In the Göteborg mail survey, 12 percent of the workers were foreign-born, and they did not differ from native Swedes on this issue.

Sex

In the Göteborg mail survey, there was no significant difference ($p = .05$) between male and female workers in support for self-management. In the Indianapolis phone survey, however, women were more favorable to self-management ($r = .17$). This difference may be due to women's traditional socialization to be empathetic with fellow human beings and sympathize with proposals to improve their lot. Supporting self-management may also be a continuation of the questioning of tradition that led the women in this sample to enter the workforce in the first place. In any case, they were not less satisfied with their jobs, more critical of employers, or less critical of workers.

Age

In the Indianapolis phone survey, age was inversely associated with support for self-management ($r = -.24$), in part because young workers were less satisfied with their jobs. Those who have recently entered the workforce often have high expectations, but they do not have seniority for entrance into the best jobs. Young workers have also been exposed to the antiauthoritarian values of the youth counterculture that blossomed in the late 1960s, which might make them more favorable to democratizing the workplace. In the Göteborg survey, young workers also tended to favor self-management more, but the difference between age groups was not nearly as great as in the United States.

Education

There was no association between education and support for workers' control in either the Indianapolis or the Göteborg survey. Some observers have suggested that the growing interest in self-management is attributable in part to the rising level of education, which makes workers more sophisticated, self-confident, and interested in using their skills to shape policy. The ranks of the well-educated do include articulate critics of established ways, but they also include managers and other privileged employees with a stake in the status quo.

Parents' occupations

The Indianapolis and Göteborg surveys included questions about the father's and the mother's occupations when the respondent was growing up.

The answers were grouped into four categories: (1) low blue-collar (machine operators, general laborers, servants, farmers); (2) high blue-collar (craftsmen and foremen); (3) low white-collar (salesmen and clerks); (4) high white-collar (professionals, technicians, managers). In both surveys, the father's job type was not associated with the respondent's views on self-management, nor was the mother's job type (among those with mothers in the workforce). Whether the parents were self-employed or employees of others also made no difference.

In the Göteborg survey, however, workers with gainfully employed mothers were significantly more favorable to workers' control than those whose mothers were housewives. If parents in the workforce served as a conduit of radical ideas articulated by leaders of the Swedish labor movement, then those with both working mothers and working fathers would have been doubly exposed to such ideas and thereby become more receptive to the idea of self-management.

Occupation

In both the Indianapolis and Göteborg surveys, blue-collar workers tended to be more favorable toward self-management than white-collar workers, but there was no significant difference within each of these two broad categories between those in the "high" (relatively skilled) and those in the "low" (relatively unskilled) groups. As table 12-2 shows, the difference between blue-collar and white-collar workers was more marked in the American sample than in the Swedish one. Blue-collar workers are more likely to support workers' control, because their jobs are generally less satisfactory (lower paid, more dangerous, more vulnerable to lay-offs) and because they have less in common with their bosses. Also in both surveys, workers with positions as regular supervisors were less sympathetic toward self-management than those who occasionally or never had supervisory tasks. This is understandable, because supervisors generally have more reumunerative and fulfilling jobs and their privileges derive from the existing authoritarian arrangements.

Union membership

In both the Indianapolis and Göteborg surveys, union members tended to be more favorable to self-management than nonmembers. Union membership may expose workers to labor movement ideology about their rights to help decide the conditions of their employment, or workers who have job grievances may decide they need influence on corporate policies and decide to form a union or join an existing one as a result. Few of the workers in either country had ever been on strike (16 percent in the Indianapolis survey, 9 percent in the Göteborg survey). Strike experience and support for

*Table 12-2. Support for workers' self-management by
occupation, within nationalities*

Occupation	Number of Decisionmaking Areas Given to Workers for Final Say*			
	1 or less out of 12 areas	More than 1 but less than 7 out of 12	7 or more out of 12 areas	Total
U.S. workers (Indianapolis survey)				
Low blue-collar	19(27%)	47(66%)	5(7%)	71
High blue-collar	11(41%)	15(56%)	1(4%)	27
Low white-collar	29(52%)	23(41%)	4(7%)	56
High white-collar	27(55%)	19(39%)	3(6%)	49
				$N = 203$
	$\chi^2 = 13.37, p < .05$			
Swedish workers (Göteborg survey)				
Low blue-collar	2(3%)	37(56%)	27(41%)	66
High blue-collar	1(3%)	20(59%)	13(38%)	34
Low white-collar	7(9%)	47(63%)	21(28%)	75
High white-collar	3(4%)	51(70%)	19(26%)	73
				$N = 248$
	$\chi^2 = 7.89, p > .05**$			

* Measure presented in table 12-1. Missing data replaced with means.
** $\chi^2 = 4.02$, $p < .05$ when blue-collar/white-collar is cross-tabulated with less than 7/7 or more areas.

self-management were not connected in the Göteborg survey, but there was a weak association in the Indianapolis survey. As with union membership, participation in strikes may lead workers to favor self-management by alienating them from their bosses and bringing them into contact with radical agitators, or it may be a result of having radical views about workers' influence on policy to begin with.

Enterprise

A significant difference between workers in different economic sectors was found in the Indianapolis survey, but this finding was not replicated in Göteborg. In Indianapolis, public-service workers were found to be more favorable to self-management than workers in the manufacturing and private-service sectors. Public-service jobs may attract applicants who have a humanistic orientation and are predisposed to be critical of authoritarian arrangements that put the interests of owners and executives before the needs of the mass of employees and their clients. Even if public-service workers did not have different values at the outset, their attitudes may diverge from those of other workers because they are relatively isolated from the profits-before-people ideology that reigns in private enterprises. Public servants also must work at jobs that private enterprise cannot or will not do effectively on its own, which may make them more conscious of the shortcomings of the status quo and more receptive to workers' control.

Another way of classifying enterprises is by size. The concentration of large numbers of workers in a single workplace is often suggested to be a radicalizing influence, because it increases contact between formerly isolated workers and makes them conscious of their collective identity and strength. The Indianapolis follow-up interview and the Göteborg mail survey included a question about how many employees worked in the local plant of the respondent's company or agency. This variable was not associated with workers' views on self-management in either study, perhaps because living in a large urban area has the same effects as those posited for working in a large factory.

Summary

With data from a series of exploratory interviews and random-sampling surveys in the United States and Sweden, it was found that the majority of workers in both countries approved of workers' self-management as an abstract idea. Among the reasons given by respondents for favoring self-management were the expectation that it would motivate employees to do a more conscientious job and the belief that it would allow them to use skills and knowledge that presently are untapped. Among American workers, however, much of the interest centered on the profit-sharing potential of workers' control, and many respondents were convinced that workers would not be qualified to decide things outside their traditional areas of competence or that democratic procedures on the job would be cumbersome and chaotic. Swedish workers, in contrast, were more interested in getting a chance to make decisions and more willing to support concrete proposals for a gradual redistribution of power in existing companies.

Discontent with working conditions and dissatisfaction with the present makers of corporate policy were found to be correlated with support for self-management among the respondents in each country, but there was little difference between the two countries on these variables. Swedish workers' higher opinion of their colleagues appeared to be a major factor in their stronger commitment to self-management. It was suggested that Swedish labor unions have adopted strategies that are more conducive to the development of a sense of solidarity within the working class than the approaches taken by American unions. Swedish unions have been more active in disseminating information about self-management and in spreading egalitarian ideas, which has probably helped to make Swedish workers more committed to industrial democracy and more uniform in their views on the matter. Similar types of workers were found to be advocates of self-management in both countries, but differences in views on self-management between various categories of workers were more frequent and more extensive in the United States than in Sweden, perhaps because of the pervasiveness of democratic and egalitarian ideology in the latter country.

References

ANDERSSON, SVEN
    1969   Vilda Strejker. Stockholm: Rabén and Sjögren.
CHINOY, ELY
    1970   Automobile Workers and the American Dream. Boston: Beacon.
HAAS, AIN
    1977   "Workers' Control in Working-Class Consciousness," Ph.D. dissertation, University of Wisconsin–Madison.
JENKINS, DAVID
    1974   Job Power: Blue and White Collar Democracy. Baltimore: Penguin.
MARTIN, ANDREW
    1977   "In Sweden, a Union Proposal for Socialism," *Working Papers for a New Society* (Summer).
MEIDNER, RUDOLF
    1978   "Employee Investment Funds and Capital Formation," *Working Life in Sweden* 6 (June).
MINISTRY OF LABOUR
    1977   Towards Democracy at the Workplace. Stockholm.
OSKARSSON, KAY and INGE
    1971   Stuvarstrejken i Ådalen 1970. Stockholm: Prisma.
RIFKIN, JEREMY
    1977   Own Your Own Job. New York: Bantam Books.
YANKELOVICH, DANIEL
    1974   "Changing Youth Values in the 70's," *Party Builder* [Socialist Workers' Party Organizational Bulletin] 8 (July).

13 Corporate Power and Urban Transportation: A Comparison of Public Transit's Decline in the United States and Germany

Glenn Yago
University of Wisconsin–Madison

Archival abbreviations used in text and references:
  APTA   American Public Transportation Association
  BA   Bundesarchiv
  DJ   Department of Justice
  FSA   Frankfurter Stadtarchiv
  NA   National Archives
  RG   record group (file coding system)

Organizations abbreviated in text:
  BPR   U.S. Bureau of Public Roads
  DIHT   Deutsche Industrie—und—Handelstag (German Industrial
    and Trade Association)
  FERRC   Federal Electric Railway Regulatory Commission
  RDA   Reichsverband der Automobilindustrie
  RVM   Reichverkehrsministrium (Reich Transportation Ministry)
  RWM   Reichwirtschaftsministerium (Reich Economics Ministry)
  SA   Sturm Abteilung (storm troopers)

Transportation technology is not some external force imposed on society, but an instance of the articulation of class power in the control of cities.[1] The decline of public transit and the rise of automobilization is a ubiquitous phenomenon in modern capitalism, but it has also advanced unevenly. To grasp comparative similarities and differences in Germany and the United States, we cannot focus merely on changes in population patterns, urban physical characteristics, or individual patterns of consumption.

I owe much to the following people for their criticism and encouragement on this research project: Michael Aiken, Manuel Castells, David Kramer, Yudit E. Jung, Bradford C. Snell, and the members of the Social Organization Colloquium, Department of Sociology, University of Wisconsin–Madison.

[1] Other studies on transit decline argue that city age, population size, and density or population characteristics of transportation consumers (age, sex, income, race, etc.) determine the level of public transportation.

Rather, the impact of broad historical changes in public policy and private corporate action must be analyzed.

Variations in the economic and class structures of Germany and the United States affected public transportation's decline, as a result of the different industrial composition of these countries' capitalist classes, which was critical in the timing of policies favoring automobilization.

What was the interaction in these two countries between long-term corporate strategy and state policy? In both countries, corporate strategy impinged on state transportation policy by creating an environment in which it was constrained. Corporations created, through their policies and those of their trade associations, limited and skewed alternatives for transportation policy makers. Though the timing of automobilization differed, we can trace the continuity of corporate control over urban transportation in both countries.

Corporate policy made it possible that even without direct representation in the political arena, there could be little doubt that public policy would answer the structural needs of those corporations in the automobile, rubber, and oil industries. However, never leaving anything to chance, corporations placed representatives directly in the political arena at all levels of the state apparatus.

The variation in transit decline in Germany and the United States is explained by differences in their pattern of capital accumulation (that is, whether based on the automobile-rubber-oil or coal-electrical-steel industrial complexes). Transportation policy was the outcome of intraclass competition between various industry groups in the capitalist class *and* the state. State policy toward transportation came to reflect ascendant interests of capital and to enhance those interests through state policies. Such policies had the consequence, if not the intention, of eliminating transportation alternatives and therefore assuring that earlier policies would not be revived and challenges by other classes to create new policies would be defeated.

The Decline of Public Transit in Germany and the United States

It is difficult to locate adequate data comparing transportation in Germany and the United States since the turn of the century. We know that transit ridership in the United States began to decline immediately prior to World War One and stagnated throughout the 1920s. Precipitous decline came with rapidly rising failures and receiverships by transit properties during the 1930s. A brief respite came during the war years, but transit ridership fell quickly after World War Two.

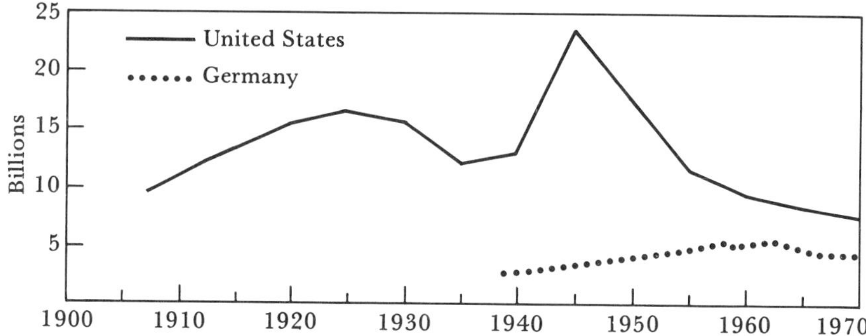

*Figure 13-1. Decline of total public transit—1900–1970
(passengers in United States and Germany)*

U.S. Source: American Public Transit Association, *Transit Fact Book,* 1975–1976. Data for 1907–1940 are from Wilfred Owen, *The Metropolitan Transportation Problem* (rev. ed.), 1966.
German Source: Rudolph Menke, Kohlhammer, Stadtverkehrplanning, Stuttgart, 1975:43.

For Germany, the impact of motorization can be seen in the decline of rail transit during the 1930s and continuing after World War Two. Aggregate ridership data for all transit modes is unavailable for pre–World War Two Germany. Although overall ridership increases slightly during the reconstruction period (1945–1959), all transit modes suffer decline in ridership since the early 1960s. This decline is hastened by buses being substituted for rail lines, resulting in reduced ridership.

In both Germany and the United States, the use of the private automobile rose dramatically. Nevertheless, the relationship between public and private transportation has not been constant and continuous. Public transit decline in both countries has fluctuated. Its decline came later and less suddenly in Germany than in the United States (figures 13-1 and 13-2).

German economic background

By the end of Germany's first wave of industrialization in 1873, a legal framework for capitalist expansion, the railroad system, shipping, and other infrastructural bases for economic growth were established. Germany had early and rapid industrial and financial concentration. Based on heavy industry, mining, railroads, electromachinery, and banking, a dominant segment of the capitalist class remained impenetrable until the crisis of the Weimar period. Together with centralized state power, it led to a rather narrow definition of transportation policy.

In the United States, land speculation and suburban settlement was possible through largely decentralized landholdings, but in Germany, con-

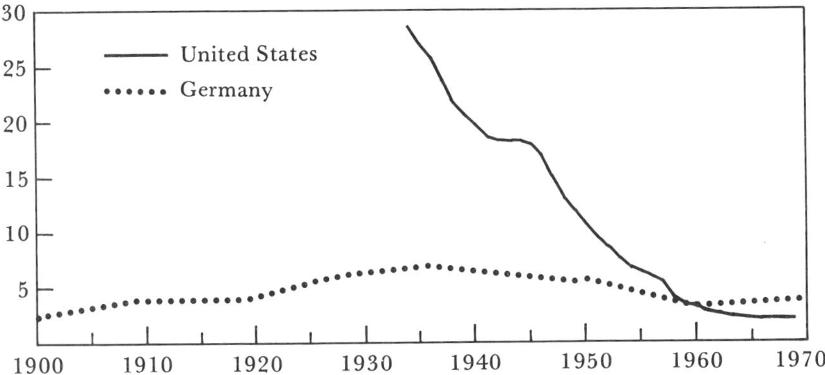

Figure 13-2. Decline of rail transit—1900–1970 (rail track length in United States and Germany)

U.S. Source: Historical Statistics for the U.S., Census Bureau, 1975.
German Source: Statistisches Jahrbücher des Deutsches Reich, 1920–1971.

centrated agrarian landownership prevented such development. Urban expansion in Germany depended on the annexation of surrounding village communities, rather than settlement and housing booms of open lands around major cities. Land speculation, housing construction, and the financing of these activities was not as much an area of profit-making as in the United States.

These characteristics of Germany's industrialization and urbanization created a stalemate over urban transportation policy. Railroad-associated interests (heavy industries and mining) emphasized rail transport and opposed the production of new transportation equipment, especially automobiles. This stalemate was broken primarily through the interpenetration of German and American capital during the Weimar period, and later, under fascism. Efforts before this to form an automobile cartel failed for lack of bank support (*Voessiche Zeitung,* November 19, 1928).

Without national financing, Adam Opel AG and many other enterprises became the target for the U.S. capital invested in Germany under the Dawes plan. The result was that the automobile and related industries became important in the realm of public policy.

German political background

Nationalizing railroads in 1879 was an early recognition of state responsibility to ensure servicing capital infrastructural expenditures. Circumscribed reforms (such as those led by Stein-Hardenberg and Bismarck) led to the centralization and rationalization of state power, and made German absolutism compatible with emerging capitalist practices. State policies reflected an often shaky coalition of industrial, financial, and agricultural capital. The state insulated them from pressures from below as well as solidifying its own economic and political support within the higher reaches of German society.

The focus of local governments, as in the "progressive era" in the United States, was to improve cities as loci of capital production, distribution, and exchange. Urban expansion had to be orderly and insulated from erratic speculative developments that might raise questions about the legitimacy of such growth. Building codes, land use ordinances, and urban planning were integrated into the functions of municipal government early on. "Municipal industrialism," the expansion of municipal ownership and control over transportation, housing, schools, and social services, became widespread. Full electrification of transit was accomplished almost completely through municipal initiative. Municipal electrification led to declining fares before World War One. Reduced fares, along with state subsidies for transit, had an enormous effect on growth in public transportation, housing, and other collective consumption expenditures.

Social measures in general, and public transportation in particular, benefited during the period following the 1918–1919 revolutionary upheavals in German cities. However, increasing public transit operation costs, the reluctance of progressive city governments to raise fares, the ensuing fiscal crisis, and the national parliamentary stalemate created a policy impasse that was not broken until the advent of fascism.

German Transportation Policy and the Decline of Public Transit

German national transportation policy excluded automobile interests prior to 1933. The transference of rail-related industrial interests into state policy occurred through fiscal, trade, budgetary and regulatory measures.

As early as 1906, automobiles were taxed for general state revenues. Taxes rose and directives from the internal revenue service allowed deductions for the journey to work *solely* for public transit. These fiscal measures clearly supported public transit at the expense of the automobile. Foreign trade policy sacrificed the automobile to foreign competition to maintain protection barriers for stronger German products. Budgetary measures prohibited the use of automobile tax revenues for the construction of public roads. Interests of rail-related industrialists and the left parties converged to oppose proautomobile measures until the early 1930s. City and business officials lobbying for more highways feared the left parties would block such financing in 1931 (Heun to Batsek 3/14/31, FA 3461/BD.1; Kaftan 1954).

Municipalizing transit was motivated by the desire to decrease and subsidize the cost of moving labor and commodities. By the 1920s, rail-related interests managed to regulate rail and motor carrier rate structures (through so-called Schenker contracts), thus insulating rail from motor traffic competition. Rising rail costs (and rising state deficits from rail subsidies) made sections of German capital reconsider transportation policy.

Business circles entered into a general Schiene/Strasse (rail/street) debate over transportation costs in German industry.[2] Which mode should receive state subsidies? Was German industry overdependent on railroads? In the midst of this, the Reichsbahn, which had industrial allies in the German National Chamber of Commerce (DIHT), bought up smaller trucking lines, exacted high tolls from rail-connected trucking lines, and sought federal approval for a rail monopoly in trucking.

German policy placed the auto industry in a remarkably weak position. That policy frustrated industrial interest in new transportation industries. Nevertheless, structural conditions were shifting towards motorization. U.S. investments, the GM purchase of Opel, and the crisis of commodity and personal transportation costs, which made state subsidies and public transit an increasing fiscal burden, all made the motorization lobby's emergence within German capital imminent.

The activities of the Reichverband der Automobilindustrie (RDA), the HAFRABA (Association for Preparing the Hansa Cities–Frankfurt–Basel Autobahn) and others created political support for motorization. By the end of the 1920s, industrial organizations were split between the traditional rail enthusiasts and those supporting motorization. The German business press and "Denkschriften" (policy papers) of the industrial interest associations indicated that any transportation mode would have to be able to accomplish both profit and spatial functions. The spatial functions of transportation policy (rationalized urban expansion) had been well served by the rails; motorization had to continue this expansion. Profit functions (i.e., profit-making in transportation equipment and related industries) could be improved by maximizing employment, establishing countercyclical sources of government spending, and assisting accumulation in other important industrial branches (such as military production).

After the advent of Nazi state power, a concerted attempt was made by the auto-linked groups to break the resistance of rail-related capitalists

---

[2] My summary of the elements of rail-related policy during the Weimar period and the Schiene-Strasse debate is based upon the records of the Eisenbahn-Kraftwagenverkehrs-Ausschuss (Rail-Motor Traffic Commission) of the Deutscher Industrie und Handelstag (DIHT), BA,R11/1516.

and state bureaucrats. A community of interests developed between the auto industry and German fascists to pursue motorization.

Fascism and national transportation policy

By February 1935, German fascism had firmly established itself and its motorization policy. In that year, the International Motor Transport Congress held its annual exhibition in Berlin, and Adolf Hitler greeted it with a bombastic pro-motorization speech. Such speeches were an annual occurrence since the first such exhibition of his chancellory in 1933. Automobile industrialists, including Louis Renault, a founder of the French automobile industry, who was well informed about converting auto manufacturing equipment to military purposes, met with Hitler during this meeting. In his long and rambling talk, Hitler lectured often about the importance of motorization, how it could serve the "primacy of the Reich idea," economic recovery, increased employment, and why it would transform German society.

> The endeavor of the National Socialist leadership is directed toward decentralizing the industrial working population from the production centers to the countryside. Factory work must be supplemented by field work. For conveyance from living quarters to work quarters a cheaper means of transportation than heretofore available must be created (2/21/35, BA, R4311/748).

By dispersing the working class to various settlements on the outskirts of major cities, suburbanization and motorization would assure a measure of social peace and a redefinition of classes in a nationalist framework though the Nazi goal, "Rebuilding the German Worker within the German State." Motorization policies would provide physical and geographic mobility instead of social mobility for a disciplined work force.

This transportation policy did not go unopposed within Fascist ranks. Only in 1931, after a meeting with representatives of the German automobile industry, had Hitler himself adopted the call for motorization. The Nazi's left wing opposed motorization. Gregor Strasser, that faction's spokesman, denounced Hitler's opportunism and opposed pro-auto measures as "at best a rising of comfort and serving the satisfaction of luxury needs" (in Kaftan 1956:152). Ernst Roehm, head of the Sturm Abteilung (storm troopers), also opposed such policies, as did his economic advisor Erich Lubbert, a member of the Reich Transportation Council representing streetcar associations. This faction of the NSDAP spoke to consumers of public transit and those elements within industrial associations opposing motorization. Despite this support, these elements were purged from the party and from the Council by 1934; Strasser and Roehm were murdered, and Lubbert imprisoned (BA, R11/1542).

For Hitler, motorization, mobilization, and militarization of society and economy were central to his policies. Motorization would stimulate the economy and create jobs. The society could be mobilized around the centrality of a motor transport system to unite the Reich. Motorization would also be a critical component in the creation of a modern military, whose expenditures, in turn, would spur economic growth, and whose pervasiveness would instill social discipline. This position was cultivated by the automobile industry.[3] Whatever the issue, the RDA, representatives of the International Motor Transport Congress (including Louis Renault and James Mooney of GM), met early and often with Hitler and his aides to formulate transportation policy.[4]

During the first years of Fascist rule, many of the legal barriers to motorization were swept away. Requisite fees (registration, license, and inspection) were set at reasonable levels. Parking regulations, traffic controls, technical inspections of automobiles, and various other measures efficiently organized motor traffic. Regulatory laws provided for training and "motorization propaganda."[5] The authorization of driving schools, Hitler Jugend activities, and the formation of the NSKK (Nationalsozialistisches Kraftfahrkorps) were all intended to popularize motor travel.[6]

---

[3] For the automobile industry's implementation of Hitler's motorization goals see Allmers (RDA) to Hitler (31.1.33,BA,R4311/4); Allmers (RDA) to Lammers (3.23.32,- BA,R4311/234); Hay (BA,R11/1542); Berliner Boersen-Zeitung (3.11.34). See also Koenig (1960:303–31); Weger (1976); Busch (1966:15–20).

[4] James Mooney was particularly active in aiding Hitler's motorization program. As President of GM Overseas Corporation and head of the U.S. Manufacturer's Export Association, he did much between 1933 and 1939 to aid Hitler's program that was to GM's benefit. Some of his philosophy about business and politics is quite revealing. At the 1933 International Motor Exhibition in Berlin, he said: "The Management Mind in the Automobile Industry has always had a great contempt for politics. The point has been missed that although we, in the Automobile Industry, have continually dismissed politics and government as quite unworthy of the attention of serious-minded men like ourselves, politics and government have been continually increasing their interest in the Automobile" (Mooney 1933:2). Despite his contempt for politics, Mooney was not beyond using politics to promote GM's interests. Aside from being warmly embraced by the Nazi bureaucracy (Snell 1974), Mooney was greatly involved with the America First Movement that attempted to keep the U.S. out of the war. The FBI kept Mooney under investigation for his Nazi sympathies. Mooney was also an early organizational theorist for U.S. business, which he wanted to see run like the Prussian military.

[5] An illuminating memorandum in the records of the Reichswirtschaftsministerium concerns "Transportation Education in National Socialist Schools" (5.11.34, BA, R11/1540); similar financial support by the auto industry, commercial trucking industry, and government for a transportation institute was forthcoming (5.4.35, BA, R11/1542).

[6] The auto industry contributed generously to motorization propaganda within NSKK and the SS (Hilgard to Lammers, 14.2.39, BA, R4311/749a); the integration of the German Auto Club (DDAC) into the NSKK (Memo 15.5.34, BA, R4311/753); and

"Fiscal Relief for Motor Transportation" became the central slogan of transportation policy. The goal was, as James Mooney had described it, "to make the masses articulate as buyers again" (Mooney 1933:4). By 1933, excise taxes on cars were removed (lowering prices 10 to 15 percent) and used-car owners were permitted to pay a one-time tax. In 1934, the journey to work by car was made tax-deductible and businesses were allowed tax breaks to replace old vehicles. Salary bonuses were given to civil servants to buy new automobiles and private employers were encouraged to do the same. Tax incentives and loans provided for expanded auto plant construction (RVM, 2/13/35,BA,R78/1542). Trade policies also greatly aided the growing automobile industry. Import tariffs were raised and an export equalization fund subsidized cheaper external export prices. In addition, various state banks bought up automobile stock (5/22/34,BA,R43/1468).

Military production through government-supported contracts was also critical to auto industry growth. Germany suffered considerably during World War One because it lacked military motorization. This lesson did not go unnoticed by the German High Command which pushed for military production of trucks, motorcycles, and tanks. The state also intervened in research and development by subsidizing the manufacture of racing cars, thus both aiding automotive development and popularizing Nazi policies (Link [Daimler-Benz] to Hitler, 3/15/33,BA,R4311/748).

Highway building as an employment policy did not originate with Hitler. The industrial and financial interests that supported highway construction preceded and survived fascism. Nevertheless, on May 1, 1933, Hitler announced with great flourish the "work and bread" goals of highway building to unite the Reich, preserve military strength, and further expand German cities with "settlement policies" to make them "physically and biologically renewed" (Die Strasse 5/1/33).

The Organization of Transportation Policy under Fascism

Motorization policy during the Third Reich subordinated rail transit by centralizing transportation planning organizations. That emerging bureaucracy reflected particular auto industrial interests by eliminating the mediation of general industrial interests through trade associations like the DIHT. Auto interests were also ensured by increasing the role of the Nazi party in forging transportation policies.

---

monetary support and technical assistance to the NSKK (Huhnlein, quoted in Mueller 1936:194; Baugart (Opel) and Nordhoff (Opel) to Krauss (NSKK) (14.7.34,4.6.37,-BA,NS 24/145); Scholtz (RDA) to Lammers (Reichskanzelei) 7.1.39).

After Hitler's motorization policies were established, the automobile industry made concerted efforts to reorganize and control policy within various ministries. Though the Eisenbahn-Kraftverkehr Ausschuss (EKA/Rail/Motor Traffic Commission) of the DIHT had been the semiofficial advisory board to the transport ministry before 1933, in 1934 that ministry ordered a special council organized within the government. At the behest of Allmers, head of the RDA, this council was to be made up of representatives of top transport industries (Hilland to Munich Commerce Chamber, 3/20/34,BA,R11/1542). This move was viewed with suspicion by other DIHT industry representatives who saw it as an attempt by the auto industry to control transportation policy. Allmers and Major Huhnlein, head of the NSKK, formed a coalition whereby the "motor industry renewed plans for a united front . . . in some ways as a forerunner of creating a unified transportation council" (Hilland to Drucker, 11/10/34, BA,R11/1542). The auto industry supplanted the general interests of capital for lower transportation costs (a spatial function of transportation) with its own profitmaking interests. The composition of the Transportation Council was heavily weighted with pro-motorization representatives (Mitgliedersliste, 8/34,BA,R11/1540). With the purge of rail representatives mentioned earlier, the DIHT engaged in intrigues with the Transportation Ministry to counteract the centralization of transportation planning that excluded other industrial interests.

Finally, the Transportation Ministry decided that the DIHT should contribute to transportation planning, but the Economics Ministry (RWM), which the RDA had more successfully penetrated, pushed for further centralization. Not surprisingly, transportation decisions moved increasingly to the RWM, the RIM (Reichsinnenministerium), and the NSKK (Posse [RWM] to Willuhn, 11/18/38,BA,R4311/749a). This concentration of planning within party and state agencies did not mean that capital's role was supplanted. The RDA was continually involved in these plans, supported various party organizations such as the NSKK, and forged economic measures to consolidate the auto industry.

Through the motorization program and the centralization of transportation policy in the Third Reich, the automobile industry and related industries dominated the formulation and administration of transportation policy. The Schiene/Strasse debate was resolved by the systematic elimination of the opposition (as in the case of Strasser, Lubbert, and Roehm) or by the cooptation of other industrial interests. Having eliminated local and regional autonomy in planning, automobile and related industries could influence policy by concentrating on the party that controlled the state. The auto industry was able, for example, to circumvent rail-biased civil servants in the Transportation Ministry.

Finally, the Nazi motorization program enabled the auto industry to demonstrate that motor transport was a viable transportation alternative for heavy industry. With state subsidies for street building, research and development, motor shipping, and cheap labor costs, the motor transportation sector could modernize and become competitive with other countries. None of this could have occurred without the decisive intervention of fascism. The Nazi motorization program broke all resistance by older industrial interests. The critical historical convergence of the emerging automobile industry, and all it meant for growth and change in German industrial structure, and the political, ideological, military, and economic goals of German fascism caused rail transit's decline. The state bureaucracy and industrial coalition that promoted motorization during this critical period survived fascism to influence policy in the Federal Republic of Germany. By 1939, the auto industry, like similar economic giants, became highly concentrated, eliminating threatening technological and industrial competition, and diversifying its production structure (Swatek 1972:68–70).[7]

Postwar transportation policy

Fascism's role in overcoming big business reluctance to state intervention was nowhere more apparent than in transportation policy (Kalecki 1972:101–102). Fascist motorization policy was unparalleled in European transportation history. It secured the auto industry and its allies' role in formulating transportation policy. Although much production was halted during and after the war, the structure of transportation production remained basically untouched after 12 years of fascism and a few years of half-hearted denazification (Vogel and Weisz 1976:902–904).

The automobile industry and its auto-directed transportation policy were restored very early after the war. The Automobile Economic Group (the Nazi production unit) and the Committee for Automobiles remained active after the war aiding the Allies reconstruct and operate various auto and truck factories. By 1948, the RDA was reincarnated as the Verband der Automobilindustrie (VDA) and became a significant voice in Occupation policies (Weger 1976:60).

During reconstruction, the auto industry became one of the central growth industries in Germany. By keeping prices low and rationalizing production and labor costs, it spurred other areas of the economy. It was

---

[7] However, in many ways, the auto-biased policies of the Third Reich were unsuccessful. Growth and concentration within the auto industry provided insufficient transportation capabilities within and between German cities. By 1942, an emergency in public transportation was declared by the Secret Police. Travel load on public transportation had increased 300 percent, replacement parts for autos and trucks were lacking, and portions of the autobahn remained incomplete (Reichsicherheitsamt, 19.3.42, BA, R58/170, BA, R58/172).

assured internal financing from its operations and capital from U.S. multinationals priming the pump of the German auto market.

A structural shift in the economy emerged during this period that paralleled the shift in the U.S. economy after World War One: the shift from the steel-coal-electrical industrial complex to an auto-oil-rubber complex of production and capital accumulation (Mertens 1962:449, table 2,- 445; Busch 1966:108).

Several conditions led to continued auto-interest control over transportation policy: the trend of urbanization, which caused demand for transportation services for labor and materials in outlying areas; the use of highway building as an instrument of fiscal policy; and the centrality of the auto industry in economic recovery.

Both SPD and CDU transport ministers continued to emphasize motorization. This policy increased auto demand while decreasing that of transit. Commuting by bus and car increased relative to commuting by rail transit (Menke 1975:43–52). Though the SPD by 1967 sought to use motor fuel tax revenues of public transportation, little had been done to reverse the neglect of public transit in state policy. Even when Brandt announced in 1973 that public transportation would receive top priority, the concerted auto lobby vitiated that positive support of public transit. Long-distance highway construction funds rose while the public transportation budget was cut drastically. The classic opposition between heavy industry, the early mainstay of German industrialization, and the complex of industries around the auto industry continued to be reflected in transportation policy struggles. The economic and political ability of capital after the war to shape transportation policy was dependent on changing state structures, the continuity of multinational investment and control over German auto manufacturing, and the profit requirements of economic reconstruction. In the United States, a more dynamic, less monopoly-constrained economy had implemented and encouraged motorization earlier.

United States: Background Factors Affecting National Transportation Policy

Two major structural factors distinguish the accumulation environment for American, as opposed to German, capital and thereby affect the more precipitous and earlier decline of public transit in the United States: (1) the longer survival of competitive capitalism, and (2) the earlier rise of an auto-oil-rubber industrial complex as the basis of capital accumulation.

For a long period, the capitalist class in the United States was characterized by intraclass competition, rather than coalition. The development of legal structures for corporations, the role of state intervention in the economy, and the development of market infrastructure by 1900 allowed the United States a more competitive manufacturing system with greater technical diversity. Corporate financing was largely internal, with banks entering the industrial stock market in the late 1870s, some 40 years after German banks began developing and controlling much of German industrial development. In this more competitive accumulation environment, the possibilities for innovative transportation technology arose much more easily than in Germany. Whether in more rapidly electrifying streetcars, or motorizing transportation, the rate at which surplus absorbing outlets for capital accumulation were provided by these innovations was faster in the United States than in Germany. There was not as much reliance on existing corporate giants for technological innovation. The technical convergence of growth in the auto, oil, and rubber industries, as well as the internal expansion of cities, made capital accumulation dynamic and the realignment of industrial power more rapid.

The growth period of public transportation in the United States

The tensions between profit and spatial functions of transportation have been exacerbated by attempts of individual corporations to dominate the transportation market. Urban transportation has been hampered by corporate attempts to achieve monopoly control in promoting one or another transportation mode. In short, the organization of urban transportation by corporations has been the greatest constraint on its development.

After an initial period of growth, the horse-drawn trolley systems saturated the market, thus making the rapid innovations of electrified trolleys with lower per unit costs and increasing supply capabilities desirable. Electrical traction intersected with the most important growth industry of that period (1888–1900), the electrical manufacturing industry. Urban transportation became part of the general growth in public utilities investment during this period.

Electrification meant growth. For most of the period between 1890–1918, transit ridership grew faster than the urban population. The streetcar network pushed urban growth toward the periphery. Land speculators and transit owners spoke almost always with one voice (and were sometimes the same person) in encouraging this expansion (Wilcox 1921:67–100). Urban transportation was viewed by transit owners and city planners alike as a "moral influence" in removing people from the deleterious effects of cities.[8]

---

[8] It was also a convenient way to displace social conflict. Henry Ford was noted for the aphorism, "We shall solve the problems of the city by leaving the city." The spatial dislocation of working populations through transportation and urban physical changes separated production and consumption struggles and made a unified *class* struggle over these issues more difficult (Katznelson 1976:28).

Because of increased investment costs, electrification encouraged the consolidation and concentration of transit ownership. Conglomerations of landowning, public utility, and financial interests (such "transit trusts" as Yerkes in Chicago, Doherty on the East Coast, or Mellon) dominated public transportation. Similarly, the private railroads also discouraged the growth of streetcar lines by either attempting to gain ownership control over such lines or by running competitive steam lines to drive commuters away from electrics. Rate wars and line-wrecking were common business strategies that constrained fiscally viable transit (Forbes 1905:35). The resulting tendency to monopolize street railways by land/public utility interests and steam railroads set the stage for electrical transportation's imminent decline.

Although the street railway building booms from 1890–1908 were well financed, transit monies were often pocketed through overcapitalization and corrupt accounting practices or thinly spread over transit lines that were unprofitable except, of course, for land speculators, banks, and brokers. This resulted in a total credit collapse between 1916–1923, when over a third of the U.S. transit companies went bankrupt. Capital was moving elsewhere toward the more profitable, less politically problematic fields of automobile investment. One major transportation financier testified before the Federal Electrical Railway Commission (FERRC) in 1919, "we insiders are selling out just as fast as we can, and when ten years are up, you will not find your Uncle Dudley or anyone of us that will own a share of stock or bond [in electrical transit]" (FERRC,1920:1058).

Another factor led to reassigning transportation investment: the political activity of the producers and consumers of transportation services. Between 1914 and 1920, the ratio between transit firms operating cost and gross income increased from 50 to 77 percent. Although part of this increase resulted from wartime inflation, labor costs also increased during this period faster than industrial wages as a whole. Transportation workers were making some gains through their trade unions, and because of many strikes, transit lines made less profits.

At this time, transit operating rights were granted by local governments. During the late nineteenth century, popular movements attempted to exercise some constraint on the transportation properties through these franchises. The result often curbed transit companies' power and had the unintended consequence of establishing monopoly barriers to new entrants into public transportation. Franchises often limited the type of equipment used, thereby slowing innovation, necessary line extension, street construction, and improvements. This usually benefited existing firms that could meet such costs and, also, auto use of streets. Finally, flat rate fares in some franchises subsidized unprofitable suburban development through inner city travel.

Attempts to circumvent or renegotiate franchises led to overcrowding and line abandonments. This situation eventually led to popular calls for public ownership. Between 1898 and 1920, virtually every major U.S. city was the scene of legal battles, referenda over rate hikes, public ownership campaigns, and investigations of transit corruption.[9] In this politically volatile atmosphere, the National Civic Federation intervened. The result of their self-serving investigation, as reported by August Belmont (owner of New York City's transit properties and president of the federation) was that public ownership would be less efficient than adequate regulation. But, the question rises: regulation for whom?

The resulting state policy was typical of urban reform during this corporate liberal period. Regulation removed the political struggle over transportation from the public sphere of city politics to appointed, business-oriented public utility and public service commissions. This was the first step in insulating transportation decisions from public pressures by de facto disenfranchising of the urban population. Transportation planning by state-appointed organizations was critically different from the previous direct public participation through referenda.

Typically, urban transportation scholars have attempted to isolate a single cause of the origins of transit's decline in corruption, in poor business practices, lack of technological innovations, overcrowding, and the rise of the automobile. Although all these factors contributed to the decline, they must be understood as part of the general social structural change reflected in transportation's shift from public to private modes. This change was not merely the technological shift from rail to rubber-wheeled vehicles, it also encompassed basic relations of labor and capital in producing transportation equipment and labor's cost of job-related travel. By shifting from public to private transportation technology, business avoided rising wage and construction costs. Organized public transit workers could be left to attrition and the production of automobiles and streets could be accomplished with unorganized and often (in the case of road construction) forced labor. Where private companies were obligated by public franchise to lay track, the federal government would construct roads. The shift to private transportation would remove the volatile political issue of urban transportation.

---

[9] Contrary to some current interpretations, the movement for public ownership of transit, utilities, and ice manufacturing at the turn of the century was not simply a petite-bourgeois movement of the Progressive Era. My archival research concerning the "Traction Question" in Chicago seems to indicate massive working class community mobilization in alliance with many small business interests in the community against "the exploitation of people's needs" (food, transportation, electricity, etc.) (Vickers 1934). Popular oppositional movements regarding transit occurred at this time in San Francisco, New Orleans, Baltimore, Detroit, Cincinnati, Philadelphia, and Milwaukee.

There would be an end to consumer movements responding to rate hikes, public ownership, and transit corruption. Finally, the shift from public to private transportation ensured the transfer of capital investment from an increasingly restrictive area to a more expansive one.

Corporate strategy and state policy: the fall of public transportation

Although corporate abuse by "transit trusts," capital flight from public transportation, and state regulation did much to start transit's decline, it did not ensure its demise. During the 1920s, when public transit stagnated, an ambiguous relationship between public and private transportation developed. Corporate interests surrounding the automobile industry found it increasingly hard to live with this ambiguity. After the initial rash of abandonments and receiverships following World War One, conditions stabilized. Receiverships fell from 9 to 7 percent annually and remained below 8 percent until the depression. Moreover, the reduction in riders and track miles could be interpreted as the first rational shrinkage in railway networks to a more financially viable economic scale (Dewees 1970:564–65). In addition, "ridership decline" may well have been merely a statistical artifact of new, more honest accounting practices under state regulation in the 1920s that deflated the inflated figures of the past.[10]

Perhaps most important to the relationship between private and public transportation was the trend toward urban growth. If we disaggregate the ridership figures between 1918 and 1927 for major cities, we find ridership increases for some major cities; St. Louis saw a 3.1 percent gain in ridership; Chicago, 10.1 percent; New York, 37 percent (Barrett 1975:418–19; APTA File 975.441). The idea that more autos resulted in less public transit, an idea prominent in regulatory hearings and among modern historians, seems grossly oversimplified. Decreases in public transportation were mostly felt by cities with less than 500,000 population. For all cities over a million population, the decrease was only 4 percent (Dewees 1970:569).

There was an inverse relationship between auto density and city size. In cities with bus and rail equipment modernizations, traffic surveys showed public transit trips increasing at a higher rate than did auto-generated trips (17 compared to 25 percent) (*Transportation Journal* 1940:4–5). A sharp decline in public transportation had been arrested. Despite finan-

---

[10] The 1920s, as I emphasize, was an ambiguous period for the transit question. One reason for the usual interpretation of the 1920s as the death knell of public transit is the aggregation of national figures, which obscures gains in transportation in specific cities.

cial disasters and rising fares, rail transit was surviving and was cheaper than the operation of buses for urban transportation.[11]

The resiliency of public transportation, along with declines in the automobile market, produced a crisis situation for corporate strategists. From 1923 on, the new car market became saturated. The auto industry agreed that the problem required a more rapid turnover of autos. General Motors led the way with strategies for style changes, advertising, franchise distribution, and financing. Despite these changes, stabilization of the auto market remained a threat to the automobile industry and the industries closely associated with it. The oil and rubber industries faced overproduction and failing prices; housing construction went into decline.[12] Corporations required effective long-range plans to neutralize public transportation and promote demand.

The spectacular investment in street railways during boom years seems to have sunk fixed capital costs, which by the 1920s could be used at reduced expense, and aided the minirecovery of public transportation in major cities. At the same time, capital invested in street railways was being devalued through lower productivity and use. The auto industry was attempting to overcome the old fixed capital investment in street railways with federally subsidized road investment (as "new" fixed capital investment) to facilitate auto traffic; however, rail transit remained a serious constraint on the expansion of the automobile and related industries at the center of capital accumulation during this period. This is why American street railways were dismantled. The transportation technology that first allowed the decentralization and expansion of cities had become a burden to that very same expansion; such expansion was critical for cities to fulfill their task as loci of capital accumulation.

Refinements in automobile production and distribution alone could not accomplish full automobilization. Competition from public carriers would not disappear. Stagnating auto demand, overproduction, the lack of "articulate consumers," and general indicators of economic crisis all required a new corporate strategy for the auto industry and its partners.

[11] For figures on operating costs of bus versus rail operations, see Dewees (1970:560–70); and Henry D. Quinby (Modern Transit Report 1950, APTA File No. 900.01). As Snell (1974:37) notes: "Engineering studies strongly suggest that conversion from electric trains to diesel buses results in higher operating costs, loss of patronage, and eventual bankruptcy. They demonstrate, for example, that diesel buses have 28 percent shorter economic lives, 40% higher operating costs, and 9% lower productivity than electric buses. They also conclude that the diesel's foul smoke . . . noise, and slow acceleration may discourage revenues and contribute to the collapse of hundreds of transit systems."

[12] On the market saturation problems of these growth industries (auto-oil-rubber, etc.), see Weiss (1965); Flink (1977:148–60); Sloan (1962:208).

Urban rail transit was to be replaced by motor buses which, in turn, were to be replaced by cars.[13]

This "modernization" of public transit was in fact the substitution of buses, which would prove ineffective in counteracting the lure of the automobile. In 1925, GM purchased Yellow Truck and Coach Manufacturing, a firm founded by former jitney owner John Hertz. Former jitney operators like Hertz (and later the Fitzgeralds, founders of National City Lines), were ideal smaller business allies for GM. They had run parallel service to streetcar lines, but had been regulated out of business. They benefited from the protection of size afforded by GM. Yellow operated a transit-owning subsidiary, Hertz Omnibus, which eventually controlled the New York railway holding company which converted the New York System to buses within 18 months between 1935 and 1936 (Snell 1974).

Simultaneously, GM was involved in other transit schemes. Through its subsidiary, Motor Transit Corporation, it became involved in converting interurban lines by forming Greyhound Corporation, of which it was the largest stockholder and sole supplier of buses until 1948. Also, in 1932, through its officers on Yellow Coach's executive committee, GM introduced a proposal "for making investments in motorized transport systems with a view to stimulating more demand for more motor coaches" (Minutes of Yellow Truck and Coach Executive Committee, GM Trial exhibit 2, NCL Civil Case).

In 1936, National City Lines was formed by GM, Yellow Coach, and former Greyhound executives. Between 1937 and 1940, National City Lines surveyed major transit operations through the country. National City then proceeded to purchase many of those lines, and to substitute buses for streetcars. This conversion was financed by a scheme whereby NCL sold its stock to GM, Firestone Tire and Rubber, Phillips Petroleum, Standard Oil of California, and Mack Manufacturing. These investors were then given sole supplier contracts for up to 10 years with the acquired companies. As one of the defense lawyers in the NCL antitrust case told me, "This was all part of a very reasonable corporate strategy to develop a market."[14] The

---

[13] The most important break in the story of public transit's decline has been the investigation by Bradford C. Snell (American Ground Transport, Hearing before the Subcommittee of Antitrust and Monopoly, U.S. Senate, Washington, D.C., 1974). I base much of this discussion on his thorough study. Snell has pointed the way to the critical questions concerning transit's decline in the United States.

[14] In many other cities, such supplier contracts of surveyed properties were an important way to develop and stabilize markets for the oil, rubber, and automotive products of these major corporations. This same process occurred with Standard Oil of California's ownership and development of United Airlines (interview with H. Templeton Brown, SOCAL Defense Lawyer in the NCL case, May 18, 1978). This defies the usual organization and economic theories that corporations "respond" to markets. Instead, they create and manipulate them [Fitzgerald to Babcock (GM), 6/8/44, NCL Case, Government Exhibit, No. 165].

decline of public transit was consciously achieved, as Snell has shown (1974), through the acquisition of transit companies, conversion, and resale.

Aside from direct control over transit companies through NCL, the auto industry found other ways to suppress technological alternatives. Many individual transit operators converted to buses with the technical and often financial assistance of GM and NCL. They gladly offered to finance bus purchases for transit firms. Similarly, sole supplier contracts made without bid often excluded other manufacturers.[15] Some transit operators were former GM or NCL executives. In other cases conversion occurred in cities where private consultants, often GM contacts, recommended changeovers on the basis of data supplied by GM and NCL. In Atlanta, Philadelphia, Dallas, Los Angeles, and elsewhere, GM pressured local banks through business connections, stock ownership, and promises of deposits to influence local transit companies to purchase buses from GM (Motor Bus Fact Memo, Department of Justice, 1956).

Where transit lines were municipally owned, GM induced officials to adopt specifications that only GM could meet. The procedure, according to GM Vice-President E. P. Crenshaw, "worked out in Cleveland, Boston, Detroit, Phoenix, and Chicago" (Motor Bus Investigation Fact Memo, Department of Justice, 1956).

Finally, NCL came to dominate the American Transit Association. Voting in the association was based on operating revenue. NCL, with $100-million annual revenues, became the largest transit operator in the country and the largest voter in the ATA. The evidence suggests that, given its position of domination within the ATA, NCL successfully suppressed opposition to bus conversions and information about rail modernization alternatives.[16] GM also exacted loyalty from those ATA officers whom it

---

[15] *U.S. v. NCL, et al.,* Civil Action 49 C 1364, Appendix to Transcripts, 47–1;47–7; also Supplementary Information Regarding Interrogatories no. 6, 9, 10, 11 and Transcript Appendix 74–4:76–3 (listing supplier, parties to contracts, etc.; also 344–1:344–11).

[16] For intance, in Rochester, N.Y., the ATA was forced to suppress a pro-rail promotional film that was being distributed to civic groups. B. E. Tilton, head of the Syracuse, Rochester, and Utica properties threatened to resign from the ATA unless the films were stopped (Wingarter to Gordon and Hecker, 2/15/1940, APTA 900.01 Syracuse). Similarly, in Newark: "Public Service has continually fought to suppress all information about these modern rail vehicles" (Modern Transit Report to the Board of Public Utility Commissioners, State of New Jersey, 12/6/50). Public Service of New Jersey was later a defendant in the GM–Bus Antitrust Case. In Buffalo, "it is only fair to point out that the people of Buffalo did not choose the bus in preference to modern streetcars, for the Buffalo public, in general, never had an opportunity to see, ride, or experience the service which the modern P.C.C. cars and Brilliners could furnish" (Gordon 1970:38).

had supported in their bids for high positions in the ATA (FBI Investigation, GM-Bus Antitrust, 1954).

There was concerted corporate opposition to bus conversions, especially from other transportation equipment producers, such as Dr. Thomas Conway (of the Cincinnati and Lake Erie Railroad), the Brill Company, Westinghouse, and other streetcar lines. Conway called meetings throughout the 1930s to defend rail lines and to popularize the use of the lightweight, aluminum Presidential Command Cars (PCC) that could reduce operating costs.[17]

Numerous stockholder suits were filed against transit companies, claiming that conversions would place the companies in jeopardy. Although the stockholders' initial injunctions were never upheld, their arguments proved true; numerous companies collapsed under the debt of bus purchases and were municipalized.

Opposition to the substitution came from consumer and civic organizations. Many riders were not enthusiastic about buses that were foul smelling, noisier, less comfortable, and slower than rail transit. Testimony at the Public Utility Commissions and city level boards of public transportation centered on these charges. At all such hearings, the local GM representative was often ready with expert testimony. The prorail representatives emphasized that rail transit could prevent further congestion, expedite local service at transfer points, use street space more efficiently, travel faster, and carry more passengers. The GM testimony usually promised cheaper fares and financing.

The response of organized transit labor was often ambiguous. Between 1945 and 1968, transit employment decreased by 57 percent. This consequence of rail abandonment was noted only by the Transportation Workers Union (TWU–CIO) and some rank-and-file members. By 1939, the TWU saw conversions as "another blow . . . struck against the TWU" (TWU Conversion Proceedings 1939:52). However, even the TWU was seduced by the propaganda of the times when it wrote "no union can set itself against progress" (TWU 1939:52).

Often, NCL entered a situation where labor negotiations threatened an already shaky transit operation. Usually, when ownership was transferred, the union suspended negotiations. Often, the international representative was sent (usually from the Amalgamated Association of Street Electrical and Motor Coach Employees–AFL) to assuage rank-and-file fears about conversions. In St. Louis, the international representative told the members: "We know that behind the Fitzgerald brothers is a tire com-

---

[17] Usually transit and urban historians maintain that the lack of public transit innovations were the cause of its demise. This ignores such developments as lightweight aluminum cars, new electrical and more efficient motors (Cavin 1976).

pany, gasoline companies, and oil companies. What effect they, as a holding company will have on the St. Louis situation, I cannot say." The following exchange occurred:

> Another member of the union, apparently a motorman employed by the Public Service Co., asked the international representative: "Don't they (NCL) always displace streetcars with buses?" The union leader replied that he knows "in many instances the Fitzgeralds have bought up old street car companies and replaced their equipment with buses and always reduced the fare and in many instances increased wages" (*St. Louis Star Times*, October 22, 1940:1).

While NCL and GM operatives were subverting transit systems throughout the country, they offered unions a temporary sweetheart arrangement: short-term pay raises in return for long-term job attrition. This arrangement was facilitated by inadequate trade union discussion, research, and strategy.

The corporate car coalition strategy was highly successful. Every possible dimension of the transit industry was integrated into the growth complex of the auto-rubber-oil industries (such as GM licensing of repair and dealerships, financing used-car purchases, and involvement in road construction through GM subsidiaries). Because future demand could be assured only insofar as auto companies monopolized transit technology, the corporate car coalition sought to eliminate technological competition from other modes. This corporate strategy coincided with emerging state policies.

State policy: the gradual shift towards automobilization

State intervention in transportation policy dates back to World War One. Though no single U.S. policy before World War Two paralleled the major impact of Nazi motorization policies, a significant number of measures established the institutional framework supporting automobilization. Transportation policy was an element in such larger policy areas as national defense, public service, economic recovery, and urban planning.[18]

State intervention was directed to both public and private modes to decrease travel time and costs for carrying goods to market and people to their jobs (NA, RG3, Box 414, General Correspondence, File 13). Street railways were supported with federal-aided line extensions. But the state

---

[18] The United States Housing Corporation was the first serious foray of state policy into providing housing. The "Own Your Own Home Campaign" was the first federal experiment in financing home ownership (NA, RG3/407). The municipal and transportation loans division provided money for transit extensions during a period of capital shortage (NA RG 3/409,401,411,408).

subsidy was for construction costs only. The line extensions, though quite useful for the factories involved, were not financially sound. Streetcar companies were locked into serving these costly and often failing lines through existing franchise agreements.

Other more indirect measures also taken at this time perhaps unintentionally inhibited public transit. Restrictive franchise agreements forced streetcar companies to bear heavy tax burdens. In 1917–1918, rail taxes used in road building reached $225 million (FERRC 1920:425). Similarly, regulatory statutes created an oppressive environment for rail transit. Bus companies often required less stringent or no public franchises and were thereby exempt from various taxation and impost arrangements because they did not need the exclusive access to right of ways. State regulatory policies and the beginnings of highway building started to offset (with the Federal Highway Act of 1921) the lower rail operating costs, which still suffered higher ground and fixed investment costs. Consequently, many cities began to shift to bus systems. A full third of those firms which had abandoned lines replaced them with bus operations (Saltzman 1977).

Early highway legislation was directed toward improving intercity truck, agricultural, and industrial traffic. It was not until the New Deal that highway policy became an important part of personal transportation and urban planning policy as well. Roosevelt extended aid to urban highways in 1934 and 1936.

Nevertheless, the New Deal was severely constrained by the depression. In this period, state intervention became established through fiscal support, technical assistance, and urban planning. The National Resources Planning Board (NRPB), the Reconstruction Finance Corporation (RFC), and the Bureau of Public Roads (BPR) all acted to construct the constraints and biases of planning that facilitated automobilization after World War Two.[19] Local and regional planning authorities were encouraged to draft proposals that would increase federal support of highway projects (Harold Ickes, 11/13/33,NA,RG 45, File 840, Box 56). State transportation commissions were set up with federal assistance.

However, could planning become democratized at state and regional levels, or would it become controlled by business and technocratic (planners and highway engineers) interests? The records of the NRPB reveal that chambers of commerce, manufacturers' associations, and other business organizations encouraged individual states and communities to build roads through state planning commissions. State legislation increased tax supports for road building, and planners and engineers argued that these roads be built parallel to railroad rights of way (NRPB, NA, RG48, File

---

[19] The Reconstruction Finance Corporation was quite active in supporting bus conversion programs during the 1930s (APTA files, 900/01,308.01, various city files).

840, Box 56). The corporate car coalition was overrepresented in all bodies of transportation planning encouraging federal financing for road building (DeCherrie to NRPB, 3/2/43, NA, RG48, NRPB, Box 56, File 840).

On the local level, measures were taken to reduce the expense and inconvenience of auto ownership. The task of regulating traffic was interpreted as the task of facilitating increasing traffic flows. Parking regulations, one-way streets, traffic signals, and other regulations were adapted to the needs of auto usage (Barrett 1975:400–401; Flink 1977; 162–63). Meanwhile, neglect of public transportation development became institutionalized.

The influence of such regulations came from the emerging profession of urban and traffic planners, automobile interests and motor clubs, and central city business interests. Planning was a response to situations and problems, not an anticipation of them. This notion of problemsolving so dominant in the urban planning tradition was exemplified by local transportation policy. Moreover, it left urban development vulnerable to corporate strategy opposing public transportation.

Everything was done by state policy to promote the automobile, nothing to constrain it. The German policy of the 1930s had demonstrated to planners that successful road building programs could not only stimulate the economy as a whole, but also promote state policies in general (CED,1965:30). The corporate car complex gave birth to the highway lobby, which informally made transportation policy. The composition of the National Advisory Commission for a National Highway Policy that designed the Federal Highway Act of 1956,[20] lobbying by the National Highway Users Conference sponsored by the motor manufacturers association, the interlocking connections among transportation associations, and the activities of individuals such as Francis V. Dupont, commissioner of the Bureau of Public Roads, and Alfred P. Sloan, Jr., all contributed to the policy financing highway construction.[21]

On the federal level, regulatory and enforcement procedures were also important in maintaining pro-automobile policy. The Holding Company Act of 1933 made it impossible for ownership concentration between

[20] The National Advisory Committee on National Highway Program consisted of General Lucius Clay, chairman, Continental Can; Stephen Bechtel, president, Bechtel; David Beck, president, International Brotherhood of Teamsters; S. Sloan Colt, president, Bankers' Trust Company; and W. A. Roberts, president, Allis Chalmers.

[21] The federal government financed but did not actually construct the highways as in Germany. This pork-barrel nature of the U.S. strategy allowed for state highway departments to dispense with federally contracted monies as a way to curry support for highway spending. This maximized support and control for highway building and ultimately for planning centralization.

transit and public utility firms. Saltzman (1977) has argued that this deprived the transit industry of needed capital for modernization. However, as the experience of utility-controlled transit firms after 1918 indicates, the deleterious effects of such control make this argument questionable. I suggest that the Holding Company Act did have the intended consequence of depriving utility monopolies of transit properties; but it also had the unintended consequence of facilitating the replacement by the corporate car complex of the electrical industry/public utility group's control over transit, and, thereby, contributing to its long-term motorization strategy. By removing the utility group from transit competition, auto-dominated interests were able to frustrate government regulatory policies and thwart the investigation of the NCL and GM bus cases by the Antitrust Division and the FBI. Both agencies faced repeated obstruction from the BPR, ATA, and individual transit operators.

Highway planning eventually reorganized transportation policy at higher levels of the state apparatus. Through federal financing and auto-sponsored planning conferences, state highway agencies were relieved of fiscal, legislative, administrative, and planning constraints in the implementation of road construction (Holmes 1973:381–83). When the 1962 and 1965 highway acts called for "comprehensive, cooperative, and continuous planning," the BPR issued directives that concentrated planning control in that bureau. The language of participatory planning was reinterpreted to emphasize the technical solutions, rather than the social effects, of highway construction. Public hearings were not intended as popular referenda, but as trial balloons for testing local opposition, developing highway support, and constructing a political strategy for any proposed highway route (Morehouse 1965).[22] The locus of planning slipped from city to state hands. A 1976 study by the Department of Transportation shows that in 24 out of 30 communities, the initiative for all planning was taken by state rather than local agencies working through metropolitan planning bodies.

This centralization of transportation planning was reinforced by court decisions in cases of highway opposition that focused upon procedural, rather than substantive issues, thereby ignoring such issues as community power in public hearings and the socioeconomic impact of highways. Similarly, proauto bias in planning was ensured by federal legislation making alternative modes virtually inconceivable. The government's apportionment formulas have been heavily antiurban, granting mass transit allocations equally to rural and urban states. Cost-benefit calculations

---

[22] This effort to ensure bureaucratic control of highway planning rather than democratic control is reflected in numerous policy memoranda (BPR Policy and Procedure Memo, 20–8, August 10, 1956; see also Morehouse 1965).

prescribed by the government have not considered improper valuations of land, pollution, residential dislocation, induced traffic, energy waste, and other social costs of auto traffic.

Conclusion

The central determinant of national transportation policy has been the corporate strategy of the auto-oil-rubber industrial complex to secure market areas and the physical infrastructure necessary to sell the commodities they produce. Transportation policy has also involved the efforts of local and regional capital to broaden the consumption of land, construction, and housing in order to secure its own profits. Thus, national capital involved in the most monopolized sectors of production, and local and regional capital involved in more speculative, less directly productive areas, are unified politically and economically in motorizing transportation.

Transportation policy reflects the profitmaking and spatial planning interests of capital accumulation in urban areas of the United States and Germany. Such policy was developed within corporate circles, expanded through public policy bodies supported by corporations, and translated into state policy. As rail transit fettered expanded production in new industries and in urban land and housing, pressures arose from corporations seeking to replace rail with motorization policies. Though electrical transit had been the climax of industrial growth associated with older industries (such as coal and steel), it became an obstacle to the emergence of an ascendant interest group within capital, the corporate car complex. That new group took steps to constrain state policies through private investment decisions, struggles against older rail-associated industrial interests, and its overall influence on emerging economic structure. With such structural determinants, corporate control over transportation policy was also secured through "instrumental" intervention in the higher levels of the state apparatus. In short, the policy leading to transit's decline in both Germany and the United States minimized public control over transportation programs and maximized private corporate benefits from them.

This experience in Germany and the United States yields several insights. Transit decline is rooted in the internal relations of old and new industrial coalitions. Germany's early monopolization and industrial concentration within older industrial groups made the corporate car coalition more difficult to forge, and it emerged later than in the United States. Moreover, this economic structure had definite consequences for the political structure necessary to achieve motorization. Although pressures for motorization were rising in Germany before 1933, fascism decisively eliminated rail biases. In the United States, for a considerable time the auto-oil-rubber group depended more on their own machinations than on state policy, which had followed the path of motorization without leading it as in Germany. However, after World War Two, continued automobilization could be promoted only through massive state intervention.

Earlier works on public transportation's decline in the United States and elsewhere are not only insensitive to the causes of falling ridership, but also to its consequences. What we have lost is not merely a type of transportation technology, but also a way of urban life. It is not overly nostalgic to observe that as urban transportation changes, so does communication between urban dwellers. The frequency of interaction between people decreases, we travel less to see friends and seek recreation, than to work and consume. The social isolation resulting from the careful parcelization of urban land through motorization and suburbanization has had its effects on us all, but especially on the poor, elderly, women, and children—all whose access to urban travel has been constrained. With freeway construction, commuter lines, and urban renewal, transportation planning has become a steady series of bypass operations that leave our cities in festering isolation.

References

BARRETT, P. F.
  1975   "Public Policy and Private Choices: Mass Transit, the Auto, and Public Policy in Chicago Between the Wars," *Business History Review* 49:473–97.

BUSCH, KLAUS
  1966   Struktur-Wandlungen der Westdeutschen Automobilindustrie. Berlin: Duncker and Humblot.

CAVIN, RUTH
  1976   Trolleys. New York: Hawthorn.

COMMITTEE FOR ECONOMIC DEVELOPMENT
  1965   Developing Metropolitan Transportation Policies. New York: CED.

DEPARTMENT OF TRANSPORTATION
  1976   Urban System Study: Report of the Secretary to the U.S. Congress. Washington, D.C.

DEWEES, DONALD
  1970   "The Decline of the American Street Railways," *Traffic Quarterly* 24:563–82.

FEDERAL ELECTRIC RAILWAYS COMMISSION PROCEEDINGS
  1920   Washington, D.C.: Government Printing Office.

FLINK, JAMES J.
  1977   The Car Culture. Cambridge, Mass.: MIT Press.

FORBES, HOWARD C.
  1905   Public Safety and the Interurban Road vs. the Railroad Monopoly in Massachusetts. Cambridge: University Press.

GORDON, WILLIAM R.
1970   90 Years of Buffalo Railways: 1860–1950. Buffalo, N.Y.: GADA.
GROTTKOPP, W.
1954   Die Grosse Krise. Duesseldorf: Econ-Verlag.
HOLMES, E. H.
1973   "The State of the Art in Urban Transportation Planning," *Transportation* 4:379–402.
KAFTAN, KURT G.
1956   Der Kampf um die Autobahnen. Berlin: Wignankow.
KALECKI, MICHAEL
1972   The Last Phase in the Transformation of Capitalism. New York: Monthly Review.
KATZNELSON, IRA
1976   "The Patterning of Class in the U.S.," paper delivered at Annual Meeting of the American Political Science Association, Chicago.
KOENIG, HEINZ
1960   "Kartelle und Konzentration." Pp. 303–31 in H. Arndt (ed.), Die Konzentration in der Wirtschaft. Berlin: Duncker & Humblot.
LINDER, WOLF
1975   Erzwungene Mobilitaet. Frankfurt/Main: Europäische Verlagsanstalt.
MANTEL, E. H.
1971   "Economic Biases in Urban Transportation Planning and Implementation," *Traffic Quarterly* 25:177–230.
MERTENS, DIETER
1962   "Veraenderungen der Industriellen Branchenstruktur in der BRD, 1950–1960," in H. Koenig (ed.), Wandlungen der Wirtschaftsstruktur in der BRD. Berlin: Duncker & Humblot.
MOONEY, JAMES
1933   Reviving Business Through Lower Automotive Taxation. Berlin: International Motor Transport Congress.
MOREHOUSE, THOMAS A.
1965   "The Determinants of Federal Policy for Urban Transportation Planning under the Federal Aid Highway Act of 1962," Ph.D. thesis, Political Science Department, University of Minnesota, Minneapolis, Minnesota.
SALTZMAN, ARTHUR
1977   "The Decline of Transit." School of Social Sciences, University of California–Irvine (mimeo).
SLOAN, ALFRED P., JR.
1962   My Years with General Motors. Garden City, N.Y.: Doubleday.
SNELL, BRADFORD C.
1974   American Ground Transport. Washington, D.C.: Subcommittee on Antitrust and Monopoly of Judiciary Committee, U.S. Senate
SWATEK, DIETER
1972   Unternehmenskonzentration als Ergebnis und Mittel der NS–Wirtschaftspolitik. Berlin: Duncker & Humblot.

Transportation Workers Union of America
1939   Convention Proceedings.
1934   *Bulletin.*

Vickers, Leslie
1934   "Fare Structures in the Transit Industry, New York." Ph.D. thesis, Department of Political Science, Columbia University.

Vogel, Walter, and Christoph Weisz
1976   Akten zur Vorgeschichte der BRD, 1945–49. München: Oldenburg.

Weger, Wolfgang
1976   Die Autobiographie. Frankfurt/Main: Verband der Automobil-industrie.

Weiss, Leonard
1961   Economics and American Industry. New York: Wiley.

Wilcox, Delos F.
1921   Analysis of the Electrical Railway Problem. New York: Wilcox.

14 The West German Working Class: Bourgeois Hegemony and the Labor Movement Since 1945

Heinrich W. Ahlemeyer
Rolf Schellhase
Institut für Soziologie der Westfälischen Wilhelms–Universität Münster

We analyze the course and consequences of class conflicts in the Federal Republic of Germany, focusing on their economic conditions, driving political forces, and social implications, in historical perspective. Within this framework, the conception of the working class must necessarily remain rather global, despite its important internal differentiations in income, living standards, and job security. The working class is a homogeneous social unit only to the extent that it is antagonistically opposed to the expansion of capital, its members have no property in the means of production, and their exclusive source of income is the sale of their capacity to work (from which profits are appropriated by the owners of capital).

Of the 61.5 million inhabitants of the Federal Republic in 1976, 26.1 million belonged to the labor force. Of these, 1.06 million were unemployed (the annual average); 21.3 million workers in the labor force were wage-dependent as workers, employees, and civil servants. The proportion of the labor force in the population declined from 45.9 percent (1950) to 40.8 percent (1976); the proportion of wage dependents in the labor force, however, grew from 63.2 percent (1950) to 81.5 percent (1976).

Is the German working class an historical force capable of impelling social change? What are the conditions and chances for it to successfully transform the German capitalist order? The development of the German working class after World War Two is shaped by three factors: the physical elimination of their most class-conscious members and leaders by the

We are especially indebted to Arno Kloenne and Hans-Juergen Krysmanski for their critical comments on earlier drafts of this article; to Ransom Bradford for his invaluable stylistic advice; and to Monika Schneidereit for her brave assistance with the typescript.

Nazis, the specific historical situation of Germany after the war, and fierce class struggle from above by the German bourgeoisie. The latter question aims at the inner connection between the strength and weakness of the working class, on the one hand, and correspondingly, of the bourgeoisie, on the other. C. Wright Mills has pointed out that "'the reality' of any one stratum is in large part its relation to the rest" (Mills 1973:221). This is particularly true for the Federal Republic, where the hegemony of the bourgeoisie in the economy, in political life, and on an ideological level is far more apparent than in comparable capitalist societies. Thus, we deal almost as much with the West German bourgeoisie and their actions as with the working class.

We distinguish three phases in the history of the Federal Republic (1945–1949, 1949–1966, and 1966 to the present). Within each phase, we analyze economic and political developments and their consequences for the material conditions of the West German working class.

When the German Wehrmacht surrendered unconditionally on May 8, 1945, Germany's executive power, and thus its future, lay in the hands of the Allied Occupation forces of the Soviet Union, Great Britain, France, and the United States. The formulation of common principles in the compromise form agreed to in the Potsdam treaty could not conceal the underlying conflict between capitalism and socialism on a global scale. This conflict reappeared at a moment when the community of interests among the Allies had been exhausted with the military defeat of Germany. National and system interests again predominated.

The overall change in the relationship between the United States and the Soviet Union had immediate consequences for the American Occupation policy in Germany. A total prostration of Germany became less important than a gradual reconstruction of at least those parts which were under Western control to contain Soviet influence and to preserve Europe as an American sphere of influence (Brauns and Jaeggi et al. 1976:28).

The substance of the Occupation policy of the United States was directed against the demands of the working class and its organizations. The trade unions demanded the socialization of basic industries, whereas the Americans ruled that socialization measures were to be deferred until a central government for Germany as a whole could be constituted.

The immediate postwar situation was characterized by immeasurable damage and losses; by millions of people killed, wounded, taken prisoner, or missing; by miserable housing conditions and scarcity of food; and by radical demographic changes. Over 4.2 million Germans had either been slain in the battlefields of an aggressive war of conquest or had become victims of Allied bombing raids; 200,000 Germans had been killed by Fascist terror for political or "racial" reasons. The structure of the population had undergone radical changes in age and gender: Germany had become a country of the aged and of women. More than 11 million refugees were pouring into the four Occupied zones from the former German territories east of the Oder-Neisse line. Paradoxically, after the bloodiest war in history, defeated Germany had 6.1 million more inhabitants living in the area of the four Occupied zones than before the war.

Traffic and transport had collapsed, production had come to a standstill, and government on all levels had practically ceased to exist. The cities were in ruins: 31 percent of the houses were completely destroyed, 45 percent more or less heavily damaged, and less than one out of every four houses in the large cities was left undamaged.

The existence of the German people after World War Two seemed to be at an absolute nadir. Yet a closer look at the productive forces and at the relations of production reveals that these two constitutive elements of the German social system remained much more intact than was visible on the surface.

The war damages suffered by industrial plants, factories, mines, and mills were surprisingly low, in particular if compared to the losses and privations suffered by the civilian population. Whereas the infrastructure, houses, and private consumption were reduced by 65 to 80 percent (Giesecke, Kloenne and Otten 1976:119), the 10 to 15 percent damages undergone by industry were considerably lower. As the war damages were even smaller than the productive capacities newly created during the war, the industrial capacity of Germany in 1945 equaled its prewar capacity in 1939.

In much the same way that the system of material productive forces remained intact, the relations of production, property relations in particular, were left basically unchanged, as private ownership of the means of production was never abandoned and the relationship between wage labor and capital remained central. Not all Germans were hit alike by the disastrous effects of the war; the material conditions of the various classes were altogether different in the postwar period.

Big capital owners, because of inflation and uncertain profit prospects, were little interested in enlarging production; they transformed the profits they had accumulated during the war into capital goods and used the extraordinarily favorable exchange rate of capital and labor to add to the value of their assets and stockpiled commodities. In contrast to business men and farmers, most wage earners and salaried employees had no objects of real value that would have enabled them to satisfy their needs by participating in the black market. They depended solely on insufficient food rations and their wages.

The living standard of the working class sank drastically below the subsistence level through rationing and worthless wages (Weiss-Hartmann and Hecker 1977:280). Until the monetary reform was introduced in 1948, the level of actual wages was less than two-thirds of the 1938 level (Kuczynski 1967:140).

Unemployment constantly increased until 1950, when it amounted to more than 10 percent of the labor force. Millions of refugees and expellees from the East served as an "industrial reserve army." By enlarging the nonagricultural wage labor force, they increased the rivalry on the job market among the working class. Compared to the prewar period, the total number of workers and employees grew from 13.2 million to 15.6 million in the Western zones, which meant an increase from 66.6 to 70 percent of the total labor force (Tjaden-Steinhauer and Tjaden 1973:85).

The weakened economic condition of the German working class affected its consciousness, organization, and strength in two ways. First, poor material conditions did not "automatically" increase class-consciousness; instead, it often encouraged individual self-centeredness. Second, despite this, it would be wrong to characterize the postwar German labor movement as defeatist and lacking in class-consciousness. Not only the verbal radicalism of working class organizations—like the Social Democrats, the German Communist party (KPD), and the trade unions—but also the numerous strikes and mass demonstrations for socialization and higher food rations, especially in the heavily industrialized Ruhr area in 1946 and 1947, show that the German working class was both ready and willing to fight for its economic and political interests.

When the Federal Republic of Germany was separately founded on the territory of the three Western Occupation zones in 1949, the restoration of capitalism had already been firmly settled; furthermore, its position was fully acknowledged and stabilized by the new constitution. This preservation of capitalist class relations, despite the contrary intentions of the majority of the German people, can be explained by the situation of the German labor movement after the war and, more importantly, by the politics of the Allied powers.

The labor movement was heavily wounded by fascism. Not only were the minds of the German people still partly affected by Fascist propaganda—whose core had always been anti-Communist and anti-Soviet—but the labor movement had also lost its most experienced and most active leaders in Nazi concentration camps. The leadership within the Social Democratic Party (SPD) and within the trade unions was left mostly to reformists who entrusted all questions concerning the economic and social order to the good faith of the Western powers. The greatest mistake, however, was their failure or refusal to recognize the fact that the capitalist relations of production continued to exist in their old form. They incorrectly identified the military defeat of fascism with the end of the capitalist system as a whole. The temporary absence of the owners and the leading role of the workers in the factories immediately after the war led to the illusion of the end of capitalism. However, the failures of the labor movement, which must be seen against the background of the objective conditions brought about by 12 years of fascism, do not sufficiently explain the development of class relations in postwar Germany.

Rather, postwar class conflicts in Germany were determined by the intervention of the occupying powers, in particular the United States. The United States intervened in a national class struggle in favor of and in the aid of one class, the German capitalist class. As part of its global strategy as well as for domestic economic and political reasons, the dominant class in the United States temporarily took over the role of the politically defeated German capitalist class and led a "class struggle from above" aimed at reestablishing capitalist relations of production and restoring the hegemony of the German bourgeoisie.

This intervention happened under historically critical conditions, when the German bourgeoisie—though economically still in control of the largest production facilities in Europe—was politically paralyzed and when the German working class was expressing its determination to create an alternative social order through demands for socialization and through waves of strikes. Three aspects of the measures and actions taken by the American occupying forces substantiate this thesis: (1) the protection and support of the German bourgeoisie, (2) the co-optation of reformist labor leaders whose loyal anticommunism was to prevent radical changes, and (3) the obstruction of the rank and file of the labor movement.

The protection of the capitalist class by the Western occupying powers found its expression at least in three measures: they cooperated with capital owners and managers in the administration of confiscated enterprises (Grosser 1974:79), they supported a political administration and a staff largely unaltered since the Third Reich, and they installed executives and experts who were clearly biased in favor of corporation interests. The Marshall Plan, by supplying urgently needed capital, enabled the bourgeoisie to invest in new machinery without risking inflation and thus it helped to increase its total assets. The separate monetary reform, introduced by the British, American and French authorities in 1948, was basically a redistribution of wealth in favor of the owners of the mines and mills. By rendering money and savings worthless, it pauperized the working class, while it guaranteed "the owners of production plants and stockpiles the preservation of the intrinsic value of their property" (Giesecke, Kloenne and Otten 1976:263). "Never before had the division of society into classes been so openly and mercilessly the basis of a decision in economic policy as was the 1948 monetary reform" (Pirkner 1960:98).

The cooperation of reformist labor leaders with Western military commanders constituted an important condition for controlling the spontaneous tendency of the Social Democrats and Communists to make their common anti-Fascist commitment the basis of a unified working-class party. A temporary ban on every kind of political activity not only gave an opportunity to the bourgeoisie to recover, gather their forces, and reorganize, but also halted the trend toward working-class political unity. Meanwhile, the Western military commanders appointed anti-Communist Social Democrats of the Weimar Republic (such as Kurt Schumacher) to administrative positions so that they could, largely unnoticed, start building up local party organizations. When final permission to establish party organizations on a district and province level was given, the movement for working-class unity had already been broken, and rank-and-file Social Democrats were firmly under the control of those leaders who supported the anti-Communist course of the exiled directory of the SPD.

This Allied policy of obstruction of the left in the labor movement can clearly be seen in the process of the reorganization of the trade unions along democratic lines (Schmidt 1973). After the war, many workers realized that their division into a series of feuding unions, parties, and factions was partly responsible for labor's defeat by the Fascists in 1933. Thus, there was a wide consensus of opinion that centralized and unified trade unions were the best organizational form to enable the working class to act effectively. The Allied powers, however, were afraid of strong and class-conscious trade unions because they corresponded with Communist aims. The Allied Occupation authorities allowed trade unions to act and organize only on the shop level, and they allowed cooperation and organization on a higher level only under carefully controlled specific conditions:

> The British military government specifically hindered the establishment of strong unified trade unions although, as in the North Rhine area and in Lower Saxony, they were established according to democratic rules. It took more than two years after the surrender before the trade unions could establish a central organization in the British zone. The Americans generally allowed organizations only within the different states of their Occupied zone. The reestablished workers' councils were harassed by the Americans, who were suspicious of the "subversive activity" of Communist forces (Schmidt 1971:14).

Delay in the organization of trade unions on a higher level minimized their influence on important decisions about the future political and economic structure of Germany. The anti-labor role of the occupying forces was not restricted to their obstruction of the establishment of trade unions: it assumed many forms, ranging from mere threats to massive intervention. When the working class developed the first major postwar strike movement to fight the continued postponement of economic reconstruction and the further decline of its living standards, the Allied powers reacted with threats of severe punishment, shortened food rations, and intervention with troops. The British and American governments also suspended the North Rhine–Westphalian law for the transfer of the mining industry to public ownership, and abrogated the Workers' Council Act, which provided the right of co-determination for trade unions in Hessen and Baden-Wurtemberg. The general strike of November 12, 1948, mobilized 9 million out of the 11.7 million workers and employees in the Anglo-American Zone, but it could not prevent an increasing shift in the balance of power in favor of capital. The favorable upswing in the economy corresponded with the consolidation of the political power of the bourgeoisie.

A separate anti-Communist German state was established on the territory of the three Western zones. Thus the new constitution of the Federal Republic of Germany, the *Grundgesetz,* passed by the Parliamentary Council in May 1949, no longer contained the progressive articles of the state constitutions; instead, it guaranteed, though in restricted form, the restoration of capitalist ownership.

The German bourgeoisie could transform their policy of restoration and of Cold War into reality only against the strong resistance of the German labor movement. When, however, the Shop Organization Law was passed in 1952 and a federal army, the *Bundeswehr,* was finally founded in 1956 after a period of fierce controversy, the working class suffered severe defeats. The remilitarizaton process and the regulation by the Shop Organization Law were not only symptomatic of the "class struggle from above" by the German bourgeoisie, but they also significantly influenced the course of further class conflicts.

The German people were almost unanimously opposed to rearming Germany. By 1950, polls indicated that more than 75 percent of the German people objected to remilitarization, and 90 percent of the young said they would refuse to serve in a general draft.

The remilitarization process in West Germany originated in the Cold War as a specific expression of the international class struggle; and it corresponded with a continuing class struggle from above on a domestic level. The resistance against rearmament within West Germany in 1950 led the federal government to issue a decree barring persons opposed to official policy from public positions as teachers or government employees. As a German equivalent to America's McCarthyism, this measure was meant particularly to hit members of the Communist party. Within the trade unions, this policy was supported by leaders of the "integrative wing," who advocated purging Communist party (KPD) members from positions within the trade unions.

On August 3, 1951, the federal government enacted the "Blitz Bill," which all but equated commitment to the peace movement with high treason. This act led to the prosecution of more than 8,000 Communists and independent members of the Peace Movement.

On November 11, 1951, the day when Chancellor Adenauer signed the European Defense Treaty, which prepared Germany's entry into NATO, the federal government asked the Federal Constitutional Court to declare the Communist party illegal to eliminate that political force within the working class which had most consistently opposed rearmament and which was, perhaps, the most dangerous antagonist of the bourgeoisie.

When the Communist party (KPD) was finally declared illegal in 1956, the Federal Republic of Germany had become the only country in Europe, except for the Fascist dictatorships in Spain and Portugal, that banned the Communist party and, only 12 years after the Nazi terror had been terminated, once again prosecuted Communist party members.

Protest against these forms of repression remained feeble. It was useless to expect active resistance by trade union leaders after the DGB, the central organization of the trade unions, had in 1949 opposed the KPD. The majority of the Social Democrats had forgotten the painful lessons learned during the common anti-Fascist struggle.

The political and social controversies that found their temporary conclusion in the Shop Organization Law of 1952 demonstrate that the working class suffered not only severe defeats on a political level during the remilitarization debate, but that it also lost in the struggle for a democratic reconstruction of the economy.

When the DGB was constituted in 1949, its program advocated a society in which the economic and political power of the corporations would be broken, democracy would be promoted in every social sphere by co-determination, and in which the satisfaction of the needs of the whole of society would prevail over the principle of private profit maximization (Schuster 1976:79).

In their legislation, the Allied powers moved constantly away from these demands of the trade unions. In 1947 the U.S. occupation forces had initiated the decartelization of the iron and steel industries and introduced co-determination (the equal representation of capital and labor on the board of directors), but Law 75 of November 1948 already indicated that the occupation authorities were no longer willing to expropriate the owners of large steel corporations like Krupp or Thyssen. Both the issue of ownership and of democratic control were left for a future German government to decide. Law 27, handed down in 1950, was an express and definite rejection of the unions' demands.

The Mining Co-determination Act of April 1951 limited co-determination to two industries alone and it broke up the unity of the demands of co-determination—a transfer of key industries to public ownership and a planned economy. Based on the ideology of the equal rights of capital and labor, this law postulated their common responsibility for the economic life of the nation and for social peace in the factories.

The Shop Organization Law was passed by the German parliament in July 1952, against strong resistance of the SPD, the KPD, and the trade unions. It not only denied the workers' equal representation on the board of directors, but also made a sharp distinction between the workers' councils and the trade unions and restricted the influence of the workers' council to social issues alone.

The bill obliged the workers' councils to cooperate with management, prohibited the encouragement of strikes, and ruled that the workers' councils must desist from any action that might endanger industrial peace. The intent of the law was obvious: The unions were to be ruled out of the factories; their actions should be restricted to merely bargaining for wages. In fact, the law's objective was "the taming of the largest class organization of the German working class" (Badstuebner and Thomas 1975:449), and its "subordination within Germany's new representative democracy and liberal capitalist economy" (Pirker 1960:242).

The defeats of the German working class in the controversies over remilitarization and the Shop Organization Law indicated how successfully the bourgeoisie had consolidated its economic and political power during the first decade after the war.

Economically, the period between 1949 and 1966 was a period of extraordinary stability, growth, and prosperity, whether it is compared with the cyclical development of capitalist economies in general, with earlier and later periods in Germany, or with other capitalist countries during the same period. Two phases must be distinguished: (1) the phase of an extensively increased reproduction, 1949–1956, and (2) the phase of an intensively increased reproduction, 1957–1966. Production during the first phase remained on a relatively constant technological level, and the growth in productivity was based on an extension of the use of human and nonhuman production elements.

Between 1950 and 1955, the gross national product (GNP) grew annually by almost 10 percent. The total labor force grew by 4 million, or more than 25 percent, during the same period. Unemployment was still relatively high, as the number of unemployed was constantly complemented by streams of refugees from the GDR.

After a long period of need and destitution, many considered the economic boom to be an economic miracle. In reality, however, it was the joint effect of numerous favorable conditions. Because relatively few production facilities were damaged in the war, the technical basis already existed; the labor basis consisted of a large industrial reserve army whose wages were kept low by competition; the financial basis was supplied by ERP-credits; and the political basis was given by the relative weakness of the labor movement and the integration of the country into the Western alliance (Huffschmid and Schui 1976:50–51; Leisewitz 1977:70 ff.).

The position of the working class was improved in absolute terms and worsened in relative terms, if compared with the position of the bourgeoisie. On one hand, wages increased much more slowly than capital income, and, correspondingly, the wage share in the gross national product decreased from 65.5 (1950) to 61.6 percent (1956). This constituted an important precondition to the rise of gross private domestic investments in the GNP from 19.1 percent (1950) to 23.6 percent (1956). At the same time private consumption decreased from 64.1 to 58.5 percent of the GNP. Wages ranked among the lowest in the Western world, and the average weekly hours still amounted to 48.8 in 1955.

For the workers and employees, however, this process was partly veiled by constant improvements in their working and living conditions. Wages after taxes increased by 6 percent annually between 1950 and 1956; price increases and unemployment diminished considerably. Many workers considered the economic boom to be the turning point to a new era of prosperity.

Until 1956, however, postwar reconstruction was marked by relatively sharp class conflict. The number of work stoppages, of workers involved, and of idle days was significantly higher than in later years (Deppe 1977: 354–55). During these strikes both sides—capital and labor—acted with the utmost determination, which indicated that the undeniable improvement of the living and working conditions of the working class was not an automatic result of the economic boom; the struggle for higher wages and better conditions was also an indication that the working class opposed the attempts of the bourgeoisie to restore its class supremacy.

After 1957, the economic development of the country entered a new stage: the phase of an intensively increased reproduction. Labor became increasingly scarce so that, on one hand, wages increased; and, on the other, production could only be expanded by substituting automated machines for human labor. This change of the technological basis of production corresponded with an extraordinary rise of capital intensity (that is, capital asset per working-hour) (Deppe 1977:375). This resulted in a further growth of industrial production and of the GNP, although the rates of growth stayed behind that of the early 1950s.

During the 1957–1966 period, the conditions of the working class considerably improved. The number of wage workers grew slowly by less than 2 percent annually. Unemployment was reduced from 4 percent (1956) to 0.8 percent (1961) and remained at that level until 1966. Because of the labor shortage, wages increased by more than 7.3 percent annually between 1957 and 1966. As inflation was limited to an average price increase of 2.4 percent, the family budget, purchasing power, and, with them, the

Table 14-1. International strike frequency: lost working days by strike per thousand workers, 1964–1968

Italy	873
United States	447
France	147
Japan	116
Belgium	114
Great Britain	109
Sweden	30
Netherlands	7
Federal Republic of Germany	5

Source: Deppe, Fuelberth, and Harrer (1977:389).

living standard of the working class were raised considerably during this period. Weekly hours could be decreased from 47.8 hours (1956) to 42 hours (1967), and the minimum annual vacation was extended to 18 working days (1967).

Because these improvements were generally achieved without major strikes or walkouts, the years between 1957 and 1966 are often characterized as a period of social peace. On a descriptive level, this seems plausible: compared to other capitalist countries, the Federal Republic of Germany had the lowest strike rate. There were only 894 strikes in the Federal Republic between 1948 and 1968, fewer in 20 years than France had in 1958 alone (see table 14-1).

The growth of trade union membership also stagnated. Between 1951 and 1966, the trade unions gained some 500,000 members, but as the total labor force grew by more than 6 million, the degree of unionization sank drastically, from 38.0 to 29.8 percent (Deppe 1977:384). The political castration of the working class in the early 1950s, the postwar reconstruction of the Adenauer administration and its aggressive anticommunism, the "economic miracle," and the increase in real wages led to an apparent loss of working-class interest in politics, declining union membership, and scarcely any active struggles for labor's economic and political interests.

Although this thesis of social peace is plausible, it does not really reflect the reality of the movement. A low strike rate does not mean that class conflict has dissolved. The struggles of the metal workers in Schleswig-Holstein in 1956–1957 and the strike of the Baden-Wurtemberg metal workers in 1963 were so intense and sharp as to reveal the underlying antagonism of labor and capital. The thesis of a final integration and embourgeoisement of the working class has also been proved wrong by studies on the political consciousness of the working class. In one of the most important empirical studies of the 1950s, two liberal sociologists summarized their results: "All the workers we talked to who had a developed conception of society . . . saw it as split in two—whether inevitable or alterable, unbridgeable or mediated by partnership; and they . . . identified themselves as part of the working class" (Popitz and Bahrdt 1956:237).

After the immediate postwar era from 1949 to 1966, lowered growth rates indicated that an end of that seemingly carefree postwar era was underway. Increased automation, labor displacement, and rapid capital accumulation resulted in the deep crisis of 1966–1967; this marked the end of a period free of depressions and the return to the cyclical development of German capitalism, in booms and busts. For the first time since World War Two, nascent social and economic change confronted the German working class with conditions that profoundly influenced the basis of their actions.

The uninterrupted economic growth and the gradual improvement of the living standard during the first two decades after the war helped to create the illusion of an affluent society no longer inflicted with crises and no longer split into classes; but the third phase in postwar German history, from 1966 to the present, has increasingly raised doubts about the efficiency, stability, and equity of the social market economy. The present period is characterized by growing economic instability, a reduced standard of living for workers, and a quantitative and qualitative increase in class conflict.

Economic development during the first part of the 1960s had been based on a further, though slowed, increase of the labor force, the growing use of technology, and a further expansion of production. Two factors, however, have had increasingly evident harmful effects on the economy. First, continued accumulation of capital made it possible for the working class to win increases in wages, but, as wages increased, it decreased the rate of exploitation. Second, fixed capital grew much faster than the labor force and productivity. Thus increasing amounts of capital met a diminishing labor force, and one whose exploitability was limited by declining working hours and rising wages. This overaccumulation led to the first serious economic crisis in the history of the Federal Republic (Huffschmid and Schui 1976: 55 ff.) In this crisis, the number of unemployed leaped to 673,000 in February 1967 from 161,000 in 1966, unemployment amounted to 4.5 percent, the GNP dropped by 1.2 percent, industrial production dropped by 2.8 percent, and a production capacity of 30 billion marks remained unused (Huffschmid 1973:7).

This economic crisis had an extraordinarily strong impact on the political life of the country. When the SPD entered the government along with the CDU on December 1, 1966 in the "Great Coalition," this acknowledged the necessity to include the Social Democrats in capitalist crisis management. The Stability Act of 1967 provided a comprehensive set of instruments for state intervention, ranging from extra imposts on wages during boom periods to government subsidies to investments up to 7.5 percent. The Stability Act also resulted in "Concerted Action," an institutionalized forum to coordinate the actions of labor, capital, and the state, which consisted of representatives from six business organizations, two labor organizations, and the government.

The policy of integration was successful. Even though the Concerted Action's projected figures could not be achieved, the proportion of profits and wages changed as intended. Capital income and profits grew by 17.8 percent before tax and rose to 22 percent after taxes in 1968; undistributed profits doubled between 1967 and 1968. But the income of the working class took quite a different turn. After stagnating in 1967, wages increased by only 5.2 percent in 1968 (while productivity increased by 9.5 percent) so that the proportion of wages in the national income fell for the first time since the war, by 2 percent. More than 200 defense strikes and protest rallies could not withstand the menace of the economic crisis, the participation of the SPD in the Great Coalition, and the cooptation of the trade unions in the Concerted Action.

Increased regimentation of the workers, combined with the enormous capital devaluation of the bust, improved export opportunities, and massive government support for profits led to a boom unprecedented in the history of the Federal Republic. As suddenly as it had appeared, the crisis—as a crisis of profits—"disappeared," leaving the costs to be borne by the working class.

The integrative course of the trade union leaders did not result in a lasting appeasement of the working class. In September 1969, a wave of wildcat strikes hit the Federal Republic, strikes of a kind such as the country had never before experienced. Between the first work stoppage on September 2, 1969, and the last job actions on September 19, 1969, more than 140,000 workers went on strike, even, where necessary, without being supported by trade union leaders. In these two and a half weeks, 532,000 working days were lost (IMSF 1971:38), more than in the entire four previous years (when only 507,000 working days were lost).

Those who had hoped that the September strikes would weaken the trade unions had underestimated the German working class, who understood the importance of their unions and their workers' councils too well to give them up for spontaneous forms of self-organization.[1]

For the German working class as a whole and for those who actively

---

[1] According to the SOFI Analysis, a comprehensive empirical study of the September strikes, the wildcat strikes did not signify the workers' abandonment of their existing class organizations: "The strikes would not have been possible without the workers' councils and the participating shop stewards, the rank and file of the trade union organizations. This is clear evidence of the strong ties of the workers to the traditional forms of class representation" (1971:163).

had participated in it in particular, the September strikes were a positive experience. The success of these job actions made similar actions easier to organize in the future: in 1970, more than 50,000 workers took part in wildcat strikes (Schmidt 1971:104). The trade unions had learned their lesson, too. Their bargaining strategy during the 1970 wage talks was much tougher than in previous years; now, when the rank and file supported their unions in these negotiations by work stoppages, it was no longer out of mere duty. Rather, it was the expression of a new quality in the consciousness and commitment of the German working class. It had begun to free itself from the embrace of the state's integrative policy and was becoming increasingly aware of its own power.

The character of political life in the Federal Republic of Germany since 1969 has been shaped by the Social Liberal Coalition. In his foreign policy, Chancellor Willy Brandt sought reconciliation with Germany's Communist neighbors, in contrast to the Cold War policy of previous Christian Democratic governments. The policy of détente culminated in international agreements, like the Moscow Treaty (1970), the Warsaw Treaty (1970), and the Treaty on Fundamental Principles between the German Democratic Republic and the Federal Republic of Germany (1972), and it has resulted in a perceptible normalization in relations between the FRG and these countries. At home, the Small Coalition pursued a reform policy that helped overcome the conservative petrification during 20 years of Christian Democratic hegemony. Yet, this Social-Democratic government, which set out "to realize more democracy,"[2] has continuously abolished basic democratic rights and introduced the unconstitutional *Berufsverbot*,[3] quite in line with capital's class struggle from above.

The economic development of Germany since 1969 has been shaped by the deepest crisis in the history of the Federal Republic. The economic crisis of 1967 was managed with the help of vast capital destruction, stagnation of wages, an aggressive export policy, and government subventions for investments; but the emerging new investment boom with growth rates of 33 percent (1969) and 17 percent (1970) sharpened internal contradictions in the process of capital accumulation. The deterioration of the conditions of capital realization led to massive overaccumulation; the recession

---

[2] Chancellor Willy Brandt in his inaugural address before the Bundestag, the German parliament, in October 1969.

[3] The "radical decree" was allegedly made to keep "enemies of the Constitution" out of jobs as civil servants, but it has turned out to be exclusively directed against the Democratic left and particularly against the new Communist party (DKP), founded in 1968, which comprises the majority of the old KPD members. The SPD has barred from membership anyone who no longer shares the party's irrational anticommunism and who cooperates with the DKP on single issues. For the consequences of the *Berufsverbot* on the social sciences, see Ahlemeyer and Schellhase (1977:9).

in 1971, temporarily retarded by private consumption but aggravated by the oil crisis of 1973, climaxed in the most serious crisis of the Federal Republic, in 1974–1975.

Economic development since then has been characterized by a considerable recovery; after the GNP growth rate had declined by 3 percent in 1975, it went up by 5.7 percent in 1976 and 2.4 percent in 1977 (Goldberg 1978:227). A new economic upsurge, however, is no longer able to solve the existing contradictions, but poses new problems. It has not only become apparent that the long postwar era is irrevocably a thing of the past, but also that the "cathartic function" of the crisis—to discipline the working class and destroy excess capital—no longer works. The development of the German economy since the early 1970s can no longer be understood in terms of normal business cycles. Rather, countless single symptoms reflect a deep structural crisis. The crisis is not restricted to the economy alone, but extends to every aspect of social, political, scientific, and cultural life. This justifies its being called a "general crisis." It is expressed in several ways that have a direct impact on the working and living conditions of the working class.[4]

First, the centralization of capital has assumed previously unknown dimensions. The number of mergers, by law subject to the consent of the federal antitrust authorities, clearly marks a new phase of the monopolization process.[5] Between 1958 and 1967, an average of 34 mergers were reported annually; between 1968 and 1975, however, 254—more than seven times as many—were registered in each year, and the latest figures show another enormous upsurge: 453 in 1976, and 554 in 1977.

According to an analysis of the federal antitrust authorities, the most active elements in this merger movement are the corporations. Between 1966 and 1972, 57 percent of the mergers were carried out by large corporations, and the 100 largest corporations alone accounted for more than every third merger in West German industry (Huffschmid and Schui 1976:84).

This process of centralization of capital enhances the economic and political power of corporate capital and enables it to restrict competition, to redistribute profits to its favor, and to realize its interests against the organized working class even more effectively. For the working class and the trade unions, these mergers indicate the necessity to continue fighting for a

---

[4] The notion of the general crisis is the backbone of a recent analysis of capitalist societies by *Autorenkollektiv* (1976).

[5] The permission of the federal antitrust authorities is required for mergers of enterprises with 20 or more percent of the market for a single product, whose turnover totals at least DM 500 million, or employ more than 10,000 workers.

qualified co-determination in these corporations in order to subject this enormous concentration of capital and its effects to democratic control.

Second, inflation in the Federal Republic was reduced from 6 percent in 1975 to 3.9 percent in 1977 and is thus considerably lower than in other capitalist countries. It is still a serious challenge, however, to the living standard of the working class. As a means of redistributing national income in favor of the corporate bourgeoisie, inflation affects the working class by devaluing real wages and savings through increased prices, by subjecting wage workers to a regressive income tax, and by reducing fiscal spending for social consumption.

Third, unemployment is definitely the most serious and the most pressing problem for the working class during the present general crisis. Unemployment is no longer linked to the cyclical development of booms and busts, but has become a permanent feature of West German society. Despite of the economic boom of 1976 and 1977, with growth rates of 5.7 and 2.4 percent, joblessness has remained constantly high: More than 1 million workers are regularly unemployed and the official unemployment rate fluctuates around the 4.6 percent level. These figures do not even take into consideration an "inner reserve" of another 650,000 men and women without jobs who are not officially registered as unemployed. Since the outbreak of the crisis, some 1.7 million jobs have been eliminated in German industry. In the long run, the prospects are bleak: The federal labor authorities expect to need some 2 million jobs by 1985.

Fourth, to counteract the squeeze on profits, the bourgeoisie is presently introducing a comprehensive system of automation and rationalization. Investment in rationalization in the Federal Republic is constantly increasing. According to the findings of the Ifo-Institut fuer Wirtschaftsforschung, more than 50 percent of the investments planned in the near future spur automation. When replacement investments, which are usually also labor-saving, are added to automation, almost 80 percent of the present investments, totaling DM 232.8 billion, are destined to eliminate existing jobs. This sharply contrasts with ideological claims of capital, which attempts to legitimate the necessity of higher profits by the alleged job-creating effect of investments.

The reign of the law of profitability prevents the use of technological progress to benefit the working class. Automation presently hits the workers in a double way: Besides creating structural unemployment on a large scale by substituting human labor, it also intensifies and increases the real burdens of work (Kern and Schumann 1977:187).

Fifth, for the last five years, the leading corporations, particularly in the chemical, electrical, and automobile industries, have markedly increased their investments abroad. The net investments of German corporations in foreign countries from 1971, when the first symptoms of the present crisis appeared, to 1976 totaled the same amount in these five years (DM 23.267 billion) as in the previous period, from 1951 to 1971 (DM 23.780 billion). By depriving the domestic economy of investments, this massive capital export bars the creation of new jobs at home.

And sixth, the conditions of the working class have also been influenced by the new role the state has assumed in the wake of the present economic crisis. Since 1974, the joint effect of inflation, the government's increasing indebtedness, and declining tax revenues have led the government to discard the Keynesian policy of global regulation, thus making way for a policy of confrontation that has radically cut back fiscal expenses for social purposes.

To overcome the crisis, the federal government accepted the demands of capital for a general limitation of government activity, for lowering the share of government expenditure in the GNP, and for the introduction of less costly social service programs, when it passed the Budget Act of 1975.

Haupt and Pauly (1976:252) have concluded that since the beginning of the crisis, "intended improvements and extensions of public goods and services have been deleted, and existing public services have been made more costly, have been reduced or have been completely eliminated. This has resulted in a reduction of the living standard of the working class."

Thus the general crisis is also a crisis of the state, both in the sense that the government's economic policy is not capable of preventing cyclical and structural crises, and in the sense that the material basis of the state has been considerably weakened. At the same time, the state and its actions are subjected ever more obviously and more immediately to the pressures of class interests.

To overcome the crisis, the measures and actions of the federal government aim at improving the profit conditions of capital; the government not only has abandoned the anticyclical policy of employment, but also has cut public expenditures for improving the infrastructure, thereby rendering the class character of the state transparent.[6]

On all levels of its living and working conditions, the West German working class is confronted with a comprehensive offensive by capital aimed at reversing the achievements of the labor movement gained between 1969 and 1973–74.

The distinctive feature of present FRG class conflicts is the employers' strategy of deliberate confrontation and polarization. In none of the other

---

[6] Specific proposals for an economic strategy to overcome the crisis have been presented by a group of 158 economists in "Memorandum '78: Toward an Alternative Economic Policy."

capitalist countries do the capital owners make use of lockouts so inten-sively.[7] And in the wage talks of 1978, the employers were determined from the very beginning to defeat the trade unions decisively.

The employers' preparations ranged from coordinating the economic and political strategies of diverse employers' associations to paying DM 252 million to individual employers for joining the lockout of 140,000 metal workers in Baden-Wurtemberg in March 1978. Employers have also tried to invalidate the Co-determination Act in the federal constitutional court in 1977.

Defensive actions of the working class do not take a straight course. Rather, after a phase of crisis shocks, separate and independent actions emerge, some of which may expand to other branches and regions, and cul-minate in successful and politically significant strikes (for example, the printers' strike in 1976 or the metal workers' strike in 1978).

FRG strike statistics (see table 14.2) support this view, and they also show that strike activity during the present crisis has been considerably higher than during the 1966–67 crisis. The paradox is that if parts of the working class have shed their illusions about the manageability of the capi-talist economy and their faith in a "social partnership" of labor and capi-tal, it is partly the consequence of the more aggressive tactics of corporate capital. A period of extraordinarily active class conflicts may have begun in 1978, when the number of workers involved and of working days lost to strikes were the highest in the last 15 years, except for 1971. During 1976 and 1977, four strikes in particular indicated that discontent and the readi-ness for political activity, which is often merely latent, may be transformed into successful actions when the trade unions take the offensive, despite cri-sis and unemployment.

In April and May 1976, up to 70,000 printers (half the 140,000 em-ployed in the industry) struck for 13 days and achieved wage raises of 6.66 percent, thus overstepping government guidelines. Capital mustered all its powers to bring about the first-ever nationwide lockout, because it realized the exemplary significance of this job action. The loss of 35,000 jobs in the printing industry between 1970 and 1975 led to the printers' union, IG Druck, challenge of the claim that higher profits meant more jobs. The 1976 printers' strike was even more significant, however, because for the first time during an SPD government, a major union had battled success-fully for its demands.

After a decline in workers' mobilization in 1977, the wage talks of 1978 were opened by the employers with particular rigidity, as both their demand for a wage freeze and their early lockout threats indicated. Con-

---

[7] Working days lost to lock-outs have risen from 73,000 (1950–1959) to 1,347,000 (1960–1969), and to 5,185,000 (1970–1978) (*Der Spiegel* 1978:31).

Table 14-2. Strikes in the Federal Republic 1966–1978

Year	Striking Workers	Working Days
1966	196,000	27,000
1967	60,000	389,000
1968	25,000	25,000
1969	90,000	249,000
1970	184,000	93,000
1971	536,000	4,484,000
1972	23,000	66,000
1973	185,000	563,000
1974	250,000	1,051,000
1975	35,000	69,000
1976	169,000	534,000
1977	34,000	23,000
1978[a]	256,000	2,700,000

[a] 1978 figures for Baden-Wurtemberg only; the first 3 months of the year only.

tract talks in the steel industry provided wage increases of only 4 percent in January 1978. It was only with the 1978 strike of the longshoremen, the first since 1896–97, that a breakthrough in negotiations could be achieved. The transport workers' union, Oeffentliche Dienste, Transport und Verkehr (ÖTV), demanded a 9 percent wage increase and new standards for a wage classification in accordance with the higher qualification requirements and increased working strain resulting from technological progress in these industries. Although the shipping load almost doubled between 1960 and 1976 (from 79 to 150 million tons), the number of longshoremen decreased by 1,000.

When employers refused to offer more than 4.8 percent, 15,000 unionized longshoremen went to the ballot boxes and 97.1 percent voted for a strike. The solidarity of foreign longshoremen prevented strike-breaking in other European harbors. A 6.4 percent wage pact was rejected by 75.8 percent of the unionized longshoremen, and when a 7 percent increase was finally won, this result made a visible impact upon wage talks in other industries.

Aside from demanding an 8 percent wage increase plus extra improvements for lower wage grades, the metal workers' union, IG Metall, demanded a contract in March 1978 with a no-layoff clause and individual job security guarantees, which would prevent individual dequalification and downgrading in the wake of technological progress. The metal employers' association, Gesamtmetall, actively resisted the union's demand for protection against the effects of automation and made arrangements for an industrywide lockout.

After negotiations failed and 90.3 percent of the metal workers voted for a strike, job actions involving some 80,500 workers in 63 factories began March 15, 1978. Five days later, the employers started a lock out campaign against 146,000 metal workers. After 20 days of active strike, IG Metall won a contract that increased wages by 5 percent, eliminated the lowest wage grade, and prohibited wage reduction in the metal industry for the next five years resulting from downgrading jobs in the wake of automation.

Rationalization and the introduction of computerized techniques were also at the bottom of the printers' strike in March 1978. Publishers also imposed a nationwide lockout. The number of working days lost by the strike (46,000) was far exceeded by the number of working days lost through the lock out (117,000). Even though the printers' union did not win all its strike aims, it did achieve a contract with significant guarantees: job retention for skilled workers for at least 8 years after their printing shops introduce computerized typesetting machines, job transfers, equivalent wage rates at the new terminals, retraining at the employers' expense without reduced wages, and a prohibition on the operation of the computerized typesetting machines by editorial staff.

The latest contracts in these industries indicate a concerted struggle by the workers to prevent technological progress from redounding only to the advantage of capital. These strikes signify a new militancy in the working class and embody an increasingly effective counterattack against the broad offensive of capital.

References

AHLEMEYER, HEINRICH W., and ROLF SCHELLHASE (eds.)
  1977   Soziologie im Arbeitnehmerinteresse. Alternative Positionen auf dem 18. Deutschen Soziologentag. Koeln: Pahl-Rugenstein.
AUTORENKOLLEKTIV
  1976   Allgemeine Krise des Kapitalismus. Triebkraefte und Erscheinungsformen in der Gegenwart. Frankfurt/Main: Marxistische Blaetter.
BADSTUEBNER, ROLF, and SIEGFRIED THOMAS
  1975   Restauration und Spaltung. Entstehung und Entwicklung der BRD 1945–1955. Koeln: Pahl-Rugenstein.
BRAUNS, HANS, ULS JAEGGI, and KLAUS P. KISKER
  1976   Die SPD in der Krise. Die deutsche Sozialdemokratie seit 1945. Frankfurt/Main: Fischer.
DEPPE, FRANK, JUTTA VON FREYBERG, and CHRISTOPH KIEVENHEIM
  1973   Kritik der Mitbestimmung. Partnerschaft oder Klassenkampf. Frankfurt/Main: Suhrkamp.
DEPPE, FRANK, GEORG FUELBERTH, and JUERGEN HARRER
  1977   Geschichte der deutschen Gewerkschaftsbewegung. Koeln: Pahl-Rugenstein.

GIESECKE, HERMANN, ARNO KLOENNE, and DIETER OTTEN
1976   Gesellschaft und Politik in der Bundesrepublik. Eine Sozialkunde. Frankfurt/Main: Fischer.

GOLDBERG, JOERG
1978   "Die wirtschaftliche Lage der BRD im Jahre 1977," in *Blaetter fuer deutsche und internationale Politik* 2(February): 227–231.

GROSSER, ALFRED
1974   Geschichte Deutschlands seit 1945. Eine Bilanz. Munich: dtv.

HAUPT, UWE, and DIETER PAULY
1976   "Die Demontage des Lebensniveaus. Zur Entwicklung der materiellen Lage der Lohn- und Gehaltsabhaengigen," in Joerg Huffschmid und Herbert Schui (eds.), Gesellschaft im Konkurs. Koeln: Pahl-Rugenstein.

HUFFSCHMID, JOERG
1973   Die Politik des Kapitals. Konzentration und Wirtschaftspolitik in der Bundesrepublik. Frankfurt/Main: Suhrkamp.

HUFFSCHMID, JOERG, and HERBERT SCHUI (eds.)
1976   Gesellschaft im Konkurs. Handbuch zur Wirtschaftskrise 1973–1976 in der BRD. Koeln: Pahl-Rugenstein.

INSTITUT FUER MARXISTISCHE STUDIEN UND FORSCHUNG
1971   Die Septemberstreiks 1969. Frankfurt/Main: Marxistische Blaetter.

KERN, HORST, and MICHAEL SCHUMANN
1977   Industriearbeit und Arbeiterbewusstsein. Frankfurt/Main: Suhrkamp.

KUCZYNSKI, JUERGEN
1967   Die Geschichte der Lage der Arbeiter unter dem Kapitalismus, vol. 7a. Berlin: Dietz.

MEMORANDUM 1978
1978   "Memorandum '78: Alternativen der Wirtschaftspolitik," in *Blaetter fuer deutsche und internationale Politik* 5 (May): 624–37.

MILLS, C. WRIGHT
1973   The Sociological Imagination. Harmondsworth: Penguin.

PIRKER, THEO
1960   Die blinde Macht. Die Gewerkschaftsbewegung in Deutschland. Munich: Mercator, 2 vols.

POPITZ, HEINRICH, and HANS PAUL BAHRDT
1956   Das Gesellschaftsbild des Arbeiters. Tuebingen: Siebeck & Mohr.

SCHMIDT, EBERHARD
1971   Ordnungsfaktor oder Gegenmacht. Die politische Rolle der Gewerkschaften. Frankfurt/Main: Suhrkamp.
1973   Die verhinderte Neuordnung 1945–1952. Frankfurt/Main: Suhrkamp.

SCHUSTER, DIETER
1976   Die deutsche Gewerkschaftsbewegung. Duesseldorf: Vorwaerts-Druck.

SOFI
1971   Am Beispiel der Septemberstreiks—Anfang der Rekonstruktions-
        periode der Arbeiterklasse? Frankfurt/Main: EVA.
DER SPIEGEL
1978   "Aussperrung: 'Sie erzaehlen ein Gruselstueck'" (June 19).
STATISTISCHES TASCHENBUCH 1977
1977   Arbeits- und Sozialstatistik. Ed. Der Bundesminister fuer Arbeit und
        Sozialordnung. Bonn: Bundespresse.
TJADEN-STEINHAUER, MARGARETE, and KARL HERMANN TJADEN
1973   Klassenverhaeltnisse im Spaetkapitalismus. Stuttgart: Enke.
WEISS-HARTMANN, ANNE, and WOLFGANG HECKER
1977   "Die Entwicklung der Gewerkschaftsbwegung 1945-1949," in Frank
        Deppe, Georg Fuelberth, and Juergen Harrer (eds.), Geschichte der
        deutschen Gewerkschaftsbewegung. Koeln: Pahl-Rugenstein,
        272-301.

15 The State and Class Conflict: Mexico During the Cárdenas Period

Nora Louise Hamilton
University of Southern California

What are the possibilities and limits of state autonomy from dominant class and foreign interests in a postrevolutionary society in which the previous dominant classes have been weakened and the major faction within the state is allied with subordinate classes? The possibilities of state autonomy are generally limited by structural constraints inherent in the class structure, but the nature and mechanisms of these constraints must be identified for a given social formation. During the government of Lázaro Cárdenas (1934–1940), Mexico was marked by a period of intensive class struggle and substantial social change in which the state (or a particular state faction) seems to have enjoyed considerable autonomy from dominant national and foreign interests.

The Mexican revolution of 1910–1917, which destroyed the former state apparatus and weakened the dominant internal classes, created conditions favoring state autonomy. In fact, the new constitution of 1917 implicitly called for an autonomous state, situated in a class society but above classes, that would represent the interests of the nation and the ideas of the revolution. Its functions included direct economic and social intervention—the establishment of national sovereignty over natural resources, the expropriation and distribution of land to peasant communities, and protection of labor rights within an implicitly capitalist system (Leal 1974: 176–77; Córdova 1973: 234).

But in the immediate postrevolutionary period, the options of the new state-in-formation were constrained—first, by divisions within its own ranks. Revolutionary leaders, who commanded their own armies and con-

---

I am very grateful to Nancy DiTomaso, Al Gedicks, Mark Kann, and Julia Wrigley for their comments on an earlier draft of this article.

[346]

trolled different regions of the country, constantly threatened those leaders in precarious control of the central state bureaucracy. Although the internal dominant classes had been weakened, foreign capital (especially U.S. and British) continued to dominate important sectors of the economy, including the major export sectors, mining and petroleum, as well as electrical utilities, communications, part of the railroad system, and substantial tracts of land. Mexico also had a considerable foreign debt with the United States and European countries, and over half its trade was with the United States. The new state also confronted the financial chaos resulting from the revolution and a consequent lack of resources, which was aggravated by international pressures for debt repayment. Finally, the revolution had been fought by the peasants, who constituted the vast majority of the population, and had brought them to the forefront of the political process where they could no longer be ignored (Meyer 1972a; Leal 1975).

The achievements of the early postrevolutionary governments had mixed implications for the possibility of state autonomy. On one hand, the revolutionary leaders controlling the executive branch of the central government succeeded in establishing their hegemony over regional military officers and other branches and levels of government. This hegemony was institutionalized with the creation of the National Revolutionary party (PNR), which became the instrument of presidential succession, eliminating other parties and bringing together all members and factions of the "revolutionary family." The new government also established conditions for capital accumulation and the financial basis of the state itself. But on the other hand, the process of accumulation involved the accommodation of groups from the prerevolutionary dominant class, as well as foreign interests, and the establishment or renewal of links between the state and private interests at all levels of society. In fact, military officers and government officials were given state subsidies to enter private business or otherwise encouraged to join the new capitalist class. Thus a pattern of recruitment between the state and the private sector was established. The state not only created the basis for the new social order, but contributed, directly and indirectly, to the creation of the new capitalist class (Córdova 1973: 353–79).

These links between factions and agencies within the state and groups within the domestic private sector (and to some extent foreign interests) constituted the basis of an implicit conservative alliance. Government leaders became increasingly reluctant to implement reforms that could affect their own expanding interests. Land distribution programs carried out in response to peasant demands were generally limited to the poorer lands of traditional estates. The government also attempted to institutionalize control over subordinate classes by the co-optation of peasant and labor organizations. These efforts met with only limited success, but by the beginning of the 1930s, the peasantry, though militant and dissatisfied, still lacked an effective national organization. The industrial working class was small, heterogeneous (with artisans and workers in small workshops as well as a militant proletariat in the railroads, mines, and petroleum fields), and, with some exceptions, relatively disorganized (Huizer 1970; Carr 1976, II: 16–21, 41–44).

But there were also elements of an implicit progressive alliance of factions within the state, the peasantry, and the working class. Certain individuals and groups at various levels of government and within the government party identified with the demands of the peasants for land and of workers for labor protection, including individual state governors who sought to organize workers and peasants and to implement land reform in their regions; rural school teachers who assisted peasant villagers in their land claims; and radical agrarians within the central government who fought attempts to restrict land distribution. In some areas, unions of industrial workers also collaborated in the organization of landless peasants.

The latent conservative and progressive alliances were obscured by a number of factors, among them the segmental divisions of the dominant class; the isolated and fragmented condition of subordinate classes and groups; vertical links between employers, local officials, and co-opted sectors of the working class; and the fact that the divisions among factions within the state were often based less on ideological orientation or class identification than on personal loyalties. Events of the 1930s clarified these alliances and the basic cleavages dividing Mexican society.

Cárdenas and the Progressive Alliance

The historical juncture of external and internal forces—that is, the effects of the world depression on Mexico—brought the progressive faction within the government party to a position of dominance within the Mexican state. Though there had been little change in Mexico's relation with foreign capital, the involvement of the U.S. and European governments in the crisis of the depression (and subsequently the threat, and actual outbreak, of war in Europe) lessened their concern with pursuing their interests in Mexico and other Latin American countries. At the same time, the depresssion seriously disrupted the Mexican economy. The rapid decline in exports resulted in production cutbacks and high unemployment in the export sector, which rapidly affected other economic sectors and led to a reduction in government revenues (still heavily dependent on export taxes), a decrease in purchasing power, cutbacks in production, and further dismissals or wage reductions in other industries. Combined with peasant dissatisfaction at government efforts to limit land distribution, the sharp increase in unemployment and wage cutbacks led to labor and peasant mobilization, including demonstrations, hunger marches to state capitals, and land invasions (Shulgovski 1968:34–36; Anguiano 1975:12–17; Córdova 1974:28; Fuentes Díaz 1959:332; García Cantú 1965:932).

These movements, although not articulated, manifested the failure of the postrevolutionary government to accommodate the most populous classes of Mexico at a time when various groups within the "revolutionary family" were becoming increasingly dissatisfied with the conservative faction in power. Motivated by frustration at their exclusion from this faction, or by genuine identification with the stated goals of the revolution, members of these groups supported General Lázaro Cárdenas as candidate for president in the 1934 elections. Cárdenas had served in various posts with the constitutional army, the party, and the government, and as governor of Michoacan had demonstrated an active concern with peasant and worker demands, promoting labor organization, land reform, and the expansion of education. The progressive wing of the PNR took over the party convention of December 1933, when Cárdenas became the official presidential candidate, and promulgated a radical six-year plan that, overriding a more moderate plan proposed by the government, gave primary emphasis to land distribution (Shulgovski 1968:80–82; Medín 1971:13; Cornelius 1969:34; Bosques 1937).

Cárdenas made the six-year plan his campaign platform. His notes and speeches during this period, and subsequently as president, indicate a return to the concept of the autonomous state implied in the constitution. This state would be concerned with independent national development and social welfare. It would direct and regulate the economy to liberate Mexico from its colonial status, carry out a rapid and extensive agrarian reform to respond to peasant demands for land, and support labor in industrial conflicts with the intent of "humanizing" capital and balancing the "factors of production" (Muñoz 1976:154; Córdova 1974:95; Mexico, Cámara de Diputados 1966, V:756). Cárdenas actively promoted the mobilization and organization of labor and the peasantry to confront obstacles to change not only within the dominant class but also within the state bureaucracy. In effect, with the encouragement of the state, the mobilizaton of these groups would be intensified to the point that the state would be *obliged* to respond. Peasant and worker mobilization was both cause and justification for the radicalization of the government program (Córdova 1974:16, 31–32).

The Progressive Alliance and the Control of Capital

During the six years of the Cárdenas administration, the progressive state faction, in alliance with the mobilized workers and peasants, brought about profound changes in Mexican society. The government supported strikes by industrial workers for wage increases, union recognition, the elimination of company unions, and collective contracts. Real wages increased, and a new labor confederation, the Confederation of Mexican Workers (CTM), was formed.

In the agrarian sector, the policy of the Cárdenas government departed from those of his predecessors in several important respects. First, more land was distributed to more peasant families than during all previous administrations: 17.9 million hectares to 810,000 families, compared to 8.7 million hectares to 778,000 families who had received land in the past. Second, whereas earlier land reform programs had generally concentrated on the poorer land of the traditional estates, Cárdenas expropriated commercial estates—previously considered immune to agrarian reform in view of their importance to the internal market and to exports (Chevalier 1967:163–68). The most important innovation was the institution of the collective *ejidos,* communally owned lands, farmed collectively, on the expropriated commercial estates. The purpose was to maintain the efficiency of the productive unit by taking advantage of economies of scale, so that a radical change in the agrarian structure would not entail a loss of productivity (Cámara de Diputados 1966, V:765; Gutelman 1974:105–106).

The new ejiditarios found themselves in a hostile environment, expressed in various forms, ranging from press attacks against "communistic" agrarian experiments, to violence, perpetuated by the armed mercenaries of the landowners, who were permitted by law to retain 150 irrigated hectares (approximately 375 acres) or its equivalent, and often controlled credit, agricultural inputs, and marketing outlets (Shulgovski 1968:254–56). In this environment, it is doubtful that the ejidos could have survived without outside support. During the Cárdenas administration the federal government provided financial assistance—including the establishment of a new Ejidal Bank to meet their credit needs—and moral support. The ejiditarios and many Ejidal Bank officials cooperated in efforts to solve administrative and technical problems; in some cases, they succeeded in expanding output and acreage under production. The early experience of the collective ejidos suggests that they were viable production units (Eckstein 1966; Landsberger and Hewitt 1970). The scope of the Cárdenas agrarian reform—and the importance given the ejidos—is shown by the shift in the proportion of land controlled by the ejidos. In 1930, they possessed 13.4 percent of the nonirrigated land and 13.1 percent of the irrigated land; by 1940 they owned 47.4 percent of the nonirrigated land and 57.3 percent of the irrigated.

Perhaps the most significant achievement of the Cárdenas government was the expropriation of the foreign-owned petroleum companies. Petroleum constituted the second major export of Mexico; the first was mineral products, also controlled by foreign companies, chiefly in the United States. The history of the petroleum companies in Mexico made them an appropriate target for expropriation. They had refused to respect Mexican legislation regarding foreign concessions. They had cut back production in Mexico and let their equipment deteriorate. Attempts of workers to unionize had been met with violence by their hired mercenaries. Cárdenas's decision to expropriate was therefore a cause of national celebration and was supported even by groups that opposed other measures of the Cárdenas government. The petroleum expropriation and nationalization was the first significant step in breaking foreign control over the export sector and in placing key industries under the state (Meyer 1972b).

Despite the intensity and scope of the process of transformation during the Cárdenas administration, some contemporary authors have questioned the government's intentions. They suggest, on the basis of the long-term effects of these programs, that the Cárdenas government was simply pursuing the interests of capitalism although with considerably more foresight and vision than its predecessors. The agrarian reform increased agricultural production—necessary for industrialization—by eliminating inefficient landowners; it also brought social peace to the countryside. The nationalization of petroleum, and subsequently of other industries, enabled the state to provide these services to private firms at reduced rates. The wage gains of the workers, as well as the agrarian reform, increased purchasing power and thus expanded the market for industrial goods. State support for demands by workers and peasants facilitated their control by the state in the interests of capitalist production. State encouragement of labor and peasant organization had the same purpose: once organized, these groups could be more easily controlled (Córdova 1974; Anguiano 1975).

The policies of the Cárdenas government have certainly had these effects. Cárdenas also continued many of the policies of his predecessors oriented to expanding conditions for capitalist development. But the goals pursued by the Cárdenas government were undoubtedly more complex. North and Raby (1977) develop an alternative interpretation of this period that emphasizes the degree of mobilization, conflict, and polarization characterizing Mexico and making it impossible for anyone to predict the final outcome. This interpretation is persuasive for several reasons. First, as indicated above, the mobilization of affected groups was an important element in the programs of the Cárdenas government, which in fact undertook no major reform without the previous mobilization of workers or peasants. The gains of industrial workers were won by strikes. The first expropriation of commercial estates took place in La Laguna, which produced half the cotton for Mexican industry, after 100 of the agricultural unions in the region went on strike for a collective contract in 1936. Subsequent expropriations were preceded by the organization of the peasants and rural workers and frequently strikes, land invasions, or other forms of mobilization. Even events culminating in the petroleum expropriation began with the demand by the industrywide petroleum union for a collective contract.

Second, Cárdenas and other members of the progressive faction within the state frequently referred to an eventual transformation to socialism or a form of workers' democracy. Although much of this can be attributed to the rhetoric of the period—and a certain element of confusion regarding the meaning of socialism, which was often invoked to describe a form of welfare state or mixed economy—Cárdenas's policies also indicate a willingness to experiment with noncapitalist, quasi-socialist forms of ownership and production. The most significant was the collective ejido. Other experiments in workers' control or administration were introduced in mines and industrial firms as well as the national railroads and the nationalized petroleum industry. Most of these experiments failed; perhaps inevitably, given the context of a capitalist society, but they indicate a willingness to encourage noncapitalist forms of production, even while conditions for capitalist production were being promoted (Cárdenas 1972a: 190–91; Shulgovski 1968:308–317; Ashby 1963:123, 131, 256–57; Anguiano 1975:89–90).

A third possible interpretation of the intentions of the Cárdenas government is compatible with the second while including elements of the first. Cárdenas's speeches suggest a concept of the state as being not only above classes but also having a mandate to control them—directing the productive process to the interests of the nation as a whole. Thus, while taking the side of labor as the weaker party in the conflict with capital, the state would assure that the struggle of labor was confined to possibilities that did not basically challenge the capitalist system. But the state would also control capital, assuring that the productive process was oriented to the goals of national independence and the social needs of the population (Mexico, Chamber of Deputies 1966, IV:753–57; PRM 1940:53, 209; Cárdenas 1972b:317). The expectation that the state would control and direct the process of capitalist production was not unreasonable, given the international crisis of capitalism and the consequent projection of "statist" solutions in most developed capitalist countries, as well as the revolutionary origins of the state and the comparative weakness of the national bourgeoisie in Mexico.

Cárdenas's policies appear to have been oriented to a form of state-directed capitalism in which traditional elements of feudalism and imperialism would be eliminated, and experiments with socialist forms of production would be tolerated or encouraged. Such an orientation was in keeping with the uncertain future of international capitalism and the ambiguities of the Mexican situation.

This rather eclectic approach was evident in the major reforms of the Cárdenas government. In the industrial sector, which was already capitalist, the role of the state was to assist the organization of labor, enabling it to confront capital so it could achieve a balance between the factors of production. The agrarian reform was to eliminate feudal relations of production; capitalist production was controlled, not eliminated, as indicated by the ability of the landowners to retain 150 hectares of the expropriated estates. The collective ejido—though a pragmatic solution to the problem of maintaining economies of scale—constituted an innovative experiment in new systems of production, as did the less successful experiments in industry. The petroleum expropriation represented an effort to control foreign capital by forcing it to respect Mexican sovereignty. It was also a first step in eliminating foreign control of key industries, notably those of the export sector, and bringing them under the control of the state.

There is little evidence of a conflict between the basic goals of the state and those of the working class and peasantry, although in isolated cases specific groups made demands that the government was unwilling to meet. The ideological leaders of the organized working class—the Communist party and the secretary-general of the CTM (Lombardo Toledano)—were under the influence of the Communist International and its conception of the Popular Front. Their analysis of Mexico was similar to that of Cárdenas in projecting a stage of antifeudal and anti-imperialist struggle to establish conditions for national capitalism (Márquez and Rodríguez 1973: 192–97). Despite the level of conflict in Mexican society, no major organized group to the left of the state pressured it to take a more radical position.

Polarization and the Limits of the Progressive Alliance

If the goals of the government and the popular classes were similar, why were efforts made to check the processes of mobilization and social transformation in the last years of the Cárdenas government? The explanation is based on the process of polarization in Mexico in this period. The policies of the Cárdenas government directly attacked the interests of certain segments of the dominant class, such as commercial landowners and the petroleum companies, and the mobilization of workers and peasants was seen as a threat to this class as a whole. It appeared that the state had abdicated its function of social control and was in fact participating in the class struggle on the side of the subordinate classes. The period of Cárdenas's administration was characterized by rapid polarization as labor and peasant mobilization were countered by an intensification of attacks by the opposition.

Beginning in 1936, proclamations issued by national business confederations lamented the climate of instability and "communist" control of the labor movement. Employers continued to try to impose company unions and in some cases provided financial support to such organizations as the Fascist, paramilitary "gold shirts," who attacked leaders and members of CTM-controlled unions (Salazar 1956:218–21; Vellinga 1975:201). By 1937, employers began to cut back investments and production. Industrialists also raised prices to maintain profits in the context of wage increases. Combined with high food prices (resulting from climatic conditions and adjustments in the agrarian sector) these increases began to cut into wage gains of workers. As the petroleum conflict intensified in the last months of 1937, the petroleum companies and other foreign interests began to withdraw their bank accounts, and capital exports increased, critically reducing Mexico's foreign exchange reserves (Anguiano 1975:81–82; Cámara de Diputados 1966, IV:68–69).

After the petroleum expropriation in March 1938, the companies retaliated with a petroleum boycott, blocking sales to the United States, England, and France, and pressured their respective governments (successfully, in England) to break off relations with Mexico. The U.S. State Department did not end relations with Mexico but exerted considerable pressure on the Mexican government for immediate indemnification of the petroleum companies. The U.S. Treasury terminated an ongoing agreement to purchase a stipulated amount of Mexican silver monthly; negotiations for a U.S. loan to Mexico were broken off; and State Department officials discouraged new loans to Mexico. Given Mexico's precarious financial condition, these acts forced the government to devalue the Mexican peso (Meyer 1972b:352, 412–13; Rippy 1972:244–55; Cámara de Diputados 1966, IV:82–83).

Aside from economic pressures and attacks in the press, the level of physical violence increased, especially in the rural areas. Aside from land reform beneficiaries and peasants petitioning for land, rural school teachers, who often supported their mobilization, became a major target; during the first half of 1938 an average of three teachers a month were killed (Raby 1972:59; *Mexican Labor News*, 28 July 1938).

The most cohesive political opposition to the direction of the Cárdenas government developed within the state itself. Conservative state governors became increasingly open in their criticism of the "excesses" of the government's agrarian reform program (blamed on the zeal of the radical agrarians of the Agrarian Department, who had been given jurisdiction over the agrarian reform in 1934) and of the CTM and its leader, Lombardo Toledano. Following the petroleum expropriation, state governors offered their support to Cárdenas in return for a promise to return jurisdiction over the land distribution program to them, a move that is generally considered as the end of the progressive phase of the land reform. Members of the Senate and Chamber of Deputies began to criticize certain government initiatives; leaders of the congressional opposition included military officers who spoke for important sectors within the army. In short, conservative factions within the state were shifting from an unwilling acquiescence in the policies of the government to active opposition. General Saturnino Cedillo led a revolt against the government (with political and possibly financial support from the petroleum companies). The revolt was quickly crushed because the military remained behind Cárdenas, indicating the importance of retaining its support (Michaels 1970; Raby 1972; North and Raby 1977).

The government attempted to reduce the growing polarization of forces by controlling the mobilization of popular groups and at the same time broadening its support base to include middle sectors and conservative factions within the state. Both ends were sought through the establishment of a new government party, the Party of the Mexican Revolution (PRM) in March 1938 on the basis of four sectors: industrial workers, peasantry, the military, and a "popular" sector. The party had been initially designed to include only the revolutionary groups of society—a form of institutionalization of the progressive alliance in which the state, in keeping with Cárdenas's conception of its function to control both capital and labor, would be dominant. One element of this control had been the organization of peasants into the National Peasant Confederation (CNC) under the auspices of the state (Gómez Jara 1970:117–25; González Navarro 1963:137–41).

The new labor confederation, established as an independent organization, had also become increasingly linked to the government, and its internal structure had become increasingly authoritarian. Because authoritarian structures characterized both the peasant confederation and the major labor confederation, these organizations were easily led into the new party by their respective leaders. The inclusion of a military sector was based in part on the hope that the military could also be controlled through the corporate structure of the party. The popular sector consisted of groups excluded from the peasant and labor sectors—such as unions of teachers and state employees that had not been permitted to join the CTM and small farmers who were not included in the peasant confederation—as well as such groups as youth and women's organizations that did not fit elsewhere.

The stated purpose of the corporate structure was to enable popular sectors to participate more effectively in the political process as cohesive groups than they could as isolated individuals. In reality, the party became a means of neutralizing and controlling its constituent organizations, particularly those of workers and peasants, as these had become instruments for the control of their members. This further limited the ability of popular sectors to continue pressures on the state that would counter the increasing pressures of dominant groups (Lieuwen 1968:124–25; Córdova 1974:147; Anguiano 1975:136; Raby 1972:52–57).

The Victory of the Conservative Alliance

The shift in government orientation from support for class conflict to efforts to control it and check the process of polarization was evident in the selection of the PRM candidate for the 1940 presidential election. Of the possible candidates being considered, the most logical choice to continue the progressive efforts of the Cárdenas government was General Francisco Múgica, who as a member of the Cárdenas government had participated in its most important decisions and had been the major proponent of the petroleum expropriation. But Múgica had powerful enemies. His reputation for honesty as much as his radical past indicated that he would not tolerate the corrupt practices and use of government for self-enrichment that had become standard procedure in Mexican politics, even among some opportunists within the progressive alliance. By the middle of 1938, conservative groups within the government had begun to organize around the proposed candidacy of Cárdenas's Secretary of Defense, General Manuel Avila Camacho. Although apparently neutral politically, and promoted as a "moderate," Avila Camacho's connections suggested a conservative orientation. His candidacy was officially announced at a banquet for state governors and military leaders given by his brother, Maximino Avila Camacho, who as governor of Puebla had clashed with the labor and peasant movements on various occasions (Michaels 1971:7–12; Raby 1972:53–56).

Officially, the PRM candidate was to be selected by the three non-military sectors of the PRM and confirmed by the party convention. But the preselection of Avila Camacho by state governors and prominent groups within the military apparently predetermined the outcome. Early in 1939 the candidacy of Avila Camacho was imposed on the membership of the CTM and the CNC by their leadership, who ignored or stifled the objections of certain unions and peasant leagues that favored Múgica. Efforts by Múgica to campaign independently were blocked by local officials of government and of the two confederations, who were in a position to take reprisals against peasants and workers who failed to support Avila Camacho. Múgica withdrew his candidacy in July (*Mexican Labor News*, March 1, March 30, May 11, and July 30, 1939; North and Raby 1977:47).

The necessity to conciliate powerful sectors of government, particularly the military, in view of the polarization occurring in Mexico, was probably the overriding reason for supporting Avila Camacho as the "national unity" candidate by Cárdenas and other progressives within the state. The war in Europe, and the imminent involvement of the United States and the Western hemisphere, had also resulted in an ideological shift by progressive groups from anti-imperialism to unity of democratic forces against fascism. Many undoubtedly saw the projected Avila Camacho administration as an "interim" government during a period of crisis: Avila Camacho would not initiate new reforms but would consolidate existing ones or at least leave them intact, and the progressive thrust of the Cárdenas government could be resumed once the crisis had passed (Raby 1972:56; Michaels 1971:14).

Avila Camacho's candidacy symbolized the expansion of the progressive alliance through the incorporation of conservative groups within the state and their allies within the private sector. But in the process it changed its character to a vertical alliance in which the conservative faction was dominant. At the same time, although the selection of Avila Camacho as presidential candidate had forced a type of unity on factions within the state, it had not had the desired effect of unifying the nation. In the middle of 1939 an opposition candidate—General Juan Andréu Almazán—appeared, and within six months had attracted a following from all sectors of the population.

Almazán, like many others, had made a substantial fortune through his military and government career in the revolutionary and postrevolutionary periods. As presidential candidate, he received most of his financial support from northern businessmen. However, his support came not only from groups opposed to Cárdenas's policies, but also from many opposed to corruption and graft within the state and to authoritarian and antidemocratic practices that had developed in state institutions and in the labor and peasant confederations (Michaels 1971:22–26, 43; Raby 1972:58).

The political platforms of the two candidates were similar. Both favored private enterprise, class conciliation, and foreign investment (with protection for Mexican capital). In the rural sector, both favored an emphasis on small holdings rather than ejidos. Both received support from North American and Mexican businessmen (Michaels 1971:22–47; Bursley 1940; Boyle 1940). In effect, the selection of Avila Camacho as the PRM candidate and the candidacy of Almazán shifted the axis of conflict within Mexico from one of class polarization to one between two vertical coalitions, both dominated by conservative forces, again obscuring the basic class cleavages. The issues dividing them were not class issues nor even ideological questions, but the nature of their relation to the Mexican state.

Aligned with Avila Camacho were a wide range of groups that had benefited (or hoped to benefit) from their connection with the state: peasants who received land, workers whose strikes and organizational efforts received state support, private business groups who received government contracts or other forms of government assistance, and opportunists within the government able to profit from their position within the bureaucracy. For many of those who supported Avila Camacho, the state represented the promise, if not the fulfillment, of the revolution. The Cárdenas regime had indicated the advances possible under a strong and progressive government.

Similarly, Almazán supporters were united by their opposition to the state, again for widely diverse reasons. Conservative businessmen feared its power over property and its intervention in the economic process, and resented its support for labor during the Cárdenas administration. Many opposed graft and corruption that, despite Cárdenas's opposition, had continued during his government. Workers and peasants resented the antidemocratic practices that had characterized the party, labor, and peasant bureaucracies.

The campaign was bitterly contested, culminating in violence on election day, with battles between Avila Camacho and Almazán forces in which several people were killed and many injured. The enthusiasm generated by the Almazán candidacy, evident in the crowds that turned out spontaneously for his speeches, indicates that he might have won a fair election. But the election day maneuvers of Avila Camacho's backers secured an overwhelming victory for their candidate that he could not have achieved otherwise (Michaels 1971:42–45).

The Avila Camacho victory assured the institutional continuity of the Mexican state and its subsequent central role in the process of Mexico's development. But it was also a victory for the conservative forces of Mexican society. Many of Almazán's supporters became reconciled to the new government as its first intitiatives demonstrated its conservative orientation. In effect, the conservative alliance again controlled the state, with the difference that the state itself had been strengthened through its control, via the new government party, of the working class and peasantry, and through the revolutionary legitimacy given the state by the Cárdenas government.

Nor could the conservative alliance, once in power, be readily ousted. Avila Camacho was succeeded not by a progressive government, but by the most conservative administration that Mexico has known since the revolution—that of Miguel Alemán. The collective ejidos, which had suffered from benign neglect under Avila Camacho, all but disappeared as a consequence of Alemán's policy of cutting off credit to ejidos that were not farmed individually. The practice of *charrismo*—the displacement of dissident, democratically elected union leaders by those imposed by the regime—became institutionalized. Assassination became an accepted means of dealing with independent peasant leaders. At the same time, the process of "recruitment" from the state to the private sector through legal and extralegal means received new impetus (Hewitt de Alcántara 1974:172–76; Hansen 1974:115–18, 167).

Since 1940, groups within and outside of the government have attempted to resurrect the progressive alliance by forming left-wing parties, peasant confederations, and labor organizations. Cárdenas himself was involved in at least one such initiative. But these organizations—if sufficiently strong to constitute a threat—have been controlled through co-optation into the government party (in some cases with limited concessions) and repression; their progressive allies within the state have been isolated (Anderson and Cockcroft 1972).

The process of development in Mexico has strengthened the dominant segment of the national bourgeoisie and tightened its relations—and those of the Mexican state—with foreign capital. The possibility of a reemergence of a progressive coalition in which factions within the state would lead subordinate classes in a challenge to this structure seems to have been effectively precluded by the strength of the ties linking members of the dominant coalition and the effectiveness of state controls over subordinate groups. Subordinate groups must be able to free themselves from state control before effectively challenging the existing system; such a challenge would have to confront the state itself in view of its position within the dominant coalition.

Conclusions

Although the experience of Mexico in the 1930s cannot be generalized, it does provide insight into questions regarding the constraints on state autonomy in a postrevolutionary society. First, real or apparent efforts of the state to challenge existing structures will confront increasing opposition by the dominant class itself. This intervention may be direct or indirect, or even latent. In Mexico, examples of *direct* intervention include the petroleum boycott, the formation of rival political movements, and the Almazán candidacy. *Indirect* intervention includes those actions taken by the dominant class which had the secondary and possibly unintended effect of influencing the state: cutbacks in investments and capital exports, which may be attributed to unstable business conditions; price increases, rationalized on the basis of higher wages and production costs; and similar economic measures, which, if sufficiently widespread, could result in destabilizing the economy.

Latent intervention consists of the possibility of threat of intervention *if* the state were to take measures against the interests of a particular class or class segment. Following the petroleum expropriation, for example, mineworkers urged Cárdenas to expropriate the U.S. mining companies, but such a move would have led to the closing of U.S. markets to Mexican minerals, at the time over half of Mexico's exports. The cost was too high, and the mining companies were not expropriated. In short, structural constraints limiting the autonomy of the state are based on direct or indirect power relations—that is, on control by the dominant class (or foreign interest) of the economic resources of the state and society. In the last instance, structural constraints are enforced by the actual or threatened political action of the relevant group, interest, or class.

Confronted by increasing polarization, the state will respond by efforts to control the mobilization of subordinate classes and groups. Whether or not it succeeds, its autonomy will be lessened. If it fails, its autonomy is threatened by subordinate groups, whose efforts to transcend the existing structure may result in revolution, anarchy, or civil conflict in which the state is eliminated or transformed. If it succeeds, its capacity to confront dominant classes in alliance with subordinate groups and classes is lessened. In Mexico, this control was relatively easy to achieve in view of the structural weakness of the working class (its small size and heterogeneity), its consequent history of dependence on the state, the stabilizing effects of land distribution, the consolidation of authoritarian tendencies within the major peasant and labor confederations, and the failure of the labor leadership to envision more radical goals than those of the Cárdenas administration. As a consequence, Cárdenas was able to institutionalize control over these groups through their incorporation into the state-controlled party structure, with the cooperation of their leadership.

Thus, a second element affecting the ability of the state to challenge the existing structure in coalition with subordinate elements is their level of consciousness and cohesion. The state is neither willing nor *able* to implement goals that go beyond those envisioned by the subordinate elements themselves.

Although the boundaries separating the state and civil society must be recognized, Mexico's recent history reveals the importance of relationships transcending those boundaries—the latent or explicit alliances between institutions and factions within the state and particular classes or class segments in civil society. Thus a third important constraint on state autonomy is the historically evolved relation between segments of the dominant class and dominant factions within the state.

In Mexico, such alliances limited the autonomy of the state and the achievements of the progressive coalition in two ways. First, government policies were often diluted or distorted at the level of implementation—for example, by local government officials in league with employers or landlords. And second, the mobilization of the conservative alliance in opposition to the reforms of Cárdenas ultimately led to a less radical policy in the last years of the administration and the selection of a conservative to succeed him. In fact, the most cohesive opposition to the Cárdenas reforms came from factions within the state—indicated in the preselection of Avila Camacho as PRM candidate for the presidency in 1940.

The Mexican case also indicates that certain factions within the state may be linked to subordinate social classes, which form the basis for a more progressive alliance. Only rarely, however, as in a postrevolutionary period, will these factions constitute the dominant group within the state. And even when they do, the entrenched alliances between state factions and dominant classes remain and set limits on what the progressive alliance can accomplish. This suggests that although alliances between subordinate classes and progressive state factions are possible, the impetus for structural change must come from outside the state. Not an autonomous state but only the autonomous organization of subordinate classes and class segments can bring about a social transformation on their behalf.

References

ANDERSON, BO, and JAMES D. COCKCROFT
  1972　"Control and Co-optation in Mexican Politics," in James Cockcroft and others (ed.), Dependence and Underdevelopment: Latin America's Political Economy. Garden City, N.Y.: Anchor Books.

ANGUIANO, ARTURO
  1975　El Estado y la política obrera del cardenismo. México: Ediciones Era.

ASHBY, JOE C.
  1963　Organized Labor and the Mexican Revolution under Lázaro Cárdenas. Chapel Hill: University of North Carolina Press.

BOSQUES, GILBERTO
  1937　The National Revolutionary Party of Mexico and the Six-Year Plan. México: National Revolutionary Party.

BOYLE, WILLIAM
  1940　Letter of April 2. National Archives, Washington (NAW), 812.00/30977.

BURSLEY, HERBERT S.
  1940　Letters of March 7, May 18, and July 25. NAW, 812.00/30968, 31055, and 31229½.

CÁRDENAS, LÁZARO
  1972a　Ideario político. México: Ediciones Era.
  1972b　Obras: I. Apuntes 1913–1940. México: Universidad Nacional Autónoma de México.

CARR, BARRY
  1976　El movimiento obrero y la política en México, 1910–1929 (2 vol.) México: Sep-Setentas.

CHEVALIER, FRANCOIS
  1967　"The Ejido and Political Stability in Mexico," in Claudio Veliz (ed.), The Politics of Conformity in Latin America. London: Oxford University Press.

CÓRDOVA, ARNALDO
1973   La ideología de la Revolución mexicana: La formación del nuevo régimen. México: Ediciones Era.
1974   La política de masas del cardenismo. México: Serie Popular Era
CORNELIUS, WAYNE A., JR.
1969   "Crisis, Coalition Building and Political Entrepreneurship in the Mexican Revolution: The Politics of Social Reform under Lázaro Cárdenas" (draft).
ECKSTEIN, SALOMON
1966   El ejido colectivo en México. México: Fondo de Cultura Económica.
FUENTES DÍAZ, VICENTE
1959   "Desarrollo y evolución del movimiento obrero a partir de 1929," *Ciencias Políticas y Sociales* V (17).
GARCÍA CANTÚ, GASTÓN
1965   El pensamiento de la reacción mexicana. Historia documental. 1810–1962. México: Empresas Editoriales.
GÓMEZ JARA, FRANCISCO A.
1970   El movimiento campesino en México. México: Ediciones Campesina.
GONZÁLEZ NAVARRO, MOISÉS
1963   La Confederación Nacional Campesina (un grupo de presión en la reforma agraria mexicana). México: B. Costa-Amic, editor.
GUTELMAN, MICHEL
1974   Capitalismo y reforma agraria en México. México: Ediciones Era.
HANSEN, ROGER
1974   The Politics of Mexican Development. Baltimore: Johns Hopkins University Press.
HUIZER, GERRIT
1970   La lucha campesina en México. México: Centro de Investigaciones Agrarias.
LANDSBERGER, HENRY A., and CYNTHIA HEWITT DE ALCÁNTARA
1970   Peasant Organizations in La Laguna, Mexico. Washington, D.C.: Inter-American Committee for Agricultural Development, *Research Papers on Land Tenure and Agrarian Reform* 17.
LEAL, JUAN FELIPE
1974   La burguesía y el Estado mexicano. México: Ediciones "El Caballito."
1975   "The Mexican State: 1915–1973. A Historical Interpretation," *Latin American Perspectives* 2(2).
LIEUWEN, EDWIN
1968   Mexican Militarism: The Political Rise and Fall of the Revolutionary Army. New Mexico: University of New Mexico Press.
MÁRQUEZ FUENTES, MANUEL, and OCTAVIO RODRÍGUEZ ARAUJO
1973   El Partido Comunista Mexicana. México: Ediciones "El Caballito."
MEDÍN, TZVI
1971   "Cárdenas. Del Maximato al Presidencialismo," *Revista de la Universidad de México* XXV.

Mexican Labor News
1936–   México: Workers University of Mexico.
1940

México: Cámara de diputados
1966   Los Presidentes de México antes la Nación: informes, manifestas y documentos de 1821–1966 (IV and V). México: D. F.

Meyer, Lorenzo
1972a   "Cambio político y dependencia. México en el siglo XX," *Foro Internacional* 50(XIII), 2.
1972b   México y los Estados Unidos en el conflicto petrolero. México: El Colegio de México (2a ed.).

Michaels, Albert
1970   "The Crisis of Cardenismo," *Journal of Latin American Studies* 2.
1971   "The Mexican Electon of 1940," Council on International Studies, State University of New York at Buffalo (September).

Muñoz, Hilda
1976   Lázaro Cárdenas: Síntesis ideológica de su campaña presidencial. México: Fondo de Cultura Económica.

North, Liisa, and David Raby
1977   "The Dynamic of Revolution and Counter-Revolution: Mexico under Cárdenas, 1934–1940," *LARU Studies* II(1), Toronto, Ontario.

PRM
1940   Cárdenas Habla. México: Partido Revolucionario Mexicano (1 septiembre).

Raby, David L.
1972   "La contribución del cardenismo al desarrollo de México en la época actual," *Aportes* 26.

Rippy, Merrill
1972   Oil and the Mexican Revolution. Luden, Netherlands: E. J. Brill.

Salazar, Rosendo
1956   Historia de las luchas proletarias en México: 1923–1946. México: Ediciones Avante.

Shulgovski, Anatol
1968   México en la encrucijada de su historia. México: Fondo de la Cultura Popular.

Vellinga, Menno
1975   "Economic Development and the Dynamics of Class: Industrialization, Power and Control in Monterrey, Mexico," Center for Comparative Sociology, University of Utrecht.

Wood, Bryce
1961   The Making of the Good Neighbor Policy. New York: Columbia University Press.

16 Class Conflict in the Chilean Countryside

Ian Roxborough
London School of Economics and Political Science

Although by the 1970s the population of Chile was largely urban, the 25 percent of the labor force engaged in agriculture constituted an important political force. Largely excluded from political participation until the 1960s (Loveman 1976), the peasants and workers on Chile's haciendas and minifundios were a potential source of support for both the Christian Democrats and the Socialist-Communist left. The passing of the Christian Democratic agrarian reform law in 1967 and the election of the Socialist Salvador Allende to the presidency in 1970 brought Chile's agricultural laborers to the front of the political arena.

The heterogeneous political coalition that supported Allende had as one of its three major programmatic targets the rapid abolition of latifundism in Chile.[1] Together with imperialism and monopoly capital, the owners of Chilean haciendas or *fundos* were singled out as the principal class enemies of the socialist government.

However, as the various parties of the Chilean left moved beyond general slogans to specific political programs, major differences began to appear. Within 18 months the parties of the Popular Unity coalition were at loggerheads with each other (and not only in the area of agrarian reform) and the government was increasingly incapable of controlling the rapidly accelerating mobilization of fundo workers. The ensuing wave of fundo seizures contributed to the growing political instability that eventually furnished the conditions for the military coup of 1973.

The differences within the left over how to deal with the agrarian problem were rooted in different analyses of the class nature of Chilean agriculture. Chilean Marxists had long debated whether Chilean agricul-

---

[1] The Popular Unity was formed from several parties ranging from the Radicals on the right to the Christian Left. The Communist and Socialist parties were the most important.

ture was still enmeshed in a feudal past or whether it could really be characterized as a form of capitalist agriculture. (There was never any suggestion that Chilean *industry* was anything but capitalist.) And if a transition to capitalism had occurred, or was occurring, the exact nature of the transition was still a matter of debate.

These discussions were not merely academic, but conditioned the policy of class alliances proposed by the various parties of the left, and were an element in determining the possibility of organizing socialist or progressive forms of agriculture.

Those who saw Chilean agriculture as emerging from a feudal past tended to accept that the most that could be done was to prepare the way for modern and efficient forms of capitalist agriculture and ensure that the bargaining position of peasants and rural workers was strengthened. Those who saw Chilean agriculture as basically capitalist were more inclined to see agrarian reform as possibly preparing the way toward socialist forms of agriculture (in the context, of course, of an overall transition towards socialism), and to be interested in mobilizing the peasants and rural workers around such a program.

Very rarely were the connections between the historical analysis of mode of production in agriculture, the formation of classes and class alliances, and concrete programs clearly spelled out by any of the parties. Rather than a set of logical postulates leading to necessary conclusions for action, the analyses of the class structure made by the various parties both initiated and reinforced propensities to act in certain general directions. The connection between historical-theoretical analysis and specific political programs was always relatively loose. Moreover, the step from program to actual action was often not direct because it depended on the vagaries of the individual situation, organizational resources available, and tactical alliances with other parties.

From its colonial beginnings as largely self-sufficient manorial demesnes, Chilean agriculture had been drawn into the expanding world market in the nineteenth century through a sudden increase in demand for wheat to feed the growing populations of California and Australia. The immediate effect was an intensification of labor discipline on the fundos (Bauer 1975:168). Previously the service tenants (*inquilinos*) had enjoyed considerable autonomy and relatively privileged positions on the great estates. Now the landowners moved to reduce the inquilinos' plots of land and increase their labor obligations. The effect was strikingly similar to the "second serfdom" in Eastern Europe (Kay 1971). According to Arnold Bauer:

> during the years following 1860, the institution of *inquilinaje* was extended and by 1930 had hardened into a conservative symbiosis with the hacienda system that was not shaken until recent years (1975:159)

Nevertheless, by the 1930s this conservative symbiosis had begun to show strains, and by the 1950s there were definite signs of an increasing proletarianization of the rural labor force. Despite increases in mechanization and an increased trend toward the reduction of the inquilinos' remaining subsistence plots, Chilean agriculture was increasingly unable to meet the needs of the growing urban population. Under the impact of the Cuban revolution this crisis in agriculture gave rise to the agrarian reforms of the 1960s and 1970s.[2]

The Christian Democratic agrarian reform law of 1967 originally intended to hand over most of the land of the inefficient latifundos to the inquilinos to be run as a cooperative, with the option after three years of dividing the farm into individual parcels. A new class of petty-proprietor beneficiaries was to develop at the same time as the large landowning class underwent an internal transformation into efficient, medium-sized, capital-intensive, capitalist farmers. (Petras and Zemelman 1972; Lehmann 1974).

Although there were considerable differences about whether Chilean agriculture had ever been feudal,[3] many agreed that, if Chilean agriculture had not always been capitalist, then at least some kind of transition to capitalism in agriculture was underway. The question remained, however, of how this process of transition had affected the patterns of class alliances.

The central plank in the Communist party's program was the achievement of four interrelated objectives: increase agricultural production, keep popular mobilization within controllable bounds, preserve the alliance with medium capitalist farmers, and isolate the principal enemy, the semifeudal latifundists.

The strategy rested on the implicit assumption that it was possible to identify two distinct social classes: the semifeudal large landowners and the industrial capitalists. It also assumed that these classes would have separate and distinct objective interests and political conflict would be structured along these lines of class cleavage. However, recent research by Zeitlin and his associates casts considerable doubt on the existence of two distinct classes; on the contrary, they were interrelated segments of a single class,

---

[2] The Alliance for Progress was in part a response to the fear that other Latin American countries would follow Cuba along the road to socialist revolution unless prophylactic reforms, of which agrarian reform was one, were set in motion.

[3] The debate over the transition from feudalism to capitalism (Sweezy 1967) is too complicated to discuss here. Some authors have argued that Chilean agriculture was a mode of production sui generis (Ratcliff 1973:66; Bauer 1975:12). It will be assumed here that the existence of a labor-service tenantry, coupled with the exclusive political power of the landowner within the boundaries of the great estates, is sufficient to define Chilean agriculture as feudal in the period between 1850 and 1930 (cf. Castex 1977; Carmagnani 1976; Saavedra 1975).

with family ties and concrete interests criss-crossing agriculture and industry (Zeitlin and Ratcliff 1975; Zeitlin, Neuman, and Ratcliff 1976). That there were not two clearly distinct dominant classes makes it difficult to accept wholeheartedly the Communist party's analysis, namely, that a semifeudal class of latifundists could be politically isolated.

This analysis of the historical development of the rural class structure implied, for the Communist party, the need to control popular mobilization to avoid alarming the rural and urban middle strata and pushing them into an alliance with the monopoly bourgeoisie and the semifeudal landowners. The party's analysis failed to note, however, the intricate web of social ties, not only between agriculture and industry, but also between large, medium, and small propertyowners.

Other parties to the left of the Communist party tended to see the owners of the large fundos as merely one stratum of a larger class of big farm owners and they were accordingly less concerned with the need to maintain the alliance with the nebulous "middle strata."[4] They were also more insistent on the need to mobilize rural workers and were less preoccupied by the immediate impact on agricultural production (Roxborough 1977:225–71). These differences were solidified around a series of immediate issues: expropriation policy, organization of the expropriated lands, and the nature of political mobilization.

The parties differed principally over whether only the very large and inefficient farms should be expropriated or whether the reform should include medium and small farms. They also differed about the desirability of leaving the owners a part of the farm as a reserve.[5] With regard to the postreform organization of the farms, the more cautious position of the Communist party was to favor the use of individual incentives and to avoid changing the organization of the farms too rapidly. The Socialist party, on the other hand, favored considerable modifications in the organization of the new productive units, which were to replace the Christian Democratic–reformed farms (asentamientos). These new Agrarian Reform Centers (CERAs) were supposed to be a step in the direction of collectivization of agriculture.

CERAs were to be formed by the amalgamation of two or more expropriated fundos and were to maximize the collective organization of production. Individual subsistence plots and pasture rights were to be kept to a

---

[4] The 1967 law had defined latifundos as all farms over 80 basic irrigated hectares or BIH (a unit which took into account soil quality and irrigation). This arbitrary definition (Barraclough 1974) was attacked by parties that wished to lower the ceiling to 40 or 20 BIH.

[5] According to the law, only the land in excess of 80 BIH was to be expropriated (unless the farm was badly managed), and 80 BIH could be left as a "reserve," for the owner to farm.

minimum. The aim was to reverse the tendency toward the formation of a class of small peasant proprietors that would be a natural bastion for conservative and Bonapartist regimes (Marx 1963). Instead, the collectivization of agriculture would, it was hoped, increasingly eradicate peasant conservatism and parochialism and reduce the differences between town and countryside. The aim was perhaps not quite so simplistic as this abbreviated summary makes it sound. Certainly it could be argued that the CERAs, with their emphasis on planning and cooperation, contained the germs of a more rational and participatory form of agricultural production. Given the rapidity with which the Chilean experiment was terminated, we shall, of course, never be able to say one way or another.

The differing attitudes toward the need for, and the forms of, popular mobilization were directly tied to the overall strategic interpretations of the Chilean road to socialism. The Communist party envisaged a slow and legal transition, with the support of the vast majority of the population, whereas the extreme-left Movement of the Revolutionary Left (MIR) and the left wing of the Socialist party believed that an insurrectionary armed confrontation with the forces of the right would be unavoidable in the immediate future. The Communist party sought not to alarm potential middle-class supporters and therefore attempted to ensure that popular mobilization was directed primarily toward electoral ends, whereas the parties farther to the left attempted to mobilize the masses in extraparliamentary ways to prepare for the coming confrontation.

The upshot of these differences was an extremely confused situation in the countryside. For several months, I lived on a fundo in the province of Santiago. During the Popular Unity period this and the neighboring fundos were organized into a MAPU-affiliated rural workers' union.[6] Although the predominant force in the area had been the Socialist party, most of the active work of political agitation was carried out by a team of MIR organizers sent from Santiago. The extent of organizational rivalry is indicated by the fact that the head of the local office of the agrarian reform agency (CORA) was a Communist party member, his staff were mainly Christian Democrats, and his zonal chief was a member of the Socialist party.

During the 1970–1973 period several fundos in this area were seized by the resident workers and then legally expropriated by the land reform agency. There was then an abortive attempt to establish a CERA. During these two struggles the various parties of the Chilean left actively intervened in an attempt to influence the course of events.

---

[6] MAPU, the United Popular Action Movement, was a party belonging to the government coalition. In 1973 it split into two separate groupings, one of which broadly followed the Communist party line and the other followed the Socialist-Mirista line.

At the center of the process of political mobilization were the MIR cadres, agitating for the seizure of the estates and, once the seizure had happened, trying to get the rural workers to pressure the agrarian reform agency to speed up the expropriation.

A team of six organizers from Santiago spent most of their time in the area, talking to the fundo workers and attending the local union meetings. As the agrarian reform agency continued to promise that the farms would be rapidly expropriated, and as the months dragged on, the MIR cadres found a receptive audience among the workers. Eventually, after receiving the go-ahead from the union, the workers and the MIR cadres seized the fundos.

A week later the fundos were declared expropriated, but there was a delay of some months before they were handed over to the workers. During this period the MIR organized some brief occupations of the offices of the agrarian reform agency. These occupations resulted in a series of confrontations with the less radical elements of the Popular Unity.

MIR's overriding aim was to exacerbate the differences between the reformist and revolutionary wings of the Popular Unity, with the ultimate intent of preparing the way for armed confrontation with the right. The MIR were quite successful in their campaign, but for various reasons failed to develop a permanent base amongst the fundo workers. One of the more important reasons was the MIR's lack of interest in the details of the organization of agriculture after expropriation. Concerned mainly with bringing the confrontation between revolutionaries and reformists to a head so they could launch an all-out assault on the state, the MIR had little time to spare for such mundane matters as the organization of production. As a result, it neglected an important area for political organization and mobilization. Once the fundos had been expropriated there was little for MIR to do, and ideological counterattack by the other parties dislodged the MIR with surprising ease and rapidity.

Not only was the MIR incapacitated by its own analysis and program but, like other parties of the left, with the possible exception of MAPU, it had few real, enduring roots in the countryside, planted and nurtured over long years of struggle. Few authentic peasant or rural worker leaders with organic links to the parties of the left had developed in the brief period between the opening up of the countryside in the 1960s and the accession of Salvador Allende to the presidency in 1970. On the contrary, both the Communist and Socialist parties had, during their participation in the Popular Front governments of the 1930s and 1940s, explicitly accepted a "hands-off" pact in the countryside as part of the price of accession to power. Only after the Cuban revolution, and the initiatives taken by the Christian Democrats and the U.S. government, did the left make any more than token efforts at organizational work in the countryside.

The MIR was also a new, untried and untested organization, still in the process of overcoming some of its early *foquista* tendencies (cf. Debray 1967). MIR's own role in the area studied by the author emphasized the distance between the young, urban, middle-class MIR organizers and the rural workers. Their first act had been to organize the seizure of a small fundo, engage in a confrontation with the rural workers' union, and then flee in disarray when the police arrived. Although the MIRistas later publicly admitted their errors, they continued to work for quick, spectacular results rather than engage in long and tedious organizational work. This explains to some extent, perhaps, their constant attempts to bypass what was the only organically rooted rural workers' organization, the MAPU-affiliated union.

But neither were the other left parties able to organize the *fundo* workers of the area effectively. The Communist party, operating through the agrarian reform agency, was swamped with bureaucratic work and could spare few resources for political organization at the grass roots. The same was true of the MAPU-controlled rural workers' union, increasingly drawn into the management of the rapidly growing reformed sector. Before expropriation, the union had been the most important political organization among the fundo workers. After the expropriation much of its previous raison d'etre disappeared, and it had great difficulty adopting a new role. The Socialist party, which at one time had several members among the fundo workers, simply failed to appear.

As a result, once the fundos had been taken over by the resident workers a process of demobilization set in. This involved an inward-turning preoccupation with the management of the reformed farms. There were constant conflicts over the management of the farms and serious and bitter factional disputes between the workers. There were struggles for the leadership of the farms, accusations of fraud, fistfights and incessant bickering. A half-hearted attempt to form a CERA never really got off the ground.

Apart from a very formal explanation of the CERA structure one weekend by the Communist cadres in the agrarian reform agency, no real effort was made to organize a CERA. Faced by a number of criticisms from the fundo workers (mainly focusing on two issues: the restrictions on the size of the private plots, and the organizational difficulties of integrating several ex-fundos into a single productive unit), the notion was quietly allowed to fade away. During the military coup of September 1973 the divided and disillusioned workers could turn to no hegemonic political organization for guidance.[7]

Some analysts argue that the processes of mobilization–expropriation

---

[7] This was not universally true. Kyle Steenland's report (1977) on the southern region of Chile gives a different picture.

of the land–demobilization that took place in this zone were the inevitable consequences of any peasant struggle. According to this line of reasoning, peasants are only revolutionary until they have satisfied their parochial demands—control of the land. Thereafter they behave as petty proprietors anywhere, supporting conservative governments, enriching themselves, and exploiting the landless peasantry (Harris 1969–70).

Such an analysis would be acceptable were it not for the great changes taking place in the rural class structure after the 1930s. In the fundos I studied, the process of proletarianization, though by no means complete, was far advanced. Subsistence plots were not large, and the differentials between the different strata of the labor force (which were characteristic of the hacienda system) were greatly reduced. The specific historical form of inquilinaje, a labor service tenantry, was increasingly undergoing an internal change in content toward the agricultural laborer living in a cottage belonging to the fundo.

As Cristóbal Kay has argued,

> It may be more appropriate to view the *inquilino* not as a lessee, but as a wage laborer being remunerated partly with land use, in kind, and with a daily wage (1974:124).

This rural proletariat, although still in the process of formation, was capable of going beyond merely peasant demands for control of the land. With the appropriate political organization and direction, the plan for a CERA might have gone ahead and the divisive process of political demobilization might not have occurred. The workers on the fundos where I lived were constantly discussing politics and holding union meetings. Whether they are best seen as peasants or rural proletarians, the workers on the great estates of Chile's Central Valley were—at least during the period of the Popular Unity government—not conservatives. They were ready for mobilization but lacked their own indigenous leadership. At this juncture the intervention of political parties was crucial. The failure to maintain a state of mobilization was not an inevitable result of peasant revolt but a specifically political failure to establish a hegemonic political leadership and organization for a nascent rural proletariat.

This political failure occurred at two levels. First, the various political parties either lacked sufficient resources to make any serious impact, or were led by mistaken analyses of the class structure into inappropriate and unrewarding actions. For example, the MIR's belief that it was dealing with a peasantry rather than a rural proletariat resulted in a relative neglect of the possibilities inherent in the new CERAs. Similarly, the Communist party's notion of a semifeudal class of latifundists reinforced its cautious approach to the political mobilization of the rural workers. With the right leadership from the Communists in charge of the local CORA office, a more unified and coordinated struggle for the expropriation of the fundos might have been undertaken with a reasonable chance of success. The correlation of class forces might have been radically altered in favor of the left.

Second, the rivalry and competition among the various parties resulted in a dispersion of effort. A crucial failure was the inability of the MIR to establish a solid base in the area because of two factors. In the first place, the policy of confrontation with the reformist elements of the Popular Unity meant that the MIR was restricted to the role of a pressure group. Real power was retained by the incumbents of positions in the state apparatus. And in the second, the MIR failed to grasp the hegemonic role played by the rural workers' union. Instead of attempting to work within the union, the MIR cadres tended to work outside, and at the margin, of the union. They thus cut themselves off from their major chance of developing a solid base at the grass roots.

As the struggle within the left between reformists and revolutionaries was fought out, the possibility for the development of advanced forms of agricultural organization slipped by, and a process of repeasantization and differentiation among the beneficiaries of the agrarian reform set in. The chance to alter the class nature of the agrarian reform was lost. And while the forces of the left fought each other to a stalemate, the right gathered its forces together and moved abruptly to put an end to the Chilean experiment.

References

BARRACLOUGH, SOLON
    1974   Diagnóstico de la Reforma Agraria Chilena. México: Siglo Veintiuno.

BAUER, ARNOLD
    1975   Chilean Rural Society. Cambridge: Cambridge University Press.

CARMAGNANI, MARCELLO
    1976   Formación y Crises de un Sistema Feudal. México: Siglo Veintiuno.

CASTEX, PATRICK
    1977   Voie Chilienne au socialisme et luttes paysannes. Paris: Maspero.

DEBRAY, REGIS
    1967   Revolution in the Revolution. New York: Monthly Review.

HARRIS, NIGEL
    1969–   "The Revolutionary Role of the Peasants." *International Socialism* 41.
    1970

KAY, CRISTÓBAL
    1974   "Comparative Development of the European Manorial System and

the Latin American Hacienda System," Ph.D. dissertation, University of Sussex.

LOVEMAN, BRIAN
1976   Struggle in the Countryside, Bloomington: Indiana University Press.

MARX, KARL
[1852]   The Eighteenth Brumaire of Louis Napoleon Bonaparte. New York:
1963   International Publishers.

PETRAS, JAMES, and HUGO ZEMELMAN
1972   Peasants in Revolt. Austin: University of Texas Press.

RATCLIFF, RICHARD
1973   "Kinship, Wealth and Power: Capitalists and Landowners in the Chilean Upper Class," Ph.D. dissertation, University of Wisconsin.

ROXBOROUGH, IAN
1977   "The Political Mobilization of Farm Workers during the Chilean Agrarian Reform, 1971–73, A Case Study," Ph.D. dissertation, University of Wisconsin.

SAAVEDRA, ALEJANDRO
1975   Capitalismo y Lucha de Clases en el Campo: Chile 1970–72. Madrid: Alberto Corazón.

STEENLAND, KYLE
1977   Agrarian Reform Under Allende. Albuquerque: University of New Mexico Press.

SWEEZY, PAUL
1967   The Transition from Feudalism to Capitalism. New York: Science and Society.

ZEITLIN, MAURICE, and RICHARD E. RATCLIFF
1975   "Research Methods for the Analysis of the Internal Structure of Dominant Classes: The Case of Landlords and Capitalists in Chile," *Latin American Research Review* 10 (Fall).

ZEITLIN, MAURICE, W. L. NEUMAN, and R. E. RATCLIFF
1976   "Class Segments: Agrarian Property and Political Leadership in the Capitalist Class of Chile." *American Sociological Review* 41(6):1006–1029.

Index